ENGLISH RENAISSANCE PROSE

History, Language, and Politics

MEDIEVAL & RENAISSANCE
TEXTS & STUDIES

VOLUME 164

ENGLISH RENAISSANCE PROSE

History, Language, and Politics

edited by

Neil Rhodes

MEDIEVAL & RENAISSANCE TEXTS & STUDIES
Tempe, Arizona
1997

© Copyright 1997
Arizona Board of Regents for Arizona State University

Library of Congress Cataloging-in-Publication Data

English Renaissance prose : history, language, and politics / edited by Neil Rhodes.
    p. cm. — (Medieval & Renaissance texts & studies ; v. 164)
  Includes bibliographical references and index.
  ISBN 0-86698-205-1 (alk. paper)
  1. English prose literature — Early modern, 1500–1700 — History and criticism. 2. Politics and literature — Great Britain — History — 16th century. 3. Politics and literature — Great Britain—History — 17th century. 4. English language — Early modern, 1500–1700 — Style. 5. Literature and history — Great Britain — History. 6. Great Britain — Intellectual life — 16th century. 7. Great Britain — Intellectual life — 17th century. 8. Renaissance — England.
I. Rhodes, Neil. II. Series.
PR769.E53 1997
828'.30809—dc21   97-15525
                                                                                                                                                        CIP

∞
This book is made to last.
It is set in Goudy, smyth-sewn,
and printed on acid-free paper
to library specifications.

Printed in the United States of America

CONTENTS

Acknowledgements	vii
Introduction: History, Language, and the Politics of English Renaissance Prose *Neil Rhodes*	1
The Sore and Strong Prose of the English Bible *Gerald Hammond*	19
The Tyrant Being Slain: Afterlives of More's *History of King Richard III* *Daniel Kinney*	35
"Take away preaching, and take away salvation": Hugh Latimer, Protestantism, and Prose Style *N. H. Keeble*	57
Richard Hooker's Discourse and the Deception of Posterity *P. G. Stanwood*	75
Sidney's Arcadian Poetics: A Medicine of Cherries and the Philosophy of Cavaliers *Claire Preston*	91
The Strang[e] Constructions of Mary Wroth's *Urania*: Arcadian Romance and the Public Realm *Paul Salzman*	109
Virgins of the World and Feasts of the Family: Sex and the Social Order in Two Renaissance Utopias *Susan Bruce*	125
"A Knowledge Broken": Francis Bacon's Aphoristic Style and the Crisis of Scholastic and Humanist Knowledge-Systems *Stephen Clucas*	147

Shapeless Elegance: Robert Burton's Anatomy of Knowledge
Jonathan Sawday   173

Milton and the Limits of Ciceronian Rhetoric
Martin Dzelzainis   203

The Powers of the Beast: Gerrard Winstanley and
Visionary Prose of the English Revolution
David Loewenstein   227

In the Land of Moles and Pismires:
Thomas Browne's Antiquarian Writings
Graham Parry   247

Bunyan's *Grace Abounding* and the
Dynamics of Restoration Nonconformity
Thomas N. Corns   259

Bibliography of Works Cited   271

Index   298

Notes on Contributors   301

* * *

The editor is most grateful to Kirsty Allen, Rita Bodlak, Jeffrey Mackowiak, and the School of English at St Andrews University for research assistance in the preparation of the bibliography and index.

NEIL RHODES

Introduction: History, Language, and the Politics of English Renaissance Prose

ENGLISH PROSE OF THE SIXTEENTH AND SEVENTEENTH CENTURIES has no "Casebook" or "Critical Heritage," and there is no general account of the critical reception of the subject. But if the term Renaissance remains serviceable as a description of a literary period, then Sidney's *Arcadia*, Burton's *Anatomy of Melancholy*, the writings of Bacon, Milton, and Browne, and above all the development of the English Bible, are clearly part of that cultural phenomenon. There are, of course, many studies of Renaissance prose written by and for specialist scholars, but little that can be offered to the student as a way into reading these rich but often challenging texts. So the present volume is designed principally to act as an introduction to some of the major figures and works in the field, though some of the essays will undoubtedly also be of interest to the specialist.

Any account of the critical reception of English Renaissance prose should probably begin with the Romantic movement, since it is within that movement that the subject was constructed as a distinct entity and granted a literary status comparable with the achievements of Renaissance poetry and drama. In particular, it was Coleridge and his circle, whose enthusiastic rediscovery of the prose writers of the sixteenth and seventeenth centuries reversed (in Coleridge's view) "the common opinion that the English style attained its greatest perfection in and about Queen Anne's reign." For Coleridge "the great models of [the classical style] in English are Hooker, Bacon, Milton and Taylor," and while this style was "easily open to corruption ... it is the existence of an individual idiom in each, that makes the principal writers before the Restoration the great patterns or integers of English style."[1] Coleridge had Sir Thomas Browne in mind here, but it was Jeremy Taylor who won the most extravagant accolades of Romantic criticism. Charles Lamb, also a Browne enthusiast, claimed that you could find in Taylor "more knowledge and description of human life and manners than [in] any prose book in the language: he has more delicacy and sweetness than any mortal, the 'gentle' Shakespeare hardly excepted,"[2] and in a final flourish to his comparative essay on Bacon, Browne, and Taylor, Hazlitt predicted that "when the name of Jeremy Taylor is no longer remembered with reverence, genius will have become a mockery, and virtue an empty shade."[3] Taylor is, in fact, less remembered now than his contemporaries, though his work was frequently reprinted in the eighteenth as well as the nineteenth centuries. This was atypical, since the eighteenth century found much Renaissance prose writing "unreadable," and a better illustration of its fortunes in that period is *The Anatomy of Melancholy* which reached a seventh edition in 1676 but was not reissued until 1800, when it was claimed for Romanticism by Lamb and Keats.[4]

Coleridge's claim that Renaissance prose writers each had an "individual idiom" is a characteristic piece of Romantic essentialism. This is reflected in further claims that they were also essentially English, formed by the nurturing properties of the native soil. Hazlitt's introduction to his *Lectures on the Dramatic Literature of the Age of Elizabeth*, which included the lecture on Bacon, Browne, and Taylor, makes this point about Renaissance literature in general:

---

[1] S. T. Coleridge, *Lectures 1808–1819: On Literature* 2, ed. R. A. Foakes, vol. 5 of *The Collected Works of Samuel Taylor Coleridge* (Princeton: Princeton Univ. Press, 1987), 235, 233, 234. I am greatly indebted to Shirley Rhodes for references to Romantic criticism of English Renaissance prose.

[2] Lamb to Robert Lloyd, 1801, *The Letters of Charles Lamb*, ed. E. V. Lucas (London, 1935), 1:257.

[3] William Hazlitt, *Lectures on the Dramatic Literature of the Age of Elizabeth*, vol. 6 of *The Complete Works of William Hazlitt*, ed. P. P. Howe (London and Toronto, 1930–34), 345.

[4] Lamb adopted Burton's sobriquet Democritus Junior; his copy of the *Anatomy* (now lost) seems to have been annotated by Coleridge. See S. T. Coleridge, *Marginalia* 1, ed. George Whalley (1980), vol. 12 of *Collected Works*, 854: "As a mark of the currency of Burton's book in C's circle, it is noticeable that the sale catalogues show that there were copies in the libraries of Green, Gillman, WW [Wordsworth] and RS [Southey]." On Keats and Burton see Janice C. Sinson, *John Keats and The Anatomy of Melancholy* (London: Keats-Shelley Memorial Association, 1971) and the essay by Jonathan Sawday in the present volume.

> Perhaps the genius of Great Britain (if I may so speak without offence or flattery), never shone out fuller or brighter, or looked more like itself, than at this period. Our writers and great men had something in them that savoured of the soil from which they grew: they were not French, they were not Dutch, or German, or Greek, or Latin; they were truly English.... The mind of their country was great in them, and it prevailed.[5]

The interchanging of the terms "British" and "English" will be irksome to modern readers, particularly Scots, but it was certainly prevalent at the time. Writing in *The Edinburgh Review* in 1812 the Scot Francis Jeffrey speculated as to whether "the force of the Reformation had much effect in producing this sudden development of British genius," before referring to "a certain raciness of English peculiarity" in Renaissance literature which "in all this splendour of native luxuriance can only be compared to what happens on the breaking up of a virgin soil."[6] Jeffrey went on to single out the prose writers, citing Taylor, Barrow, Hooker, and Bacon as examples of a native *poetic* genius which outdid any verse that had "since been produced in Europe."[7] Coleridge complained that these views had been appropriated from himself, but the significant point is that, whatever their other differences, Romantic critics agreed that English Renaissance prose was a distinctive national product which had been superseded by the homogeneous European taste developed in the Restoration and eighteenth century.[8] And the most distinctive national product of all was the English Bible, as De Quincey sums up: "Amongst our many national blessings, never let us forget to be thankful that in that age was made our final translation of the Bible, under the State authority. How ignoble, how unscriptural would have been a translation made in the age of Pope!"[9]

The Coleridge circle devised various projects to demonstrate the supremacy of English Renaissance prose writing. One was the extensive study of English prose style proposed by Coleridge for the *Bibliotheca*

---

[5] Hazlitt, *Complete Works*, 6:175.

[6] Peter F. Morgan, ed., *Jeffrey's Criticism: A Selection* (Edinburgh: Scottish Academic Press, 1983), 106–7.

[7] Ibid., 108–9.

[8] See S. T. Coleridge, *Biographia Literaria*, ed. James Engell and W. Jackson Bate (1983), vol. 7 of *Collected Works*, 50–52.

[9] Thomas De Quincey, "The English Language," in *The Collected Writings of Thomas De Quincey*, ed. David Masson (London, 1897), 14:154.

Britannica, which went the same way as many other Coleridgean projects.[10] Another was the anthologizing of especially luminous extracts from the chosen writers of the period. Lamb wrote to Robert Lloyd in 1801 to say "To your inquiry respecting a selection from J. Taylor I answer — it cannot be done ... for who can disentangle and unthread the rich texture of Nature and Poetry, sewn so thick into a stout coat of theology, without spoiling both *lace* and *coat?*"[11] But it was done, four years later, by Coleridge's friend Basil Montagu, whose *Selections from the Works of Taylor, Hooker* [etc.] began with a hundred and fifty pages from Taylor and continued (anachronistically) with Latimer.[12] Montagu's anthology was successful, being reprinted in 1807 and again in 1829. A later Coleridge-influenced anthology was Robert Aris Willmott's *Precious Stones* (1850), which was more wide-ranging than Montagu, containing extracts from Sidney, Spenser, and Jonson, as well as religious writing. Willmott had heard Coleridge lecture at Trinity College, Cambridge, recording his impressions in *Conversations at Cambridge* (1836), and he had also published a biography of Jeremy Taylor. His anthology began with Latimer and Cranmer and continued into the eighteenth century, but it was the Renaissance which excited him: "The greatest preachers and authors of the period between Elizabeth and the second Charles, like their Master of Antioch, wore purple over armour. The controversial sword cut through the folds of a decorated and learned fancy, only to be blunted on the impenetrable argument beneath it."[13] Willmott's metaphor is an interesting variant on the topos of language as the dress of thought, and also on Lamb's "stout coat of theology." Both conceive of writing as dress only, but whereas for Lamb the decorative and the functional are inextricable, for Willmott a soft and opulent dress covers a hard dress. Presumably what blunts the "controversial sword" is the "whole armour of God" (Eph. 6:11), but Willmott's metaphor is also designed to deflect readers from the suspicion that they are merely being offered purple passages, while his ornamental title suggests the reverse, and invites the sort of observation

---

[10] See Coleridge, *Marginalia* 1, ed. Whalley, 156.

[11] Lamb to Lloyd, 1801, *Letters of Charles Lamb*, 1:285.

[12] See Basil Montagu, *Selections from the Works of Taylor, Hooker, Hall and Lord Bacon* (London, 1805), expanded in subsequent editions to include Latimer and others.

[13] Robert Aris Willmott, *Precious Stones: Aids to Reflection from Prose Writers of the Sixteenth, Seventeenth and Eighteenth Centuries* (London, 1850), viii. Willmott borrowed his title from Coleridge's lecture on Taylor at Trinity College, Cambridge; see Robert Aris Willmott, *Conversations at Cambridge* (London, 1836), 25.

that Coleridge made, in a different context, about disconnectedness: "a popular Book is now a mere bag of marbles."[14]

With purple passages and precious stones, or marbles, we are about to enter the late Victorian world of belles-lettres which for "English prose" lasted well into the twentieth century, but the notion that Renaissance prose reflects a peculiarly English or "British" genius would have to be qualified by its reception in nineteenth-century America.[15] Noah Webster excoriated Johnson's use of Browneisms in the dictionary, and held Browne up as an example of precisely the kind of decadent, unnatural Old World learning and writing which the brave new American language would overthrow.[16] So he would presumably have been distressed to discover the extent to which Browne, Bacon, and Burton were a source of inspiration for what was to become the classic American novel, *Moby Dick*. The *omnium gatherum* quality of *Moby Dick* is almost certainly an imitation of Browne in all his styles: the Ishmael autobiographical sections are related to *Religio Medici*; the encyclopedic quality to *Pseudodoxia Epidemica*; the *vanitas* theme and the obsessional completeness of the documents on whaling to *Urn-Burial*. *Pseudodoxia Epidemica* is one of Melville's principal sources for the chapters "Cetology," "Monstrous Depictions of Whales," "Less Erroneous Depictions of Whales," and "Of Whales in Paint," and this pedantic antiquarianism is reflected in stylistic borrowings — sentence structure, rhetorical flourishes, gallows humor, conceits, sententiousness — which also show the influence of Bacon and Burton. These influences were noted by Melville's early reviewers with mixed feelings. A London critic remarked on "a quaintness reminding us of Sir Thomas Brown, and anon a heap of curious out-of-the-way learning after the fashion of the Burton who 'anatomised' 'melancholy,'"[17] while the *New*

---

[14] E. H. Coleridge, ed., *Letters of Samuel Taylor Coleridge* (Boston and New York, 1895), 2:551.

[15] I am most grateful to Claire Preston for allowing me to borrow from an unpublished paper on American responses to Browne.

[16] "Sir Thomas Brown seems to have been a favorite; yet the style of Sir Thomas is not English; and it is astonishing that a man attempting to give the world a standard of the English Language should have ever mentioned his name, but with a reprobation of his style and use of words." Webster then lists examples which "will afford a specimen of his pedantry and ill taste," *Letter to Dr. David Ramsay* in *Johnson: The Critical Heritage*, ed. James T. Boulton (New York: Barnes & Noble, 1971), 129.

[17] Henry F. Chorley in *Athenaeum*; reprinted in *Melville: The Critical Heritage*, ed. Watson. G. Branch (London: Routledge & Kegan Paul, 1974), 252. Melville had bought copies of Burton and Coleridge in 1848; ibid., 14.

Monthly Magazine (1853) managed to hear in Melville's cadences "the dip of the sun-stilled, Pacific waves, — and sometimes the grave music of Bacon's Essays! Thou wert right, O Howadji, to add, 'Who but an American could have written them.' "[18] Other reviewers, however, did not share the view that this Baconian or Browneian quality in Melville gave his work a distinctively American flavor: Fitz-James O'Brien, for example, commented in *Putnam's Monthly Magazine* (1853) that "we give Mr. Melville every credit for his deliberate plagiarisms of old Sir Thomas Browne's gorgeous and metaphorical manner," but concluded, "Let him diet himself for a year or two on Addison, and avoid Sir Thomas Browne, and there is little doubt but that he will make a notch on the American Pine."[19]

Melville was not the only writer to make his notch on the American pine who neglected to follow O'Brien's prescription. An early reviewer of Hawthorne, E. A. Duyckinck, who was to become a close friend of the author, claimed that "The distinctive mark of Hawthorne's writings, is a fanciful pathos delighting in sepulchral images" and related this to Taylor's *Holy Dying* and Browne's *Urn-Burial*.[20] Thoreau, too, is a Browneian: *Walden* has meditative digressions on life much like those in *Religio Medici* and *Urn-Burial*, and he is clearly modeling some of his *sententiae* on Browne's. Indeed, the reflections on clothing in *Walden* are virtually a pastiche of Browne:

> Our moulting season, like that of the fowls, must be a crisis in our lives. The loon retires to solitary ponds to spend it. Thus also the snake casts its slough, and the caterpillar its wormy coat, by an internal industry and expansion; for clothes are but our outmost cuticle and mortal coil. Otherwise we shall be found sailing under false colors, and be inevitably cashiered at last by our own opinion, as well as that of mankind.[21]

Despite the lexicographical strictures of Webster, then, and the uneasiness of some nineteenth-century reviewers, the quaint and curious style — the

---

[18] Ibid., 332.

[19] Ibid., 325, 329. Webster had also contrasted Addison and Browne in the *Letter to Dr. David Ramsay* and Henry S. Salt, the English biographer of Thoreau, prescribed Addison rather than Browne in his article on Melville in *Scottish Art Review*, 1889; *Melville: The Critical Heritage*, 416.

[20] *Hawthorne: The Critical Heritage*, ed. J. Donald Crowley (London: Routledge & Kegan Paul, 1970), 77.

[21] Henry David Thoreau, *Walden* (Harmondsworth: Penguin Books, 1983), 66.

"grave music" of Renaissance English writers — found its way into the mainstream of American prose.

Returning to England at the end of the nineteenth century, we find the Romantic rediscovery of Renaissance prose consolidating into an institutionalized belletrism. Anthologies such as Montagu's or Willmott's were superseded by Henry Craik's five-volume selection; Bacon and Browne appeared as "English Men of Letters" and, fulfilling Coleridge's project, the first general histories of the subject were written.[22] The quintessence of belletrism is captured in Sir Arthur Quiller-Couch's 1925 anthology, which adds imperial purple to the Romantic sense of Englishness:

> Our fathers have, in the process of centuries, provided this realm, its colonies and wide dependencies, with a speech malleable and pliable as Attic, dignified as Latin, masculine, yet free of Teutonic guttural, capable of being as precise as French, dulcet as Italian, sonorous as Spanish, and of captaining all these excellencies to its service.[23]

So writes Q in his preface. That voice was about to be challenged by Leavis, but Q's influence as a connoisseur of English prose survived, paradoxically, in the American Helene Hanff's *84 Charing Cross Road*, which charts the author's transatlantic love affair with a London bookshop during the 1950s. "I just happen to have peculiar taste in books, thanks to a Cambridge professor named Quiller-Couch, known as Q, whom I fell over in a library when I was 17," she explains in one of her first letters to the shop.[24] The books she orders tend to be by Romantic essayists or Renaissance prose writers, and among them, of course, is Donne. Hanff is indignant about the fact that she can only get Donne's prose in bits, complaining that she will have nightmares about academics "carrying long butcher knives labelled Excerpt, Selection, Passage and Abridged."[25] She refers here to Logan Pearsall Smith's *Donne's Sermons: Selected Passages*,

---

[22] See Sir Henry Craik, ed., *English Prose: Selections*, 5 vols. (London, 1894); George Saintsbury, *A History of English Prose Rhythm* (London, 1912); G. P. Krapp, *The Rise of English Literary Prose* (New York, 1915).

[23] Sir Arthur Quiller-Couch, ed., *The Oxford Book of English Prose* (Oxford: Clarendon Press, 1925), xvii.

[24] Helene Hanff, *84 Charing Cross Road* (1971; repr. London: Warner Books, 1992), 17. See also Helene Hanff, *Q's Legacy* (London: Futura, 1986).

[25] Hanff, *84 Charing Cross Road*, 75.

which had appeared in 1919 when Donne was being rediscovered. Donne had not been included in Basil Montagu's *Selections*, but Pearsall Smith refers to this as "the best of ... our prose anthologies,"[26] probably on account of its Coleridgean provenance, and if Donne did not form part of the Romantic pantheon of English Renaissance prose writers he was certainly romanticized in Pearsall Smith's introduction. Despite Hanff's hilarious frustration with his practice of excerpting, that introduction sums up perfectly the spirit of Q, of *84 Charing Cross Road*, and the fusty charm of the belletrist tradition:

> As we read these sermons, amid much that is remote and meaningless to us, we seem now and then to hear the timbre of a living voice, and then for a moment the past returns; and in the vast, dim-lit cathedral of old St Paul's we seem to see that awe-struck congregation as they gaze up at the courtly, spectral figure standing with his hour-glass in the pulpit, and pouring forth in impassioned eloquence his inmost thoughts of remorse and ecstasy.[27]

As Hanff says, "that's for me, I'm a great lover of I-was-there books."[28]

In the early 1920s, when Q was compiling his anthology and lecturing at Cambridge, Morris Croll was running a graduate course at Princeton on English prose style, 1500–1680. The essays which resulted from this represent the beginning of modern academic study of the subject, and they effectively set the critical agenda for Renaissance prose studies for the next fifty years.[29] So in terms of reception, the belletrist, anthology-piece approach to the subject, which was the legacy of Romanticism, continued in parallel with an approach that was characterized above all by its intellectual and scholarly rigor. The outlines of Croll's thesis are well-known. Essentially, he was concerned to describe the "anti-Ciceronian" or, as he preferred, "Attic" prose styles of the seventeenth century, based on Seneca and Tacitus, which came to replace the Ciceronian model of eloquence encouraged by humanism. Elaborate, periodic constructions were abandoned in favor of more aphoristic, "curt" and "loose" styles. Modern prose style, then, begins around 1600 with Bacon. What is less

---

[26] Logan Pearsall Smith, *Donne's Sermons: Selected Passages with an Essay* (Oxford: Clarendon Press, 1919), xxi.
[27] Ibid., xxxviii.
[28] Hanff, *84 Charing Cross Road*, 85.
[29] See Morris W. Croll, *Style, Rhetoric and Rhythm: Essays by Morris W. Croll*, ed. J. Max Patrick and Robert O. Evans (Princeton: Princeton Univ. Press, 1966).

often emphasized is that, *pace* the Romantic insistence on the Englishness of English Renaissance prose, Croll's perspective is very much a European one. Where Q claimed Attic for England, Croll's account of Attic prose places Bacon alongside Muret, Montaigne, and Justus Lipsius and states that Attic "was to dictate the prevailing form of prose style in all the countries of Europe."[30] Croll's theories were extended by George Williamson in his account of English Senecanism and, in the field of drama, by Jonas Barish in his brilliant adaptation of the term "baroque" to an analysis of Jonson's prose style.[31] But they were also challenged by R. F. Jones who argued that it was science rather than the anti-Ciceronian movement which principally effected the transition to modern prose style, and that this shift occurred around 1660 rather than 1600.[32] Jones's argument was in turn qualified by Robert Adolph who stressed the importance of utilitarianism in the development of plain style, and implicitly challenged by Brian Vickers who sought to re-establish Bacon as a "literary" writer by stressing the importance of rhetoric in his work.[33] Hoping to have the last word in this debate Stanley Fish added an epilogue on "The Plain Style Question" to his *Self-Consuming Artifacts* (1972) where he claimed that

> it seems to me that seventeenth-century style is not polarized by a distinction between Ciceronians and anti-Ciceronians, or by a controversy between Puritans and Anglicans, or by the incompatibility of the rhetorical and scientific ideals, or by the difference between a prose that is useful and a prose in the service of "self-revelation".... In short, for a political, social or religious opposition, I substitute an opposition of epistemologies, one that finds its expression in two kinds of reading experiences: on one side the experience of a prose that leads the auditor or reader step-by-step, in a logical and orderly manner, to a point of certainty and clarity;

---

[30] Ibid., 167. Croll's first essay, "Juste Lipse et le Mouvement Anticicéronien à la Fin du XVIe et au Début du XVIIe Siècle" was published in *Revue du Seizième Siècle* in 1914.

[31] See George Williamson, *The Senecan Amble: A Study in Prose Form from Bacon to Collier* (Chicago: Univ. of Chicago Press, 1951); Jonas A. Barish, *Ben Jonson and the Language of Prose Comedy* (Cambridge: Harvard Univ. Press, 1960).

[32] See R. F. Jones et al., *The Seventeenth Century: Studies in the History of English Thought and Literature from Bacon to Pope* (Stanford: Stanford Univ. Press, 1951).

[33] See Robert Adolph, *The Rise of Modern Prose Style* (Cambridge: Harvard Univ. Press, 1968); Brian Vickers, *Francis Bacon and Renaissance Prose* (Cambridge: Cambridge Univ. Press, 1968).

and on the other, the experience of a prose that undermines certainty and moves away from clarity, complicating what had at first seemed simple, raising more problems than it solves.... To the paired terms of my predecessors — Anglican-Puritan, Painted-Plain, Ciceronian-Senecan, Scientific-Rhetorical, Utilitarian-Frivolous — I add a new pair, Self-Satisfying and Self-Consuming.[34]

Fish's triumphant coinages may not have settled the debate, but they perhaps helped bring it to an end; the passage is worth quoting at length not least because it offers a convenient resumé of the terms of the debate up to that point.

With Fish we enter a period of academic discussion which is recognizably contemporary, and it was Fish who edited the only previous collection of critical essays on the subject, from Croll onwards.[35] In the intervening twenty-five years, there have been numerous specialist studies of individual writers, some by contributors to the present volume; we have seen the founding of the journal *Prose Studies*, and there is at last an up-to-date single volume history of the subject.[36] But there has been no further attempt at a critical overview of English Renaissance prose. It is an odd feature of the theoretical developments of the last two decades, and of new historicism and cultural materialism in particular, that their ostensible claims to rescue the marginal and to deny a privileged status to "literature" have not resulted in any significant increase in attention to the prose writing of the period (with the exception of writing by women). Prose writing is typically represented in new historicist criticism as context for yet further discussion of Shakespeare. *Plus ça change.*

Since the aim of the present volume is principally to encourage a reinstatement of the subject within our pedagogy it is necessarily catholic

---

[34] Stanley E. Fish, *Self-Consuming Artifacts: The Experience of Seventeenth-Century Literature* (Berkeley: Univ. of California Press, 1972), 377–79. The terms of Fish's distinction are implicit in Stephen Clucas's essay on Bacon and aphorism in the present volume.

[35] See Stanley E. Fish, ed., *Seventeenth-Century Prose: Modern Essays in Criticism* (Oxford Univ. Press; New York, 1971).

[36] See Roger Pooley, *English Prose of the Seventeenth Century, 1590–1700* (London: Longman, 1992); see also his article "Prospects for Research in Seventeenth Century Prose," *Prose Studies* 10 (1987): 9–17. Though not a "single-volume history" John Carey's extremely lively account, "Sixteenth and Seventeenth Century Prose" in *English Poetry & Prose, 1540–1674*, ed. Christopher Ricks (London: Sphere Books, 1970) should also be mentioned.

in terms both of subject matter and critical methodology. Inevitably, there are writers who might have had a chapter to themselves who for reasons of space do not, and there will be subject areas which may seem to be under-represented. But the scope of the book comprises historiography, romance, political oratory, and the sermon; antiquarianism, utopian fiction, theology, and scientific writing; Bible translation, psychology, spiritual autobiography, and visionary prose — a list which is testament to the rich diversity of this field and suggestive, also, of the encyclopedic character of much Renaissance prose writing. Nor does the volume attempt to advance a thesis or to rewrite the subject in terms of contemporary literary theory. Feminist concerns are voiced by Susan Bruce in her discussion of utopias and by Paul Salzman in his account of Lady Mary Wroth's *Urania*, while Jonathan Sawday offers a different kind of materialist perspective through his investigation of Burton's use of print technology in constructing *The Anatomy of Melancholy*. But it is true to say that the majority of essays represented here work within a broadly traditional framework of literary scholarship and criticism and intellectual history. Where the present volume differs from Stanley Fish's *Seventeenth-Century Prose*, the only comparable collection, and from earlier criticism of Renaissance prose, is in its move away from a focus on purely stylistic issues. No editorial directive discouraged the use of the term "style," but it is noticeable that it makes a rather limited appearance in this book. What the title of this introductory chapter points to is the inseparability of history, language, and politics in Renaissance prose writing, and the essays that follow are largely, though not exclusively, concerned with the intersections between these areas.

Another way in which this differs from Fish's collection is in its historical scope. This is not a book about seventeenth-century prose, but about prose writing from the early sixteenth century to the Restoration, the period which is usually termed the Renaissance in English literary culture. It is noticeable that studies of prose, as opposed to poetry and drama, have firmly avoided the term "Renaissance," privileging instead the seventeenth century as the period when prose *had* its Renaissance. This is true even of the recent single-volume history of the subject, Roger Pooley's *English Prose of the Seventeenth Century, 1590–1700*, which in fact stretches back to Lyly's *Euphues*, 1578.[37] "Seventeenth century," there-

---

[37] In fairness to the author of this excellent volume it should be pointed out that the term "seventeenth century" was presumably a publishers' requirement for the series in which it appeared.

fore, has come to stand for the term "Renaissance" within the field of English prose studies. The reason for this is almost certainly the unique status granted to the Authorized Version of the Bible, 1611, as the noblest monument of English prose and the elevation by association of such immediately subsequent writings as the sermons of John Donne. In order to redress the balance the present volume focuses not upon the King James Bible, but on Tyndale's, and not upon Donne, but Latimer. As Gerald Hammond points out in the opening essay, Tyndale, as originator of most of the text of the Authorized Version, is "the most widely read of all English prose writers and he, more than anyone, may claim to be an originator of modern English prose," while N. H. Keeble reminds us that Latimer was the first English Protestant preacher to have his collected sermons published, concluding that "in Latimer's sermons English prose begins to discover its modernity."

In historical terms, however, our starting point is the inception of the Tudor dynasty. Daniel Kinney's essay on More's *History of Richard III* shows how that text is constructed to appear as an exemplary history, becoming "the most seminal statement of the Tudor myth amplified and rewritten from Hall down to Shakespeare and beyond," while at the same time being fraught with ironies which render that history duplicitous. But if the Morean adage "Time trieth truth" is itself tried by the afterlives of More's text, it is one which could also serve as an epigraph for several of the later chapters in this book. P. G. Stanwood takes the title for his essay "Richard Hooker's Discourse and the Deception of Posterity" from the beginning of Clarendon's *History of the Rebellion*, "That posterity be not deceived, by the prosperous wickedness of these times," words which echo Hooker's own opening to *Ecclesiastical Polity*. Such claims to objective truth-telling, setting the record straight, are nonetheless misleading. In Hooker's case they disguise tendentiousness and polemic, and, as Stanwood argues, his "reputation as the author of the *via media* [and] . . . even the notion of the English church as being peculiarly comprehensive" are relatively recent inventions. Of course, the events of the civil war and Interregnum — the rebellion, as Clarendon has it — produced their own tendentious versions of the truth. Thomas Corns describes Sprat's "brazen rewriting" of the early history of the Royal Society in which Sprat claims that its scientific activities were pursued as a distraction from the "misfortunes" of the Interregnum, when in fact the originators of the Society had been Cromwellian placemen, comfortably ensconced in Oxbridge colleges during the 1650s. As Graham Parry points out in his essay on Browne and antiquarianism, it was rather the Royalist gentlemen who sought distraction from the misfortunes of that time in the study of antiquities — an escape from history into history. And in a further twist to the representation of the events of the mid-century we have David Loewenstein's account of Winstanley's visionary prose writing, which precisely reverses the political escapism of the antiquarians. For Winstanley, contemporary political events were to be transcribed into biblical mythology, so that the Fall itself becomes "not a distant event to be blamed on Adam who died six thousand years ago, [but] ... a historical process unfolding within us all."

With "the revisions of the history of the 1650s," to quote the final sentence of our final essay, Thomas Corns echoes our chronological starting point in the afterlives of More's *Richard III* and the representation of another slain "tyrant." The death of Richard at Bosworth, followed by the consolidation of the Tudor dynasty, and the execution of Charles, followed by the Interregnum and Restoration, mark the historical boundaries of this book. Both these watershed events prompted the rewriting of history for political reasons. The word "revisions," however, points also to a very specific way in which the truth of the prose texts of this period is tried. Textual instability is not, of course, a phenomenon peculiar to the Renaissance, but some instances are of particular significance. We have, for example, texts such as More's *Richard III* and *Utopia*, and many of Bacon's, which exist in both Latin and English versions, and the theory and process of translation is obviously central to the reconstruction of biblical truth in English. The two great monuments of Elizabethan prose, Hooker's *Laws of Ecclesiastical Polity* and Sidney's *Arcadia*, are textually unstable: the first because the integrity of the posthumously published books 6–8 has been questioned (a view which P. G. Stanwood challenges here), and the second because Sidney embarked on an unfinished revision which resulted in the posthumous publication of a composite text. Three of the essays on seventeenth-century subjects in the present volume deal specifically with textual revision. Martin Dzelzainis considers Milton's entry into government service with *The Tenure of Kings and Magistrates*, published the month after Charles's execution in 1649 and concerned *inter alia* with the legitimacy of tyrannicide, and shows how textual revisions to the second edition reveal Milton accommodating himself "to being an insider working for a regime which was, if anything, anxious to shed its revolutionary aura." The actual context for Thomas Corns's reference to "the revisions of the history of the 1650s" is Bunyan's *Grace Abounding* which, he points out, is "not one text but three"; looking back to the 1630s, '40s, and '50s from the vantage point of the Restoration, Bunyan alters and supplements his spiritual autobiography in response to the changed political and religious climate of the restored order. But the most remarkable — indeed, exorbitant — case of textual revision in Renaissance prose is surely that of Burton's *Anatomy of Melancholy*, "the nearest we can come, in the world of texts, to a *process*," Jonathan Sawday suggests. And Sawday goes on to show how Burton's compositional method, along with his enthusiastic manipulation of print technology, finds a theoretical model in "the Renaissance culture of dissection," anatomy itself. The *Anatomy*, in fact, is both backward-looking, to Renaissance humanism, and forward-looking, to post-Cartesian human science.

The Janus face of Burton's text(s) also invites us to consider the meaning of the term "Renaissance." The title of the present volume uses the term in part to indicate that we are not merely concerned with the seventeenth century, and it may be excessively scrupulous to attempt an intellectual justification of a title of convenience. But since "Renaissance" is currently losing favor within the field of English studies it requires some comment. New Historicism, moving on from Greenblatt's *Renaissance Self-Fashioning*, has tacitly discarded the term, presumably on the grounds that it sounds unhistorical, and prefers instead the historians' "early modern."[38] But the substitution brings paradoxes and problems. One problem, even if we leave aside that of the nature of modernity, is that the latter term is used by historians to cover a period which goes far beyond the restoration of the Stuart monarchy in England, an event which was transitional in terms of English literature but scarcely of global significance. The paradox, more interestingly, is that new historicism claims to be engaged in an enterprise called cultural poetics.[39] If this is so, then however problematic the concept of "Renaissance" may be, it can hardly be discarded, since its determining characteristic lies precisely in the field of cultural poetics. This does not really require elaboration, but one instance from the present volume will illustrate the point. Claire Preston's essay on Sidney's Arcadian poetics, while reminding us that prose writing

---

[38] See, for example, Leah S. Marcus, "Renaissance / Early Modern Studies," in *Redrawing the Boundaries: The Transformation of English and American Literary Studies*, ed. Stephen Greenblatt and Giles Gunn (New York: The Modern Language Association of America, 1992), 41–63. Heather Dubrow searchingly questions how we use these terms in her letter "The Term *Early Modern*," PMLA 109 (1994): 1025–26.

[39] This is explicit in the University of California Press Series edited by Stephen Greenblatt, *The New Historicism: Studies in Cultural Poetics*.

too has its poetics, is concerned with an "emblematic habit of mind [which] developed throughout the sixteenth century and reached its zenith between the time of Sidney's literary maturity in the 1580s and the outbreak of the Civil War sixty years later." Preston argues that the narrative development of *Arcadia* is governed by an emblematic poetics which is morally functional, not merely decorative, and that reading the emblems involves an act of interpretation on the part of the reader which is related to Protestant scriptural exegesis. In these respects *Arcadia* is essentially an English Renaissance text.

In European terms the Renaissance involved the rediscovery of classical ideals of eloquence. In terms of cultural poetics we can say that the sixteenth century produced a culture which gave an enormously privileged status to rhetoric and, in particular, to the pursuit of *copia* in discourse.[40] Renaissance readers were trained to equate *copia* with eloquence. Issues concerning rhetoric appear throughout this book and provide some critical continuity between it and the "Style, Rhetoric and Rhythm" which Croll's editors chose as a title for his collection. The most crucial issue raised by rhetoric in this period is the legitimacy of amplification, encouraged by Renaissance humanism, in Bible translation, and Hammond shows how Tyndale developed "a sore and strong" prose for the English Bible in tension with humanist ideals of copious eloquence. Similarly, and shortly afterwards, Latimer was creating for Protestantism a plain style of sermon which preferred the colloquial and anecdotal to crafted periods and patristic authority. As both Keeble and Hammond point out, this was a seminal development in English prose which influenced the Puritan writing of the 1640s and '50s, and, looking towards the end of this book, we find David Loewenstein emphasizing Gerrard Winstanley's almost obsessive distrust of rhetoric. In his attacks on "verbal worship" and the "verbal profession" of the preaching clergy Winstanley is constantly aware of the way in which rhetoric in the service of scriptural interpretation can become an instrument of institutional oppression.

What emerges from this is the recognition that the period produces both a rhetoric culture and an anti-rhetoric culture, or, perhaps more accurately, that it produces a rhetoric culture engaged in a debate about the nature of rhetoric, which ends with the dominance of the plain style in the Restoration. The Romantic reception of English Renaissance prose

---

[40] See, most recently, Neil Rhodes, *The Power of Eloquence and English Renaissance Literature* (Hemel Hempstead: Harvester Wheatsheaf, 1992), especially 41–50.

stressed the achievements of Anglican eloquence — Hooker, Taylor, and, later, Donne — but this is only a part of the Renaissance. At the same time, the Anglican/Puritan opposition in terms of ornateness or simplicity is also potentially misleading: Latimer may have rejected Latinity in the 1540s, but Milton, writing a century later, certainly did not; Hooker's Ciceronianism may have helped to legitimize the Anglican church, but Milton's Ciceronianism was put to the service of a revolutionary Puritan government. While reminding us that Latin is also a part of English Renaissance prose, Martin Dzelzainis demonstrates Milton's adherence to humanist ideals of oratory as action and the vital relationship between eloquence and the demands of public office. Cicero had declared of epideictic rhetoric that "there is no class of oratory capable of producing more copious rhetoric or of doing more service to the state," and in following this dictum Milton illustrates how the Renaissance, in the received sense of the term, outlived even Charles I. The fact that Winstanley would have put a rather different construction on Cicero's statement at exactly the same time (1649–1650) indicates the inseparability of history, language, and politics in any discussion of English Renaissance prose.

The other field in which the rhetorical values of Renaissance humanism come under pressure is science. Bacon is obviously central in this regard, and discussions of seventeenth-century prose have frequently focused on his role in the reorientating of rhetoric in the interests of scientific discourse.[41] Classic statements of the anti-Ciceronian position, often quoted, are his attack on the "affectionate study of eloquence" and the humanists' privileging of *verba* over *res* in the *Advancement of Learning*, and, deriving from this, Thomas Sprat's call for "mathematical plainness" and the banishment of eloquence in his *History of the Royal Society*.[42] In fact, Bacon's attitude to rhetoric is rather more complex than this would suggest, as Stephen Clucas acknowledges in his essay on the function of the aphorism. Clucas is not, however, concerned with altering traditional perceptions of the way in which science stripped rhetoric of its claims to authority so much as with demonstrating Bacon's innovative use of aphorism in the formation of a new scientific discourse. Humanist and scholas-

---

[41] See Jones, *The Seventeenth Century*; Adolph, *The Rise of Modern Prose Style*; Vickers, *Francis Bacon and Renaissance Prose*; also Brian Vickers and N. S. Struever, *Rhetoric and the Pursuit of Truth* (Los Angeles: Univ. of California Press, 1985).

[42] Francis Bacon, *The Advancement of Learning*, ed. G. W. Kitchin (London: J. M. Dent, 1973), 24; Thomas Sprat, *History of the Royal Society*, ed. Jackson I. Cope and Harold Whitmore Jones (St. Louis: Washington University Studies, 1959), 113.

tic writers had seen aphorism as a *sermo brevis*, an essentially closed locution which was a suitable vehicle for the transmission of knowledge as dogma. Bacon, by contrast, saw aphorism as a method rather than as a stylistic or rhetorical feature, and as a method which would act as a stimulus to scientific enquiry and progress. In place of the closed knowledge systems of humanism and scholasticism, buttressed by the complacency of rhetoric, Bacon presents aphorism as "a knowledge broken," a method designed to "stir" and "provoke" people to enquiry. Clucas argues that this redefined function of aphorism is a neglected factor in the development of a plain style in the seventeenth century. The conflict between humanist values and the values of empiricist science is also discussed, though in a strikingly different context, by Susan Bruce. Bruce sets Bacon's utopia of knowledge in *New Atlantis* against More's utopia of reason, showing how "between More's text and Bacon's we move from an early Renaissance humanist vision of an ideal world, to a late Renaissance utopia whose intent is to illustrate the power of a community based on scientific principles." The very different context is provided by Bruce's discussion of the role of sexuality and the family in the construction of these utopias. While More creates a society where there is no clear distinction between family and state, and where desire is contained, Bacon subordinates family to state and creates a society where the discourse of sexuality cannot be contained. The underlying value of *New Atlantis* is knowledge of the natural in the pursuit of power, and Bacon insists that patriarchy is part of the natural order. Scientific progress and patriarchy, therefore, go hand in hand.

Bruce's essay offers a feminist approach to two utopias constructed by men, and issues of gender are necessarily prominent in Paul Salzman's essay on Lady Mary Wroth. At the same time both essays implicitly evoke the presence of Queen Elizabeth herself at the historical center of this period. In *New Atlantis* Bensalem's status as "virgin of the world" (in the text Bacon calls the country Bensalem, not New Atlantis) is clearly linked to its objectives of knowledge and power, and that association inevitably brings to mind the woman whose name used to be attached to the entire period of the English Renaissance. In the field of prose itself Elizabeth's own speeches demonstrate her ability to employ the power of rhetoric for political ends. But the mastery of eloquence was, of course, traditionally represented as a specifically male attribute, and one therefore which Elizabeth had to appropriate. After all, the word itself derives from *e-loquor*, to speak out, and speaking out in public was certainly not something to be encouraged in women. That, however, is what Lady Mary Wroth did in her Arcadian romance *Urania*, without the authority of sovereignty, and Paul Salzman explains the difficulties she encountered in entering the public arena. Salzman suggests that *Urania* depicts the rival claims of the queen's two bodies and relates this dilemma to a public/private debate, but he also sees Wroth collapsing such an opposition through her "careful use of multivalent narratives, voices, characters, situations" which unfix "the univocal nature of patriarchal discourse." In a statement which reflects interestingly on both Bensalem and Elizabeth herself, Salzman claims that "Within Wroth's narrative, political sovereignty, be it male or female, is always challenged by the power of desire." These essays, then, remind us of the role of gender in the relations between history, language, and the politics of English Renaissance prose, and if we glance back to Quiller-Couch's lofty ascription of masculinity to English prose, that reminder may seem an appropriate point on which to end this introduction.

GERALD HAMMOND

The Sore and Strong Prose of the English Bible

A CERTAIN ENGLISHMAN, IN THE EARLY YEARS of the sixteenth century, traveled around Europe on a great humanist enterprise. By his own account it cost him much labor and time, and he lived much of the while in poverty; but after ten years he could reasonably claim to know at least as much about the Hebrew language as any other Christian, and as much as most Jews for that matter. How extraordinary his achievement was may be measured by the lateness of Hebrew studies in Christian Europe. The first university chair in the language had been founded in 1488 in Bologna, and Johann Reuchlin's *De Rudimentis Hebraicis*, the first very basic guide to the study of Hebrew, appeared in 1506. Scarcely a generation later here was an Englishman in the forefront of study of this great, original language, as Hebrew was then imagined to be. Given the general lateness of the English Renaissance, this man's claim to be one of our chief humanist pioneers is great. He may lack the breadth of Sir Thomas More, but in his intense focus upon the primary language of the Bible, Old Testament and New, he embodies the great Renaissance cry, *ad fontes*, back to the sources.

Knowledgeable readers may well have guessed that this certain Englishman is William Tyndale, the first English translator of the Bible from its original languages, and the originator, in most of the Old Testament and all of the New, of the text of the English Bible as it finally emerged in the 1611 Authorized Version.[1] So influential has this text been, upon all

---

[1] For accounts of the extent and nature of Tyndale's influence upon later English

sections of society, from the unlettered who could only hear the Bible read to them, to the most creative of our writers, that Tyndale has no rival to claims of preeminence. Put simply, he is the most widely read of all English prose writers and he, more than anyone, may claim to be an originator of modern English prose. He is not, however, the Englishman who is the subject of my opening paragraph. That man was Robert Wakefield, a scholar of such standing that he filled Reuchlin's chair of Hebrew at Tübingen in 1522, after the latter's death, and who then returned to England to take up the first lectureship in Hebrew at Cambridge in 1524.[2] To compare Wakefield and Tyndale is to get some insight into the nature of modern English prose as it developed in the sixteenth century, and, in particular, to realize how essentially inhumane a medium it was in its Reformation years.

Inhumane may seem a loaded term to apply to a form of writing, so an example may help explain what I mean. This is Tyndale, in the prologue to his translation of the book of Jonah, in the process of listing the advantages of reading an Old Testament book such as this one:

> And thirdly ye see in that practice, how as God is merciful and long suffering, even so were all his true prophets and preachers, bearing the infirmities of their weak brethren, and their own wrongs and injuries, with all patience and long suffering, never casting any of them off their backs, until they sinned against the holy ghost, maliciously persecuting the open and manifest truth: contrary unto the example of the pope, which in sinning against God and to quench the truth of his holy spirit, is ever chief captain and trumpet blower to set other a-work, and seeketh only his own freedom, liberty, privilege, wealth, prosperity, profit, pleasure, pastime, honour and glory, with the bondage, thraldom, captivity, misery, wretchedness, and vile subjection of the brethren: and in his own cause is so fervent, so stiff and cruel, that he will not suffer one word spoken against his false majesty, wily inventions

---

versions, see C. C. Butterworth, *The Literary Lineage of the King James Bible* (Philadelphia: Univ. of Philadelphia Press, 1941) and Gerald Hammond, *The Making of the English Bible* (Manchester: Carcanet Press, 1982).

[2] Wakefield's life is recounted in the preliminary matter to the recent edition of his *Oratio*: G. Lloyd Jones, ed., *Robert Wakefield: On The Three Languages [1524]*, Medieval & Renaissance Texts & Studies, vol. 68, Renaissance Texts Series, vol. 13 (Binghamton, N.Y., 1989). If Wakefield's own account is to be trusted, he began to learn Hebrew around 1514.

and juggling hypocrisy to be unavenged, though all Christendom
should be set together by the ears, and should cost be cared not
how many hundred thousand their lives.[3]

In spite of its content, one quarter praise of God's mercy, three-quarters
venomous attack upon the pope and his followers, this is humane prose.
Verbally exuberant, its syntax a masterpiece of improvisation, this one
sentence delights in showing off itself and its writer's control over the
language he speaks. All fury and passion, it stretches the language in ways
which would be developed by later Renaissance writers like Thomas Nashe
and Robert Burton. Tyndale's real influence, however, derives from his
work in translation, and the prose which he produced in this role was
something quite different. Here is a passage of his translation, of roughly
equal length, from 2 Kings 2, the first half of which promises comfort
while the second half is disconcertingly vicious:

Then the men of Jericho said to Eliseus: behold the city standeth
pleasantly as my Lord saith, but the water is nought and the
ground barren. And he said: bring me a new cruse and put salt
therein. And they brought it to him. And he went unto the spring
of the water and cast the salt in thither, and said thus saith the
Lord: I heal this water, there shall not come henceforth either
death or barrenness. And the water was healthsome ever after
according to the saying of Eliseus which he spake.

And he went from thence up to Bethel. And as he was going
up in the way, there came little lads out of the city and mocked
him, and said to him: go up thou baldhead, go up thou baldhead.
And he turned back and looked on them and cursed them in the
name of the Lord. And there came two bears out of the wood and
tare forty-two of the boys. And he went from thence to mount
Carmel, and from thence went again to Samaria.[4]

That this little anecdote might have disconcerted early sixteenth-century

---

[3] From David Daniell, ed., *Tyndale's Old Testament* (New Haven: Yale Univ. Press, 1992), 630–31.

[4] Ibid., 504. The text is 2 Kings 2:19–25 (4 Kings in Tyndale). Two years after Tyndale's death the pseudonymously titled Matthew's Bible appeared, containing what is now generally accepted to be Tyndale's translation of the historical books of the Old Testament (from Joshua to 2 Chronicles) including this passage. The rest of the Bible is made up of Tyndale's Pentateuch and New Testament and Miles Coverdale's translation of the remainder of the Old Testament.

readers is borne out by the note which was appended to the verse beginning "And there came two bears" in the Matthew's Bible text in which Tyndale's translation first appeared:

> The contempt of godly men, chiefly preachers, is an offence most grievous: whose authority ought to be most holy and reverent to all the people whom he that receiveth, or again saith, receiveth or rejecteth God. Fathers while they correct not the wantonness of their children, while they hold them not under nurture, while they suffer them to jest and scoff with every man, and let them attempt every thing unpunished, the Lord punisheth them with the children many ways.

What interests me here is not so much the sentiment as the difference in style. The annotator may or may not have been Tyndale himself, but in his need to fill out the text, by offering a fourfold amplification of what parental neglect means, he is glossing the inhumane syntax of the original, in which action follows action with no explanation and no subordination of clauses, with a syntax which implies that things are more complex than the text makes them seem.

Perhaps I should use the favorite word of critics of Hebrew narrative, that is "reticent," to describe such prose as Tyndale creates in his Old Testament translations, but "inhumane" will serve as a reminder that the English Bible developed alongside English humanism, and that it was, in many more respects than styles of writing, a counter movement. It is in this context that Robert Wakefield's example is instructive. He, as a humanist scholar, was firmly opposed to the whole idea of translation. Speaking in Latin to his audience (his *Oratio* is a transcript of his inaugural lecture at Cambridge) Wakefield aimed to get them to appreciate the wonder and complexity — the mystery — of the Hebrew language. To translate it is to destroy it: and 'it' means not just the original language but the only text in which it survives. As he told his Cambridge audience:

> when you are able to read and understand the fountain of truth, by which I mean those sacred books of the Old Testament, in its own original language ... then you will feel a general contempt for all translations and expositions.[5]

---

[5] Lloyd Jones, *Robert Wakefield*, 172–73: Lloyd Jones's translation: "translations and expositions" stands for *interpretationum expositionumque* in Wakefield's text.

I shall not now go into the mysteries which Wakefield attributes to this great original language, the source of all wisdom and knowledge and the language which God's finger actually wrote; but one of his themes is relevant. Wakefield stresses the peculiar force of Hebrew words, emphasizing that each word contains multiple meanings. Some of this takes the form of kabbalistic mumbo-jumbo whereby transposition of the three letters which make up the root of every verb sometimes leads to six different meanings.[6] We can dismiss this as nonsense now but Wakefield's scholarly audience would have been keenly attuned to notions of hieroglyphic magic and many would have taken it seriously. Other elements of his argument still make sense, however. Classical Hebrew is a language of limited vocabulary, even in comparison with early sixteenth-century English, and on the few occasions when he translates a biblical phrase or verse, Wakefield invariably does so by using two, three, or even more synonyms for single words. For instance, translating the Hebrew adjective *oz*, he renders it "strong and powerful," and the noun *melitsah* as "eloquence or ornate speech."[7]

Such use of synonyms is consistent with humanist practice. Thomas More does the same when he translates his own Latin life of Richard III.[8] And we can see something of the same reflex in a contemporary like Tyndale when he is not translating, as in the passage from the prologue to Jonah which I quoted earlier, where the pope is described as not merely seeking his own way, but seeking "his own freedom, liberty, privilege, wealth, prosperity, profit, pleasure, pastime, honour and glory," at the expense not simply of others' servitude, but with their "bondage, thraldom, captivity, misery, wretchedness, and vile subjection." The ideal is one of *copia*. But when it comes to the Bible, the text itself has stern injunctions against adding to or subtracting from what is written there, and although a dogmatic, fundamentalist adherence to the literal word of

---

[6] E.g., from *baqar*, "herd" or "ox," Wakefield produces *baraq*, "lightning"; *raqabh*, "rottenness"; *rabhaq*, "become fat"; *qarebh*, "approach"; and *qabhar*, "bury." See Lloyd Jones, *Robert Wakefield*, 104–5.

[7] Ibid., 132–33 and 76–77 respectively.

[8] See Richard S. Sylvester, ed., *The Complete Works of Sir Thomas More* (New Haven: Yale Univ. Press, 1963), 2:lvi–lvii. In discussing More's use of doublets Sylvester states: "The practice is almost universal among English translators in the late fifteenth and early sixteenth centuries.... In adopting it a translator, consciously or unconsciously, affirmed his descent from the mediaeval glossator; at the same time he made his own contribution towards the augmentation of the English language."

God is more a seventeenth-century phenomenon than a sixteenth-century one, it still behooves a believing translator not to offer more than the original does. The Authorized Version, accordingly, has an amazingly small range of vocabulary, given the size of its text. Just one Shakespeare play throws up a greater variety of words and, more to the point, stretches the resources of the language in terms of semantic range and improvisation.[9]

So, while Tyndale's editors praise him, understandably, for his contribution to English vocabulary, they ought rather to recognize how verbally costive he was. To what extent this is a matter for praise is debatable, but the example set by Tyndale's translation was followed by the various sixteenth-century English Bible versions into the 1611 Authorized Version. It was followed by many others than Bible translators too. John King has charted in some detail the influence of the early printed English Bibles upon "the emergence of the Protestant plain style," a movement which extends at least into the eighteenth century.[10] He cites Nicholas Udall's preface to Tome 1 of Erasmus's *Paraphrases* as a "defence of Protestant plainness." In it, Udall explains the providing of biblical paraphrase as:

> a plain settyng forth of a texte or sentence open, clere, plain, and familiar, whiche otherwyse should perchaunce seem bare, unfruictefull, hard straunge, rough obscure, and derke to bee understanded of any that wer ... unlearned.[11]

As King notes, however, the plain style is not Udall's normal mode of writing, and even this brief snatch of a long sentence shows that his style here is not as plain as it pretends, in its piling up of adjective upon adjective and its syntactic ambitiousness.[12] If Udall's plain style is bibli-

---

[9] Since part of the purpose of this paper is to point towards the influence of sixteenth-century English Bibles upon English prose in the next century, Nigel Smith's comments on Ranter prose are relevant here: "This writing ... displays a high degree of accomplishment, though it has a tendency to become tongue-tied by using a limited vocabulary to handle different concepts.... Apart from Coppe's colloquial and proverbial phrases, Ranter pamphlets do possess a restricted vocabulary, with a particular concentration upon Biblical words connected with the notion of becoming and illumination, as well as the horrors of prophecy." From Nigel Smith, ed., *A Collection of Ranter Writings From The Seventeenth Century* (London: Junction Books, 1983), 38.

[10] John King, *English Reformation Literature: The Tudor Origins of the Protestant Tradition* (Princeton: Princeton Univ. Press, 1982), 138.

[11] Ibid., 130–31.

[12] See also Udall's explanation of the need for a plain style, quoted by King, ibid.,

cal, it is so in a Pauline way, for it is only in the New Testament epistles that Tyndale uses a varied, cumulative vocabulary with a complex syntax, as in these verses from Col. 1:

> We give thanks to God the father of our Lord Jesus Christ, always praying for you, since we heard of your faith which ye have in Christ Jesus and of the love which ye bear to all saints for the hope's sake which is laid up in store for you in heaven, of which hope ye have heard before by the true word of the gospel, which is come unto you, even as it is into all the world, and is fruitful as it is among you, from the first day in which ye have heard of it, and had experience in the grace of God in the truth, as ye learned of Epaphras our dear fellow servant, which is for you a faithful minister of Christ, which also declared unto us your love which ye have in the spirit.
>
> For this cause we also, since the day we heard of it have not ceased praying for you and desiring that ye might be fulfilled with the knowledge of his will, in all wisdom and spiritual understanding, that ye might walk worthy of the Lord in all things that please, being fruitful in all good works and increasing in the knowledge of God, strengthened with all might, through his glorious power, unto all patience and long suffering with joyfulness giving thanks unto the father which hath made us meet to be partakers of the inheritance of saints in light.[13]

But even Paul is not commonly so convoluted, and if we look elsewhere in Colossians we find, in Tyndale's rendering of it at least, a direct prose in which every word stands by itself, needing no synonym, and where the sentences are largely monoclausal or biclausal:

> Wives, submit yourselves unto your own husbands, as it is comely in the Lord. Husbands love your wives and be not bitter unto

---

141: "Albeit in this English paraphrase the translators have of purpose studied to write a plain style, than to use their elegancy of speech ... partly because there was a special regard to be had to the rude and unlettered people, who perchance through default of attaining to the high style, should also thereby have been defrauded of the profit and fruit of understanding the sense, which thing that they might do, was the only purpose why it was first translated.... For as the learned are able enough to help themselves without any translations at all."

[13] Col., 1:3–12; from David Daniell, ed., *Tyndale's New Testament* (New Haven: Yale Univ. Press, 1989), 295.

> them. Children, obey your fathers and mothers, in all things, for that is well pleasing unto the Lord. Fathers, rate not your children, lest they be of a desperate mind. Servants, be obedient unto your bodily masters in all things: not with eye-service as men-pleasers, but in singleness of heart, fearing God. And whatsoever ye do, do it heartily as though ye did it to the Lord, and not unto men, forasmuch as ye know that of the Lord ye shall receive the reward of inheritance, for ye serve the Lord Christ. But he that doth wrong, shall receive for the wrong that he hath done: for there is no respect of persons. Ye masters, do unto your servants that which is just and egal seeing ye know that ye also have a master in heaven.[14]

In his address to his Cambridge audience Robert Wakefield reminded them that, in essence, the Greek of the New Testament was an Hebraic language: *hebraicograecum* was his term for it.[15] Tyndale came to the same realisation through his own experience of translation and took care that his readers should appreciate the fact. He had, after all, initially presented himself to the bishop of London as a translator of Greek, taking with him to the bishop's house a version of Isocrates which he had already done. With no encouragement from the bishop he went into exile on the Continent, translating the New Testament in 1525.[16] He then turned to the Old Testament, and between 1525 and 1530 learned Hebrew well enough to translate the Pentateuch. When he returned to the New Testament to revise it, issuing his revision in 1534, he began his new preface "W.T. unto the Reader" like this:

> Here thou hast (most dear reader) the new testament or covenant made with us of God in Christ's blood. Which I have looked over again (now at the last) with all diligence, and compared it unto the Greek, and have weeded out of it many faults, which lack of help at the beginning, and oversight, did sow therein. If ought seem changed, or not altogether agreeing with the Greek, let the finder of the fault consider the Hebrew phrase or manner of speech left in

---

[14] Col., 3:18–4:1; ibid., 197–98.

[15] Lloyd Jones, *Robert Wakefield*, 72: *quaque totum novum testamentum hebraicograecum scriptum est.*

[16] Tyndale's account of his efforts to get sponsorship for translating the New Testament in London is to be found in his preface to his Pentateuch, "W.T. to the Reader"; see Daniell, *Tyndale's Old Testament*, 5.

> the Greek words. Whose preterperfect tense and present tense is oft both one, and the future tense is the optative mode also, and the future tense is oft the imperative mode in the active voice, and in the passive ever. Likewise person for person, number for number, and an interrogation for a conditional; and such like is with the Hebrews a common usage.[17]

This would have struck his merely English readers as a forbidding comment. Words like "optative" and "preterperfect" scarcely figured in the daily conversation of the ploughboys who Tyndale, following Erasmus, wished to read his New Testament − indeed, they were brand new English words.[18] Normally Tyndale chose not to make any kind of technical comment on his translation, his prefaces being taken up with the much more serious matter of telling his readers how they should understand and respond to the words of scripture, and this is a rare example of a place where he inclines towards the kind of commentary which Wakefield offered to his learned audience. That it comes at the very opening of his New Testament preface makes it all the more striking. Tyndale clearly thought it more important to tell his readers about the Hebraic nature of New Testament Greek than to worry about frightening them off as they began to read.

This passage from St. Paul to the Corinthians may represent one Hebraic element of Pauline style, the tendency to think in a binary mode:

> All things are lawful unto me: but all things are not profitable. I may do all things: but I will be brought under no man's power. Meats are ordained for the belly, and the belly for meats: but God shall destroy both it and them. Let not the body be applied unto fornication, but unto the Lord, and the Lord unto the body. God hath raised up the Lord, and shall raise us up by his power. Either remember ye not, that your bodies are the members of Christ? Shall I now take the members of Christ, and make them the members of an harlot? God forbid. Do ye not understand that he which coupleth himself with an harlot, is become one body? For two (saith he) shall be one flesh. But he that is joined unto the Lord, is one spirit.

---

[17] Daniell, *Tyndale's New Testament*, 3.
[18] The OED's first attestation for *optative* is 1530; for *preterperfect* Tyndale's use here is the first recorded example.

> Flee fornication. All sins that a man doth, are without the body. But he that is a fornicator, sinneth against his own body. Either know ye not how that your bodies are the temple of the holy ghost, which is in you, whom ye have of God, and how that ye are not your own? For ye are dearly bought. Therefore glorify ye God in your bodies and in your spirits, for they are God's.[19]

From its opening balance of "lawful" and "profitable," followed by "may do all" set against "no man's power," the argument develops through parallels and antitheses. In his study of Hebrew poetics James Kugel pointed out that parallelism, while it has long been acknowledged as a defining principle of Hebrew poetry, was a basic feature of much biblical prose too, so that parallel and antithesis may almost be described as essential to the Old Testament mind.[20] In this respect, even the punctuation of Tyndale's prose deserves comment. While it is normally dangerous to attribute any certain meaning or set of principles to printed sixteenth-century texts, there is evidence to believe that the Bible was exceptional, and that even so early a translator as Tyndale took care to achieve consistency and coherence in his practice.[21] In this passage, note how words which normally link clauses and help construct complicated sentences become, instead, markers of division and separation, as in the end of the first paragraph where first "For" and then "But" introduce separate, distinct sentences. Tyndale uses colons and full-stops to cut potentially complex sentences into binary structures.[22]

Such structures are proverbial. Theoreticians puzzle over what it is that constitutes a proverb, dictionaries of proverbs habitually beginning with a defensive statement to the effect that the proverb, while easily recognizable, is essentially undefinable. But behind all of the elements which are adduced — pithiness, authority, experience, ambiguity — the one necessary element seems to be that proverbs have a binary structure. In Alan Dundas's formulation, "all proverbs are potentially formulations which

---

[19] 1 Cor., 6:12–20; Daniell, *Tyndale's New Testament*, 248–49.

[20] James L. Kugel, *The Idea of Biblical Poetry: Parallelism and its History* (New Haven: Yale Univ. Press, 1981); see especially 59–95.

[21] For comment on the implications of punctuation practice in Renaissance English Bibles, see Samuel Hornsby, "A Note on the Punctuation in the Authorized Version of the English Bible," *English Studies* 54 (1973): 566–68.

[22] In practice Tyndale is anticipating the division into verses which only appeared in English versions in the 1560 Geneva Bible.

compare and/or contrast."[23] Such comparisons and contrasts may, for all of their pithiness, be repetitive and developmental. Indeed, St. Paul's prose works in just such a way, when "meats" and "belly" are initially contrasted — "Meats are ordained for the belly"; then compared — "and the belly for meats"; and then fitted into a greater contrast — "but God shall destroy both it and them." Then again, the proverbial structure may exist at the simplest level of the two word sentence, as in Tyndale's rendering which begins the second paragraph, "Flee fornication." To flee is to hurtle away from; to fornicate is to press together. The alliteration which should bind helps instead to force the words apart.

To identify in Tyndale's Bible translation his proverbial syntax as something opposed to the humanist enterprise is apparently paradoxical, for was not the recovery and transmission of proverbs an enterprise most dear to the early Renaissance humanists? Erasmus's *Adages*, to take the most obvious example, became a set-text throughout the schools of sixteenth-century Europe. One look at the *Adages*, however, is enough to reveal that the collection and study of proverbs is quite different from the use of them. True, Erasmus is sometimes proverbial in his own style, but most often his strategy is to circle round and round a proverb, amplifying and extending it, tracing in great detail its history, in particular the authority which lies behind it, and the complexity of its meaning: a practice not far removed from the marginal glosses to bare biblical verses which I quoted earlier. While the material which Erasmus works with seems commonplace, his purpose is to ennoble it; and he makes a careful point, in the earlier editions of the *Adages* at least, to play down biblical material, as if associating the word of God with such expressions would bring it into disrepute.[24] Tyndale leaned the other way. "Flee fornication" is more obviously proverbial, along the lines of, say, *festina lente* or *ollas ostentare*, two of the adages given extensive comment by Erasmus, than is Luther's rendering of the sentence, "Flihet dir hurerey"; or, even more tellingly, than the effect of a modern English translation like the Revised English Bible's "Have nothing to do with fornication."[25]

---

[23] In Wolfgang Milder and Alan Dundas, eds., *The Wisdom of Many: Essays on the Proverb* (New York: Garland, 1981), 54.

[24] See Margaret Mann Phillips's discussion of Erasmus's gradually increasing use of biblical material in her edition of *The 'Adages' of Erasmus* (Cambridge: Cambridge Univ. Press, 1964), 25–34.

[25] Here Tyndale is uncharacteristically preferring the Vulgate's rendering, *Fugite fornicationem*, over Luther.

When he came to translate St. Paul's description of his own epistolary style Tyndale echoed Luther's "schwere und starck" in his own rendering:

> For the pistles (saith he) are sore and strong: but his bodily presence is weak, and his speech rude.[26]

The "but" which introduces the second and third parts of this sentence indicates a contrast between the "sore and strong" written style and the "rude" speech. And, certainly, if one looks at a later translation, such as the Authorized Version, the gap between the written and the spoken is virtually a chasm:

> For *his* letters, say they, are weighty and powerful; but his bodily presence *is* weak, and *his* speech contemptible.[27]

Set against this contrast between weighty and powerful writing and contemptible speech, Tyndale's opposition of sore and strong writing and rude speech is much less striking; and, interestingly, "rude" was a second thought, for in his original New Testament translation he had described the speech as "homely."[28] I would like to argue, therefore, that, in spite of the "but," Tyndale sees some connection between "homely" or "rude" speech and a written style which is "sore and strong," the latter phrase being as good a definition of proverbial compression as one might wish.

Not only Paul but Christ too, is sharp and strong, speaking in proverbs whose essence is the rude and homely. Tyndale's Englishing of his speech, in vocabulary and syntax, is nearly always aiming for the simplest words within a potentially proverbial structure. The sermon on the mount offers obvious examples, as in these verses from the beginning of Matt. 7:

> Judge not, that ye be not judged. For as ye judge so shall ye be judged. And with what measure ye mete, with the same shall it be measured to you again. Why seest thou a mote in thy brother's eye, and perceivest not the beam that is in thine own eye. Hypocrite, first cast out the beam out of thine own eye, and then shalt thou see clearly to pluck out the mote out of thy brother's eye.
>
> Give not that which is holy, to dogs, neither cast ye your pearls

---

[26] 2 Cor., 10:10; Daniell, *Tyndale's New Testament*, 269–70.

[27] The Greek words used by Paul mean, respectively, "heavy in weight, severe, stern"; "strong, firm"; "utterly despised."

[28] The OED cites, from Caxton's introduction to his *Eneydos* (1490), "Some gentlemen . . . desired me to use old and homely terms in my translations."

before swine, lest they tread them under their feet, and the other turn again and all to-rent you.

Ask and it shall be given you. Seek and ye shall find. Knock and it shall be opened unto you. For whosoever asketh receiveth and he that seeketh findeth, and to him that knocketh, it shall be opened. Is there any man among you which if his son asked him bread, would offer him a stone? Or if he asked fish, would he proffer him a serpent? If ye then which are evil, can give to your children good gifts: how much more shall your father which is in heaven, give good things to them that ask him?

Therefore whatsoever ye would that men should do to you, even so do ye to them. This is the law and the prophets.

Enter in at the strait gate: for wide is the gate, and broad is the way that leadeth to destruction: and many there be which go in thereat. But strait is the gate, and narrow is the way which leadeth unto life: and few there be that find it.[29]

It is fair to say that even the most prolix and syntactically sophisticated translation will find it hard to mess this up, but a comparison with a very modern version like the Revised English Bible shows a watering down of the basic antitheses presented by Tyndale's short sentences.[30] And even the Authorized Version, which follows Tyndale virtually word for word here, shows a slight temptation towards expansion. In verse eleven Tyndale's absolutely clear antithesis "if ye then which are evil, can give to your children good gifts," has become, by 1611, "if ye then, being evil, know how to give good gifts unto your children"; and in verse twelve Tyndale's "whatsoever ye would that men should do to you, even so do ye to them" is amplified to "all things whatsoever ye would that men should do to you, do ye even so to them." In each case the Authorized Version translators, as is their wont, are translating more literally, but this in itself is revealing. Tyndale will compress even the highly compact Greek in order to make the binary structure of Christ's sentences more striking.

---

[29] Matt., 7:1–14; Daniell, *Tyndale's New Testament*, 28–29.

[30] E.g., in The Revised English Bible, verses 1–2: "Do not judge, and you will not be judged. For as you judge others, so you will yourselves be judged, and whatever measure you deal out to others will be dealt to you"; and in verses 7–8: "Ask, and you will receive; seek, and you will find; knock, and the door will be opened to you. For everyone who asks receives, those who seek find, and to those who knock, the door will be opened."

In the margin to the paragraph beginning "Ask and it shall be given you" Tyndale writes "Covenants," in line with his promise, in the 1534 preface, to mark out such places:

> Faith now in God the father through our Lord Jesus Christ, according to the covenants and appointments made between God and us, is our salvation. Wherefore I have ever noted the covenants in the margins, and also the promises.[31]

As W. Clebsch has demonstrated, Tyndale's movement towards a contract theology through the 1530s is marked most of all by his prioritizing of the word "covenant."[32] It even seems, from the opening sentence to his revised New Testament (quoted above, p. 8) that he was tempted to retitle his Bible as being made up of the Old Covenant and the New Covenant. The theology of this is only important here insofar as it impinges upon matters of style and syntax. As Tyndale explains in his preface:

> The right way: yea and the only way to understand the scripture unto our salvation, is, that we earnestly and above all thing, search for the profession of our baptism or covenants made between God and us. As for an example: Christ saith (Matt. 5) Happy are the merciful, for they shall obtain mercy. Lo, here God hath made a covenant with us, to be merciful unto us, if we will be merciful one to another: so that the man which sheweth mercy unto his neighbour, may be bold to trust in God for mercy at all needs. And contrary-wise, judgement without mercy, shall be to him that sheweth not mercy (James 2).[33]

In effect, a covenant is a contract, a binary structure: you do this and I shall do that; you show mercy to others and I shall show mercy to you.

The syntax of covenant, promise, and contract is, when pared down, the syntax of the proverb, the most commonplace of our forms of speech. That there was a "Tudor hunger for gnomic sayings, proverbs, aphorisms, and parables" is itself a commonplace, but that this hunger shifted through the classes as the sixteenth and seventeenth centuries developed

---

[31] Daniell, *Tyndale's New Testament*, 5.

[32] William A. Clebsch, *England's Earliest Protestants 1520–1535*, Yale Publications in Religion 11 (New Haven: Yale Univ. Press, 1964); especially 185–95.

[33] Daniell, *Tyndale's New Testament*, 4.

is also worth note.³⁴ James M. Osborn sums up the shift in his introduction to the autobiography of Thomas Whythorne (1528-1595):

> At times Whythorne seems to write almost exclusively in proverbial phrases, well-worn sayings such as the *Adagia* of Erasmus, lore from compendia, and phrases from the Bible. In this he was of course characteristic of the mid-sixteenth-century gentleman...; during the next century the quoting of proverbs began to be typical of artisans, and below the taste of the wellbred man.³⁵

By the 1640s and 50s the proverbial structures established in Tyndale's Bible translation and consolidated in the various Bibles which built upon his work, up to and including the Authorized Version, were most natural to the men and women who made up the popular movements which helped turn the world upside down. Here is one such, the Ranter Joseph Salmon offering an apologia for his writing:

> I have stept out of my silent Mansions, to offer these few words to the Vulgar view: how hardly I was persuaded to it, my own heart can evidence, and many in my behalf can testify: some engagements urged me to it, more than any desire of mine to become public.
>
> I am quite aweary of popular applause, and I little value a vulgar censure; the benefit of the one, cannot at all affect me, nor the prejudice of the other much molest me:
>
> I enjoy greater treasures in my happy silence, than all their cruelty can make me capable of the want of.
>
> 'Tis true I have lost a good name, and honourable esteem in the world.
>
> I have also another name, which is a new one, which none can read, but he that hath it; none can blast with the least blot of infamy.
>
> I can cheerfully bear the indignation of the Lord, for I have sinned:
>
> It is not for me to reply against the dealings of the Eternal Wis-

---

³⁴ The description of the Tudor hunger for proverbs is from King, *English Reformation Literature*, 360.

³⁵ James T. Osborn, ed., *The Autobiography of Thomas Whythorne* (Oxford: The Clarendon Press, 1961), lvi.

dom: it is rather good for me to bear the yoke in my youth, with a Christian silence and gravity.

I am made willing to give my cheek to the smiter, to sit alone, (keeping silence) and put my mouth in the dust: any thing with the Lord, it is to me very acceptable; nothing (without God) dares approach my quiet and still Mansions.

In a word: I am both to do and to suffer all things through an Eternal Almightiness: And resolved I am to gain a conquest over the World, by prostrating myself a subject to their weakness.

I must submit to them, that I may reign over them; and even then I trample them underneath my feet, when I am most subdued to their will and pleasure.[36]

This kind of syntax was one of the major effects of the English Bible, leaving its mark on English prose in the residues of puritan discourse which survived into the growth of the novel. Whether Tyndale would have enjoyed such a development is questionable. Robert Wakefield certainly would not. His vision of Biblical Hebrew was of a mysterious language in which there was nothing "crude and improper," which had no capacity to express "human allurements and unworthy passions," but whose words contained "an endless store of meanings ... full of nuances" — it was a language which always "expresses itself in a refined manner."[37] This was the humanist ideal. The sixteenth-century Bible translators, in spite of their scholarship, did not share it, favoring instead the sore, the strong, and the rude.

---

[36] Smith, *Ranter Writings*, 216–17.
[37] Lloyd Jones, *Robert Wakefield*, 109–10; Lloyd Jones's translation.

DANIEL KINNEY

The Tyrant Being Slain: Afterlives of More's *History of King Richard III*

> You sleep in peace, the tyrant being slain. —
> Campaign-promise at Bosworth
> (Shakespeare, *Richard III* 5.3.257)

OUR OWN STORY BEGINS WITH AN ENDING, a ragged ending, or rather a pair of them. Richard III, King of England, was killed in battle on Bosworth Field August 22, 1485; Sir Thomas More was beheaded in the Tower of London July 6, 1535. Three years later, in a record from 1538, comes the first dated mention of More's *History of King Richard III*, in an interrogation of a certain George Croftes:

> I have asked him [Sir Geoffrey Pole] if one might without jeopardy have More's books in keeping. He said "Yea, for they treated not of the King's matters," and lent me a chronicle of More's making of Richard III.[1]

---

[1] *Letters and Papers... of Henry VIII*, ed. J. S. Brewer et al., 21 vols. (London, 1862–1932), 13/2:334–35, no. 828. More's English history appears in vol. 2 of More's *Complete Works* (15 vols. [New Haven and London, 1962–, hereafter "CW"]) with two highly corrupt forms of the Latin text; a superior version of the Latin from a newly recovered manuscript appears with my own English translation in *CW* 15. Though the English history at least in the much-reworked Hardyng-Hall version was destined for far greater currency than the Latin, the Latin's alternative phrasings as well as a number of points where the two texts diverge in their treatments of "fact" make the Latin an often

The consensus today is that More's history at least indirectly had a great deal to do with the King's matters, no less Henry VIII's than his father's, the king who supplanted King Richard III; yet Croftes' answer apparently satisfied Henry VIII's agents, and the history or chronicle in English "of More's making of Richard III" was first published in 1543 as a sequel to John Hardyng's medieval verse chronicle of England. It would seem that More's death somehow checked or disguised the subversive potential of the history, at least for a time, and made it fairly easy for all the best-known Tudor chroniclers to take up More's text as a charter for Tudor ascendancy, this in spite of the fact that a Tudor king ordered More's death and the fact that in some ways More's all-but-canonical treatment of Richard's accession may be just as subversive of Henry VII's ascendancy as it is of the king's he supplanted. More's portentous description of Richard's purported caesarean delivery — "a knife was the midwife" (CW 15:333) — appears almost as apt for the vexed and belated emergence of More's history in both English and Latin, for the posthumous legends of Richard as well as of More, and indeed for the birth of most dynasties including the Tudors; for all these in some way owe their birth or traumatic rebirth to high-level political violence, and to violence now viewed partly thanks to More's history as a force which is never either fully or finally decisive, as a process which generates new questions as fast as its throes or its strokes make short work of the old.[2]

---

indispensable guide to the work or the play of allusion in More's history and the play-work of shaping conjecture. Thus at need I cite either More's English from CW 2 or his Latin or my English rendering (or both) from CW 15; since the Latin of CW 15 is keyed marginally to the English of CW 2 it is easy to make a comparison in either direction. Unless otherwise stated all modern English renderings are mine. The relation between the various English and Latin recensions of More's history is examined in CW 15:cxxxiii –cliii; see especially cxxxv, cxlii and n. 2, cxlv, and cxlix–cli, documenting the claims that the new Paris manuscript cannot be derived by mere copying from any other known form of the text and that the manuscript text of the Latin includes many telling additions which are found in no form of the English. It may be that the Latin is also the most "final" form of a text More indeed left unfinished in Latin *and* English, since the Latin directly assails as naïve one important claim made in the English (clii n. 3) and includes two insertions not found in the English which aid both continuity and closure, at least of a sort (480/20–23 with note and 482/25–484/25). Possibly as a modest precaution against angering Henry VIII (d. 1547) Richard Grafton did not actually mention More's authorship when he first published More's text with John Hardyng's chronicle in 1543 (cf. H. Ellis' reprint-edition [London, 1812; repr. New York, 1974]); later printings beginning with Edward Hall's chronicle of 1548 did acknowledge More's authorship.

[2] Marjorie Garber's fine chapter, "Descanting on Deformity: Richard III and the

More's text sets up conventional expectations about violence and its shaping functions in history at least partly in order to upset them; right of conquest, the watchword of triumphant monarchs from Edward IV to the first Tudor king and beyond, here turns into an all-purpose tool of political conjuring opportunely engaged to bear out any number of *faits accomplis*, whereas virtuous defeat becomes even more oddly destabilized, issuing in both the innocent deaths laid to Richard en route to his final defeat and the desperate but outstanding courage that he there displays.[3] If the blood of the martyrs is the seed of the church, here the blood of a series of partisan martyrs has tended to yield mainly seed for subversive conjecture, a view borne out not least by the odd fact that More's text in English has long been a text little less fundamental for Ricardian revisionist writers than for mainstream pro-Tudor defenders of an anti-Ricardian status quo.[4]

Shape of History" (in *The Historical Renaissance: New Essays on Tudor and Stuart Literature and Culture*, ed. Heather Dubrow and Richard Strier [Chicago and London, 1988], 79–103) takes up Shakespeare's stage version of More's history as a point of departure for a more comprehensive account of written record as distortion, displacement, and "de-featuring"; Garber's chapter, though it never explicitly treats Shakespeare's sources, is one of the best illustrations of how often More's own (mis)shaping designs, and not only his statements of "fact," find close parallels in Shakespeare. More perhaps got the image of the sword or knife (*ferrum*) as midwife from a source he indeed must have known, since that gathering of poems supplies models for many of More's Latin epigrams, namely one *Greek Anthology* poem (A. P. 9.311) on a hunting-bitch (cf. here n. 20) who gives birth to her pups by caesarean: "Artemis is no longer the kind mistress of birth; / instead, Ares serves females as midwife." Cf. also Pliny the Elder, N. H. 7.45–47, where breech-birth is pronounced inauspicious, but caesarean birth (at least from a dead mother!) is professed to bode well for the offspring.

[3] More refers to right of conquest ("victoria deciso iure") in *CW* 15:438. For Edward IV's appeal to the principle in his 1471 declaration of right see Thomas Rymer, ed., *Foedera, Conventiones et Litterae*, 20 vols., (London, 1704–35), 11:710A, and cf. Sydney Anglo, *Spectacle, Pageantry and Early Tudor Policy* (Oxford, 1969), 8; for Henry VII's analogous appeals see the various texts noted in Sir George Buck's *History of King Richard III* [1619], ed. A. N. Kincaid (Gloucester, 1979), 88–89, with note, and more generally R. Bartlett, *Trial by Fire and Water: The Medieval Judicial Ordeal* (Oxford, 1986), esp. 107–19.

[4] Both Cornwallis and Buck, Richard's first self-professed literary defenders, transpose speeches and arguments to be found in More's history from a context of blame to its opposite. See also the most measured pro-Richard response to More's history in Jeremy Potter, *Good King Richard: An Account of Richard III and his Reputation 1483–1983* (London, 1983), Chap. 12 ("More Myth-making") and *passim*. Of course More's reputation as a martyr not only for Catholic orthodoxy but also for freedom of political conscience much enhanced the prestige of his testimony against Richard III, even when appraised by a Deist like Edward Gibbon; see his comments on Walpole's *Historical Doubts* (Edward Gibbon, *Miscellaneous Works*, ed. Lord Sheffield, 4 vols. [London, 1814], 3:342).

Since More even explicitly stresses the uncertain historical basis of much of his text, and since one London chronicle More adopts as a skeletal template for his own account was already in print as of 1516, it seems clear that More's version's tenacious vitality is far more than a matter of neutral or prior historical record, or for that matter even the enduring appeal of an untroubled doctrinaire digest of "fact."[5] It is rather as if some intractable element of differing opinion is what makes the More version from either perspective *the* version to conjure with, as if More's artful mock-up of primary sources' incoherence has made his entire discourse, however belated, pass muster more often than not as a primary source.[6] Without treating More's text, as some have, as mere hoax or as merely "More Myth-making," I propose to approach More's duplicitous history and its own opposed posthumous doubles as a lesson in historical doubt and historical irony, irony at the Tudors' expense very nearly as

---

[5] On More's factual disclaimers see Alison Hanham (*Richard III and his Early Historians 1483–1535* [Oxford, 1985], esp. 157–60, 165), who generally treats the whole text as a Lucianic spoof on more earnest historians' distortions; see also Potter, "More Myth-making," and n. 26 below. The skeletal template for much of More's history is Robert Fabyan's *New Chronicles of England and France* (London: R. Pynson, 1516), though More may well have have used another Fabyan collection, *The Great Chronicle of London*, now ed. A. H. Thomas and I. D. Thornley (London, 1938). Fabyan's *New Chronicles* were apparently finished by 1504, the *Great Chronicle* however not before 1509; see *Great Chronicle* lxix–lxxii and n. 17 below.

[6] From a kindred perspective More's "self-censorship" (Denys Hay, *Annalists and Historians* [London, 1977], 120) in withholding the text all his life and his deftly ambiguous treatment of Richard's ascent both reflect More's precocious approach to deploying literary indirection and irony as a potent political force; on the political "discovery" of literature and literary indirection in early modern England, but mainly by much later authors, see Annabel Patterson, *Censorship and Interpretation* (Madison, 1984). The tenacious hold of both *Richard III* and *Utopia* on those same authors' visions suggests that the gradualist ironic re-visions implicit in both of More's texts slowly translated the monarchist dogmas of early Tudor discourse into something quite close to a "populist" alternative idiom. For this "populist" idiom in *Utopia*, see Brendan Bradshaw in *The Cambridge History of Political Thought 1450–1700*, ed. J. H. Burns (Cambridge, 1991), Chap. 4; for More's *Richard III*, see especially Hanham 183–85, as well as A. Patterson, *Reading Holinshed's Chronicles* (Chicago and London, 1994), 208–10; for some noteworthy Morean and populist resonances in late-Tudor drama see Richard Helgerson, *Forms of Nationhood: The Elizabethan Writing of England* (Chicago and London, 1992), especially 210–12, 221, 234–35, and 237–40. H. A. Kelly some time ago noted the way Richard's preemptive, preposterous bids for the sanction of Providence in More's history constitute not a myth (as in "The Tudor Myth") but an "anti-myth" structurally at odds with most time-serving monarchist pieties; see *Divine Providence in the England of Shakespeare's Histories* (Cambridge, MA, 1970), 130–32, 137, 282.

much as at Richard's, a methodically two-edged approach to deciding the issues of both violence and temporal authority.[7]

The high stakes of this sort of approach to More's history or self-conscious para-history become clearer when we take up a formula of cultural optimism that in one variant ("Time trieth truth") supplied More with a personal motto. The assertion that truth, and thus right, will eventually ("in due time") prevail could indeed be described as not far from a humanist credo persisting on through the Enlightenment. Not

---

[7] See the previous note and my article, "Kings' Tragicomedies" (*Moreana* 86 [1985]), 131-32, for a survey of previous approaches to More's history. Hanham's always suggestive if sometimes strained treatments of More's styles of allusive invention are often uncommonly useful, as are Alistair Fox's discussions of allusion and larger design (*Thomas More: History and Providence* [New Haven and London, 1982], Chap. 3); on the closely linked problem of "uncanny" affinities and doublings in Shakespeare and More consult Garber as well as the article by Peter Rudnytsky ("More's *History of King Richard III* as an Uncanny Text," in *Contending Kingdoms: Historical, Psychological, and Feminist Approaches to the Literature of Sixteenth-Century England*, ed. M.-R. Logan and P. Rudnytsky [Detroit, 1991], 149-72), and cf. again "Kings' Tragicomedies" 138. On Richard's monstrous emergence in Shakespeare as a prideful negation of natural and feminine origins see the often complementary discussions of Robert N. Watson (*Shakespeare and the Hazards of Ambition* [Cambridge, MA, 1984], Chap. 1) and Janet Adelman (*Suffocating Mothers: Fantasies of Maternal Origin in Shakespeare's Plays, "Hamlet" to "The Tempest"* [New York and London, 1992], "Introduction"). Other useful discussions of Shakespeare's (and thus More's) engagement with subtexts appear in recent books by Rebecca W. Bushnell and Robert S. Miola (*Tragedies of Tyrants* [Ithaca and London, 1990], chap. 4, and *Shakespeare and Classical Tragedy* [New York and London, 1992], chap. 3). On dramatic as (sometimes) opposed to historical representation see Chris Hassel, Jr. (*Songs of Death* [Lincoln and London, 1987], chap. 5), Phyllis Rackin (*Stages of History* [Ithaca and New York, 1990]), and Barbara Hodgdon (*The End Crowns All* [Princeton, 1991], chap. 4). On the general problem of historical representation in the period see Joseph M. Levine (*Humanism and History* [Ithaca, 1987], esp. chap. 1), D. R. Kelley (in *The Cambridge History of Renaissance Philosophy*, ed. C. B. Schmitt et al. [Cambridge, 1998], 746-61), John D. Lyons *Exemplum* [Princeton, 1989]), and Timothy Hampton (*Writing from History: The Rhetoric of Exemplarity in Renaissance Literature* [Ithaca and London, 1990]), with nn. 24-25, below, and my treatment of More's controversy with the French poet Brixius about poetry, history, and partisan bias in CW 3/2:553-62 and 572-89. An impressive synopsis of the fortunes of Richard III's posthumous legend, and thus of More's standard recasting of Richard III's story, may be found in A. J. Pollard's mass-market large-format book *Richard III and the Princes in the Tower* (New York, 1991). For a useful synopsis of constitutional questions connected with each stage of Richard's rise and fall see Charles Wood's *Joan of Arc and Richard III* (New York and Oxford, 1988). Leonard Tennenhouse's discussion of two forms of exemplary stage violence and the person of Elizabeth I ("Violence Done to Women on the Renaissance Stage," in *The Violence of Representation*, ed. Nancy Armstrong and L. Tennenhouse [London and New York, 1989], 77-97) has a surprisingly close bearing on how Tudors and Tudor historians both staged and construed the dead body of Richard as spectacle.

surprisingly in view of the Renaissance humanists' own fairly sweeping designs on posterity, the same adage has also appealed to many other ambitious or marginal causes intent on prevailing at *some* point at least, at some privileged moment of truth pregnant with a new right and new *faits accomplis*; and among marginal causes of this sort the Yorkist cause — Richard III's cause — has long had an exceptionally close link with this same proverbial appeal. In the form of a telling metaphor of descent it indeed comes to furnish the title for Josephine Tey's well-known pro-Richard novel, *The Daughter of Time*; for Time's daughter, *this* variant insists, is The Truth. Tey's own cue for this title was probably a line More assigns to a time-serving preacher engaged in an effort to bastardize all Yorkist claimants *but* Richard III: "... the trouth comming to light, the rightful inheritors be restored, & the bastard slip pulled up, ere it can be roted depe" (CW 2:67). As in other revisionist borrowings from More's history the main point of Tey's title is to save — by excising — the truth of Ricardian material from More's own in the main hostile context. Probably unknown to Tey, though perhaps not to More (cf. CW 2:6), was the pedigree-lesson before Parliament in the year 1460 on which Richard III's father, Richard, Duke of York, largely based his own bid for the crown, "... for though right for a tyme rest and be put to silence, yet it rot[t]eth not nor shall not perish."[8] Truth is not dead but sleeping, and finally will

---

[8] *Rotuli Parliamentorum*, ed. J. Strachey et al., 6 vols. (London, 1767–77), 5:377, also cited in *English Historical Documents 1327–1485*, ed. A. R. Myers (Oxford, 1969; hereafter "Myers"), 418. Richard Duke of York was descended from Edward III's third son on his mother's side and fifth son on his father's side; Henry VI was descended on his father's side only from Edward's fourth son, John of Gaunt, Duke of Lancaster. York's legitimist claim thus included something more than the double-edged argument that Henry VI was demonstrably unfit to rule, and was thus further still from the desperate and double-edged argument employed before Bosworth by the soon-to-be Henry VII, scion of John of Gaunt's bastards, that the crown fell to him since he planned to expropriate it from a tyrant (S. B. Chrimes, *Henry VII* [London, 1972], 39, R. A. Griffiths and R. S. Thomas, *The Making of the Tudor Dynasty* [Gloucester, 1985], 139); cf. Richard III's proclamation on the Tudors' descent in *Richard III: The Road to Bosworth Field*, ed. P. W. Hammond and A. F. Sutton (London, 1985), 209, from the Paston letters. As J. Dunbabin argues (in *The Cambridge History of Medieval Political Thought c. 350–c. 1450*, ed. J. H. Burns [Cambridge, 1988], 493–98), the excuse of deposing a tyrant was generally an argument of last resort for pretenders, and an argument fertile in "bloody instructions" because other pretenders could make the same claim; but the Tudors made shift as they could, it seems, not least by spilling any stray Yorkist blood they could not absorb in the new dynasty (A. F. Pollard, *Henry VIII*, 2nd ed. [New York, 1966], 9, 143; for a similar view of why York dispatched Henry VI see Charles Ross, *Edward IV* [London, 1974], 175).

come out, resurrected and newborn at once; if in some sense the truth was there dormant and waiting all along, it was virtually not there at all for all practical purposes until York's own ambitious researches first brought it to light. Clearly Richard III's own family-history research is productive as well as incisive in much the same way, though More savors the irony that an argument bastardizing Richard's brother and nephews all but dictates a crowning surprise bastardizing him too: Richard's new truth is already pregnant with its own undoing.

The Yorkist penchant for precedent-searching by way of substantial innovation is not only akin to the self-authorizing maneuvers of Renaissance culture in general, digging up ancient precedents in order to make newness seem old and espousing forward movement by way of return to the sources;[9] it is also a neat illustration of the doubleness inherent in virtually any appeal to the notion that truth and thus right must in due time emerge and prevail. Truth will always out; out of what? Error? At the outset of his very useful account of revision and disjunction in history, *The Estrangement of the Past*, Anthony Kemp treats as "clearly a misreading" a disjunctive, late-Renaissance use of the adage that time brings forth truth; nonetheless it is clear from More's cherished Erasmus among numerous others that the Renaissance sense of how time yields up truth is more often disjunctive than not.[10] Though the due time for some vital truths to emerge might have been long ago, even a moderate revisionist outlook assumes other truths worth revealing are just now in the course of emerging or are still wrapped in error as yet. The more drastic one's sense that enlightening new personal visions are kept in — or down — by the past, and indeed by the present, the more drastic becomes one's own style of delivering them; it was Milton, not some feckless dynast, who wrote that "Truth ... never comes into the world, but like a Bastard, to the

---

[9] On making newness seem old see the first words of Machiavelli's *The Prince*, Chap. 24 (cf. Lyons, especially 40, 49–50), and on retrograde progress as a dynamic paradox of humanist praxis cf. Erasmus's adage-essay "Festina lente" and CW 15:lxviii, lxxvii, and now Timothy Hampton's introduction.

[10] For this typical Renaissance gloss of the adage see F. Saxl in *Philosophy and History*, ed. R. Klibansky and H. J. Paton, 2nd ed. (New York, 1963), especially 200 n. 1, and cf. Bacon's strongly revisionist title, *Temporis partus masculus*, "The Masculine Birth of Time"; for an effort to distance this sort of productive perceptual disjunction from the less edifying emergencies of physical conflict see Erasmus's Adage 1523 ("Bellum haudquaquam lachrymosum") as contrasted with 2436 ("Bellum omnium pater") and the long adage-essays of 1515, in particular 3001 ("Dulce bellum inexpertis").

ignominy of him that brought her forth ..."[11] In this image, which links the portentous emergence of Wisdom-Minerva from Jupiter's brain with the trenchant discovery-practices of Socratic judicial midwifery, we are clearly by now a long way from viewing Truth as Time's untroubled firstborn, and not nearly as far from the Marxian extremity of naming Violence the male-midwife of History.[12]

But what then of strategically contrary founding directives which both sanction and outlaw such violently primal expedients, as in bolstering a Tudor ascendancy while forestalling new Yorkist reprisals? What about More's own project, one in which clearly candor must compromise with Tudor dynastic anxieties even as it examines the slippery foundations of dynastic authority in general? Here indeed Richard functions for both Henry VII and for More as a "lightning-rod," "scapegoat," and blind (Watson 16; cf. CW 2:10); and indeed, at least some demonizing and brutalizing, especially *post mortem*, is virtually bound to attend on an effort as drastic as Richard's to recast and challenge his precursors' version of truth. More, however, not only indulges the scapegoating-impulse; he also reflects on its power to distort and its use in confounding not only historical hindsight but emergent political insight as well, insight which could strip Tudor pretensions of right as completely as the Tudors stripped Richard. An indictment of Richard is no unambiguous endorsement of Henry VII[13]; here as elsewhere, More mounts a more local polemic with

---

[11] *Complete Prose Works*, ed. D. Bush et al., 10 vols. (New Haven, 1953–), 2:225. Milton may even be aware of his own true-born bastard's affinity with Richard III's dubious right; compare PL 2.653–56 (Milton's Sin, also patterned on Spenser's personified Error) with Shakespeare's contentious description of Richard III's mother in *Richard III* 4.4.47–48: "From forth the kennel of thy womb hath crept / a hell-hound that doth hunt us all to death ..."

[12] *Das Kapital* (1867), part 7, chap. 24 [28]: "Die Gewalt ... der Geburtshelfer" (emphasis added). Marx may also have had in mind Heraclitus's old saying (B 53, B 80 Diels-Kranz, clearly also congenial to Hegel) that conflict or war is the father of all; but the midwife analogy (cf. Plato, *Theatetus* 149a–151d, and n. 2 above) is still closer to Shakespeare or Milton, and thereby to More. Highly relevant to Marx's analogy, though remarkably they do not cite it, are three rich recent studies of masculine anxiety about unruly feminine productiveness both historic and otherwise; see Neil Hertz, *The End of the Line* (New York, 1985), chap. 9; Gail Kern Paster, *The Body Embarrassed: Drama and the Disciplines of Shame in Early Modern England* (Ithaca, 1993), especially chaps. 4 and 5, and Marie-Hélène Huet, *Monstrous Imagination* (Cambridge, MA, and London, 1993), especially chap. 1.

[13] In a letter to Ulrich von Hutten of 1519 Erasmus called More a hater of tyrants in general, not a champion of this or that king; he was certainly no personal favorer or favorite of Henry VII or his dubious alternative to tyranny. On More's attitude toward

a vastly more daring oblique emphasis.[14] The Tudors' brutalized and demonized Richard, like every good scapegoat, showed an uncanny staying-power right from the start; in provoking his readers' reflection on the posthumous shaping and misshaping of this needful scapegoat, on the scapegoat as monstrous official projection with the new ruling order its own Frankenstein, More effectively doubled the dead king's disconcerting historic persistence, now no less an exemplary victim of history than a monstrous exemplary victimizer.

In a kind of detachable coda to his history as written in English, More adds this edifying conclusion to a long, bizarre hearsay account of how Richard III killed his young nephews, the "princes in the Tower":

> ... Which thinges on euery part wel pondered: god neuer gaue this world a more notable example, neither in what vnsuretie standeth this worldly wel, or what mischief worketh the prowde enterprise of an hyghe heart, or finally what wretched end ensueth such dispiteous crueltie.... King Richarde himselfe [was] as ye shal herafter here, slain in the fielde, hacked and hewed of his enemies handes, haryed on horsebacke dead, his here in despite torn and togged lyke a cur dogge.... (CW 2:86–87)

Since More's history in English breaks off with a speech in which More's sometime patron, the prelate John Morton, helps Buckingham, Richard's chief backer, decide to rebel, it would seem More himself never got to

---

Henry VII and his policies see CW 2:lxv–lxi, CW, 3/2 index (More's verse criticisms of Henry VII), and CW 15 index (further parallels between Henry VII's own policies and tyranny according to More's history, with More's call for deposing unworthy officials examined on 525).

[14] See CW 3/2:559, and D. Baker-Smith, "'Inglorious Glory': 1513 and the Humanist Attack on Chivalry," in *Chivalry in the Renaissance*, ed. S. Anglo (Woodbridge, Suffolk), 140, on the motives of More's controversy with the warmongering French poet Germanus Brixius. This particular account of More's overt and covert designs in *The History of King Richard III* helps account for the odd fact that one and the same reader can see in More's text both a *pièce à thèse* scourging King Richard as tyrant and a lampoon on partisan history of the sort even then being written at Richard's expense; see Hanham, especially 159, 195. It is worth noting here that More's basically populist point in exposing the scapegoating-impulse as focussed on Richard is much less to indict an anonymous collective for its slaughter of an innocent victim than to lay bare the ultimately self-compromising ambition of mighty lords, Richard included; for the former perspective on scapegoating-practice see René Girard in *Violent Origins: Ritual Killing and Cultural Formation*, ed. R. G. Hamerton-Kelly (Stanford, 1987), esp. 109–18 (but see also 248–49, on the rather different case of *Othello*); for the latter, n. 20 below.

expand on this list of instructive indignities. But More's chronicle sources supply more detail, and so do the continuations of More's history as included in Shakespeare's chief source-texts, the standard collections of Edward Hall and Raphael Holinshed, who adapt and expand More's own text to supply a neat bridge between other more standard regnal narratives. The first published recension of More's English, from a manuscript probably furnished by Hall, even adds one last crowning indignity to the lines we have just finished citing: the king harried on horseback is not merely dead; he is naked as well.

This last detail is variously reported in the two London chronicles on which More apparently relied, not reported at all in the earlier ill-preserved Crowland chronicle; instead, it merely states that "the said Richard's body ... and other insults was brought inhumanely with a rope around its neck into Leicester" (*Crowland* 182). In the often inaccurate account of a Spanish purported eyewitness at Bosworth we are told that the king's corpse lay three days in Leicester draped with only a paltry black loincloth; such near-naked display, which stops just short of total divestment as well as deliberate abuse, has no lack of close parallels in England, most meant to confirm that some king's rival really is dead.[15] But indeed both the Crowland account and two separate and early disparaging comments about the dead king as a "dog" who was "slain in a ditch"[16] make it clear the symbolic uncrowning and degrading of Richard at Bosworth was no decorous halfway-divestiture. *Fabyan's Chronicle* is

---

[15] For this narrative, the so-called De Valera letter, see Pamela Tudor-Craig, *Richard III* (London, 1973), 68. There are numerous examples of such treatment in its milder forms, for example the posthumous treatment of Edward II, Richard II, and Henry VI, as well as Warwick the Kingmaker (P. W. Hammond, *The Battles of Barnet and Tewkesbury* [Gloucester, 1990], 79) and James IV of Scotland (CW 3/2:386). Even Edward IV lay in state clad in only a loincloth, presumably to lay to rest lingering suspicion of any foul play in his death (James Gairdner, ed., *Letters and Papers . . . of Richard III and Henry VII*, Rolls Series 24, 2 vols. [London, 1861–63], 1:4; on the practice in general cf. C. A. J. Armstrong, "Some Examples of the Distribution and Speed of News in England at the Time of the Wars of the Roses," in *Studies in Mediaeval History presented to F. M. Powicke*, ed. R. H. Hunt et al. [Oxford, 1948], 437). But historians from the Crowland chronicler (*The Crowland Chronicle Continuations: 1459–1486*, ed. N. Pronay and J. Cox [London, 1986], 182) to Holinshed (3:446), Buck (105, 120), Ross (*Richard III* [Berkeley and Los Angeles, 1981], 225–26), and Griffith (164–65) all remark on the singular abusiveness of the treatment afforded King Richard.

[16] The Welsh bard Dafydd Llwyd ap Llewelyn's prophetic ode on Bosworth, written c. 1485–1486 (Tudor Craig 95), and a late-1490 drunken outburst in York (records summed up in Hanham 63); Richard also dies a dog's death in More (CW 2:87) and Shakespeare (*Richard III* 5.5.2; cf. also nn. 20, 23).

at any rate decorously biblical in describing the dead Richard "naked as he was born" (Fabyan, 2, sig. XX₃v; cf. Job 1:21, Eccl. 5:14), but the *Great Chronicle*, another London collection by Fabyan which More perhaps also employed, is far more crudely carnal or feral in its way of conveying the king's nakedness:

> And Richard, late king, as gloriously as he in the morning departed from that town [Leicester], so as irreverently was he that afternoon brought into that town. For his body was despoiled to the skin, and nothing was left about him so much as would cover his privy member, and he was trussed behind a pursuivant called Norroy as a hog or other vile beast. And so all bespattered with mire and filth he was brought to a church in Leicester for all men to wonder upon, and was there finally irreverently buried. And thus ended this man with dishonor as he that sought it. (*Great Chronicle* 238)[17]

Polydore Vergil's history of England, first written in Latin, softens this stark new genital emphasis and remarks on the naked king's dead body, almost defensively, "a miserable spectacle in good sooth, but not unwoorthy for the mans lyfe" (Vergil 226). The vernacular version in Hall-Holinshed, the least guarded and most prejudicial of all in the way it

---

[17] Modernized version found in Myers 347; Edward Hall's *Chronicle* is here cited according to H. Ellis' edition (London, 1809), Polydore Vergil's *English History* in a Tudor translation according to Ellis' (partial) edition (Camden Society Publications 29, London, 1847), and Ralph Holinshed's *Chronicles* (2nd ed. of 1587) according to Ellis' edition in 6 vols. (London, 1807-8). On the dating of Fabyan's two chronicles and the more skeletal Cotton MS. Vitellius A XVI, also based on a "Main City Chronicle" and compiled about 1496, see texts cited in n. 5 above. The Vitellius version, as well, reports Richard being borne off "all naked" behind someone on horseback (*Chronicles of London*, ed. C. L. Kingsford [Oxford, 1905], 193). The contemporary "Ballad of Bosworth Feilde" (cf. Ross [1981] 235-37) also speaks of Richard "naked as be borne might be"; it is hard to say who first adopted this biblical phrasing. The Burgundian chronicler Jean Molinet, whose own work ends in 1506, gets the facts of the Bosworth encounter impressively wrong but again mentions Richard's corpse borne off behind someone on horseback, bespattered with mire and filth, "shown to the people all naked, without any clothes" [*tout nud et sans quelque vesture*] (*Chroniques*, ed. G. Doutrepont and O. Jodogne, 3 vols. [Brussels, 1935-37], 1:436); this almost formulaic convergence suggests these details form a separable unit of vivid description, historically accurate or not, circulating most freely a number of years after Bosworth. Overall, though in differing degrees, More and Polydore Vergil like Shakespeare much later seem to play down the chroniclers' near-emblematic insistence on the dead Richard's literal nakedness and to focus instead on what less crudely localized secrets of kingly descent were laid bare by the reckoning at Bosworth.

expands on this "miserable spectacle," correspondingly yields an especially good opening for our own discussion:

> For his bodye was naked and despoyled to the skyne, and nothynge left aboue hym not so much as a clowte to couer hys pryue members, and was trussed behynde a persiuaunt of armes called blaunche senglier or whyte bore, lyke a hogge or a calfe, the hed and armes hangynge on the one syde of the horse, and the legges on the other syde, and all by spryncled with myre and bloude, was brought to the gray fryers church within the toune, and there laie lyke a miserable spectacle: but suerly consyderyng his mischeuous actes and Facinorous doynges, men may worthely wonder at such a caytiue, and in the sayde church he was with no lesse funeral pompe, and solempnitie enterred, then he woulde to be done at the berying of his innocent nephiwes whome he caused cruellie to be murthered and vnnaturally to be quelled...so yll was his lyfe that men wished the memorie of hym to be buried with his carren corps.... Thus ended this prince his mortall life with infamie and dishonor, which neuer preferred fame or honestie before ambicion tyranny and myschiefe. (Hall 421, with additional slurs [!] echoed in Holinshed 3:446)

Tudor chroniclers never have done having done with such scenes, clearly climax as well as embarrassment, and at times even primal enough to outface the best primary testimony.

Something more is at stake here than the "infamie and dishonor" stressed by Hall; this is singularly outrageous treatment even for a bad king. We are not unfamiliar with the Renaissance (and not only Renaissance) custom of calling on God as a kind of chief justice to warrant harsh handling of judicial prisoners both living and dead, but the gingerly way in which Richard's abusers exploited this time-honored warrant or sanction is almost as telling as the actual fact of abuse. For the dead king's alleged crimes included high treason of more than one sort, usurpation compounded with regicide, yet the actual abuse of his corpse as both countenanced by Henry VII and dragged on through the Tudor tradition for all its excesses stopped short of the usual horrors reserved for a traitor, and indeed stopped at only those injuries one might just contrive to explain or defend as all part of the chances of war.

Henry's prudence and ruthlessness joined in electing a new form of "miserable spectacle" in which even as an overthrown king was abused and degraded the whole work of abuse and degrading appeared to be less the design of the victor himself than the notionally transcendent force which assigned him the victory.[18] In this vein the new king's propagandists made opportune use of whatever might strengthen their cause, from the judgment of victory itself to the furious last charge Richard led against Henry's own guard, a charge Henry might not have survived if retainers of Richard's had not turned on him. Even though there was certainly a limit to how far Henry dared to disfigure his dead rival's corpse, he and his propagandists could not be more perfectly placed to abuse Richard's memory in place of it. For the very betrayal that might seem to taint Henry's success could be made to accentuate Richard's isolation, and indeed his abandonment by even his own better judgment, with his fatal last charge opportunely construed as the last, suicidal extremity of a brute gone mad — even "berserk" — or a beast run amok; this does much to account for the first pronounced "uncanny doubling" in these (professed) records apart from the generative doubling of violent birth and death, namely doubling the dead king himself with the doubly eponymous pursuivant (herald, attendant) who bears off his body.[19]

---

[18] The term "miserable spectacle" ("Miserabile spectaculum") is already employed in the thirteenth century for the severest form of punishment for high treason, drawing, hanging, and quartering, which it seems routinely included castration; see J. G. Bellamy, *The Law of Treason in the Middle Ages* (Oxford, 1970), 23 n. 2 and chap. 3 passim. All of this is of course quite distinct from the more decorous early Tudor spectacle addressed in Anglo's study, though on 11-13 it does note the singular irony that with only a few interlined alterations the program for Richard III's coronation was restyled for Henry's. On King Richard's post-mortem attainder by Henry for high treason see Chrimes 50, 63; on God's judgment by victory in battle see n. 3 above.

[19] Hall-Holinshed names this figure the "White Boar" or "blaunche senglier" pursuivant, Richard's personal heraldic attendant (cf. Hammond and Sutton 128-29); in this version of fact Richard's lethal charge leaves him as finally no more than his own heraldic token, textualizing him into precisely what Tudor accounts wish to make of him. *The Great Chronicle* calls this attendant "Norroy" instead, a professional title and nickname conventionally reserved for the "king of the [heralds of the] North"; of course this pairing, too, would dispose of Richard with his own heraldry. The Norroy herald at this time was a certain John More, no relation (presumably) to our More despite this new unsettling convergence of names, with a More emblematically "bearing out" Richard's dead body (see CW 2:7, and for John More, Norroy herald, and the "blaunche senglier" pursuivant conjecturally styled John More's son [!] on the basis of the variants here cited see the entries by Walter H. Godfrey et al., *The College of Arms, Queen Victoria Street* [London, 1963], 106, 238). Indeed our author More may redouble this ironic doubling in his story of Hastings' encounter with the pursuivant Hastings en route to his own execution; see CW 2:51 and Godfrey 265-66, and cf. my n. 31 below.

Tudor records made Bosworth a boar-hunt (the boar being Richard's heraldic device) or a hunt to dispose of a wolf or mad dog who would need to be put down in any case.[20] Even so, the dead monarch was spectrally still recognized as a king, though a king who undid his own dynasty, and the scandal of Richard's post-mortem ill-treatment might well help to offset or outwear the old mystery of what had become of the young heirs that Richard displaced. It seems likely that both new respect and new disrespect shown to Richard's memory some ten years after Bosworth reflected a twofold campaign to dispose of a lingering Yorkist opposition and its stubborn premise that one of the princes yet lived; for dead Richard was given a tomb at about the same time Tudor texts began dwelling with such fascination on Richard's bared privates, a crude mark of the end of the line for the whole house of York, but a vital if demonized prop for the new Tudor dynasty.[21]

---

[20] On Richard's boar insignia, probably based on a punning allusion to York (Latin "Ebor[acum]"), see A. J. Pollard 86–89 and J. R. Planché, *The Pursuivant of Arms* (London, 1873), 262, 273–75; for additional early polemical references see *CW* 2:214, Tudor-Craig 95 with refs., *Crowland* 184, and Bernard André in James Gairdner's *Memorials of Henry VII* (Rolls Series, vol. 10 [London, 1958], 31 and 138 ("Marsus aper") [from Horace, *Carm.* 1.1.28, linked with Mars in the Renaissance glossaries] and the "senglier Archadique" [the third labor of Hercules/Henry VII]). On the boar's generally negative symbolism see B. Rowland, *Animals with Human Faces* (Knoxville, 1973), 37–43, and Joyce E. Salisbury, *The Beast Within: Animals in the Middle Ages* (New York and London, 1994), 80–81, and on the boar throughout Shakespeare as voracious and lustful intruder see the reference in *CW* 2:223 (with *H5* 4.7.13, "Alexander the Pig"!). More's own note in his prayerbook identifies with "Mahomet" the biblical *aper de sylva* or "boar from the wood" found in Ps. 79 (A. V. 80):14. Numerous visual instances of Richard's insignia in Hammond and Sutton quite graphically bear out the *OED*'s first definition of "boar" as "the wild or tame male swine (uncastrated)"; also see the next note. Cf. also More's phrasing in *CW* 15:328 = *CW* 2:10 ("inter dissidentes factiones suo ipsius sanguine foedus sanciretur") with Servius' comments on Vergil, *Aen.* 1.61, 8.641; Servius claims the term *foedus* or "treaty" refers to the "foul" (*foeda*) death of the beast killed to clinch an alliance or truce, with the implicit wish that whoever broke faith would then die the same sort of foul death as the beast, specified as a *pig*, either female or male. On Richard characterized as a wolf or (mad) dog, see *CW* 2:24, 87 and nn. 2, 11, and 16 above; cf. also *CW* 3/2, no. 115, on good rulers and tyrants as watchdogs and wolves, a suggestively volatile contrast based on Plato, *Rep.* 416a.

[21] On the now-destroyed tomb the first Tudor commissioned for Richard, complete with a statue (no doubt a fine likeness indeed!), see the note in Buck 280–81, with R. Edwards, "King Richard's Tomb at Leicester," *Ricardian*, 3/50 (September 1975), 8–9, and N. Llewellyn, "The Royal Body: Monuments to the Dead, for the Living," in *Renaissance Bodies: The Human Figure in English Culture c. 1540–1660*, ed. L. Gent and N. Llewellyn (London, 1990), 226–27; on the probable epitaph, see Buck 217–18 and note; on a statute of 1495 also seemingly aimed at the "pacification" of Yorkists by way

More began his own history some twenty years later, when the Yorkists were more or less crushed.[22] Even so, he proceeds as if making short work of dead Richard III were as urgent a business as ever, and the lively Tudor market for modified forms of More's text makes it clear that this sense of fresh business is apt, and perhaps apt in more ways than one. Shaming Richard III's corpse and abusing his memory were not much more at odds with heroic magnanimity than with even the more primal "heroic" desire to the annihilate the enemy's fame altogether, since the force of the Tudors' own claims owed so much to the spectral vitality of the "tyrant" to whom Tudor historians assigned the main mortal initiative, and sometimes indeed even the main moral initiative, for the Tudors' violent seizure of power.[23] Dwelling as they *must* dwell, to ward off rival claims,

---

of a qualified recuperation of Richard see Chrimes 178-79; on the dating of texts stressing dead Richard's sexual exposure see nn. 5 and 17 above. It is naturally no easy task to pin down all the symbolic functions of this perplexed sexual emphasis in most Tudor texts' treatment of Richard, though their authorized style of construing his "last stand" does habitually feature an odd blend of collapse and defiance as its central theme; cf. CW 15:484/18-21 and note, with Wood's comment (119) on how vandals and votaries of Richard still vie for control of his image in Leicester, in this case a heroic modern statue and its upthrust sword. On the notion of sexual impasse as interpretive point of departure see most notably Hertz with discussion by Catherine Gallagher; on the joined symbolism of weakness and strength in exposures of Christ's sexuality in Renaissance art see especially Leo Steinberg, *The Sexuality of Christ in Renaissance Art and Modern Oblivion* (New York, 1983), 46-48, 86-91, 187. Given Steinberg's distinctive indifference to the common description of Christ as a seminal *Word* (see especially Gregorius Magnus, *Moralia* 23.15.28 [PL 76:267CD]), it is also worth noting how for instance the Latin *fascinum* (Greek *baskanon*) is both phallus and spell-binding word, equally apotropaic and threatening, being a token which both binds and looses all manner of unruly issue(s) including the issues of speech. Late-medieval and Renaissance etymologies derived *aper* (our "boar") and *aporia* (our "impasse") from "opening" (*ab aperiendo*), one more seminal clue as to what makes uncanny empowerments of Richard's impairments throughout his long, vexed posthumous history.

[22] For the *terminus post quem* of More's history see CW 2:lxiii-lv and especially xc, on the 1515 *editio princeps* of Tacitus's *Annales* 1-5, More's main source for the links he allusively draws between Richard III and Tiberius.

[23] In imputing to Richard not only the death of King Henry VI but the death or assumed death of two Yorkist princes, as well, and in treating the latter as a fair but harsh judgment afflicting the whole Yorkist cause for together condoning the former, Bernard André provides an especially incisive account of the leading role this Tudor Richard performed in undoing the whole Yorkist cause, first in moral terms, then in dynastic ones: "sicque mors morte, exitium exitio pensatum est" (*Vita Henrici VII* [c. 1502], Gairdner 24). In sharp contrast with this bustling bane of his family is the nondescript figure of the soon-to-be Henry VII who in Shakespeare and elsewhere seems largely defined by his power to stand by to inherit. On Homeric attempts to obliterate a hero's prestige by disfiguring his body see J.-P. Vernant, *Mortals and Immortals: Collected*

on a much-demonized martial hero-as-scapegoat, Tudor texts limit Henry's performance in arms to heroic *withstanding* of violence, and at times even come close to damning in Richard active martial performance in general; this implicit Erasmian discounting of old-fashioned chivalric aggressiveness may also do much to explain what drew More to this story in the first place. More joins previous Tudor writers and even outdoes them in diverting the reader's attention (overtly, at least) from the violence perpetrated by Henry himself, in transforming Richard's death-wounds to grisly birth-defects prefiguring his crimes, self-destruction, and death (*CW* 2:7), and in animalizing, isolating, and exposing what Shakespeare makes Richard himself call his own "naked villainy" (*Richard III* 1.3.335); but where earlier Tudor writers avoid ever reflecting at length on the manifold ironic ways in which Henry's own "rights" merely crown Richard's wrongs, More takes some pains to heighten and activate this irony at virtually every stage of his narrative. More's indictment of Richard works much less like a straightforward charter for Henry VII than a pointedly unbalanced study-in-contrasts by way of implicit critique; it treats Richard's traditional faults as an opening for a glancing but well-aimed Erasmian assault on the violent charade of dynastic contention in general.[24] The text slowly but relentlessly opens out its own case against Richard in a way which may best be illuminated by even a quick sketch of More's double-edged rhetoric of exemplification and allusion.

One of the most striking features of More's history in both English and Latin, a feature borne out but still far from exhaustively charted in the

---

Essays, ed. F. Zeitlin (Princeton, 1991), chap. 2, especially 60–73; on the different, ferocious and yet indecisive tradition of post-mortem assaults on Richard's body and memory see especially Buck 105 and 120, and compare the king-criminal polarity examined in R. C. Finucane's essay, "Sacred Corpse, Profane Carrion" (in *Mirrors of Mortality: Studies in the Social History of Death*, ed. J. Whaley [London, 1981], 47–51). On 122 Buck describes More as a Cynic reviler who takes up in effect where Vernant's (and Homer's) "dogs of war" leave off; on 123–24 Buck proposes to "pay him [More] in his own coin" and adduces the way More's own corpse was abused in a bid to discredit his memory. For the compromised recuperation of More's scattered members as relics see Clark Hulse, "Dead Man's Treasure: The Cult of Thomas More," in *The Production of English Renaissance Culture*, ed. David L. Miller et al. (Ithaca and London, 1994), 190–225.

[24] The most crucial Erasmian parallels for More's glancing exposé of dynastic contention (cf. nn. 10 and 14 above) are the adage-essay "Dulce bellum inexpertis" (1515) and *Institutio principis christiani*, a text published the following year. Bradshaw studies the latter text's barely concealed general challenge to hereditary monarchy and connects it at length with the "populist" features of More's own *Utopia*, another text first published in 1516.

Yale annotated editions, is its seemingly endless allusiveness. On one level the way that More's text implicates so many other, distinct texts seems to bolster its own representative claims; as a gallery of behavioral and rhetorical types, recognizable types, the text frequently seems to encourage the sense that both it and the course of events it relates are exemplary histories, patterns often encountered before and quite sure to surface often again. It undoubtedly much helps to naturalize the partisan perspectives of More's history and to generalize the vision based here on the murky events which preceded Richard's crowning that so much here appears to proceed in accord with historical and narrative constants of various kinds; we might even speak of the tenuous thread of historical evidence (the "historical evidence" in our sense) being fortified and enriched by the frequent appeal to (in our sense) extraneous precedents. In this way More's authorial providence replicates the harmonious complexities of the figural patterns inhering in biblical history and in history in general according, for instance, to St. Augustine in the *City of God*; More's authorial providence thus appears to corroborate God's own even as God's shaping presence returns the favor.[25] With such powerful credentials written into its own very texture and with More's *bona fides* borne out by his death under Henry VIII, it is none too surprising that More's history as incorporated in the great Tudor chronicles is in certain respects Tudor history *par excellence*, the most seminal statement of a Tudor myth shaping and reshaping historical perspectives from Hall-Holinshed to Shakespeare and beyond.[26]

---

[25] On the whole range of medieval historiographic conventions so unsettlingly redeployed in More's history see Ruth Morse, *Truth and Convention in the Middle Ages: Rhetoric, Representation, and Reality* (Cambridge, 1991), and nn. 5-7 above; on Providential design in relation to More's history and its imitators see most notably Kelly, Fox, and Hassel; on medieval providentialism and new disjunctive styles of historical consciousness of the sort also active in More's history see Kemp, chap. 3; on early-modern survivals and extensions of medieval providentialism see M. E. James, *Society, Politics and Culture: Studies in Early Modern England* (Cambridge, 1986), esp. 12-15. Clearly I do not share Kelly's sense that More's "anti-myth" fully preempts the more pious account of the Tudors' legitimacy which has come to be known as "the Tudor myth" (n. 6 above; cf. also nn. 23 and 30).

[26] For such judgments of More's history see CW 2:275 n. 4 (contrast lxxvii), 3/2:579, and Buck cxxix n. 5, the last reference attributing the Latin to Cardinal John Morton. The old claim that More's history in Latin is really John Morton's is briefly reviewed and exploded in CW 15:cxxxvi and cxlv; still, for prudential reasons More might well have seen fit to *suggest* that the work owed a great deal to Morton as Henry VII's chief adviser. As A. Patterson observes (*Reading Holinshed's Chronicles*, 36) Tudor chroniclers after Grafton's unascribed first edition are uncharacteristically careful in acknowledging their own borrowings from More's history.

Another aspect of allusiveness in More's history complicates and bedevils this version of events; its allusiveness is also at times disconcertingly counter-Providential, not so much edifying as intently illusive, the metier of figures like Richard himself who are best at deploying and exploiting the allure of suspicious conjecture.[27] More's chief patterned allusions are no less disruptive than they are suggestive; they suggest that to make correct sense of the narrative we must learn to dispense with a number of the values that given events are assigned on the narrative's surface, most of all those which claim to present a sharp contrast between other kings and Richard III. I have already noted that Richard himself may be seen as a kind of instructively clouded allusion to the ruling directives not only of York's entire line but of kingly contenders in general; in a sharp, saving contrast with these male aggressors construed as a group More eventually fields a complex and seductive amalgam of Cressida, Eve and Griselda all joined in the peace-loving charms and good deeds of "Jane" Shore, Edward's "merriest" and best-beloved mistress, whose victimization by Richard merely draws down new blame on himself.[28] But apart from the sexual complications which trouble this contrast in principle there is also one crucial and unhappy note which confounds it in practice as well: all "Jane" Shore's selfless good deeds in youth render her in the end perhaps still more disfigured and still worse-remembered than Richard in all his self-seeking, yet More finally gives up trying to salvage her memory as a task which is strictly at odds with the narrative project in which it would seem all the more fortunate survivors of those days compete: ever more prejudicial remembering.[29] We might say that More's text thus subversively unfolds "history" into fiction, or rather into overtly reflexive, self-critical history, in almost the same way that King Richard's life-story unfolds Edward's or Henry VII's; as a variably candid and reticent gloss on the Tudor construction of Providence to

---

[27] "The allure of suspicious conjecture" is a paraphrase of Lucian, *De calumnia* 21: "the appeal of unlikely assertions" (*to pros ta paradoxa tōn akousmatōn hepomenon*, a text for our own School of Suspicion!). See More's own commentaries on subversive allusion in *CW* 3/1:5–7 and 15:272, with the notes on the latter, and on Richard himself and his ways with subversive allusion see the treatment of "anti-myth" in Kelly (n. 6) and the now-numerous treatments of King Richard in Shakespeare as parodist.

[28] See discussions in *CW* 15:622–23 and Fox 83–84 of "Jane" Shore and Elizabeth Woodville as two somewhat bizarrely convergent allusive amalgams, and on More's "protofeminist" treatment of "Jane" (actually Elizabeth) Shore in particular see A. Patterson, *Reading Holinshed's Chronicles*, 217–20.

[29] *CW* 2:55–57, 15:424–30.

which it overtly subscribes, More's authorial irony no less clearly anticipates Shakespeare's dramatic departures from the Tudor myth proper than the orthodox line which More's history in its "finished" forms did so much to establish.[30]

To arrest this beginning account of More's textual strategies in the same summary style we began, I will end with a brief look at how More combines and offsets these opposed protocols of allusion in one crucial scene, the famed "strawberries-scene" with its sequel in Richard's bloody coup in the Tower. Hanham rightly describes Richard's coup against Hastings, the most powerful still-surviving supporter of Edward IV and his heirs, as the central and pivotal movement or "Act" of More's history right up to the unfinished coda.[31] Richard's pivotal seizure of power in this scene lets More balance ironically two quite different perspectives on the previous king's reign, one impossibly glowing and the other impossibly dark, representing, of course, two successive official points of view. From here on until he wears the crown, Richard meets no significant outward resistance; from here on, in fact, Richard's effrontery starts to make him his own worst detractor. Hanham notes how one local counterpoint of allusions serves to trivialize Richard's new order in contrast to what he destroys; Hastings' death means that "chivalry," too, is now dead and defunct.

Counterpoint though this is, it chimes well with one overt refrain of the text as a whole: Richard's gain is a dead loss for everything true and worth fighting for. But another effect less remarked on in this case by Hanham proceeds from ironic convergences which show up even Hastings' own chivalry as regrettably and even perniciously far from ideal. In this scene, after all, Hastings reaps as he sows, seized and killed even as he exults in the immminent death of the Queen's kin he helped to entrap. Their own chivalrous leader, Lord Rivers, we learn, once set out to snare Hastings in much the same way; these chivalric exemplars are thus also, we learn, both inveterate practitioners of perfidy. More's description of

---

[30] Cf. n. 25. Garber's article is especially useful in charting these striking Shakespearean departures; Rackin 80, however, still treats Shakespeare's *Richard III* as unlike the later histories in advancing the Tudor myth uncritically.

[31] CW 2:46–58; CW 15:406–32; Hanham 159, 166–85, 188. As observed in CW 2:226, there are close parallels between the edict against Hastings as reported by More and by the foreign eyewitness Mancini; this is more documentary basis than we generally have for the "facts" as reported in More's history. For the structural affinity which I here allege between Hastings' and Richard's undoing according to More see the further convergence proposed in n. 19 above.

Hastings' malicious incaution appears based on the very first lines of Lucian's essay *On Slander*; some years later, More writes of the treachery and blindness of Judas Iscariot in much the same terms (CW 15:418/19-22 and note; cf. note on 324/14-15). Hastings, Rivers, and Richard are all waging the same sort of war-out-of-season, and indeed all for much the same stakes; the first two merely lose before Richard does.

This suggestion does much to explain what perhaps are the strangest of all the subversive allusions to be found in this part of the text, a whole range of allusions quite clearly suggesting that Richard's tyrannical-seeming behavior toward Hastings may indeed uphold more than a few forms of *law*.[32] A subliminal sense that there must have been *something* behind Richard's charges has brought some to suppose that indeed Hastings was then conspiring against Richard[33]; but what I want to stress is the *form* of the charges and how far it offsets More's overt allegations of tyranny. At this point still officially Protector, not King, Richard starts by obtaining the Council's and Hastings' agreement that plotting against the Protector still counts as high treason. He then implicates Edward IV's former mistress "Jane" Shore in a plot to spell-bind (*fascinare*) Richard's arm, and indeed his whole body, by witchcraft; but since Hastings the ex-king's bosom-friend has by now taken over his mistress, he tries to shield "Jane" by appending a tactfully dubious "If" to the charges being leveled against her. As if Hastings had flatly defied him, Richard calls him a

---

[32] On the scope of Richard's powers as Protector of England see J. S. Roskell, "The Office and Dignity of Protector of England," *EHR*, 68 (1953), esp. 227-28. The most relevant discussions of treason-proceedings in late-medieval and early modern England under the common law as well as so-called law of arms (something like what we call martial law, but in those days a curious amalgam of Roman civil law and the standard rules of chivalry) are in Bracton (*De legibus et consuetudinibus Angliae*, ed. G. F. Thompson, 4 vols. [Cambridge, MA, 1968-77], 2:334-37, 394-403) and in Bellamy (1970) and *The Tudor Law of Treason: An Introduction* (London, 1979), especially 21-22, 36 (on the first Tudors' famous proceedings against treason by "If") and "Appendix: Martial Law." More's attention to forms of law here (cf. also *CW* 2:45, on Catesby and law) counters Bellamy's sense ([1970] 215) that according to most of the sources "there does not seem to have been any legal process at all, proper or improper, before the execution of William Lord Hastings...." Cf. also Ross (1974) 240-43, 397-98, on the equally summary treason proceedings of Edward IV against Clarence and Burdet (cf. *CW* 2:7, 70) and More's *CW* 10, notes on 265, 286, and 290, showing how More himself in his term as Lord Chancellor began to adopt a more rigorous approach to enforcement, including enforcement of laws against "treason by words," not unlike the approach here imputed to Richard III.

[33] Wood 170.

traitor, declares he will "prove it on [his] body," and signals his men, who lead Hastings out straight to the block; Richard then with his main ally Buckingham pulls on some old armor, addresses the suddenly skeptical civic leaders of London, and explains that since Hastings was caught in the act of rebellion they of course felt no qualms in despatching him. Then a long edict summing up each of these legal developments is read by the herald to the furtive derision of the populace.

All More's gibes at the trumped-up, preposterous character of the case against Hastings should not be allowed to obscure how much it in fact shares with well-known treason-cases pursued under Edward IV and the two earliest Tudors, in particular the summary case against Edward's brother Clarence (a case More here recalls through the linked case against Thomas Burdet) and the equally tenuous case against more than one magnate (including at last More himself) whom the Tudors condemned for obstructing some regal design with an untimely, tentative "If." Similarly, More's destructive analysis of the edict against Hastings construed as material evidence is not unlike the sort of destructive analysis to which More's entire history seems especially vulnerable assessed strictly as matter of "fact"; as More hints (at CW 2:66), it is largely a question of *whose* history or whose preferred version of fact we can safely confute. If we grant Richard's case for proclaiming a state of emergency, then according to then-current norms, summary justice is clearly in order; if we grant that proclaiming a state of emergency seconded with the Council's swift backing is just what a Protector *should* do, it is hard not to grant Richard's case for proclaiming a state of emergency. And as not just Protector, but also Lord Constable of England, surely Richard can claim the same powers of discretion as earlier and later Lord Constables of England with regard to how summary justice should be carried out. Forms of law, common law and the knightly law of arms, are in fact more intact at the heart of this text than they are in the "judgment of victory" at Bosworth, and if what Richard did in fact "prove on the body" of Hastings is simply that one against many is not a fair trial, Sir George Buck long ago pointed out that what Henry and Henry's men proved on the body of Richard once ambushed at Bosworth amounted at best to an equally unchivalrous object-lesson.[34]

Even so, we can scarcely discount the increasing if furtive derision with which Richard's common subjects in More view his outwardly legal

---

[34] Buck 98–105.

designs. York's and Richard's dynastic emergency is in essence *not* England's emergency, and indeed becomes England's emergency only thanks to an uncivil gang of great lords who reduce the law's warrants to pretexts or shields for their own rival captious assertions of "right." This republican judgment of most working law and most dynastic right as no more than a weapon or screen for ambition and privilege is indeed the same judgment advanced in *Utopia* and in numerous related Erasmian essays, as well as in Edward IV's rueful deathbed oration according to More (CW 2:11-13); and in terms of this judgment, what Richard becomes, or is made, merely brings to the surface what rival dynastic designs tend to be all along. In this one crucial sense, exposed Richard, like More, bears ambiguous yet seminal witness to the power of consensus against tyranny.

N. H. KEEBLE

"Take away preaching, and take away salvation":[1] Hugh Latimer, Protestantism, and Prose Style

> I told you before of *scala coeli*, the ladder of heaven; I would you should not forget it. The steps thereof are set forth in the tenth of Romans. The first is preaching, then hearing, then believing, and last of all salvation. *Scala coeli* is a preaching matter, I tell you, and not a massing matter. (S, 178; cf. S, 155)

PROTESTANTISM'S SUBSTITUTION OF AN HOMILETIC for a sacerdotal ideal of Christian ministry is particularly marked in the sermons of the English reformer Hugh Latimer, bishop of Worcester from 1535 till, unable to comply with Henry VIII's attempt to stay the process of reform through the promulgation of the Six Articles, he resigned in 1539.[2] John Foxe's account of his burning for heresy during the Marian persecution ensured that in English Protestant martyrology Latimer would hold a preeminent place as an exemplary and heroic witness to the reformed faith.[3] That

---

[1] *Sermons by Hugh Latimer*, ed. George Elwes Corrie, The Parker Society (Cambridge, 1844), 155; cf. 123. This volume is hereafter referred to parenthetically in the text as S.

[2] Allan G. Chester, *Hugh Latimer, Apostle to the English* (Philadelphia: Univ. of Pennsylvania Press, 1954), 144–51; Harold S. Darby, *Hugh Latimer* (London: Epworth Press, 1954), 155–58.

[3] For discussion of Foxe's contribution to the English martyrological tradition in general and of his presentation of Latimer in particular see John R. Knott, *Discourses of Martyrdom in English Literature, 1563–1694* (Cambridge: Cambridge Univ. Press, 1993).

faith and witness are validated in Foxe's account through his association of the Roman Catholic Marian authorities with pagan Rome and of Latimer with the testimony of the early church. Just before their pyres are lit, Foxe has Latimer comfort his fellow martyr, Nicholas Ridley, with words which echo Eusebius's account, reprinted by Foxe himself earlier in his *Book of Martyrs*,[4] of the heavenly voice of encouragement heard by St. Polycarp, bishop of Smyrna, on the occasion of his martyrdom by burning in AD 155/56: "Be of good comfort, master Ridley, and play the man. We shall this day light such a candle, by God's grace, in England, as I trust shall never be put out."[5] Latimer had, however, already done as much as any man to light the flame of Protestantism in early Tudor England. As Tyndale was its biblical genius and Cranmer its liturgical, so Latimer was its homiletic genius. It was as the preeminent preacher among the first generation of English reformers that his reputation was established and endured. Augustine of Canterbury's title, "Apostle to the English," was being used of him within a year of his death.[6] His first editor presented him as "a singular instrument to set forth [God's] truth" who was able "by his preaching to open the eyes of such as were deluded by the subtle and deceitful crafts of the popish prelates" (S, 319, 320). For Foxe he was "*The famous preacher* and worthy martyr."[7]

This reputation reflected a commitment which identified Christian ministry with the office of preaching.[8] In his "Sermon of the Plough," delivered at St. Paul's in January 1548, Latimer rebuked himself for having once been one of those who had "racked" the dominical saying, "No man, having put his hand to the plough, and looking back, is fit for the kingdom of God" (Luke 9:62), by applying it to the monastic ideal, "whereas indeed it toucheth not monkery, nor maketh any thing at all for any such matter; but it is directly spoken of diligent preaching of the word of God" (S, 60). The foolishness of preaching (1 Cor. 1:21) is the divinely

---

[4] Noted by Warren W. Wooden, *John Foxe* (Boston: Twayne, 1983), 52.

[5] John Foxe, *The Acts and Monuments*, ed. Stephen Reed Cattley, rev. Josiah Pratt, 4th ed., 7 vols. (London, [1877]), 7:550, recalling 1:133. The fullest account of the proceedings against Latimer is in D. M. Loades, *The Oxford Martyrs* (London: Batsford, 1970).

[6] Darby, 214–15.

[7] Foxe, 7:437 (my italics).

[8] Latimer, who had begun preaching regularly in London and before Henry VIII in 1530, "continued all king Edward's time, preaching for the most part every Sunday two sermons" (S, 320; cf. Foxe, 6:501). From this preaching career, forty-three sermons are extant, all but six from the reign of Edward VI.

ordained means of salvation (S, 291; cf. 349, 358). "We cannot be saved without faith, and faith cometh by hearing of the word; it is a necessary way to salvation" (S, 200). Regeneration "is not to be christened in water ... and nothing else"; it is to be born again "by the word of God preached and opened" (S, 202; cf. 471). The parable of the sower in Luke 8:5-15 confirms that preaching is the Christian minister's main business, and the preacher, like the ploughman, cannot afford to be idle: "ye that be prelates, look well to your office; for right prelating is busy labouring, and not lording. Therefore preach and teach, and let your plough be doing" (S, 65).

Neglect of this office is consequently a distinguishing mark of unreformed Christianity. "This is the thing that the devil wrestleth most against: it hath been all his study to decay this office.... He hath set up a state of unpreaching prelacy in this realm this seven hundred year; a stately unpreaching prelacy" (S, 202). The worldliness of unpreaching prelates is repeatedly contrasted with the selfless commitment of the apostolic church: "since lording and loitering hath come up, preaching hath come down, contrary to the apostles' times: for they preached and lorded not, and now they lord and preach not. For they that be lords will ill go to plough: it is no meet office for them; it is not seeming for their estate" (S, 66; cf. 77). "Paul was no sitting bishop, but a walking and a preaching bishop" (S, 68). So to insist that the prelate's place is in the pulpit was to come into direct conflict with the ecclesiastical hierarchy of the late medieval church, for it was also to insist that "a bishop cannot be two men" (S, 70). Episcopal involvement in politics, in foreign embassies, in government administration, court affairs, estate management, is incompatible with a bishop's true evangelistic ministry (S, 67-70).[9]

A good many feathers were ruffled by Latimer's development of such themes in Paul's Cross sermons. He himself frequently adverts to reports abroad of the seditious or heretical tendency of his sermons and to the hostile reception of his preaching (e.g., S, 131, 141, 154). This, however, was no cause of dismay. On the contrary: for Latimer preaching was of its very nature subversive, not the servant of the dominant culture and ideology but its critic and chastiser. It was the preacher's business to

---

[9] When released from prison at the beginning of Edward VI's reign under the customary general amnesty at the accession of a new monarch, Latimer himself resisted pressure to return to the episcopal bench, preferring to devote himself to preaching (Darby, 167-72).

disturb, unsettle, upset complacencies, and not merely those of pompous bishops. Opposition from those in power is hence testimony to the preacher's effectiveness: "It rejoiceth me sometimes, when my friend cometh and telleth me that they find fault with my discretion; for by likelihood, think I, the doctrine is true" (S, 241); "Christ himself was noted to be a stirrer up of the people against the emperor; and was contented to be called seditious. It becometh me to take it in good worth: I am not better than he was" (S, 134). Conformity, complacency, and submission are for Latimer marks not of commendable humility but of spiritual torpor. He can display an almost Miltonic scorn for the stupefying tyranny of custom:

> In the popish mass-time there was no gainsaying; all things seemed to be in peace, in a concord, in a quiet agreement. So long as we had in adoration, in admiration, the popish mass, we were then without gainsaying. What was that? The same that Christ speaketh of, *Cum fortis armatus custodierit atrium* &c., 'When Satan, the devil, hath the guiding of the house, he keepeth all in peace that is in his possession.' When Satan ruleth, and beareth dominion in open religion, as he did with us when we preached pardon-matters, purgatory-matters, and pilgrimage-matters, all was quiet. He is ware enough, he is wily, and circumspect for stirring up any sedition. When he keepeth his territory, all is in peace.... When he hath the religion in possession, he stirreth up no sedition, I warrant you.
>
> How many dissensions have we heard of in Turky? But a few, I warrant you. He busieth himself there with no dissension. For he hath there dominion in the open religion, and needeth not to trouble himself any further. The Jews ... look whether ye hear of any heresies among them? But when *fortis supervenerit*, when one stronger than the devil cometh in place, which is our Saviour Jesus Christ, and revealeth his word, then the devil roareth; then he bestirreth him; then he raiseth diversity of opinions to slander God's word. And if ever concord should have been in religion, when should it have been but when Christ was here? Ye find fault with preachers, and say, they cause sedition. We are noted to be rash, and undiscreet in our preaching. Yet as discreet as Christ was, there was diversity .... There was never prophet to be compared to him, and yet was there never more dissension than when he was, and preached himself. (S, 129-30)

It is precisely their devotion to "old wont, customs, forefathers" which reveals the formalism and hypocrisy of the Pharisees, as of Rome (S, 287).

To disturb this Satanic quietude and to awaken drugged consciences requires "a nipping sermon, a pinching sermon, a rough sermon" (S, 240), such as Jonah delivered to the Ninevites (Jon. 3.4). Here Latimer found his model. The denunciatory oracles of the Old Testament prophets authorized the preacher's excoriations of moral turpitude and depravity: Latimer has "a companion of sedition; and wot ye who is my fellow? Esay the prophet" (S, 137); he is "content to bear the title of sedition with Esay" (S, 140). It is the property of a preacher to be "a true man ... and not to regard the personage of man; not to creep into his bosom, to claw his back; to say to the wicked he doth well, for filthy lucre's sake" (S, 292). "Drawing the sword of God's word" he is inevitably a trouble maker, "much like as Elias was the cause of trouble in Israel; for he was a preacher there, and told the people of all degrees their faults, and so they winced and kicked at him, and accused him to Achab the king, that he was a seditious fellow, and a troublous preacher" (S, 249-50). Nor ought a preacher any more to restrain himself from intervention in political and social matters than had the prophets. "Some say preachers should not meddle with such matters" (S, 184) but "Moses, fearing no man, with this sword [of the word] did reprove king Pharao at God's commandment. Micheas the prophet also did not spare to blame king Ahab for his wickedness" (S, 86; cf. 82); Jesus himself reproved corrupt judges (S, 184). Upon such authority, Latimer can cry to London to repent as vehemently as Jeremiah to the cities of Moab (S, 64-65, referring to Jer. 47:1ff.), but it is the specificity of his damning rehearsal of the particularities of malpractice which sharpens his denunciations: the prevention of the poor from working on holidays (S, 53), the extortionate fees charged by physicians and lawyers, rack-rents (S, 98), enclosure (S, 100), prolonged delays in legal proceedings and neglect of suits put by those not gently born (S, 126-27), perversions of justice and the judiciary's dependence upon bribes (S, 142-46, 179-83), the sale of offices (S, 185-86) which threatens to make "the yeomanry slavery" (S, 100).

Latimer expends far more energy upon the excoriation of such tyrannical abuses of power in either church or state than he does upon the exposition of doctrine. There is remarkably little theology in his sermons. Their field is rather ethics, the practice of a Christian life. He makes occasional reference to the sufficiency of Christ's sacrifice, to solifidianism and to the problems of assurance posed by the doctrine of election,[10] but these do not hold his attention. He speaks with respect of Peter Martyr, John à Lasco, and Bernard Ochino (S, 141), and of that "wonderful instrument of God," Luther (R, 52; cf. S, 212), but neither the soteriological subtleties of "the new learning" (S, 30-31; cf. 203, R, 318-19), as Protestantism (not Humanism) was then disparagingly known,[11] nor the developing intricacies of systematic Reformed theology ever appear. That "most dangerous question of the predestination of God" (R, 205) and other such teasing matters are given short shrift: "thou shalt not be able to search the counsels of God" (R, 205). Latimer's is a liberation theology: what fires the sermons is not the challenge of elucidating doctrine but outrage at an oppressive and exploitative system in which "judges be afraid to hear a poor man against the rich" (S, 145).

That outrage can sound radical notes: "The poorest ploughman is in Christ equal with the greatest prince that is" (S, 249; cf. 199-200). Preaching to Edward VI in 1549, Latimer de-centers the court, denying the nobility its precedency: "by yeoman's sons the faith of Christ is and hath been maintained chiefly" (S, 102; cf. 141). We must not overstate the case: equality *in Christ* is not social equality. Latimer distinguishes his attacks on the abuse of power from the alleged rejection of authority *per se* by Anabaptists (S, 157). Speaking of stewardship and of charity to the poor he is careful ("lest some of you would report me wrongfully, and affirm, that all things should be common") to defend the holding of private property (S, 406). He suspects that beggars are mostly "idle lubbers" (S, 376). He is as committed as the *Book of Homilies* to passive obedience to proper authorities: "thou must obey thy king, do not take upon thee to judge him," even when he is tyrannical or acts illegally (S, 300, preaching on Matt. 22: 21; cf. 355-57, 371, 373). "Our whole conversation should be agreeable unto the laws" (R, 81).[12] It is not,

---

[10] E.g., *Sermons and Remains of Hugh Latimer*, ed. George Elwes Corrie, The Parker Society (London, 1845), 125-26, 137-42, 146-51, 175-76. This volume is hereafter referred to parenthetically in the text as R.

[11] The definition in *The Compact Edition of the The Oxford English Dictionary*, ed. Sir James Murray *et al.*, 2 vols. (Oxford: Oxford Univ. Press, 1979) *s.v.* "Learning," 3b ("the studies, esp. of the Greek language, introduced into England in the 16th century; also applied to the doctrines of the Reformation") is belied by the *Dictionary*'s own supporting quotations, which illustrate the second sense from c. 1530 (from Latimer) but the first only from 1874.

[12] Latimer was equally firm on the inferiority of women: S, 252-54.

however, possible both to assert that "a poor woman in the belfry hath as good authority to offer up this sacrifice [of the Lord's Supper], as hath the bishop in his *pontificalibus*, with his mitre on his head, his rings on his fingers" (S, 167-68) and unequivocally to support hierarchical notions of church and state polity. There is a line from Latimer's social concern to the radical Puritan sentiments famously voiced by Colonel Thomas Rainsborough at the Putney debates of the New Model Army in 1647: "I thinke that the poorest hee that is in England hath a life to live as the greatest hee."[13] Latimer speaks for "the poorest hee," on behalf of the misguided, the impoverished, the disadvantaged and the oppressed against those who would abuse them.

This spokesman has a distinct rhetorical identity. Although briefly a bishop and a London and court preacher, whose pulpit was regularly Paul's Cross, "the most important vehicle of persuasion used by the government during the period 1534-1554,"[14] Latimer presents himself as an outsider and an interloper in the episcopal and courtly world. He belongs not there but with those on whose behalf he speaks. He is with them in his religious experience ("a great number of *us*" have trusted in masses and pilgrimages [R, 58, my italics]), in his vulnerability to despotic power ("I was travailed in the Tower myself" [S, 163]), and in his social background: "My father was a yeoman, and had no lands of his own, only he had a farm of three or four pound by year at the uttermost, and hereupon he tilled so much as kept half a dozen men. He had walk for a hundred sheep; and my mother milked thirty kine" (S, 101). Though Latimer may preach to the king at Paul's Cross, he does so not as a townsman – and certainly not as a courtier – but as a countryman: "They say in my country, when they call their hogs to the swine-trough, 'Come to thy mingle-mangle, come pur, come pur'" (S, 147). The autobiographical reference there is typical, but this is not merely a matter of biography: such recollections of his own humble origins set his moral and social critique in the tradition of *Piers Plowman* (S, 61).[15] Constructing himself in the image of this recognized type of the

---

[13] C. H. Firth, ed., *The Clarke Papers* (London: The Royal Historical Society, 1992), 301.

[14] Millar MacLure, *The Paul's Cross Sermons, 1534–1642* (Toronto: Univ. of Toronto Press, 1958), 20.

[15] See further Robert L. Kelly, "Hugh Latimer as Piers Plowman," *Studies in English Literature* 17 (Winter 1977): 13–26. For the pervasive influence of *Piers Plowman* upon early Tudor Protestant writers, see Helen C. White, *Social Criticism in Popular Religious Literature of the Sixteenth Century* (New York: Macmillan, 1944), chap. 1; John N. King,

religious ideal authenticates and legitimizes his discourse. It was also a circumspect negotiation of Latimer's problematic position as both castigator and representative of the Tudor regime. The voice of the preacher sounds from another moral and social order. We hear not a lord of the church turning upon his peers but a voice from the margins, "a voice in the wilderness" as it were, like that of John the Baptist recalling Elijah, crying that the ways of the Lord should be made straight (Luke 3:2-4; Isa. 40:3). We might compare the almost contemporaneous use by Skelton of the mask of the countryman Colin Clout to voice his anticlericalism.[16]

This bluff, at times almost oafish, piece of self-fashioning affronts and confronts both court manners and clerical dignity.[17] When, in the final years of his life, Latimer was called upon to dispute with university doctors in their academic gowns, or to appear before ecclesiastical commissioners and bishops, resplendent in scarlet and gold, he presented himself

> holding his hat in his hand, having a kerchief on his head, and upon it a night-cap or two, and a great cap (such as townsmen use, with two broad flaps to button under the chin), wearing an old thread-bare Bristol frieze-gown girded to his body with a penny leather girdle, at the which hanged by a long string of leather his Testament, and his spectacles without case, depending about his neck upon his breast.[18]

In Foxe's account, this "somewhat bizarre"[19] dress serves as a rebuke to

---

English Reformation Literature: the Tudor Origins of the Protestant Tradition (Princeton: Princeton Univ. Press, 1982), index.

[16] John Skelton, "Collyn Clout" (1523?), in John Scattergood, ed., *The Complete English Poems* (Harmondsworth: Penguin, 1983), 246–78. "Colin" derives from Latin *colonus*, "farmer"; a "clout" is an old rag (Scattergood, 466). The name was afterwards taken up by Spenser (as was Piers) in *The Shepheardes Calendar* (1579) and "Colin Clouts Come Home Again" (1595). Spenser's familiarity with the English tradition of ecclesiastical satire and anticlericalism extended to Latimer's sermons, as well as to Langland and Skelton: see John N. King, *Spenser's Poetry and Reformation Tradition* (Princeton: Princeton Univ. Press, 1990), 22.

[17] By ignoring this persona and the other means (explored hereafter in this essay) by which Latimer creates a demotic and oppositional discourse, Stephen Greenblatt is able ingeniously and misleadingly to argue that Latimer "functions as part of a highly educated, male, professional élite" (*Shakespearian Negotiations: the Circulation of Social Energy in Renaissance England* [Oxford: Clarendon Press, 1988], 131). What Greenblatt contrives to present as an example of the manipulative exercise of patriarchal power is an autobiographical tale told to discountenance misogynistic suspicion of women (S, 336).

[18] Foxe, 7:529.

[19] Loades, 209.

Latimer's antagonists through its recollection of the unworldly ideals of the primitive church; its eccentricity delineates "an emblem of apostolic simplicity and truthfulness."[20] In an act of self-dramatization[21] Latimer presents a visually striking contrast with the worldliness of his opponents, signifying difference, dissent, otherness in terms which that exemplary preacher John the Baptist had used: he "had his raiment of camel's hair, and a leathern girdle about his loins" (Matt. 3:4). Just so, in his sermons Latimer constructs for himself the persona of a plain countryman. He may, through the foresight of his parents, have been educated and attended Cambridge, "or else I had not been able to have preached before the king's majesty now" (S, 101), but it is not from Cambridge that his authority as preacher derives. Latimer's B.D. oration in 1524 had been directed "against Philip Melanchthon and against his opinions"; his early academic career was that of "as obstinate a papist as any was in England." That he came "to smell the word of God" was due not to his preceptors but, as he more than once declared from the pulpit, to "[Thomas] Bilney, little Bilney" (S, 222), "or rather Saint Bilney" (S, 334), Fellow of Trinity Hall, Cambridge, and an auditor of Latimer's oration, afterwards one of the first English Protestant martyrs. He "was the instrument whereby God called me to knowledge"; through his example and influence, Latimer turned his back on Cambridge and "forsook the school-doctors and such fooleries" (S, 334–35). He preaches as one who finds scant satisfaction in expositors and theologians and who, confronted with a knotty point of doctrine, "will bungle at it as well as I can" using his commonsense (S, 267). Distanced from the culturally shaping institutions of late medieval England, Latimer speaks not with the authority of a D.D. — which he probably did not possess[22] — but "as I find by experience" (S, 205; cf. R, 67) of conversion, of faith, and of the malpractice of the imperfectly reformed church.

Sources of information and authorities cited in the sermons are consequently as likely to be autobiographical or topical as biblical or Patristic. Augustine and Chrysostom, "the ancient doctors," are occasionally cited, but otherwise there is very little reference to the Fathers, whom Latimer would not have unduly revered (S, 218), and none at all to the medieval Schoolmen, "holy Thomas ... subtile Duns," "your [Papist] old doctors,"

---

[20] Knott, 76.
[21] Cf. Darby, 233: "Latimer was never slow to dramatize situations."
[22] Chester, 8–9.

"who for all their wisdom, godliness, holiness and subtilty, deceived, were deceived, and lied" (R, 317, 319). Rather than the "fooleries of doctors," contemporary events and shared experience are adduced to confirm a point. Indeed, they may serve as proof text as frequently as the Bible. "I must tell you more news yet" (S, 138), and there is reportage, current affairs, hearsay, anecdote, and reminiscence in plenty: "I will tell you what a bishop of this realm once said to me" (S, 121); "I will tell you what I remembered yesternight in my bed" (S, 149); "I heard once a tale of a thing that was done at Oxford twenty years ago" (S, 163); "Here I have to tell you what I hear of late, by the relation of a credible person and a worshipful man" (S, 151); "I walked one day with a gentleman in the park" (S, 278); "I heard of credible men ..." (S, 160); "there was a woman..." (S, 180); "I heard of a bishop..." (S, 207); "I came myself..." (S, 208); "I chanced to meet..." (S, 209); "When I was in Cambridge..." (S, 440). When Biblical cases are adduced, they are given the same contemporaneity and immediacy: the "froward" Jews were "much like our Englishmen now-a-days, that in the minority of a king take upon them to break laws, and to go by-ways" (S, 112); Isaiah "speaking of the judgments done in his time in the common place, as it might be in Westminster-hall, the Guildhall, the Judges-hall, the Pretor-house; call it what you will — in the open place" (S, 156); Capernaum was "such a town as Bristow or Coventry is" (S, 533). Latimer's own "examination before five or six bishops" illustrates the Machiavellian deceitfulness of the Pharisees' questioning of Jesus (S, 294-95). The "arch-Pharisees, Provincials, and Abbots-Pharisees" (S, 296), "reputed most godly men ... as our monks were of late," were "much like the Observant Friars," "watchers, tooters, spies" for ecclesiastical authority (S, 287). The parable of the Good Samaritan transmutes into a contemporary ecclesiastical tale of the absentee and negligent bishop of Exeter and Miles Coverdale, "the bishop indeed" (S, 272).

Coverdale keeps company with a host of other early Tudor figures in these newsworthy texts — Wolsey (S, 301), Erasmus (S, 46), Colet (S, 440) and More (S, 250-51); Protector Somerset (S, 118, 126-27), Admiral Thomas Seymour (S, 160-62, 181-84) and the young Edward VI (S, 117-18). Such named figures are surrounded by a teeming cast of bishops, monks, friars, chantry priests, archdeacons, abbots, and priors; judges, magistrates, and justices of peace; king's counsellors, courtiers, lords, duelling gallants, women of fashion in French hoods with their hair in "tussocks and tufts" (S, 253-54), and noble revellers abed "till eight, or nine, or ten of the clock" (S, 255); yeomen, Thames wherry-men, smiths, carpenters, labourers, cobblers, soldiers; servants, apprentices, thieves, and prisoners. These are a far noisier and pressing presence than Biblical figures. Similarly, the material circumstances of Tudor England, both countryside and capital, bulk larger in the sermons than those of ancient Israel: the stews of Bank-side (S, 196), the sanctuary of St. Martin-le-grand (S, 196), Ludgate prison (S, 223), and the Bocardo in Oxford (S, 250). And the events recalled are as likely to be those of recent (and particularly English) history as of Jewish or early Christian history: medieval English long bow victories (S, 197), the life of "the good duke Humphrey" of Gloucester (S, 118-19), the defeat of Cornish rebels at Blackheath field in 1497 (S,101), the Pilgrimage of Grace (S, 29), Seymour's execution (S, 160-62, 181-84), Bilney's martyrdom (S, 222), the case of Joan of Kent (R, 114), the fall of Rhodes to the Turks in 1523 (R, 33).

The neighbourliness of this persona and range of reference is engaged in making Christianity familiar and in familiarizing the auditory with Christianity. What is strange and novel is presented as a natural part of the known, felt world. The arcane mysteries, esoteric subtleties, and elaborate rituals, which for Latimer were the instruments of ecclesiastical oppression, give way to the commonplace and the recognizable. This tendency towards the mimetic and representational is most pronounced in the frequent narratives Latimer introduces into his sermons: retellings of Biblical story (necessary when the laity had only recently been granted access to the vernacular Bible),[23] recollections of personal experience, tales and stories from both oral and written sources, all tend to that circumstantial detail and authenticity of dialogue which were to mark later Elizabethan pamphleteering. Colloquiality demystifies biblical story: Ham "made a mocking-stock" of his father Noah (R, 16); Joseph's brothers "thought all was cock-sure" (S, 259); the Pharisees, those "wily pies" (S, 288), would have "snarled" Jesus with their question concerning the tribute money, "they would have caught him by the foot" (S, 283); Jesus gives the Jews "a good quip" (R, 9), "a goodly privy nip" (R, 76). In Latimer's expansion of the mention in 1 Cor. 5:1-2 of one that "should have his father's wife," the conversational register brings home (a particularly apt locution) the abomination from ancient Greece to Tudor England by situating it within contemporary social habits:

---

[23] As remarked by J. W. Blench, *Preaching in England in the late Fifteenth and Sixteenth Centuries* (Oxford: Blackwell, 1964), 41.

In the city of Corinth one had married his step-mother, his father's wife: and he was a jolly fellow, a great rich man, an alderman of the city; and therefore they winked at it, they would not meddle in the matter, they had nothing to do with it: and he was one of the head men, of such rule and authority, that they durst not, many of them. (S, 257)

Dialogue in the narratives Latimer constructs from his Biblical sources is similarly idiomatic. The Pharisees' exclamation to their officers, *Num et vos seducti est?* (John 8:47) is paraphrased: "What, ye brain-sick fools, ye hoddy-pecks, ye doddy-pouls, ye huddes, do ye believe him? are you seduced also?" (S, 136); the Pharisees' hypocritical address to Jesus in Matt. 22:16 is rendered: "Master, we know thou art a true man, and teachest the way of God truly. Master, we know that thou art Tom Truth, and thou tellest the very truth, and sparest for no man. Thou art plain Tom Truth" (S, 289).

Such story-telling recalls oral tradition rather than literary narrative, and there is a good deal of generic instability in Latimer. Homiletic structure is under threat from the intrusive tales, frequent digressions, and parenthetical anecdotes. Latimer is having constantly "to return to my matter" (S, 246), only to be lured away again. There is no hint of the shape of a classical oration, nor of such a design as the seven-part structure derived from it which Andreas Hyperius, professor of theology at Marburg, recommended: "reading of the sacred scripture, Inuocation, Exordium, proposition, or diuision, Confirmation, Confutation, conclusion."[24] By the time of William Perkins this had become the three-part structure variously recommended for the next century by *artes concionandi* of all persuasions as "doctrine, reason and use," "explication, confirmation, application," "proposition, confirmation and inference."[25] No such tripartite division is adumbrated in Latimer, nor has he any other plan of his own. The immediacy and unconstrained familiarity of the mode of address cannot stay for any systematic division of the biblical text; no list of heads

---

[24] Andreas Hyperius, *The Practise of Preaching*, trans. John Ludham (London, 1577), fol. 22.

[25] William Perkins, *The Arte of Prophecying*, in *The Workes*, 3 vols. (London, 1616–18), 2:673; John Wilkins, *Ecclesiastes* (London, 1646), 5; Richard Baxter, *A Christian Directory* (London, 1673), 2.xix.575; James Arderne, *Directions concerning... Sermons*, ed. John Mackay (Oxford: Blackwell, 1952), 9. On the development of sermon structure, see Blench, chap. 2; W. Fraser Mitchell, *English Pulpit Oratory from Andrewes to Tillotson* (London: SPCK, 1932), 93–100.

is given at the opening of the sermon. Rather, he will make his way "partly being out of my matter, partly being in" (S, 170). In the course of a general disquisition upon a Biblical passage, topics arise as if unbidden: "here we have occasion to speak of midwives" (R, 114); "here I might take occasion to speak of all estates" (R, 95) — or perhaps, it seems, I might not. If not in fact extempore,[26] the thought of the moment appears to have as much weight as what may have been premeditated: "a saying of St. Chrysostom," which "might come hereafter in better place," is inserted "whilst it cometh to mind" (S, 203-4). The sermons present themselves as texts in process, constructed and deconstructed as they proceed: in the previous sermon "I should have told you" of the Anabaptists (S, 151); "But before I go forward with this, I must first tell you a tale" (S, 180); objections will be dealt with "hereafter, and if I forget ... not" (R, 68); an address is curtailed because "I am not very well at ease this morning" (S, 370). Loose and digressive,[27] the self-reflexive instability of the resultant movement has the unpredictability of confessional writing. Its catholic curiosity tends to the circumambulatory comprehensiveness of cornucopian Renaissance texts; contained within little room, however, it anticipates the discursive movement of that secular sermon, the essay.

Stylistic niceties are as little regarded as the proprieties of formal homiletic discourse or the dignity of the preacher.[28] The radical Protes-

---

[26] Amongst Foxe's MSS there is a story (not included in the *Book of Martyrs*) of Latimer preaching extemporaneously in 1525 in response to the unexpected arrival in church of his diocesan, Bishop Nicholas West (Darby, 27), but the account's authenticity may be questioned (Chester, 24-26). In view of Latimer's Cambridge education and the pulpit custom of the time, it is most unlikely that his apparent carelessness was uncontrived (Kelly, 11). Cf. C. S. Lewis, *English Literature in the Sixteenth Century* (Oxford: Clarendon Press, 1954), 193: "An appearance of casualness ... is one of the rhetorician's weapons: and I suspect that everything which seems to fall by chance from Latimer's lips is consciously devised."

[27] Taken to be a fault by Blench, 92.

[28] Though he referred with equanimity to their collection and publication by "a diligent person" (S, 511) Latimer himself seems not to have supervised the publication of any of his sermons, nor does it appear that his own manuscripts ever supplied the printer's copy. The texts we have were recorded and reconstructed by various intermediaries, chiefly the devoted Augustine Bernher, Latimer's servant, or "more accurately ... disciple" (Loades, 171), often with an apology that they are "not so fully and perfectly gathered as they were uttered": see, e.g., S, 3, 82, 447n, 455n. The caution which must hence hedge any statement of what was delivered from the pulpit or of Latimer's precise responsibility for the texts published over his name does not, of course, extend to discussion of the details of the texts themselves.

tant imperatives of the sermons demand a style as little awed by, as little concerned to impress, the world as is Latimer's plain gown. Against materialism, hypocrisy, and formalism is set an ideal of simplicity, authenticity, and integrity: "religion, pure religion, I say, standeth not in wearing of a monk's cowl, but in righteousness, justice, and well-doing" (S, 392; cf. R, 332-33). The Christian's true pilgrimage is not from place to place but following the "very godly and ghostly pilgrimage" traced out by the Beatitudes (S, 490), the way of meekness and poverty. Plainness marks the literary as well as the devotional style of this model of the Christian life. Rhetorical sophistication is as suspect as the "fooleries of doctors" and the ritualistic formalism of Rome: did not Jonah preach efficaciously with "no great curiousness, no great clerkliness, no great affectation of words, nor of painted eloquence" (S, 240)?[29] There is occasional punning and wordplay — on homily/homely, for example (S, 121), or honourable/horrible, honour/horror (S, 153) — and a penchant for using compounds to create such satiric caricatures as "purgatory pick-purse" (S, 50) or "merit-mongers" (R, 200), but, as quotations throughout this essay illustrate, the lexis of the sermons shows none of that fondness for inkhorn terms and aureate diction fashionable in the early century, and perhaps especially a mark of the discourse of ecclesiastical authorities.[30] Latimer speaks "with a wanniaunt"[31] (S, 119), with colloquial directness and proverbial trenchancy applying the "common sayings" of England (R, 140; cf. 150): "I have ript the matter now to the pill" is his conclusion of a passage of textual exposition (S, 117). Nor has Latimer a humanist's satisfaction in well-crafted periods. Discrete clauses (and phrases), usually quite brief, are marshalled sequentially with very little subordination. There is a fondness for couplings, for repeating ideas in slightly varied phrasing, both to allow the auditory time to assimilate a point and to achieve various kinds of emphasis, hortatory, denunciatory, exclamatory, and these are often enforced by alliteration and by some of the simpler schemes of repetition (*anaphora* most commonly, but also *epanalepsis*, *epizeuxis*, and *polyptoton*). There is some parallelism (or *parison*) and sentences can anticipate the

---

[29] For the contrary high valuation of eloquence in the Humanist tradition, and its stylistic consequences, see Neil Rhodes, *The Power of Eloquence and English Renaissance Literature* (Hemel Hempstead: Harvester Wheatsheaf, 1992).

[30] Janel M. Mueller, *The Native Tongue and the Word: Developments in English Prose Style, 1380-1580* (Chicago: Univ. of Chicago Press, 1984), esp. 162-77.

[31] Colloquial exclamation equivalent to "with a vengeance" (OED).

style shortly to be known as Senecan (though looser and less cryptic).[32] The rhythms of Latimer's paratactic style, however, follow oral rather than literary models, with frequent interjections, exclamations, interrogatives.[33]

Plain the resulting style may be, but not, as will already have appeared, bald, dull, or predictable. The language of experience, of authentic Christian faith, is demotic, unruly, apparently unpremeditated.[34] It is an undress style, a make-piece seemingly cobbled together from what lies to hand, like Latimer's attire, and, like that, an offence to decorum. His dialectal and everyday words (with a taste for archaisms) — *tooting, louting, hurly-burly, doddypoll, bibble-babble, blanching, springold*, and their like — disregard linguistic propriety. When he ventures on a trope, it is of a piece with his "plain Dunstable way" (S, 113), appealing to popular culture, its pastimes and preoccupations.[35] The analogy between the Christian life and a game of cards in the "Sermons on the Card," known only from the report of them by Foxe, is typical in its kind, but early (c. 1529) and unusually developed; thereafter, tendencies towards either allegory or extended figures are few. The spiritual corrosion caused by a "bag of rusty malice" (S, 20), the "scouring" of truth till it shines (S, 30) are characteristically terser metaphors. And there is Latimer's humor, his *facetiae* preventing homiletic solemnity. In his section "Of deliting the hearers" in his *Arte of Rhetorique* (1553), Thomas Wilson included Latimer's mock presentation of the Devil as the most diligent bishop in England (S, 70) as an example of "pleasant dissembling, when we speake one thing merily and thinke an other earnestly,"[36] as well he might. There is a good deal

---

[32] See on this stylistic fashion George Williamson, *The Senecan Amble: A Study in Prose Form from Bacon to Collier* (London: Faber, 1951).

[33] Many of these features are illustrated by the passage quoted above, p. 60. For the Biblical inspiration of this style (especially its fondness for doublets and parallelism), and the argument that it has distinctively Protestant characteristics, see Mueller, passim, and King, esp. 138–44 (citing Latimer); for its medieval (homiletic) antecedents, both stylistic and satirical, see G. R. Owst, *Literature and Pulpit in Medieval England*, 2nd ed. (Oxford: Blackwell, 1961), esp. 98–100 (on Latimer), and Blench, 113–42.

[34] See further Blench, 142–53, which praises Latimer as "the greatest pulpit exponent of the colloquial style in the century" (142).

[35] He nevertheless shared that wariness of popular culture as a rival to godliness common among Protestants, lamenting the "reading of profane histories, of Cantorbury tales, or a fit of Robyn Hode" (S, 106–7; cf. 208). See further King, 209ff.

[36] Pp. 146–47, cited by Mueller, 365. Wilson's other example is from Sir Thomas More.

of drollery "to refresh my auditory" (S, 136), of "pretty stories" told "to refresh you withal" (S, 524), for "I had rather ye should come of a naughty mind to hear the word of God for novelty, or for curiosity to hear some pastime, than to be away.... I had rather ye should go a napping to the sermons, than not to go at all ... the preacher may chance to catch you on his hook" (S, 201).

It is of a piece with his determination to have done with "the fooleries of school-doctors" that English is Latimer's uncluttered medium. Although at this early stage of the history of English Protestantism Latimer still quotes the Latin Vulgate Bible, he always translates, and there are otherwise very few Latin tags or citations. Augustine appears in English dress. Though Latimer can refer to Hebrew usage (R, 105), there is no Hebrew cited, and he professed to understand no Greek (R, 263; but cf. S, 447; R, 163). There is consequently no more of the humanist about Latimer's pulpit persona than of the theologian. He can occasionally cite Horace, Terence, Livy, and Ovid, but this is hardly to stray beyond the Latinity common to any literate person of the period, and it is, he confesses, recalled from "almost forty years ago" (S, 415). He knows Erasmus's New Testament (S, 219; R, 263, 341) and can refer to Ficino, but "it is a great while since I read him now" (S, 197). When they are cited, classical authors appear not as cultural or linguistic mentors but as sources of proverbs (e.g., S, 431), of cautionary counsel (e.g., S, 287) and of tales (e.g., S, 457, 491): "We read in stories" is his form of introduction to an (unidentified) passage from Eusebius (R, 47; cf. 80). Rather than give the impression that he lived in antique authors, Latimer was at some pains to distance himself from Latinity. Admonished to explain his views on transubstantiation in a disputation at Oxford in 1554, he replied, "I pray you good master prolocutor, do not exact that of me, which is not in me, I have not these twenty years much used the Latin tongue."[37] Doubtless this petition, like his garb, was a strategy to refuse the cultural hegemony of his interrogators, and we may query its literal truthfulness; but it is an entirely characteristic piece of self-fashioning, consistent with his homiletic rhetoric and his literary bias. Latimer's sermons are a significant contributor to that movement whereby English established itself as a medium of authoritative discourse.[38]

---

[37] Foxe, 6:501; repr. in R, 251.
[38] On this subject see R. F. Jones, *The Triumph of the English Language* (London: Oxford Univ. Press, 1953).

English homiletic styles (especially at court) were soon to indulge in something altogether richer, more elaborate, and ostentatiously erudite than Latimer's "tub thumping," as C. S. Lewis called it,[39] but the Renaissance flirtation with various ornate, copious, and mannered styles in Andrewes, Hooker, Donne, and Taylor was to prove but a passing fashion. The predominant tradition of English prose to emerge at the end of the seventeenth century does not derive from them; it is rather in the line from Latimer. At the Restoration, their manner was rejected even by divines of their own episcopal persuasion, even by such an ardent royalist and passionate anti-Puritan as Robert South. Though the refinement and urbanity of a John Tillotson is far from Latimer, his eschewing of linguistic and exegetical ingenuity and his commitment to an unadorned prose are not. The models here (particulary Tillotson's) were Puritan. The manner of Latimer — the "rustick thunderer" as Richard Baxter called him[40] — had continued in the Puritan tradition of plain preaching and in the literature of social concern produced by the Levellers, and by Gerrard Winstanley. It passed to Bunyan and the nonconformists, and, through them, to Defoe.[41]

This contribution to the development of English prose style was made possible not by the preaching but by the publishing of Latimer's sermons. He was the first English Protestant preacher to be accorded collected editions of his sermons in print,[42] and, in this, is a signal instance of

---

[39] Lewis, 196.

[40] Richard Baxter, *Catholick Communion Defended against Both Extremes* (London 1684), pt. 1, p. 32. I owe this reference to the kindness of Professor William Lamont.

[41] For more particular discussion of these rather large generalizations, see: Juliet Dusinberre, "Bunyan and Virgina Woolf: A History and Language of their Own," *Bunyan Studies* 5 (1994), 15–46; Harold Fisch, "The Puritans and the Reform of Prose Style," *Journal of English Literary History* 19 (1952): 229–47; Fraser Mitchell, esp. chaps. 9–10; Christopher Hill, "From Marprelate to the Levellers," in Christopher Hill, *The Collected Essays* (Brighton: Harvester Press, 1985), 75–95; N. H. Keeble, *Richard Baxter: Puritan Man of Letters* (Oxford: Clarendon Press, 1982), 48–68, and *The Literary Culture of Nonconformity in Later Seventeenth-century England* (Leicester: Leicester Univ. Press, 1987), 240–62; Owst, 97–109; Roger Pooley, "Language and Loyalty: Plain Style at the Restoration," *Literature & History* 6 (1980): 2–18; Gerard Reedy, *Robert South (1634–1716)* (Cambridge: Cambridge Univ. Press, 1992), passim; Isabel Rivers, *Reason, Grace and Sentiment: the language of religion and ethics in England, 1660–1780* (Cambridge: Cambridge Univ. Press, 1991), chap. 1–3.

[42] *27 Sermons* (1562; STC 15276), enlarged as *Frutefull Sermons* (1571–72; STC 15277), enlarged in 1578 (STC 15279). The earliest English preacher to have a collected edition published appears to have been the Roman Catholic Roger Edgeworth (1557), who was, of course, then favored by political circumstances as Latimer was not.

Protestantism's revaluation not only of English prose but of both the book and the act of reading. The substitution of an homiletic and ministerial ideal for a sacramental and priestly one changed not only relations between priest and people, preacher and congregation, but between author and audience, reader and text. The immediate recourse of Protestantism throughout Europe to the printed book showed a prescient awareness of the significance of mass communication and was very largely responsible for its becoming a definitive feature of the culture of the early modern period. The technological and ideological aspects of this commitment to spreading the word (a locution which bears reflection) generated new conceptions of the nature and business of texts and of their readers, imposing on both new kinds of responsibility. It demanded of the former new methods and techniques and generated in the latter new expectations and criteria of judgement. A priest may bestow, but a preacher must persuade; to succeed, the ministry of the Word must both respect its people and reach as many of them as possible. It was here that print came to the aid of the Protestant evangel. Preacher and congregation become writer and reader: God would, said Latimer, "that christian people should hear my doctrine, and at their convenient leisure read it also, as many as would"; the "care" of traditionalists on the other hand, of the Roman hierarchy, of opposers of Bible translation and defenders of Latinate culture, is "not that all men may hear it, but all your care is, that no lay man do read it: surely, being afraid lest they by the reading should understand it, and understanding, learn to rebuke our slothfulness" (S, 38; cf. 55). It is "devilish ploughing" to "have things in Latin" (S, 71). Books in print in native tongues are no longer rare repositories of mysteries to be safeguarded from the *hoi polloi* but exercises in mass communication. An equality is implied between author and reader, destroying the fundamental medieval distinction between cleric and lay (cf. S, 46). If in Latimer's sermons English prose begins to discover its modernity, in Augustine Bernher's concern to publish those sermons a print culture is taking hold. English books and readers would never be the same again.[43]

---

[43] On this whole subject (but particularly its technological and professional aspects) see Elizabeth Eisenstein, *The Printing Press as an Agent of Change*, 2 vols. (Cambridge: Cambridge Univ. Press, 1979), esp. chap. 4.

P. G. STANWOOD

Richard Hooker's Discourse and the Deception of Posterity

> *Though for no other cause, yet for this; that posteritie may know we have not loosely through silence permitted things to passe away as in a dreame, there shall be for mens information extant thus much concerning the present state of the Church of God established amongst us, and their carefull endevour which woulde have upheld the same.*
> — Richard Hooker, opening statement to "A Preface"
> *Of the Lawes of Ecclesiasticall Politie* (1593)

I

CLARENDON BEGINS HIS *HISTORY* by recalling Hooker's opening words, directing them to a time of disappointed hopes and bitter nostalgia: "That posterity may not be deceived, by the prosperous wickedness of these times," Clarendon writes, he shall uncover for the world's view "the grounds, circumstances, and artifices of this Rebellion," disclosing also the "seed-plots" from which the present mischiefs have grown.[1] Out of his vivid and personal experience, Clarendon is composing an historical narrative of his times; and his allusion to Hooker reinforces the melancholy he wants to convey. Yet the reference is misleading; for Hooker, in setting out his own contemporary intellectual and cultural situation, is

---

[1] See Edward, earl of Clarendon, *The History of the Rebellion and Civil Wars in England*, ed. W. Dunn Macray (1888; repr., Oxford: Clarendon Press, 1969), 1:1.

being essentially descriptive and polemical. Perhaps with some shade of irony he does begin the most controversial and fiercely partisan section of the *Lawes*; and if Clarendon saw a wistful mood in these lines — or if we in our turn feel a sense of ruined hope in a still-born treatise — then we are all deceived. Hooker is here writing tendentiously, mischievously, and eagerly on behalf of a cause both topical and universal which was not, except in particular items, ever really to fail.

Hooker has been oddly regarded by posterity since his death in 1600.[2] He was not looking back, as Clarendon would evidently do, to a better time that seemed about to pass away; for Hooker surely did not see the years around 1593 and 1597 — the dates of publication of the *Lawes*, preface with books 1-4, and book 5, respectively — in such terms. Under the early influence of Bishop John Jewel (1522-71) and the later patronage and encouragement of Archbishop Whitgift (c. 1530-1604), Hooker set out to answer the objections of the Admonitionists, especially John Field and Thomas Wilcox, presumed authors of the first manifesto which was intended for presentation to Parliament, and later Thomas Cartwright, author of the Second Admonition to the Parliament (1572). These persons, and many other clergy who joined them, represented the radical side of reformed protestantism; they attacked episcopal government and a number of ceremonies thought to be romanist, such as the use of wafer-bread at communion, reception of the sacrament while kneeling, making the sign of the cross at baptism, and so on. Walter Travers was another principal figure in this controversy, for he wrote his *Book of Discipline* (1574)[3]

---

[2] Richard Hooker was born in or near Exeter in April 1554, was educated at the Exeter Grammar School, and, through the influence of Bishop John Jewel, admitted to Corpus Christi College, Oxford (B.A. 1574, M.A. 1577). He became a probationary fellow of Corpus Christi in 1577, a full fellow in 1579, and was appointed deputy professor of Hebrew in 1579. He was ordained deacon, 1579, and priest, 1580. In 1584, he was presented to the living of Drayton Beauchamp, Buckinghamshire, and in 1585 he was appointed Master of the Temple, where he publicly opposed the presbyterian views of Walter Travers, the current Reader. In 1591 he was instituted subdean of Salisbury, prebend of Netheravon, and rector of Boscombe, Wiltshire, offices which he resigned in 1595 when he was presented by the Queen to the living of Bishopsbourne, near Canterbury, where he died on 2 November 1600, and is buried. Hooker was married to Joan Churchman in 1588; two sons (b. 1589 and 1596) predeceased him; he was survived by his wife and four daughters. The best recent biography is by C. J. Sisson, *The Judicious Marriage of Mr. Hooker and the Birth of* The Laws of Ecclesiastical Polity (Cambridge: Cambridge Univ. Press, 1940). Georges Edelen is preparing a new and full *Life of Richard Hooker* (forthcoming).

[3] Travers published his principal work as the *Ecclesiasticae Disciplinae et Anglicanae Ecclesiae ab illa Aberrationis plena e verbo Dei et dilucida Explicatio* anonymously at La

which outlined most of the reformers' contentions; and Hooker here is responding to their arguments in his *Lawes*. He is therefore confronting ecclesiastical antagonists in a way highly dismissive and, by impugning their sincerity, loyalty, and intellectual integrity, he is probably at times unfair. But Hooker is to some extent deliberately writing a document that captures the prevailing view of the established church of his time.

Hooker died before he was able to publish all eight books of the *Lawes*, which are necessary for understanding the true scope of the work and the magnitude of its argument. Hooker's aim, as a reading of the whole work makes clear, was not simply to undermine the leading proponents in the Admonition controversy but to move beyond particular contentions into the defining of political and ecclesiastical authority and yet further into promoting a systematic and sacramental theology. Hooker was supposed to have embodied Anglican wisdom and passed it on as an inheritance for the post-1600 generations, in the thinking summarized by the comfortable formulation of the preface to the revision of the Book of Common Prayer of 1662 (written by Robert Sanderson, Restoration bishop of Lincoln): "It hath been the wisdom of the Church of England, ever since the first compiling of her publick Liturgy, to keep the mean between the two extremes, of too much stiffness in refusing, and of too much easiness in admitting any variation from it." Hooker was commonly believed to have negotiated between these extremes, but this view is false; for he really set out to mock the reformers, with an especially lively caricature of the Genevan Calvinists (especially in section 3 of the preface, "By what meanes so many of the people are trained into the liking of that discipline"), and a persistently critical treatment of the "unsound yet true" Church of Rome, full of evils that need to be cured. "They which measure religion by dislike of the Church of Rome," Hooker suggests, "thinke every man so much the more sound, by how much he can make the corruptions thereof to seeme more large."[4] Hooker sets a course that gener-

---

Rochelle; it was simultaneously translated by Cartwright and known formally as *A full and plaine declaration of ecclesiasticall discipline*. Travers, who was dismissed from his position at the Temple in 1585, subsequently wrote and circulated *A Supplication made to the Privy Counsel by Master Walter Travers* (1586), but not published until 1612, with Hooker's *Answer* (also of 1586). These works, along with Hooker's treatises central to the controversy, especially *Of Justification*, have been newly edited for The Folger Library Edition of The Works of Richard Hooker, vol. 5, by Laetitia Yeandle with commentary by Egil Grislis (Cambridge: The Belknap Press of Harvard Univ. Press, 1990).

[4] See Richard Hooker, *Of the Lawes of Ecclesiastical Politie*, 4.8.2, in The Folger Library Edition of The Works of Richard Hooker, gen. ed. W. Speed Hill (Cambridge:

ally condemns false teaching: Rome is consistently wrong on many issues; but reformed religion, toward which he naturally feels drawn, also errs in certain fundamental ways.

Hooker's reputation as the author of the *via media* may be unfounded — the term itself originated in the Tractarian movement of the earlier nineteenth century — even the notion of the English church as being peculiarly comprehensive is recent and hardly relevant to Tudor and Stuart times.[5] The first collected edition of Hooker appeared in 1662, with an introductory life by Bishop John Gauden, who hoped for an episcopal see more prominent than Exeter. But Gauden's verbose account is oddly, perhaps unintentionally, disparaging of Hooker. When an undergraduate at Corpus Christi College, Oxford, for example, Gauden writes that he was "a good *plodding Student,* one that *lay heavy* on the plow" (ed. 1662, p. 10); as Master of the Temple in the Inns of Court, "he preached like *a living,* but scarce *moving statue*: His eyes *stedfastly* fixed on the same place from the beginning to the end of his *Sermons*; his *body* unmoved, his *tone* much to an *Unisone,* and very *unemphatick"* (p. 30). Such remarks are at odds with the reputation that Hooker had by this time acquired among most leading churchmen, especially Gilbert Sheldon, archbishop of Canterbury from 1663, who probably directed Izaak Walton to write a more fitting life. Walton's "holy" *Life of Hooker,* indeed, displaced Gauden's in the next edition of Hooker's *Works* of 1666, and it appeared in every subsequent reprinting through John Keble's edition of 1836. Walton treats Hooker reverentially — "he that praises *Richard Hooker,* praises God, who hath given such gifts to men" — but also casts doubt on the integrity

---

The Belknap Press of Harvard Univ. Press, 1977), 1:299. All subsequent references to Hooker are taken from this edition and cited in the text, first by Hooker's book, chapter, and section, then to The Folger Library Edition by volume and page. Vol. 1 (noted here), comprising Hooker's preface and books 1 to 4, was edited by Georges Edelen; vol. 2 (also 1977) which gives book 5, was edited by W. Speed Hill; vol. 3, books 6, 7, 8 (1981), was edited by P. G. Stanwood. See also vol. 4 (1982), "Attack and Response," edited by John E. Booty, and vol. 5 (1990), "Tractates and Sermons," texts edited by Laetitia Yeandle and commentary by Egil Grislis (cited in n. 3). Vol. 6, in two parts (Binghamton, N.Y.: Medieval & Renaissance Texts & Studies, 1993), contains introductions and commentary for all of the *Ecclesiastical Polity* (preface, William P. Haugaard; book 1, Lee M. Gibbs; books 2 to 4, William P. Haugaard; book 5, John E. Booty; book 6, Lee M. Gibbs; book 7 and 8 and Hooker's notes and fragments, Arthur S. McGrade). A concluding vol. 7, with bibliography and indexes, is forthcoming.

[5] See Robert K. Faulkner, *Richard Hooker and the Politics of a Christian England* (Berkeley: Univ. of California Press, 1981), who discusses Hooker's moral and religious stand in the context of his times.

of the posthumously published books 6–8 of the *Lawes*, in which Hooker may be seen to question the episcopacy and the royal authority. Certainly he is ambivalent and unemphatic about these and many points which the Restoration church had no wish to dispute.

Hooker has been made to serve the interests of various groups, sometimes with opposing views, but in general Walton's hagiographical life and his inventive dismissal of one-third of the *Lawes* has misled many subsequent readers. Walton especially helped to begin a tradition of uncritical adulation, for he reports in his *Life of Hooker* that the pope (Clement VIII) was so moved to hear the first book *Of the Lawes of Ecclesiasticall Politie* (supposed to have been translated *extempore* into Latin by Thomas Stapleton) that he exclaimed, "This man indeed deserves the name of an Author; his Books will get reverence by Age, for there is in them such seeds of Eternity, that if the rest be like this, they shall last till the last fire shall consume all Learning"; and with similar credulity, Walton makes King James say that "there is in Mr. Hooker no affected language, but a grave, comprehensive, clear manifestation of Reason." Every page reveals pictures of "Truth and Reason," which assure their "Learned, or Judicious, or Reverend, or Venerable" author an immortal remembrance.[6] Such appreciation is never far from the more measured yet vague assessments of modern writers on Hooker, such as those of C. S. Lewis, who may be typical in calling Hooker's style "for its purpose, perhaps the most perfect in English."[7] Hooker's capacity for stimulating reverent admiration with-

---

[6] See *The Life of Mr. Richard Hooker* (1665), in *Lives*, ed. George Saintsbury, The World's Classics (1927; repr., London: Oxford Univ. Press, 1956), 212–13. For a description of the circumstances that led to Walton's writing about Hooker, see David Novarr, *The Making of Walton's Lives* (Ithaca: Cornell Univ. Press, 1958), 197–298. There is, in fact, no evidence that Stapleton ever went to Rome. See *Dictionary of National Biography*, 54:101.

[7] See C. S. Lewis, *English Literature in the Sixteenth Century Excluding Drama* (Oxford: Clarendon Press, 1954), 462. Cf. this nineteenth-century assessment of Hooker's *Lawes*: "The chief characteristic of the work is its elevated calmness of luminous and reasonable thought.... No writer ever conducted a great argument in a higher, purer, and more enlightened spirit. None ever dwelt in a more lofty, serene, and truthful atmosphere, or raised himself more directly, by mere grandeur and largeness of conception, above all the petty and vulgar details which beset controversy even on the greatest subjects" (John Tulloch, *Rational Theology and Christian Philosophy in England in the Seventeenth Century*, 2nd ed. [Edinburgh: Blackwood, 1874], 1:53). John Carey is reacting against such appraisals in his dismissive account of Hooker's style, which he finds manipulative and disingenuous; but Carey seems to miss the largeness and complexity of Hooker's argument (see "Elizabethan Prose," in *English Poetry and Prose 1540–1674*, ed. Christopher Ricks [London: Sphere Books, 1970], 368–73).

out sufficient attention to his meaning may be explained in part by the great length and ambition of his work; for few other English writers have attempted to provide a systematic cultural, political, and theological treatise based upon so broad and deep a foundation of learning and history.

Hooker reveals through his prose what Georges Edelen has properly described as "a cast of mind which is reflected everywhere in the *Lawes*,"[8] and which illuminates a rational process and a logical order. That cast of mind results in language that features periodicity or extended grammatical suspensions and an extraordinary facility for joining many parts of a single very long sentence together with virtuosic coherence and persistent clarity.[9] His distinctive blend of complexity, balance, and expository brilliance has indeed been the subject of frequent scrutiny; yet the relationship of these characteristics to the objectives of the *Lawes* as a whole still needs more explanation. We are right to urge the essentially polemical outlook of the *Lawes* and its controversial aim within the context of the later sixteenth century; but this viewpoint does not necessarily lessen the great imaginative and literary power of Hooker's work in its totality.

My present wish is to observe the intellectual movement and development of Hooker's theme and the way in which his discourse, broadly and stylistically speaking, reveals his overall purpose. By "discourse," I mean to refer narrowly, or at least in terms that Hooker and his contemporaries would understand, to those aspects of rhetorical practice and invention important to the construction of sermons and treatises. "Discourse," in this sense, contains style, in the special features that embody it, from the syntactic and grammatical arrangements of words, to such devices as antimetabole and epanalepsis. I mean "style" to comprehend these particular embellishments while yet being capable of defining the overall arrangement and quality of an argument.[10] We now refer to the coher-

---

[8] See Georges Edelen, "Hooker's Style," in *Studies in Richard Hooker: Essays Preliminary to an Edition of His Works*, ed. W. Speed Hill (Cleveland: Press of Case Western Reserve Univ., 1972), 257. I am generally indebted to Edelen's excellent study.

[9] In his *Church History* (1655), 9:216, Thomas Fuller described Hooker's writing as "long and pithy, driving on a whole flock of several separate clauses before he came to the end of a sentence." The comment is reprinted by John Keble in his edition of *The Works of ... Hooker*, 7th ed. (Oxford: Clarendon Press, 1888), 1:79 n. 2.

[10] "The term style comprehends all at once a multiplicity of things — manner in language and diction, texture, so to speak, and further, thought and judgment, line of argumentation, inventive power, control of material, emotion, and what the Greeks call ἦθος, — and within each one of these notions a profusion of shadings, no fewer, to be

ence of Hooker's *Lawes,* by which we mean that all of its parts are necessarily related, or as Hooker himself claimed at the beginning of his work, "I have endevoured throughout the bodie of this whole discourse, that every former part might give strength unto all that followe, and every later bring some light unto all before" (1.1.3; 1:57). I want to discuss this wide design and suggest certain ways in which Hooker orders it with his style of seeing "two-sidedly," in terms of bifurcation and dichotomy. I believe that through such attention we may see better how Hooker displays a bold imagination in a style that ideally upholds Renaissance literary discourse. But first we need to observe Hooker's typical rhetorical invention, for the sentences obviously contain and provide the fundamental structural units of the work as a whole and illustrate its concerns in microcosm.

II

Hooker is deservedly known for his long sentences, which he frequently constructs periodically, that is, holding in suspension the finite verb until nearly the end of the statement, anticipating the conclusion with a series of compound-complex clauses. Hooker is also often supremely ironic and witty, succinct and cogent, and a master of the apothegmatic style. Examples of proverbial statements abound. He says early in the first book that "the lawes of well doing are the dictates of right reason" (1.7.4; 1:79); that "we all make complaint of the iniquitie of our times: not unjustly; for the dayes are evill" (1.10.3; 1:98); and wittily, "I am perswaded, that of them with whom in this cause we strive, there are whose betters amongst men would bee hardly found, if they did not live amongest men, but in some wildernesse by themselves" (1.16.6; 1:140); and later, "he that will take away extreme heate by setting the body in extremitie of cold, shal undoubtedly remove the disease, but together with it the diseased too" (4.8.1; 1:298); and "No man which is not exceeding partiall can well denie, but that there is most just cause wherefore we should be

---

sure, than the differences in talent, which are as numerous as men themselves": so Erasmus in his edition of Jerome (quoted from *Collected Works of Erasmus,* ed. James F. Brady and John C. Olin [Toronto: Univ. of Toronto Press, 1992], 61:78). In addition to Edelen's study of Hooker's style, see also Brian Vickers in his introduction to an abridged edition *Of the Laws of Ecclesiastical Polity,* ed. A. S. McGrade and Vickers (London: Sidgwick & Jackson, 1975), 41–59, and cf. P. E. Forte, "Richard Hooker as Preacher," in The Folger Library Edition of The Works of Richard Hooker, vol. 5, *Tractates and Sermons,* 657–82.

offended greatly at the Church of Rome" (4.9.2; 1:302), this last comment employing the ironic understatement that is typical of much of Hooker's writing. We meet such irony in many places, especially, for example, in book 4 (chap. 2.1; 1:276-77), where he is answering the Admonitionist objection that the Church of England lacks "ancient Apostolicall simplicitie":

> For it is out of doubt that the first state of thinges was best, that in the prime of Christian Religion faith was soundest, the scriptures of God were then best understood by all men, al partes of godlines did then most abound: and therefore it must needs follow, that customes lawes and ordinances devised since are not so good for the Church of Christ, but the best way is to cut of later inventions, and to reduce things unto the aunciente state wherin at the first they were.

And further to the same point:

> It is not I am right sure their meaning, that we should now assemble our people to serve God in close and secret meetings, or that common brookes and rivers shoulde be used for places of baptisme, or that the Eucharist shoulde bee ministred after meate, or that the custome of Church feasting shoulde be renewed, or that all kinde of standing provision for the ministerie shoulde be utterly taken away, and their estate made againe dependent upon the voluntary devotion of men. (4.2.3; 1:278)

Periodic sentences occur on almost every page of the *Lawes*. In book 1 is the long and important tenth chapter on the formation through reason of human laws. In order to show clearly the organization of one particularly arresting sentence (of section 10), I shall set it off by clauses. There is first of all a kind of prologue: "That which plaine or necessarie reason bindeth men unto may be in sundry considerations expedient to be ratified by humane law: for example,"

> if confusion of blood in mariage,
>   the libertie of having many wives at once,
>   or any other the like corrupt and unreasonable custome
>   doth happen to have prevailed far
>   and to have gotten the upper hand of right reason
>   with the greatest part, so that no way is
>   left to rectifie such foul disorder without

>   prescribing by lawe the same thinges
>   which reason necessarilie *doth* enforce
>   but is not *perceyved* that so
>   it doeth,
> or if many be grown unto that, which thapostle did lament in some,
>   concerning whom he wryteth saying, that
>   *Even what things they naturally know, in*
>   *those very thinges as beasts void of*
>   *reason they corrupted them selves;*
> or if there be no such speciall accident,
>   yet for as much as the common sort are led by the
>   swaye of their sensuall desires,
>   and therefore do more shun sinne for the
>   sensible evils which follow it amongst
>   men, then for any kinde of sentence
>   which reason doth pronounce against it:
> **this verie thinge is cause sufficient**
>   why duties belonging unto ech kinde of vertue,
>   albeit the law of reason teach them,
>   shoulde notwithstanding be prescribed even by humane law.
> Which lawe in this case wee terme *mixt*,
>   because the matter whereunto it bindeth, is the same
>   which reason necessarily doth require at our handes,
> and from the law of reason
>   it differeth in the maner of binding onely.[11] (1:105-6)

This elaborate sentence, typical of the *Lawes,* begins with a series of three adverbial "if" clauses, each with its own dependencies, at the end of which Hooker introduces the long-awaited independent clause (here in bold italic); but this "cause sufficient" is a temporary conclusion, for not only does it complete one sentence but it also provides the pivot upon which rests a further succession of dependent clauses. Hooker intends to balance the earlier part of the sentence with the later part, and to reflect grammatically the weighing of the sides, even as he is carefully discriminating "mixt" laws, or defining the conjunction of human (or positive)

---

[11] Georges Edelen quotes the long passage that follows this sentence as an example of Hooker's expository mode (Edelen, "Hooker's Style," 264-65).

law with natural (or divine) law. The effect is expressive of Hooker's logical method, with its suspension of opposing ideas in a steadying equilibrium of confident poise.

III

Hooker divided the eight books of the *Lawes* in half, the first four dealing with "generalities," the last four with "particulars" (4.14.7.*advertisement*; 1:345). Such a division is natural, just as the one More makes in *Utopia*, or Bacon in his *Advancement of Learning*, or Milton in *The Reason of Church Government*, or Browne in *Religio Medici*, and in *Hydriotaphia* and *Garden of Cyrus* (as the first and second parts of separate but complementary works). These partitions may seem fortuitous or inevitable, yet they enable their authors to arrange material that is evidently hemispherical so that we have two views of a single object. Hooker means to do this, but his conception must be sustained over an enormous length, like a colossal and far more coherent *Religio Medici*. That he succeeds in his ambition, not only in the large ordering of the *Lawes*, but also, as we have briefly seen, in the management of its discrete parts, needs to be recognized and named as one of the great achievements of English literature.[12] Hooker starts with the abstract or natural law, with God himself who is that law which man may know through right reason. He is careful to distinguish the different, yet interlocked, kinds of law; for all men are subject to many laws, which ask for a variety of responses. There are thus eight kinds of law, the first four relating particularly to the natural law, the last four to the positive or man made law, with the eighth forming the foundation of the rest:

> [1] The lawe which God with himselfe hath eternally set downe to follow in his owne workes; [2] the law which he hath made for his creatures to keepe, [that is,] the law of naturall and necessarie agents; [3] the lawe which Angels in heaven obey; [4] the lawe whereunto by the light of reason men finde themselves bound in that they are men; [5] the lawe which they make by composition for multitudes and politique societies of men to be guided by; [6] the lawe which belongeth unto each nation; [7] the lawe that

---

[12] But see W. Speed Hill, "Editing Richard Hooker: A Retrospective," *Sewanee Theological Review* 36 (1993): 187–99, esp. 198.

concerneth the fellowship of all; [8] and lastly the lawe which God himselfe hath supernaturally revealed. (1.16.1; 1:134)

Each law is unique yet laws together rest in the "bosome of God":

> Her voyce [is] the harmony of the world, all things in heaven and earth doe her homage, the very least as feeling her care, and the greatest as not exempted from her power, but Angels and men and creatures of what condition so ever, though ech in different sort and maner, yet all with uniforme consent, admiring her as the mother of their peace and joy. (1.16.18; 1:142)

Hooker is here defining that one law which harmonizes the rest, toward which Providence moves all people, and heals the disjunction and conflict between the positive law of "politique societies" and the divine law of God.

Having founded his whole treatise on the natural law, and also assumed man's informed reason in the making of his own laws in accordance with that law, Hooker turns to the authority of the scriptures (books 2-3), of the church and its "proceedings" (book 4), its ceremonies and its government (books 5-7), and finally to the authority of the king or "Civil Governour" in matters civil and ecclesiastical (book 8). To collect and integrate the details that follow from Hooker's general discussion of the natural law in book 1, which finally leads to and supports his argument about the jurisdiction of kings in book 8, requires a complicated kind of patience and the judgment of detached observation. All authority derives from the natural law and from God himself; "all men are not for all thinges sufficient." The prince may not act for the bishop, nor the bishop for the prince, yet both are subject to the universal law:

> And therefore publique affayres being devided, such persons must be authorized Judges in each kinde as common reason may presume to be most fitt. Which cannot of *Kings* and *Princes* ordinarily be presumed in causes meerly Ecclesiasticall, so that even *Common* sense doth rather adjudge this burthen unto other men.[13]

---

[13] 8.8.8; 3:430. Hooker's church polity is normative, I believe, for the Anglican communion. The fact that so many Laudian churchmen ignored or misrepresented his message does not change its essential meaning or significance. See Patrick Collinson, *The Elizabethan Puritan Movement* (Oxford: Clarendon Press, 1967), on the later sixteenth century from the standpoint of Hooker's opponents; and *The Religion of Protestants* (Oxford: Clarendon Press, 1982), which demonstrates the continuity of the church from Elizabethan through Jacobean times. See also Robert Eccleshall, "Richard Hooker and

Hooker argues that the king is supreme while nevertheless he points out his limitations both in the spiritual and political realm. This double nature of the royal supremacy is in fact an analogical extension of the positive and the divine law, of the church militant and heavenly, of Christ himself in two natures, the incarnate word, in *hypostasis*, realized in the "real presence" of the eucharist itself. All things work together in a mysterious duality which embraces simultaneous separateness and unity.[14]

In considering the totality of the *Lawes*, we must especially recognize the essential contribution of the last three (posthumous) books to the whole work, yet their curious history makes this task difficult. Books 6-8 seemed orphans for so long because of their unfinished or dubious state, and to some readers they reflected a falling off from Hooker's best expository skill. But Hooker's careful description both of the natural and of the positive law in book 1 states the general principles which make possible his later distinction in book 8 between the two kinds of headship of the church, that is, the differences between the governance of Christ and of the king.[15] The intervening books enable us to see the application of the different species of the law from a variety of two-eyed standpoints, such as the relation of reason to revelation, the visible church to the immutable faith of Christ, and so on. These relationships are reciprocal and they are fundamental to Hooker's grand scheme, and to a style that develops ideas

---

the Peculiarities of the English: The Reception of the *Ecclesiastical Polity* in the Seventeenth and Eighteenth Centuries," *History of Political Thought* 2 (1981): 63-117; Hugh Trevor-Roper, *Catholics, Anglicans and Puritans* (London: Secker and Warburg, 1987), esp. chap. 4, "The Great Tew Circle"; and W. J. Torrance Kirby, *Richard Hooker's Doctrine of the Royal Supremacy* (Leiden: E. J. Brill, 1990), 34-35.

[14] See Kirby, *Richard Hooker's Doctrine of the Royal Supremacy*, 116-17, who forcefully elaborates this point. By appealing to the personal unity of the divine and human natures in Christ, "Hooker demonstrates the unity of sovereign power or dominion over both Church and the secular political order" (and chap. 4, "*Supremum Caput*: Hooker's Theology of Headship").

[15] On the fundamental unity of the *Lawes*, see the important studies by A. S. McGrade, "The Coherence of Hooker's *Polity*: The Books on Power," *Journal of the History of Ideas* 24 (1963): 163-82, and also his introduction to an edition of Hooker's preface, books 1 and 8, in "Cambridge Texts in the History of Political Thought" (Cambridge: Cambridge Univ. Press, 1989); and W. D. J. Cargill Thompson, "The Philosopher of the 'Politic Society,'" in *Studies in Richard Hooker: Essays Preliminary to an Edition of His Works*, ed. W. Speed Hill (Cleveland: Press of Case Western Reserve Univ., 1972), 3-76, repr. in Cargill Thompson, *Studies in the Reformation*, ed. C. W. Dugmore (London, 1980). I give a detailed explanation of the authorial integrity of books 6-8 of the *Lawes* in my textual introduction to them in The Folger Library Edition, vol. 3 (1981).

already exposed. Any difficulty in reading and responding to the *Lawes* occurs on account of our traditional disinclination to realize the extent to which Hooker is able to join all the parts that he also separates; at the same time, we easily become disoriented within the work, like travelers in a dark wood who see one tree illuminated only to find the rest of the forest in obscurity.

Hooker's seeming ambivalence over so many issues expresses what Sir Thomas Browne later called the "divided and distinguished worlds" which amphibious mankind must negotiate. These worlds are mortal, on the one hand, and spiritual, on the other; and while we live in both, we are not always aware of such a dual existence. Nor is Hooker always helpful in leading us through this strange landscape of earth and spirit, and so I must be selective in illustrating what can be found there. The great scheme and its supporting style does seem to break down by book 6, which is, in its present state, primarily about penitence and confession, and it serves mainly as a kind of preface to the jurisdiction of lay elders. Book 7, however, which is essentially complete, deals at length with the state of bishops and the episcopal function. Here it is easy to see that Hooker upholds the episcopacy principally because of its "publique benefit" and long tradition, an estimation that falls far short of the divine right theories upheld by Richard Bancroft or Hadrian Saravia.[16] Bishops gather to themselves virtues uncommon among other kinds of leaders: "Devotion, and the feeling sence of Religion are not usual in the noblest, wisest, and chiefest Personages of State, by reason their wits are so much imployed another way, and their mindes so seldom conversant in heavenly things" (7.24.15; 3:299). Hooker's support of the episcopacy is based mainly upon the conservative view that traditional forms if not obviously harmful should be preserved. The "regiment" by bishops is "a thing most lawful, divine and holy" (7.2.3; 3:153). Hooker warily rejects the limitations on their authority proposed by the reformers (especially in chapter 15 of book 7), and he is at pains to show how the same person combines a civil and ecclesiastical function as long as this is a matter of positive law. The

---

[16] See Richard Bancroft, *Daungerous Positions and Proceedings published and practised within this Iland of Brytaine, under pretence of Reformation, and for the Presbiterial Discipline* (London, 1593), and Hadrianus Saravia, *De diversis ministrorum Evangelii gradibus* (London, 1590; Frankfurt, 1591). See the detailed study of Saravia by Willem Nijenhuis, *Adrianus Saravia (c.1532–1613)* (Leiden: E. J. Brill, 1980), and also J. P. Sommerville, "Richard Hooker, Hadrian Saravia, and the Advent of the Divine Right of Kings," *History of Political Thought* 4 (1983): 229–45.

immutable law of God and Nature is silent on this issue and by implication the episcopacy itself: "From contrary occasions, contrary Laws may grow, and each be reasoned and disputed for by such as are subject therunto, during the time they are in force.... Wherefore... Canons, Constitutions, and Laws which have been at one time meet, do not prove that the Church should always be bound to follow them" (7.15.14; 3:241).

The adroitness with which Hooker manages these distinctions, applying to them his great scheme of positive and natural law, is entirely characteristic of his style, whether we mean the particularity of the diction and the periodic sentences, or the broader formulations of theme. For the present, I am most concerned to see Hooker's style as thematic function, and in having recalled book 7, one of the least read and appreciated parts of the *Lawes*, to suggest that this style — a kind of architectural maneuvering — pervades the whole work. An understanding of this point may release us from posterity's false teaching. Hooker, indeed, would poise his arguments for the episcopacy on standards that change while remaining the same, a fact which may have caused the deliberate "loss" of book 7 until the Restoration "found" it, nearly sixty years after Hooker's death. Yet Hooker's "double vision" is the means whereby he sees everything, with ambivalence its characteristic mode, "periodicity," or the simultaneous balancing of divergent points, its strength. Perhaps this idea can be still better presented by illustration from the longest and most detailed of the books of the *Lawes*; this fifth book is just as conceptually and fundamentally clear as any of the others, while signalling and epitomizing the issues of the entire work.

Book 5 seems superficially to be an extended discourse on the forms of religious worship, especially according to the Book of Common Prayer. While it does, of course, function in this way, Hooker is offering much more than a commentary. The book begins by affirming its own importance: "Pure and unstayned religion ought to be the highest of all cares apperteyninge to publique regiment" (5.1.2; 2:16), Hooker writes. The commonwealth depends on justice united with religion, and on the rule of reason that depends on the interaction of the positive and the divine law. After twenty-two chapters about the outward form of churches and on public worship and preaching, chapter 23 opens another aspect of the subject: "Of Prayer" gracefully directs us "betwene the throne of God in heaven and his Church upon earth" (5.23.1; 2:110). This harmonious touching of the two realms of heaven and earth, with its angelic commendation, looks forward to George Herbert who defines prayer as "the

Churches banquet, Angels age" in his poem on "Prayer" (1633); and Hooker inspired John Cosin who borrows his phrases in the preface of the celebrated *Private Devotions* (1627).[17] Hooker eloquently describes prayer as a "worke common to the Church as well triumphant as militant, a worke common unto men with Angels...so much of our lives is coelestiall and divine as we spend in the exercise of prayer" (5.23.1; 2:111). Now this second principal division of book 5 continues until we reach chapter 50, "Of the name, the author, and the force of Sacraments," which provides a further, and final introduction for the concluding, yet unequal third of the book. Hooker ends this chapter cautiously by advising us of the importance of what is to come: "And for as much as there is no union of God with man without that meane betwene both which is both, it seemeth requisite that wee first consider how God is in Christ, then how Christ is in us, and how the sacramentes doe serve to make us pertakers of Christ. In other thinges wee may be more briefe, but the waight of these requireth largenes" (5.50.3; 2:208-9).

Hooker amply justifies his admonition, and for most of the considerable length of book 5 that remains he explores sacramental theology in detail. To comprehend what remains largely ineluctable we must exercise our abilities to the utmost: "The strength of our faith," Hooker says, "is tryed by those thinges wherein our wittes and capacities are not stronge" (5.52.1; 2:211). Essential to our understanding of faith — or truth more plain than it is clear — is the doctrine of the Incarnation defined by the Chalcedonian formula, "in fower words ἀληθῶς, τελέως, ἀδιαιρέτως, ἀσυγχύτως perfectly, indivisibly, distinctly; the first applied to his beinge God, and the seconde to his beinge man, the third to his beinge of both one, and the fowrth to his still continuinge in that one both" (5.54.10; 2:227). This fundamental distinction forms the basis of Christ's presence to us by means of that participation inherent between Him and this world. Sacraments are therefore necessary because "they are heavenlie ceremonies, which God hath sanctified and ordeined to be administred in his Church, first as markes wherebie to knowe when God doth imparte the vitall or savinge grace of Christ unto all that are capable thereof, and secondlie as meanes conditionall which God requireth in them unto whome he imparteth grace" (5.57.3; 2:245-46). Hooker steers us carefully between the spiritual realm and the ordinary or external realm in all of

---

[17] See *A Collection of Private Devotions*, ed. P. G. Stanwood (Oxford: Clarendon Press, 1967), 14.

these distinctions, as he has done and continues to do throughout the *Lawes*. *Participation* is the generally descriptive term for what he says about the sacramental presence, and indeed about all of life, where "we may evermore dwell in him, and he in us."[18]

Participation, of course, depends upon the dual activity of one going forward to meet another who has simultaneously advanced, with the mingling of two identities defined as one which yet remain the same and apart. Hooker gracefully evokes this curious linking in his chapter, referred to already, "Of Prayer": "For what is thassemblinge of the Church to learne, but the receivinge of Angels descended from above? What to pray, but the sendinge of Angels upward? His heavenly inspirations and our holie desires are as so many Angels of entercorse and comerce betwene God and us" (5.23.1; 2:110). Hooker here sustains in the imagery of earthly ascending and heavenly descending, and their transposition, a mysterious process that tells of order, simultaneity, and interaction, the defining features of the *Lawes of Ecclesiastical Polity*. Within a discourse of such coherence exists the life that Hooker would not have us miss or allow dreamily to pass away.

---

[18] See John E. Booty, in *Commentary*, introduction to book 5 (Binghamton, N.Y.: Medieval & Renaissance Texts & Studies, 1993), 6:197–99. Cf. also Booty's "Hooker and Anglicanism: Into the Future," *Sewanee Theological Review* 36 (1993): 215–26.

CLAIRE PRESTON

Sidney's Arcadian Poetics: A Medicine of Cherries and the Philosophy of Cavaliers

> What can saying make them beleeve, whom seeing cannot perswade? Those paines must be felt before they ca[n] be understood; no outward utterance can command a conceipt.[1]

IN ONE OF MANY RETROSPECTIVE NARRATIVES in book 2 of the *New Arcadia* Pyrocles, disguised as the Amazon Zelmane, recounts his past adventures to Philoclea; among these he recalls his brief and tragic encounter with the original Zelmane. That young noblewoman, in love with Pyrocles and eager to make amends for her father's bad faith, disguises herself as a page and becomes attached to him in service. He recalls her costume and bearing, both of which contain clues to her sex and motive, though not specifically to her identity:

> Her apparrell of white, wrought upon with broken knots, her horse, faire & lustie, which she rid so, as might shew a fearefull boldnes, daring to doo that, which she knew that she knew not how to doo. (2.12.291)

Her inexpert equestrianism gives her away as a neophyte; her white clothing — always in Sidney a sign of innocence or inexperience — confirms it; the broken lovers' knots show her state of mind. "Me thought

---

[1] *New Arcadia*, 2.3.161. All references to the *New Arcadia* refer to book, chapter, and page numbers in Feuillerat's edition (Cambridge, 1912).

I had seen that face," Pyrocles remembers thinking, "but the great alteration of her fortune, made her far distant from my memorie." Probably her distracting subliminal charms also make her obvious deception all but illegible to him. "How often (alas) did her eyes say unto me, that they loved? and yet, I (not looking for such a matter) had not my conceipt open, to understand them." It is only with hindsight that he remarks she "well shewed, there is no service like his, that serves because he loves." (2.22.291) The image of lovelornness presented by Zelmane is one which is obscure to Pyrocles until she explains it to him; only much later does he supply the gloss: "she serves because she loves" virtually stands as a motto to this emblematic spectacle.

Because the whole episode is retold by Pyrocles well after the event, when he is aware of Zelmane's subterfuge, it is narratively slack. Had it been recounted at first hand, the iconographically proficient reader might have supplied the meanings for white clothes, and read the message of the broken knots. And unlike Pyrocles, temporarily blinded by sexual *frisson*, the reader might have seen that "Daiphantus" was really the girl Zelmane. This superior interpretive ability might have outstripped Pyrocles', had the story not been told retrospectively.

The situation of this recollected event recapitulates the circumstances of the teller and his auditor: Philoclea, like Pyrocles, also has none of the penetrating wit or acuity to decipher visual information, and like the original Zelmane, her cross-dressed lover must finally provide his own gloss for her. The Zelmane story is retold to Philoclea *after* the puzzle is solved so that there is nothing to interpret, an activity which she is quite unfit to perform anyway. These resonances of the dead Zelmane's tragedy within the mainly comic tale of the putative Zelmane are lost both to Philoclea and to Pyrocles, but not to the reader.

Part of the purpose of such recollective narratives is to allow the speakers to organize information coherently which was before chaotic and apparently meaningless. In retelling they order their experience into a pattern which yields a lesson — in this case, Pyrocles turns his encounter with Zelmane into an emblem whose primary gloss ("there is no service like his, who serves because he loves") reminds him in future to keep his "conceipt" open to such emblematic impressions. "Conceipt" comes from the Latin *concipere*, in Ciceronian diction "to imagine" or "to image." To put it another way, Pyrocles has organised the confused and analytically vacant set of responses initially elicited from him by the Zelmane sequence into a picture of the causal consistency between the signs of lovesickness and her emotional predicament, between his culpable failure to read those signs and her death. This act of reordering which produces didactic consistency and clarity is precisely the task assigned to fictions in the *Defence of Poetry*.

Sidney's poetic image is an organic one. He employs the metaphor of body and soul, of inward character embodied in outward appearance, to show that ultimately "the skill of each artificer standeth in that *idea* or fore-conceit of the work, and not in the work itself."[2] This bifurcated poetic image, where abstraction becomes visible only in a vesture of words, is a morphology reminiscent not only of Aristotle's simile of plot and characters as bones and flesh,[3] but of the emblem-theorists' equation of image and motto with body and soul.[4] The instrument of instruction, according to the *Defence*, is a "doctrinable" poetry which *shows* abstractions in concrete and physical images, and only secondarily names and discusses them.

Delightful and instructive poetry as it is defined in the *Defence*[5] is that which teaches by example, and only subsequently offers precept, an idea first introduced in its exordium: his riding master Pugliano "according to the fertileness of the Italian wit, did not only afford us the *demonstration* of his practice, but sought to enrich our minds with the *contemplations* therein, which he thought most precious."[6] Demonstrable precepts require a concreteness which is available to Sidney through *ekphrasis*, the rhetorical figure most characteristic of the *New Arcadia*, the trope which by minute description puts before the mind's eye an object or a work of art.[7] Like Pugliano's equestrianism, Sidney's narrative is rarely more than

---

[2] Philip Sidney, A *Defence of Poetry* in *The Miscellaneous Prose of Sir Philip Sidney*, eds. Katherine Duncan-Jones and Jan van Dorsten (Oxford: Clarendon Press, 1972), 79. All references to the *Defence* refer to this edition.

[3] Aristotle, *Poetics*, ed. James Hutton (Ithaca: Cornell Univ. Press, 1982), 51. See also Wesley Trimpi, "The Meaning of Horace's Ut Pictura Poesis," *Journal of the Warburg and Courtauld Institutes* 36 (1973): 26; and Jean Hagstrum, *The Sister Arts: The Tradition of Literary Pictorialism and English Poetry from Dryden to Gray* (Chicago: Univ. of Chicago Press, 1958), 7.

[4] "Primum id est, ut inter animam & corpus iusta quaedam incedat proportio & analogia." (Abraham Fraunce, *Insignium, Armorum, Emblematum*... (London, 1588), M2ʼ); see also Guilliermo Ruscelli, quoted in Henri Estienne, *The Art of Making Devises*, trans. Thomas Blount (London, 1646), 22.

[5] Sidney uses the word "poetry" to mean "imaginative fictions" either in verse or prose.

[6] *Defence*, 73 (my emphasis).

[7] George Puttenham calls this trope "icon" (*The Arte of English Poesie*, eds. Gladys

descriptive (though densely ramified), or only secondarily discursive and explanatory.

The requirement that ideas be invested with rhetorical dressings is hardly singular. Puttenham, like Sidney, also invokes a dichotomous poetical mechanics to ask whether

> our vulgar Poesie shew it selfe either gallant or gorgious, if any lymme be left naked and bare and not clad in his kindly clothes and coulours.[8]

But Sidney's concept of the poetic image is distinctly *not* ornamental. Where Puttenham's poetic dress of rhetorical figures happily covers up an unseemly plainness, Sidney's embodies an otherwise inexpressible or only metaphorically available concept. Puttenham's is decorative; Sidney's is functional. Puttenham seeks to prank up a bare thought in "courtly habiliment"; Sidney's more neoplatonic image is the glass through which we are to see, darkly, a sublime world of pure Idea. Sidney's fictions are figurative in the most exact sense: he suggests meaning through a moral language of pictures. The judging of these pictures by readers and characters is the central activity of the *New Arcadia*.

The necessity for the late sixteenth-century Protestant poetic theorist to justify fictions by granting them an underlying but dominant moral purpose is unmistakable in *The Defence of Poetry*; in the *New Arcadia* this necessity manifests itself in a plot in which events are determined by the expectation of an organic unity of the image, the (as it were) grammatical agreement between its outward presentation and its governing foreconceit. This agreement, also characteristic of emblematic art, offers a means of imposing a structured order on the otherwise "undoctrinable" and arbitrary world of experience, of creating what Cartari describes as *gentil'imago vero*, the elegant and *true* or perspicuous image.[9] And the true poetic image, like the emblem, demands an interpretive act from the viewer; it prompts good reading, or what Tesauro calls *ingegno naturale*,[10] what Pyrocles accomplishes only in the figure of *anamnesis*: the "purifying of wit, enriching of memory, enabling of judgement, and enlarging of conceit."[11]

Doidge Willcocks and Alice Walker (Cambridge: Cambridge Univ. Press, 1936), 241.)

[8] Puttenham, 137.

[9] Vincenzo Cartari, *Le Imagini de i Dei de gli Antichi* (Venice, 1571), a4v.

[10] Cited by Ernest Gilman in *The Curious Perspective: Literary and Pictorial Wit in the Seventeenth Century* (New Haven: Yale Univ. Press, 1978), 76.

[11] *Defence*, 82.

The *Defence* and *Arcadia* powerfully assert the dire moral consequences of false images (signs disengaged from or misrepresenting a controlling idea); therefore *good* fictions should either observe the principle of unity between idea and image, or should demonstrate the consequences of disjoined fictions by producing a visually exact and detailed lexicon of images which can be "read" and judged for the degree of such dissociations. In the emblematic device, a moral abstraction or fore-conceit is pictured iconographically and is accompanied by a verbal account of it in the form of a motto or an inscription which endorses the picture as its interpretation or gloss.[12]

The visual, pictorial mode of the *New Arcadia* is essentially emblematic, since the ekphrastically produced *pictura loquens* is a kind of transparent hieroglyph which efficiently directs the reader straight to the idea which it represents, or, as he says, "clearly to see through" the outward poetical dressing to the inner, abstruse idea.[13] The poet, like the good painter, he says, "painteth not Lucretia whom he never saw, but painteth the outward beauty of such a virtue."[14] As Politian had argued, Sidney believes that poetry's "feigning of notable images" is the most powerful of all didactic tools.[15] By comparison, the philosopher's "wordish descriptions" are tedious maxims "rudely clothed for to witness outwardly . . . contempt of outward things," and the historian is "captived to the truth of a foolish world." Philosophy is not efficient, history not sufficient for moral instruction. But the poet, like the good portraitist described by Hilliard, can depict essential, idealized versions of Nature's

---

[12] Verbal pictures may be "emblematic" rather than simply pictorial because they are to some extent iconic or hieroglyphic and not merely descriptive; their meaning is not literally, but only iconographically, present; and like emblem-book devices they require a conscious act of interpretation from the beholder. In the theoretical writing about emblems, the motto was thought to "explain" the picture secondarily; the subscriptive verse was tertiary in the order of apprehension. See, however, Mario Praz, *Studies in Seventeenth Century Imagery*, 2nd ed. (London: Warburg Institute, 1964), 25–31; and Rosemary Freeman, *English Emblem Books* (London: Chatto and Windus, 1948), 54.

[13] *Defence*, 86. See also Lawrence C. Wolfley, "Sidney's visual-didactic poetic: some complexities and limitations," *Journal of Medieval and Renaissance Studies* 6 (1976): 225; and Forrest G. Robinson, *The Shape of Things Known: Sidney's Defence in its Philosophical Tradition* (Cambridge, Mass.: Harvard Univ. Press, 1972), 1–3.

[14] *Defence*, pp. 80–81.

[15] Leonardo, citing Politian in *Trattato della Pittura*, in *The Literary Works of Leonardo da Vinci*, eds. Jean Paul Richter and Irma A. Richter, 2 vols. (Oxford: Oxford Univ. Press, 1939), 1: 46.

creations and so may "strike, pierce, [and] possess the sight of the soul."[16] In its clarity and exactitude, Sidney's poetic image claims controlling hermeneutic power for the maker.

Michael McCanles has observed that readings of the complex rhetorical structures of the *New Arcadia* mainly attempt to say what such descriptive passages *mean* rather than discover *why* they are constructed as they are.[17] But tenor and vehicle are not — at least by Sidney's account — mutually exclusive. Inherent in the emblematic rhetorical strategy outlined by the *Defence* and executed in the *New Arcadia* is a rhetoric whose specialized form of expression urges us to visualize its objects and to engage in vigorous acts of interpretation.

The emblematic habit of mind developed throughout the sixteenth century and reached its zenith between the time of Sidney's literary maturity in the 1580s and the outbreak of the Civil War sixty years later. This habit of mind allowed the phenomenal world to be organized and read as sentences and paragraphs.[18] "The notion of ensignment is universal, and natural," says Edmund Bolton; " ... but cast your eye ... upon the goodly booke of the world."[19] Similarly, Paracelsus in *Prognosticatio* (1536): "in every thing there is some external sign by which we detect that which, not subject to the eye, is internal."[20] The wit that uncovers the innate "ensignments" of things is the same ingenuity required to fashion emblematic devices. The reading of fiction needs an equivalent canniness, a blend of erudition and wit, because reading emblematic art is designedly and self-consciously difficult, a difficulty

---

[16] *Defence*, 85; and Nicholas Hilliard, *The Arte of Limning*, eds. Arthur Kinney and Linda Bradley Salomon, with foreword by Sir John Pope-Hennessy (Boston: Northeastern Univ. Press, 1983), 22–24.

[17] Michael McCanles, *The Text of Sidney's Arcadian World* (Durham, N.C.: Duke Univ. Press, 1989), 16–17.

[18] Even a brief account of this sensibility would have to refer to an enormous cultural development which cannot be covered here. This essay can but refer to the origins of emblematics by noting that the humanists were interested in pre-linguistic or non-linguistic forms of signification, in the conviction that such a discourse could transcend in power ordinary human language (see Praz, 23), and that the search for such a discourse triggered a rage for a modern equivalent of the hieroglyph, for "speaking pictures," which was to inform every kind of cultural endeavor from hat-badges, chivalric devices, garden design, architecture, costume, armour, frontispieces, funerary monuments, portraits, masques, and entertainments, to poetry, physiognomics, and landscape painting.

[19] Edmund Bolton, *The Elements of Armories* (London, 1610), 7–11.

[20] Paracelsus, *Prognosticatio* ([Augsburg?], 1536), *figura* 1.

which reminds the reader of the need for interpretation and of the moral stature implied by the ability to do this correctly.[21]

The spectacular increase in ekphrastic material is one of the most noticeable features of Sidney's revision of the romance,[22] and this increase produces a fictional universe of legible pictures in which all artificial and natural phenomena have potential "countenance." As the humanists anatomized facial expression and gesture as *natura specialis*, a rhetoric of the soul,[23] so the Arcadian rhetoric of landscape, physiognomy, gardens, buildings, costumes and disguises, armour, equine accoutrements, and jewels can be deciphered as if they figured forth their own ideas. Consequently, the most profoundly active verbs in the Arcadian vocabulary are "to show," "to figure," "to witness," "to deck," "to testify," "betoken," "become," "paint," "seem," "bewray," "portray," and the like, all terms of visual *display*.

When Pyrocles, dressed as Zelmane, discovers Prince Musidorus, now Dorus the shepherd, they commiserate with one another as they stroll in a grove of palm trees "which being loving in their nature, seemd to give their shadow the willinglier, because they held discourse of love"(2.2.152). Since palm trees are a well-known emblem of married love, the carefully

---

[21] This active, participatory function of emblems and of images is one well-developed throughout the sixteenth and seventeenth centuries; *versibilità* is the seventeenth century Italian rhetorical term for the ability to engage in *acts* of understanding by contemplation and differentiation of all aspects of a subject. Arthur Kinney identifies this activity with the rhetorical term *methexis* (*Humanist Poetics: Thought, Rhetoric, and Fiction in Sixteenth-Century England* (Amherst: Univ. of Massachusetts Press, 1986), 231). Such analysis by the "versible" reader is not only emblematic, but also related to the Protestant tradition of biblical exegesis, where infolded meaning of figurative scriptural language must be coaxed out through a dynamic, earnest process of contemplation and response by the diligent believer, who is enjoined thereby to follow right action. Indeed, techniques of biblical reading were strengthened and reinforced by such textual emblems, for biblical exegesis or "prophesy" sought partly to uncover archetypal patterns which might direct and inform common life. Such providential patterning is analogous to Sidney's notion of "poetic patterning" in fiction which in his words moves men toward "the end of well-doing."

[22] An account of Sidney's pictorial revisions of the *Old Arcadia* is given by Norman K. Farmer, Jr., *Poets and the Visual Arts in Renaissance England* (Austin: Univ. of Texas Press, 1984), 2–18.

[23] See G. S. Brett, *Brett's History of Psychology*, ed. and abridged by R. S. Peters (London: George Allen & Unwin Ltd, 1953), 293–322; Baldesar Castiglione, *The Book of the Courtier*, trans. Thomas Hoby, ed. Walter Raleigh (London, 1900), 348; Paolo Lomazzo, *A Tracte Containing the Arte of Curious Painting*, trans. Richard Haydocke (London, 1598), 95; B. L. Joseph, *Elizabethan Acting* (Oxford: Oxford Univ. Press, 1951), 106; and W.J.T. Mitchell, *Iconology: Image, Text, Ideology* (Chicago: Univ. of Chicago Press, 1986), 41.

designated setting suggests that these two be read as matrimonial partners, a proleptic misreading of Pyrocles' identity which causes hilarious results elsewhere in the forest.[24] But many of his investigative descriptions are more difficult, less easily pictured. The delineations of the shipwrecked Musidorus, "though he were naked, nakednes was to him an apparrell" (1.1.8), and the imperious Pamela "of high thoughts, who avoides not pride with not knowing her excellencies, but by making that one of her excellencies to be voide of pride" (1.3.20), are both halted by a recalcitrant *antimetabole*, a figure of tautologous, self-referential equilibrium which effectively ends description.[25] Most of Sidney's ekphrastic descriptions, even his most physical catalogues of costume and landscape, are beyond the draughtsman's pencil and even the literature fancy. The critical task he devolves upon the reader is therefore not of material but of moral imagination, the task of assigning abstract meaning to imagined countenance.

Sidney's emblematic poetics of fiction governs narrative development in the *New Arcadia*. He gives a rich pictorial rendering of the fictional world, and then allows the plot to revolve around the analyses of such information by various characters. In this way, at least two distinct registers of recognition are established: that of the characters, who are required to make their own unassisted judgements based on concrete but unorganized evidence before them, and that of the reader, who responds to Sidney's artful rhetorical presentation of that evidence. We are, however, constantly reminded of our epistemological advantage over the characters, who are bound to their immediate and chaotic set of impressions, unaided by the shaping diegetic voice of the narrator. The gulf between the apprised and the ignorant is often the locus of narrative crisis in the revised romance.

Fundamental to these distinct processes and registers of reading in the *New Arcadia* is the presence of interior and exterior verbal emblems. The

---

[24] For palm-tree emblems, see Paolo Giovio, *The Worthy Tract of Paulus Giovius*, trans. Samuel Daniel (London, 1585), H2v; Thomas Palmer [Vegetable emblems] Bodleian Library Ashmole MS. 767, fol. 181r: "*Tyll deathe us departe*: The female palme dothe beare no fruite unless the male be by / Whose lynked braunches never parte tyll one or bothe dow dye."

[25] See John Carey, "Structure and Rhetoric in Sidney's *Arcadia*," in *Sir Philip Sidney, An Anthology of Modern Criticism*, ed. Dennis Kay (Oxford: Clarendon Press, 1987), 245–264, for Sidney's use of *antimetabole* and *synoeciosis*.

interior emblem, as an element of plot, tests the ability of the character to observe ingeniously and to act accordingly. Interior emblems are mostly items of conscious personal display such as costume. Kalander, Pamela, and Musidorus are most effective interior emblem-readers; Cecropia, Basilius, and Pyrocles are not. The exterior emblem, as an external, narratorial communication to the reader, works in a separate register by generating expectation and suspense from information to which the characters are not privy. The vignette of Dorus and Zelmane shaded by palm trees is exterior because the implicit comedy is legible only to the reader.

The registers of meaning and legibility associated with interior and exterior emblems are demonstrated by the houses of Kalander and Basilius. Kalander's house, garden, and park reemphasize the virtues first noticed in the opening panorama of the Arcadian landscape. The house is of

> strong stone, not affecting so much any extraordinarie kinde of finenes, as an honorable representing of a firme statelines ... each place handsome without curiositie, and homely without lothsomnes. (1.2.15)

This house is a microcosmic emblem of the well-disposed state, the Aristotelian *via media*. Textually (and probably geographically) proximate to this abode is the forest lodge of Basilius and his family, in which the practice of architectural anatomy is extended. Pyrocles, eager to catch sight of Philoclea, introduces the potential of expressive buildings:

> Desirous I was to see the place where she remained, as though the *Architecture* of the lodges would have bene much for my learning. (1.13.85)

The royal lodge, it turns out, is star-shaped, its garden and the forest immediately around it cultivated to mimic its pentangular form; a house, it seems, of highly "curious" design. These two special houses and their gardens, one belonging to the prince, the other to one of his leading subjects, operate as a pair of antithetical emblems which reiterate the basic difficulty in Arcadia.

Whenever Sidney offers a descriptive passage, we are on notice that his picture is probably legible. The message of the unlikely Basilian lodge is at first one of order in the midst of wilderness, but its elaborate design also suggests the fortifications of medieval castles, an exterior irony, since this supposedly secure and barricaded dwelling is constantly being penetrated. In his *Elements of Architecture*, Henry Wotton deems many-angled buildings to be "fittest for *Militar*[y] ... then for *Civill* use," and invokes the Basilian lodge:

> *Sir Philip Sidney*, (whose *Wit* was in truth the very rule of *Congruity*) ... well knowing that *Basilius* (as he had painted the *State* of his *Minde*) did rather want some extraordinary *Formes* to entertaine his *Fancy*, then *roome* for *Courtiers*; was contented to place him in a *star-like Lodge*; which otherwise in severe *Judgment* of Art, had been an incommodious *Figure*.[26]

In comparing the royal lodge with Kalander's stately Palladian-style villa, Sidney encourages us to see the joke in outdated, outlandish, and unstylish medieval architecture,[27] and to reflect on the momentous misreading of the oracle by Basilius, an error which has entailed the isolation his eldest, princely daughter and heir from her needful education and experience. As Wotton recognizes, Sidney chooses architecture to paint the state of Basilius's mind. The silliness of the stellate house also implicitly suggests the most important property of emblems: they reiterate and confirm, rather than reveal. To intelligent readers, emblems deal in the currency of the already known. The inability to read an emblem correctly is a sign of profound ignorance or stupidity. Basilius is a comic but disabled reader, even of his own emblematic constructions; but such inability also has serious consequences later in the *New Arcadia*.

When in the final pages of book 1 Phalantus displays his triumph of pictures, Sidney invites us to study a visual enactment of his poetics which is at once a powerful reminder of the central trope of the *New Arcadia* as well as its rhetorical impoverishment. Puttenham uses the word "countenance" to describe the apparelling of poetry in rhetorical figures;[28] but in the Arcadian universe countenance is the *only* harbinger of inward meaning, and it is appropriate that Phalantus, the misappropriator of show, should be the unwitting victim of Sidney's visual joke. Phalantus has turned up with a general challenge to anyone who will fight him for the honor of his lady, the prize being the portrait of the loser's lady. But

---

[26] Henry Wotton, *The Elements of Architecture* [London, 1629] in *Reliquiae Wottonianae* (London, 1651), 216 and 304.

[27] Victor Skretkowicz, however, regards the star as an image appropriate to a ruler; but also suggests that Basilius's stellate lodge portends his death, as comets and other astronomical phenomena were thought to do ("Symbolic Architecture in Sidney's *New Arcadia*," *Review of English Studies* n.s. 33 [1982]: 177-79).

[28] Puttenham, 137.

the collection of portraits he has won are paltry countenances, of no more intrinsic merit bundled together in this way than a set of baseball cards. This is a devalued cache of pictures because Phalantus neither loves the woman whose beauty he has defended and in whose name he has acquired them, nor cares much whose portraits he has got. He simply wants to have more pictures than everyone else, "to keep," as he later confesses, "his valour in knowledge." He venerates show over substance; and Sidney obligingly colludes with him by measuring up the pictured ladies in vulgar and hilarious precision, dwelling on the smallness of an eye or the length of a chin as if he were judging horseflesh, and studiously giving each one of them in the process no profounder compliment than an anagram of a good face.

Phalantus's relatively harmless pretensions in book 1 become dangerous in book 3, eventually distorting and deforming the culture of emblematic presentation so profoundly that tragedy inevitably ensues. This distortion through emblematic malpractice is clearest in the behavior of Amphialus and his opponents, and of Cecropia in her cruel stratagems against her nieces. Critics of the revised romance have complained, in the words of Ronald Levao, of "a mounting torrent of images that ultimately challenges any mastery, whether by protagonist, poet, or reader"; that "the attempt to interpret images...can become a bewildering shuffling of significances."[29] But let that confusion, instead, be read as a deliberately darkened and abused emblematic world, where the dialectical harmony of meanings and their symbols is subverted, and book 3 looks less like the pastoral of book 1 and more like a moral landscape ruined by poetic toxins; the remedial "medicine of cherries" described as the good poet's cordial in the *Defence* has been appropriated by "the deceitfull physition [who] geveth sweete syrropes to make his poyson goe downe the smoother."[30] Book 2 pictures the consequences of careless poetry.

The primary situation in book 3 is the captivity of the two princesses and Pyrocles in the castle of Cecropia and Amphialus. The besieging Basilian knights (for whom the captivity of the princesses suggests a characteristic chialric predicament) respond with the appropriate chivalric forms and behavior. In all her activities Cecropia *is* that deceitful physi-

---

[29] Ronald Levao, *Renaissance Minds and their Fictions: Cusanus, Sidney, Shakespeare* (Berkeley: Univ. of California Press, 1985), 216, 220.

[30] Stephen Gosson, *The Schoole of Abuse* [London, 1598], in O. B. Hardison, ed., *English Literary Criticism: The Renaissance* (New York: Appleton-Century-Crofts, 1963), 87.

cian, who notably falsifies appearances and promotes misunderstanding. She is said to "hale kindnesse into her countenance" (3.5.376) and to make "curtesie the outside of mischiefe" (3.2.362); her stock-in-trade is a horrible dissembling in which the abduction of the princesses is engineered by minions disguised as harvest celebrants, and a fairground illusion called "the Decollation of John Baptist" is used to make Pyrocles think Philoclea is dead.[31] We learn quickly enough that where Cecropia is involved things are never what they seem, that her displays are designed not to be illegible but to be misread. Cecropia's devotion to visual deceit is so complete that it causes her downfall: she is unable to comprehend that Philoclea's refusal to entertain her son's suit is honest, absolute, and final. She misreads the monolithic and unified message being given to her both verbally and visually, and eventually goes too far when she persuades Amphialus that "no is no negative in a womans mouth" (3.17.452).

The narrative pattern of much of book 3 alludes to the particular badness of Cecropia. It shifts between events within and without the castle, making the fruitless exterior battles a distraction from the equally fruitless torture of the princesses within it; and this discontinuity between the genuinely horrific punishments to which Cecropia subjects her nieces and the elegant formalities of the *pas d'armes* in which the duelling knights engage reminds us of the harmful potential in "bad" emblems or *imprese* (the stylized personal devices most characteristic of chivalric ensignment). After the bitter initial battle between the armies of Basilius and Cecropia, the representational impropriety of signifying the dangerous position of the princesses with the formal and innately playful tournament games is an irony made even more unpalatable by Amphialus's decision to hold them before the captive women for their entertainment.

The *impresa* (a kind of coterie emblem whose meaning is deliberately and learnedly obscure) and its attendant culture of legible costume and armour — what Estienne calls "the Philosophie of Cavaliers"[32] — is the central feature of the fatal indecorum in book 3; the introduction of this

---

[31] Reginald Scot, *The Discoverie of Witchcraft* (London, 1584), book 13, chap. 34, pp. 349–50.

[32] Henri Estienne, *The Art of Making Devises*, trans. Thomas Blount (London, 1646), 10. The *impresa* is specific to the bearer and often to the occasion on which it is worn. Composed of a mutually dependent motto and picture, the *impresa* should be unintelligible if either element is missing. The meaning of *imprese* requires recondite information to be deciphered, such as languages, classical chronicles, and catalogues of natural history and mythology.

specialized, personal emblematic form into the fray is the most obvious instance of the misglossing and consequent misprision which infect the events of book 3. The highly thought out detail of tournament symbolism necessitates an ekphrastic specificity even more precise and concrete than the descriptions in earlier episodes. The more palpable physical appearances of book 3 seem to be inversely placed against the increasing decadence and insufficiency of these symbols to act as speaking pictures.

In the dominant brutality of the initial battle, the spectacle of hacked bodies lying on the field reproves any more heroic or courtly behavior, and the only knight who is distinguished in any way is one whose accoutrements yield no information; or rather, whose emblematic message is that he will not be known by any message other than his deeds:

> a Knight in armor as darke as blacknes coulde make it, followed by none, and adorned by nothing; so far without authoritie that he was without knowledge. But vertue quickly made him knowne. (3.8.392)

Essential and unadorned violence is appropriately represented by one whose virtue and authority — indeed, whose identity — derives only from his success at killing. His emblem, such as it is, is ostentively[33] blazoned in the splashes of blood on his armor. This is the most primitive of icons, an elementary and deathly hieroglyph which seems to mock the culture of personal devices and the misplaced chivalric response which follows. Sheer slaughter, it seems to say, can require no emblems because it has finished with diplomacy; and emblems are a kind of silent speaking. The Black Knight, the only knight who refuses to adopt the traditionally courtly forms, is really Musidorus, the only knight in book 3 genuinely attempting to liberate the princesses, the only knight truly "in service" to one of them.

Courtesy, however, appears to gain ground over warfare when, after the initial battle, Amphialus challenges the Basilians to individual ornamental duels. But as honorable sport is restraining the carnage, Argalus (newly married champion of the king) is prevailed upon to join it, and his disastrous participation reintroduces death and destruction. The other knights note that the Black Knight is unemblazoned and wonder at his deliberate anonymity. Argalus, in blazoning himself, is less canny and reflective.

---

[33] I use this philosophical term for primitive signification, the language of showing objects, the language of simple display. See Keir Elam, *The Semiotics of Theatre and Drama* (London: Methuen, 1980), 29–30.

Argalus has so far been spared by Basilius the duty of attending the siege, "in respect of his late mariage" to Parthenia.

> But now [Basilius's] honour, and (as he esteemed it) felicitie standing upon it, he could no longer forbeare to chalenge [Argalus] of his faithfull service. (3.12.420)

Narratively, martial gives way to matrimonial as the scene shifts from the hostilities to the household and their respective claims upon Argalus. He and Parthenia are found at home reading a story of Hercules, a hero of some fascination for Sidney, who uses his enslavement to Omphale elsewhere as a potent emblem of infatuation.

Signs of what is to occur are embedded in this vignette: Parthenia's eyes stray adoringly from the book to Argalus as she listens to the tale, apparently in a tableau of domestic harmony. Yet the reader is aware that Argalus's honor is about to be solicited; and his rapt attention to the story he is reading hardly suggests Herculean infatuation with his wife, since, after all, *his* eyes do not stray from Hercules to Parthenia. Sidney's word-picture shows Parthenia's eye fastened upon her husband and their marriage, while his is fastened upon images of heroism. Argalus, a more perfect Hercules, will not linger near the distaff once Basilius's envoy arrives. And when the messenger arrives Parthenia instantly recognizes the dilemma "written," so to speak, in Argalus's face:

> her husbands countenance figured some resolution betweene lothnesse and necessitie ... (like a man in whom Honour could not be rocked on sleep by Affection). (3.12.420)

Honour indeed turns out to be more dear to him than his wife's affection, and his decision to forsake her is taken in spite of her forebodings. But even Argalus chooses to ignore in her weeping face "a presage ... of that, which you would not should happen" (3.12.421).

Each detail serves as a partial revelation, and in this way the process of *anagnorisis* can develop at different speeds among different readers. We know what the message imports; Parthenia is alerted to it by her husband's facial expressions; with least "conceipt," Argalus all but laughs away her prophetic concern. The prognostication which he is able to read in *her* face he dismisses as inconvenient and incompatible with the martial impulse.

Henri Estienne says that "a Devise exposeth the rare conceipts, and gallant resolutions of its Author, far more perspicuously, and with more certainty, then *Physiognomy* can";[34] and the more stylized elements of the martial emblems borne by Argalus only serve to confirm publicly what is already privately and physiognomically revealed. Argalus's accoutrements signify his doom. His name, an echo of "orgulous" — proud — is an exterior communication to the reader.[35] His horse bears two further emblems of pride: it has the wings of Pegasus, the steed of Bellerophon who attempted to ride to heaven; and his saddle is shaped like an eagle, the only bird who dares gaze at the sun.[36] His white armor, however, is decorated with lover's knots made of a woman's hair; and his shield bears the device of two palm trees, a repetition of the marriage emblem seen earlier.[37] The favor worn around his arm is embroidered by his wife with bleeding hearts. The effect is of heroic aspiration coupled with transcendent but doomed love. These disquieting images advance the competing claims of love and honor in Argalus; and, notified by the presence of such descriptions, we may suspect that though his armor seems tangled in a woman's hair, this metaphorical net will prove too frail to restrain his appetite for glory.

Parthenia's tomb armor is among the most remarkable of all Sidney's descriptions of chivalric detail. At the occasion of her death, Parthenia for the only time in her history chooses to put on significant clothing; elsewhere she is presented as one whose appearance, like Philoclea's, is "but a faire embassadour of a most faire minde" (1.5.32) which "the mistres thought ... either not to deserve, or not to need any exquisite decking" (1.16.103-4). In her previous appearance she had been restrained from defacing herself, from undoing her identity as Parthenia. Mortally damaged by Argalus's death, she can no longer be Parthenia and therefore, by the logic of emblems, she had better not look like Parthenia.

When Parthenia describes herself in pictorial terms as "the gasing-stock of endles miserie" (3.12.426), she claims to be the outward form of utter woe. And when she appears in the tomb armor she quite literally

---

[34] Estienne, 14.

[35] That Argalus should be so named ought to give us pause as early as book 1, in which his remarkable courtship of Parthenia, including her disfigurement and restoration, is retailed. It is as though the potential tragedy of their early history — miraculously reversed for the time being — is latent in his name.

[36] The eagle is equated with honorable ambition. Of all animals, only it can look at the sun without blinking, and tries to fly to it.

[37] See n. 24 passim.

makes a spectacle of herself. Arriving processionally, almost triumphally, with attendants in mourning, she rides in the center of this retinue in a ghastly armor painted to resemble a gaping sepulchre, funereal cypress branches and life-like worms decorating her furniture and bases, and a monstrous *impresa* of a two-headed child half-dead. She had looked upon the honors done her dead husband as "but the triumph of her ruine" (3.12.427), and what was metaphorically stated is now physically embodied. Parthenia as Tomb Knight is a powerful image of *contemptus mundi*.

Virtually everything about her appearance betrays her identity, and yet this is the one thing that her emblematically proficient adversary fails to decipher. In his ignorance he kills her. The comedy of Philoclea's inability to identify the Amazon Zelmane as Pyrocles, and the grimmer story of the real Zelmane's unrequited love for Pyrocles, are the antecedents of this terrible misreading by Amphialus. The reverberation is still more ominous and tragic, since in this case Amphialus is wholly culpable in the disaster which ensues.

Parthenia's death, "inough to have taught sorrow to the gladdest thoughts, and have engraved it in the mindes of hardest metall" (3.12.426), represents the climactic misglossing of all the ceremonial battles: her death deprecates their expressive and pacific efficiency. Argalus is a knight destroyed by his own emblematic behavior; he is capable of assuming significant devices but unable to read them correctly. This pattern has already been figured less tragically by the actions of Phalantus, the knight who initially proposes the duels and most clearly dissociates the poetry of image from any substantial purpose. Moreover, Argalus's decision to affect the emblematic forms of chivalry and to accept the symbolic role of king's champion (thereby rejecting his conjugal responsibilities), is reprehensible: as Stephen Orgel notes, service to a lady should be the most *disarming* of all the ritual activities associated with chivalry, and it is she whom Argalus explicitly disobeys.[38]

Amphialus and his other opponents injure emblematic propriety even more comprehensively. Instead of rescuing the sisters from danger, they collaborate in keeping them there. Their dabbling in the attractive but ill-timed courtesies of the staged tournament duels narratively enacts the moral nightmare of poetastery, of the fictional image cast adrift from any corresponding foreconceit. The chivalric behavior of the knights is like

---

[38] Stephen Orgel, "Making Greatness Familiar," *Genre* 15 (1982): 43.

bad poetry; and as if to pronounce this emphatically, Sidney introduces a parodic version of the knightly duel between Clinias, the sycophant of Cecropia and Amphialus, and Dametas, the rustic "protector" of the now-captive Pamela. With their absurd posturings, their pusillanimity, and their miscellaneous accoutrements, their meeting is studiously devised to make a nonsense of the conventional and elegant formalities of challenge and reply, of choreographed battle, and of courteous passages of arms, an invalidation of chivalric custom as complete as that of Phalantus or Parthenia. This semi-comic interlude seems sternly placed by Sidney, as if to remind us through farce that Amphialus and his antagonists do not acknowledge the gravity of the situation, that they, like Dametas, bear emblematic signs which they are not equipped to read, that to insist on playing superficial courtly games to resolve matters of life and death is a metaphor of the prussic acid delivered by the bad poet.

Emblematic structures of *Arcadia* — both explicit in chivalric devices, and implicit in ekphrastic, emblematic passages inviting analysis — are initially presented in simple and straightforward examples. The comparison between Kalander's house and Basilius's lodge is unproblematic and, like much emblem material, reiterates and summarizes what we already know. As the novel progresses, however, such naive presentations of emblematic images become scarcer, giving way to subversions of the expected unity of image and foreconceit. These dangerous subversions are culpably inadvertant in the general program of knightly duels and in the thoughtless donning of emblematic signs by Phalantus and Argalus; but deliberately deceitful in Cecropia's feigned benevolence and actual violence.

In the ethical twilight of book 3, the movement from efficient and indicative uses of emblematic expression in books 1 and 2 towards functionless and vitiated ceremony figures forth the consequences of bad poetry. In the brazen world of human nature, good poetry can still move men toward well doing and not well knowing only; the example is Musidorus as Black Knight, a hero contemptuous of chivalric frivolity and acting instead on the precepts of a strong education consisting of "excellent devises...to move [him] to do nobly, & teach [him] how to do nobly; the beautie of vertue still being set before [his] eyes" (2.7.189-90). This concord of idea and action is apparently challenged by the many knights who respond to Amphialus's general invitation to fight duels but is in fact only one of many images of disagreement in book 3:

> according to every ones humour, so were the causes of the challe[n]ge grou[n]ded: one laying treason to his charge; another

preferring himselfe in the worthines to serve *Philoclea*; a third, exalting some other Ladies beautie beyond ether of the sisters; a fourth, laying disgraces to Love it selfe, naming it the bewitcher of the witt... a fifth, disdayning to caste at lesse than at all, woulde make the cause of his quarrell the causers of love. (3.12.419)

Like this one, each disjunction in book 3 refers back to the emblematic display of information, a language which, like good poetry, must be unitary in outward form and inward meaning. When the poetical feigning of ideas lacks such agreement it is decadent and, in Sidney's Protestant poetics, thoroughly unethical. His assembled rhetoric of gesture, display, in short, of countenance, demands the collusion of the reader to supply its meanings and to scout its abuses. For Sidney, the truest poetry is the most feigning, a conceit but not a deceit, a way of figuring the ineffable, of investing it in some more visible cloth.

PAUL SALZMAN

The Strang[e] Constructions of Mary Wroth's *Urania*: Arcadian Romance and the Public Realm

THE FEMINIST CHALLENGE TO ESTABLISHED LITERARY CANONS reached Renaissance literary studies rather later than many other areas, but now it is possible to discern a dramatic discovery (or re-discovery) of an increasing number of women writers from the period. Mary Wroth is perhaps the most significant of these writers thus far, given the scope and amount of her production in so many important genres. Her new stature is acknowledged by the editorial work of Josephine Roberts, and by a recent volume of essays dedicated solely to Wroth's oeuvre.[1] In particular, Wroth's romance, *The Countess of Montgomery's Urania*, is at last becoming the object of the kind of intensive critical analysis formerly reserved for the *Arcadia*, the romance produced by her uncle, Sir Philip Sidney. Indeed, with the same kind of light being shed upon the writing of the Countess of Pembroke, and the editorial work on the poetry of Wroth's father, Robert Sidney, the Sidney family as a whole may now be examined as a

---

[1] Josephine A. Roberts, ed., *The Poems of Lady Mary Wroth* (Baton Rouge: Louisiana State Univ. Press: 1983); Roberts is editing a complete version of *Urania*, to be published by Medieval & Renaissance Texts & Studies; Naomi J. Miller and Gary Waller, eds., *Reading Mary Wroth: Representing Alternatives in Early Modern England* (Knoxville: Univ. of Tennessee Press, 1992). This recent attention to Wroth could be seen as answering Carol Neely's feminist challenge to new historicism, both through her suggestion that there is a need to "overread men's canonical texts with women's uncanonical ones" and the need to example the implications of gender in Renaissance literature and its criticism. See Carol Thomas Neely, "Constructing the Subject: Feminist Practice and the New Renaissance Discourses," *English Literary Renaissance* 18 (1988): 5–18.

writing community, crossed and interconnected by a complex network of relations, including those of politics and gender.² In this context, *Urania* can be seen as a romance which enters into a dialogical relationship with the *Arcadia*, interrogating some of Sidney's assumptions about the nature of romance, particularly in relation to issues of gender and sexuality.³

The publication of *Urania* in 1621 involved Wroth in much more than a familial dialogue. As is by now well-known, the depiction in *Urania* of some actual scandals from the life of the Jacobean court provoked a sharp response, especially from the notoriously hot-tempered Edward Denny, who demanded the romance's withdrawal, and who produced a scurrilous poem about Wroth, attacking her for daring, as a woman, to enter the world of secular literature.⁴ Denny's verse characterized Wroth as: "Herm-

---

² See especially Mary Ellen Lamb, *Gender and Authorship in the Sidney Circle* (Madison: Univ. of Wisconsin Press, 1990); Gary Waller, "Mother / Son, Father / Daughter, Brother / Sister, Cousins: the Sidney Family Romance," *Modern Philology* 88 (1991): 401–14, "The Sidney Family Romance: Mary Wroth and Gender Construction in Early Modern England," in Miller and Waller, and *The Sidney Family Romance: Mary Wroth, William Herbert and the Early Modern Construction of Gender* (Detroit: Wayne State Univ. Press, 1993); P.J. Croft, ed., *The Poems of Robert Sidney* (Oxford: Clarendon Press, 1988). Gary Waller contends that "The Sidney family ... was not merely a collection of individual men and women linked by kinship, but also a major site of contradictory cultural forces, a discursive formation in miniature in which the broader conflicts of the age were being enacted," in "The Countess of Pembroke and Gendered Reading," in Anne M. Haselkorn and Betty S. Travitsky, eds., *The Renaissance Englishwoman In Print* (Amherst: Univ. of Massachusetts Press, 1990): 334.

³ For this approach see, for example, Lamb, *Gender and Authorship*; and, in a context wider than simply Sidney, see Naomi Miller, " 'Not much to be marked': Narrative of the Woman's Part in Lady Mary Wroth's *Urania*," *SEL* 29 (1989): 120–37; Maureen Quilligan, in an extremely suggestive article, points to the empowerment for Wroth of her alliance with her cousin, and of "brother-sister" ties in general: "Lady Mary Wroth: Female Authority and the Family Romance," in *Unfolded Tales: Essays on Renaissance Romance*, ed. George Logan and Gordon Teskey (Ithaca: Cornell Univ. Press, 1989): 257–80; Josephine A. Roberts, "Labyrinths of Desire: Lady Mary Wroth's Reconstruction of Romance," *Women's Studies* 19 (1991): 183–92; and a judicious summing up in Helen Hackett, " 'Yet Tell Me Some Such Fiction': Lady Mary Wroth's *Urania* and the 'Femininity' of Romance," in *Women, Texts and Histories*, ed. Clare Brant and Diane Purkiss (London: Routledge, 1992): 39–68.

⁴ See John J. O'Connor, "James Hay and the Countess of Montgomery's Urania," *Notes and Queries* 200 (1955): 150–52; Josephine A. Roberts, "An Unpublished Literary Quarrel Concerning the Suppression of Mary Wroth's *Urania*," *Notes and Queries* 222 (1977): 532–35; Paul Salzman, "Contemporary References in Mary Wroth's *Urania*," *Review of English Studies* 29 (1978): 178–81; there is a full account in Roberts's edition of Wroth's poetry, which includes complete transcripts of the poems exchanged by Wroth and Denny, pp. 31–35.

aphrodite in show, in deed a monster."[5] It is significant that Denny sees Wroth as a hermaphrodite, a threatening figure of sexual ambiguity who has traversed the safe confines of gender boundaries.[6] He makes this even clearer in a letter which compares Wroth's activities to those of the Countess of Pembroke:

> But lett your Ladyship take what course yt shall please you with me, this shall bee myne with you [that] to ever wish you well and pray that you may repent you of so many ill spent years of so vaine a booke and that you may redeeme the tym with writing as large a volume of heavenly layes and holy love as you have of lascivious tales and amorous toyes that at the last you may follow the rare, and pious example of your vertuous and learned Aunt, who translated many godly books and especially the holly psalmes of David.[7]

While the letter at least allows women the "safe" and contained literary activity of pious translation, Denny's poem concludes on a note of total exclusion: "Work o th' Workes leave idle books alone/For wise and worthyer women have writte none."[8] There is a curious contradiction emerging within this couplet: how is an "idle" book able to cause Denny so much distress? What are the implications of the *Urania*'s power to provoke such a response? (And Denny's response was evidently not unique, as a remark of John Chamberlain's makes plain: "in her book of Urania she doth palpablie and grossely play upon him and his late daughter the Lady Hayes, besides many others she makes bold with, and they say takes great libertie to traduce whom she please, and thincks she daunces in a net.")[9] Wroth herself, in her poem responding to Denny's, takes the notion of hermaphrodite and turns it against him: "Hirmaphrodite in sense in Art a monster." (The whole notion of the monstrous becomes very important in the course of *Urania*. While there are a number of literal monsters in the narrative, the notion of the monstrous as implicated in gender issues emerges in the manuscript continuation, when

---

[5] Roberts, *Poems of Mary Wroth*, 32.

[6] This aspect of Denny's response is discussed cogently by Mary Ellen Lamb, who stresses the sexual ambivalence present in Denny's imagery, in *Gender and Authorship*, 156–59.

[7] Roberts, *Poems of Mary Wroth*, 239.

[8] Ibid., 33.

[9] *Letters of John Chamberlain*, ed. N. E. McClure (Philadelphia: American Philosophical Society, 1939), 2: 427.

Amphilanthus calls women "monsters" (2.i.49v) as a response to his [mistaken] idea of Pamphilia's unfaithfulness, but then calls himself a monster in a typical moment of reversal in connection with such issues (2.i.51).[10] Philippa Berry cites Stubbs's reaction to gender disturbance in *The Anatomy of Abuses* [1583]: "Hermaphroditi; that is, Monsters of bothe kindes, halfe women, halfe men.")[11] Wroth describes *Urania* as a "harmless book". At one level, this perhaps concedes the "amorous toyes" allegation, in an ambivalence about the moral/immoral nature of literature which recalls Sidney's anxieties about the worth of his literary pursuits.[12] For the author to see *Urania* as a harmless book is a clear example of disingenuous argument, but this whole issue becomes more complex if we turn to Wroth's letter to Buckingham, written after the agitation of Denny clearly began to have some effect on court — and King James's — opinion of Wroth's actions.

Wroth's apologetic letter to Buckingham is dated 15 December 1621, and it addresses what she calls "the strang constructions which are made of my book contrary to my imagination, and as far from my meaning as is possible for truth to bee from conjecture."[13] By "strang," Wroth presumably intends to mean "strange," although there is a Bloomian felicity in the idea of "*strong* constructions" wresting a particular interpretation of her book from her intention. Again, the protestations about intention may be read as disingenuous, but a more interesting ambiguity is present in the revelation that Wroth, while protesting that she never intended *Urania* to be published ("which from the first were solde against my minde"), had sent Buckingham a presentation copy, which she now asks him to return in order to set a good example for *all* those who may refuse to surrender their copies: "besides that your Lordship wilbe pleased to lett mee have that which I sent you, the example of which will without question make others the willinger to obay."[14]

---

[10] Throughout this essay references are to the printed text of *Urania* (1621), cited as 1, and to the manuscript continuation held in the Newberry Library, described as the "second part," cited as 2. The continuation is in two parts.

[11] Philippa Berry, *Of Chastity and Power: Elizabethan Literature and the Unmarried Queen* (London: Routledge, 1989): 69.

[12] On this aspect of Sidney see Katherine Duncan-Jones, "Philip Sidney's Toys," *Proceedings of the British Academy* 46 (1986): 161–78, repr. in Dennis Kay, ed., *Sir Philip Sidney: An Anthology of Modern Criticism* (Oxford: Clarendon Press, 1987): 61–80.

[13] Roberts, *Poems of Mary Wroth*, 236.

[14] Ibid.

The whole episode of Urania's publication, the response of its courtly readership, its withdrawal, and the subsequent manuscript continuation, which was never published, offers a significant paradigm for the complex issue of how an early modern woman writer like Wroth might negotiate the relationship between an enclosed sphere of allowable activity and the more dangerous entry into a public literary (and political) arena: an activity which we are gradually beginning to realize was undertaken with greater frequency than scholars once acknowledged. Ostensibly seeking Buckingham's critical opinion of her work, Wroth was actually using the publication of Urania in 1621 as an intervention in the court world from which she had been excluded. One approach to this issue, which I believe casts some light on a complex series of questions about women's writing in early modern England, as well as answering some of the challenges thrown out by recent feminist and new historicist criticism of the period, is to examine what the implications of Arcadian romance were when Wroth wrote, and how Wroth is able to extend the genre to suit her own ends.

In the early years of the seventeenth century, Sidney and his work became associated with a nostalgia for Elizabethan heroic values, which were utilized in protest against King James, especially in relation to his policy of pacifism and religious neutrality in Europe. As Annabel Patterson states, "Sidney's *Arcadia* . . . was constantly rewritten by later readers (as well as by Sidney himself) in the light of their own historical circumstances and ideological needs."[15] The *Arcadia* was presented to the reading public as a printed text in two forms: the *New Arcadia*, offered in 1590 by Sidney's friend and biographer, Fulke Greville, as Sidney's revised but unfinished epic, and the composite version prepared under the direction of Sidney's sister and published in 1593. The composite text was the version reprinted during the seventeenth century, but this text offered considerable opportunities for continuations and completions, which duly followed.[16] Recently scholars alert to the political implications of

---

[15] Annabel Patterson, *Censorship and Interpretation: The Conditions of Writing and Reading in Early Modern England* (Madison: Univ. of Wisconsin Press, 1984): 18. For Sidney's influence in the seventeenth century, see, among other studies, John Buxton, *Sir Philip Sidney and the English Renaissance* (London, 1964); W. H. Bond, "The Reputation and Influence of Sir Philip Sidney," (unpublished Ph.D. diss., Harvard, 1941); Dennis Kay, "Sidney — A Critical Heritage," in Kay, *Sir Philip Sidney*, 3–41; and Jackson Boswell and H. R. Woudhuysen, "Some Unfamiliar Sidney Allusions," in Jan Van Dorsten et al., *Sir Philip Sidney: 1586 and the Creation of a Legend* (Leiden: E.J. Brill, 1986): 221–37.

[16] For a general account of these, see Paul Salzman, *English Prose Fiction 1558–1700: A Critical History* (Oxford: Clarendon Press, 1985), chap. 10.

Jacobean literature have pointed to the significance of pastoral poetry as a mode of protest, and this may also be linked to the role played by the *Arcadia* and the figure of Sidney. David Norbrook notes that "The years 1613-14 saw a revival of pastoral poetry, and in adopting the persona of the plain-thinking shepherds the Spenserians were indicating their dissatisfaction with contemporary events."[17] Mary Wroth herself was placed within a complex nexus of familial/political positions in relation to the Jacobean court. The Sidney/Herbert families did not form a simple or single political group, although they can be viewed as holding Protestant views which emerge most strongly in William Herbert's position at court.[18] Wroth's own position as Herbert's cousin and lover (she bore two illegitimate children by Herbert) must be taken into account, as well as her relationship to her husband, who was knighted by James in 1603, and whose father had served in the House of Commons since 1562/63.[19]

With the accession of James, Wroth took up a position in Queen Anne's court, which was established in 1606 (her father was appointed Anne's lord chamberlain).[20] In 1603 Anne had established what her biographer calls a "lasting friendship" with William Herbert during her stay at Wilton, once again pointing to the intertwining of the Herbert/Sidney alliance with a court in some ways set up in opposition to James's.[21] Anne's court provided a female counter to James's male, not

---

[17] David Norbrook, *Poetry and Politics in the English Renaissance* (London: Routledge, 1984): 207; see also Michael Brennan, *Literary Patronage in the English Renaissance: The Pembroke Family* (London: Routledge, 1988): 134.

[18] See Margot Heinemann, *Puritanism and Theatre: Thomas Middleton and Opposition Drama Under the Stuarts* (Cambridge: Cambridge Univ. Press, 1980): 264–83, for the strongest statement of this view of Herbert, a view which may be countered somewhat by David Norbrook, who sees the Herbert group as less coherently oppositional, in *Poetry and Politics*, 185. The complex and ongoing debate between historians over the nature of political factions at this time is obviously relevant to my account of Wroth's position at court. The most convincing adjustment of the views of revisionist historians (e.g., Kevin Sharpe, ed., *Faction and Parliament: Essays on Early Stuart History* [Oxford: Clarendon Press, 1978], and Kevin Sharpe, "Faction at the Early Stuart Court," *History Today* 33 [1983]: 39–46) is Linda Levy Peck, *Court Patronage and Corruption in Early Stuart England* (Boston: Unwin Hyman, 1990), esp. chap. 3. Peck stresses "the fluidity and fragility of patronage networks," 54.

[19] See Wallace Notestein, *The House of Commons 1604–10* (New Haven: Yale Univ. Press, 1971): 63.

[20] Roberts, *Poems of Mary Wroth*, 12.

[21] Ethel Carleton Williams, *Anne of Denmark* (London: Longman, 1970): 76.

to say misogynistic, preserve.²² The brief flowering of Prince Henry's court further emphasized this political alignment with the implications of the Sidney legend and the position of Arcadian romance. Henry set up a court which, like Anne's, could be seen as a counter to James's, but Henry's court was like his father's in its masculine (not to say macho) character. Roy Strong has emphasized how Henry deliberately associated himself and his court activities with Sidney, stressing a "direct link between the new circle of the Prince and that centring in the previous reign on Sir Philip Sidney."²³ Henry's love of the symbolic tilts reminiscent of those of Elizabeth's reign is evident in *Prince Henry's Barriers*, a masque of 1610 described by Strong as presenting "the new court of St James's as the thinly veiled focus for a revival of the Elizabethan war party, fiercely Protestant and anti-Hapsburg," and in the 1610 Accession Day Tilt, at which William Herbert appeared dressed in "two Caparisons of Peach-coloured velvet embroidered all over with oriental Pearls."²⁴ It is notable that in *Urania* Wroth depicted versions of both the masque-centered court of Anne and James, and the tilt-centered world of Henry's court, as part of her examination of the interaction between female and male realms within a context of revived chivalric, as well as pastoral, romance motifs.²⁵

Arcadian romance was available as, in some respects, a discourse already saturated with the criticism Sidney himself had directed against Elizabeth's policies.²⁶ The 1593 composite *Arcadia* itself was reprinted eleven times up until 1638, during the period when Fulke Greville helped

---

²² In this respect, James's court may be contrasted with Elizabeth's; see the interesting discussion in Philippa Berry, who stresses the challenge of Elizabeth to "conventional ideas both of masculine and feminine identity," and notes the roles allowed for noble women, in contrast to their marginalisation under James, *Of Chastity and Power*, 68 and 79; see also Peck, *Court Patronage*, 68–74.

²³ Roy Strong, *Henry, Prince of Wales and England's Lost Renaissance* (Thames and Hudson, 1986): 145; and see also Graham Parry, *The Golden Age Restor'd: The Culture of the Stuart Court 1603–1640* (Manchester: Manchester Univ. Press, 1981), chap. 3.

²⁴ Strong, 141 and 158.

²⁵ For some examples of significant masques in *Urania*, see 1.144, 2.i.14v–15v, 2.i.41–41v, 2.ii.26; for tilts see 1.77, 92, 120, 196, 415.

²⁶ There are many studies on this; see in particular Richard C. McCoy, *Sir Philip Sidney: Rebellion in Arcadia* (Brighton: Harvester, 1979); Alan Sinfield, "Power and Ideology: An Outline Theory and Sidney's *Arcadia*," *ELH* 52 (1985): 259–77; Christopher Martin, "Misdoubting His Estate: Dynastic Anxiety In Sidney's *Arcadia*," *English Literary Renaissance* 18 (1988): 369–88.

to sharpen the political critique inherent in the *Arcadia*, commenting on how the romance shows the "dark webs of effeminate Princes" in a state that declines as states do "when Soveraign Princes, to play with their own visions, will put off publique action."[27] Sidney's sister, whose 1593 edition of the *Arcadia* superseded Greville's, also played a role in the continuing Protestant aesthetic/political allegiance.[28]

When Wroth produced her romance, the homage to Sidney implied by the title (even if it may have been complicated by the nature of *Urania* itself) had, at least potentially, a serious political implication. *Urania*'s depiction of real events like those that enraged Denny can also be connected to the vogue for political romances, exemplified in John Barclay's *Argenis*. *Argenis* appeared in Latin in the same year as *Urania*; although King James commissioned a translation from Ben Jonson, an English version did not appear until 1625, with a second following in 1628. *Argenis*, with its detailed account of French political history within the mode of romance, offers an expansion of the possibilities of the genre, which in some ways can be seen in Wroth's careful elaboration of the dynastic politics throughout the "Europe" of *Urania*, as well as within the court society of England, which found itself caught and exposed in her narrative.

Wroth's act in producing *Urania* is rightly seen as a significant example of female intervention in the masculine world of secular literature. But her own strange constructions within *Urania* involve an even more unsettling critique directed at a series of distinctions within her society underpinning the exclusion of women from the public realm. A great deal of the ideological tension associated with the rule of Elizabeth failed to dissipate after the throne reverted to a male sovereign. As Leah Marcus has pointed out, in relation to the stage, "The cultural memory for Elizabeth's mannerisms and characteristic strategies was longer than we are likely to find credible, and continued to exert a subtle shaping on stage depictions of female dominance — particularly those with a reformist bent — even decades after her death."[29] In a discussion of the nature of female rule in *Urania*, Jose-

---

[27] Sir Fulke Greville, *Life of Sir Philip Sidney*, ed. Nowell Smith (Oxford, 1907): 13 and 11.

[28] See Margaret P. Hannay, *Philip's Phoenix: Mary Sidney Countess of Pembroke* (New York: Oxford Univ. Press, 1990), passim.

[29] Leah S. Marcus, *Puzzling Shakespeare: Local Reading and Its Discontents* (Berkeley: Univ. of California Press, 1988): 104. Among the many important accounts of how Elizabeth's reign unsettled assumptions about gender and ideology, see especially Louis Adrian Montrose, "'Shaping Fantasies': Figurations of Gender and Power in Elizabethan

phine Roberts suggests that Wroth depicts, particularly within the character of Pamphilia, a dilemma over the rival claims of the "Queen's two bodies," offering "a highly ambivalent view of female rule in which the central character struggles vainly to fulfill the dual nature of sovereignty."[30]

However, while Wroth is certainly interested in the nature of sovereignty, both male and female, she is also able to overturn the opposition between public and private in relation to both the question of direct political power, and the issue of where female autonomy may be located. At present there is a debate emerging among critics over the nature of Wroth's "intervention" in this area. In a provocative account of Wroth's sonnets, Jeff Masten sees them as an essentially private literary act, a withdrawal from the circulation of the market (which of course has more than literary implications for women): "Wroth's texts...do not merely reflect the emergence of a public/private distinction 'in the culture,' but also work to create that distinction," and he believes that *Urania* encapsulates "the opposition of a public, male world and Pamphilia's withdrawal into a privatised locus of female poetic expression."[31] This view may be directly contrasted with the position of Ann Rosalind Jones, who sees Pamphilia and her sonnets as examples of political power and intervention.[32] I believe that it is important to examine the whole public / private dichotomy much more carefully in order to determine how *Urania* may be read in such a context. At the most basic level, as commentators are increasingly emphasizing, it is almost impossible to assign a fixed "position" to *Urania*, because of Wroth's careful use of multivalent narratives, voices, characters, situations. (This aspect of *Urania* itself can be valuably read as an unfixing of the univocal nature of patriarchal discourse, and certainly as the questioning of any essentialized position on political or gender issues.)[33]

Culture," *Representations* 1 (1983): 61–94; Berry offers a counter view to Montrose, suggesting that Elizabeth's reign was a much more "radical event" (see *Of Chastity and Power* chap. 3).

[30] Josephine A. Roberts, "Radigund Revisited: Perspectives on Women Rulers in Lady Mary Wroth's *Urania*," in *Haselkorn and Travitsky*, 202; the concept of the Queen's two bodies is analysed in Marie Axton, *The Queen's Two Bodies* (London: Royal Historical Society, 1977), which in turn draws on Ernst H. Kantorowicz, *The King's Two Bodies* (Princeton: Princeton Univ. Press, 1957).

[31] Jeff Masten, " 'Shall I turne blabb?': Circulation, Gender and Subjectivity in Mary Wroth's Sonnets," in Miller and Waller, 70 and 76.

[32] Ann Rosalind Jones, "Designing Women: The Self as Spectacle in Mary Wroth and Veronica Franco," in Miller and Waller, 135–53.

[33] For an excellent example of this, see the unpublished paper by Marion Wynne

The current examination of the public/private dichotomy in early modern England is fuelled by Francis Barker's argument about the construction of the subject in the course of the seventeenth century (or perhaps the reconstruction of the subject) in his study *The Tremulous Private Body*.[34] During the period when Wroth was writing she was moving between life inside the court of Queen Anne, and life outside it — albeit not unconnected with it, given, for example, the increasingly important position of the Herbert faction and of William Herbert himself under James and Charles. At that historical juncture, the relationship between public and private was extremely problematic. In Jonathan Goldberg's succinct formulation, "In the seventeenth century, privacy all but merged into the public"; or, to take a historian's less dramatic verdict, "the dichotomy so familiar to us today between private and public is necessarily false when applied to the experience of early modern England."[35] Wroth's intersection with the court may not seem to be an encounter with anything like a public sphere, but an event such as the presentation of *Urania* to Buckingham by a woman writer is an intervention in a public realm: a place outside the private, silent/pious, "proper" place for an early modern woman.

Within *Urania*, this interconnection between the public and private is everywhere evident, particularly in the intersection between what might be formulated as the love of power and the power of love. Within Wroth's narrative, political sovereignty, be it male or female, is always challenged by the power of desire. In *Urania*, every court is subject to the menace of desire (like the Jacobean court Wroth knew so well, which was challenged by the intersection of desire and political calculation in incidents like the Overbury scandal). In the language of *Urania*, passion rules as (usually) a tyrant:

> Surpassing passion, excellent, still gouerne, how delicate is thy force? How happie thy rule, that makes such excellent women thy

---

Davies, " 'Et in Arcadia Ego': Lady Mary Wroth's Excursion into Renaissance Pastoral," delivered at the "Voicing Women" conference, Liverpool, April, 1992.

[34] Francis Barker, *The Tremulous Private Body: Essays on Subjection* (London: Methuen, 1984).

[35] Jonathan Goldberg, *James I and the Politics of Literature* (Baltimore and London: Johns Hopkins Univ. Press, 1983): 150; Susan Dwyer Amussen, *An Ordered Society: Gender and Class in Early Modern England* (Oxford: Basil Blackwell, 1988): 2; for similar accounts see Debora Kuller Shuger, *Habits of Thought in the English Renaissance* (Berkeley: Univ. of California Press, 1990): 190; Kevin Sharpe, Criticism and Compliment: The Politics of Literature in the England of Charles I (Cambridge: Cambridge Univ. Press, 1987): 272.

subjects? made so by thy gouernement, instructed by thy learning, and indeed made by thee. (1.315)

In this context, it is worth returning for a moment to Denny's response to Wroth's portrayal of his family scandal; a scandal both personal and political. Denny can only read Urania as a product of a (warped) desire which challenges assumptions about appropriate gender roles in relation to writing; yet by replying with a poem ("How easy wer't to pay thee with thine owne,"[36] he writes, apparently without irony), Denny enters into the conjunction of the public and the private which Wroth pursues throughout her romance.[37] This sovereignty is not simply patriarchal rule over female subjects, even if the powerful central story of Pamphilia is focused on female constancy set against male inconstancy (this very trait of Amphilanthus still proves him subject to the rule of desire). The entire narrative of Urania is, after all, presided over by a woman: Mellissea, a powerful enchantress who (perhaps evoking the memory of Elizabeth) rules alone, all-seeing, if not exactly all-powerful. At the macrocosmic level in the romance, Mellissea's power is always behind the multifarious narrative threads, the wanderings and crossings of all the huge cast of characters. Mellissea is also responsible for reinforcing the intersection between the apparently "private" world of passion and the public world of politics; each enchantment she sets up and then allows the characters to solve has repercussions at the level of state politics and at the level of dynastic (and therefore personal) attachments.

To take this interrogation of dichotomies such as public/private into the realm of gender, Wroth engages in a complex account of the relationship between female victims, and female power and solidarity. Rather than see this as a clear, univocal statement in Urania, which has led to a critical debate couched in either/or terms, I would prefer to read the romance as a deliberately unsettled and unsettling strategy concerned to question the power of such categories.[38] One might start by underlining

---

[36] Roberts, *Poems of Mary Wroth*, 34.

[37] Mary Ellen Lamb stresses the sense of sexual anxiety behind Denny's response; see *Gender and Authorship*, 154–59.

[38] The two most dramatically opposed views on this debate are contained in Caroline Ruth Swift, "Female Identity in Lady Mary Wroth's Romance *Urania*," *English Literary Renaissance* 14 (1984), which sees the female characters as victims, and Naomi Miller, "Not much to be marked," and "Women's Voices in Wroth's *Urania* and Shakespeare's Plays," in Miller and Waller, who sees female solidarity and resistance. Accounts more sympathetic to the argument I am putting forward here include Hackett, "Yet Tell Me

the contrast between Pamphilia and Urania as a corrective to a reading of the romance which insists on a unitary narrative with a single pair of protagonists, namely Pamphilia and Amphilanthus. Urania's more pragmatic view of love and its effects is contrasted to Pamphilia's almost obsessive constancy. In terms of their political power, however, their positions are reversed, as Pamphilia rules over her kingdom in her own right, rather than through marriage (though she does inherit the kingdom from her uncle). Josephine Roberts has argued that Pamphilia's attachment to Amphilanthus has an adverse effect on her "commitment to the body politic," but she still wields the power in her state, and is always conscious of the need for her good government: "she lost not her selfe; for her gouernment continued iust and braue, like that Lady she was, wherein she shewed her heart was not to be stirr'd, though her priuate fortunes shooke round about her" (1.411).[39] At the same time, Urania herself is praised by her husband Steriamus for her political perspicacity: "how did her counsell rauish our eares, more Judiciall, more exquisite then the whole great counsells of the greatest Monarchies" (2.i.57).

The most complex interrogation of such dichotomies occurs when gender and genre interact in the *Urania*. At one level, Wroth has her characters and also the narrator use conventional gender contrasts between the weakness of women and the strength of men, to the degree that the reader seems to be presented with essentialized traits. For example, while we are given portraits of judicious women, able to offer counsel to men, this very ability is seen in gendered terms: "The lady, who had so great a spiritt, as might be called masculine" (2.ii.57v). Displays of emotion are frequently seen as "womanish lamenting" (2.ii.58); and when a man weeps he says that he "playd the woman"

Some Such Fiction," and Roberts, "Labyrinths of Desire." For a fascinating account of Wroth's "manipulation of cultural constructions of the woman reader to provide some degree of dignity to women's reading," thereby enabling a precarious negociation of the pressures of the masculine world of letters, see Mary Ellen Lamb, "Women Readers in Mary Wroth's *Urania*," in Miller and Waller, 225, and see also Lamb's analysis of *Urania* in *Gender and Authorship*. Patricia Parker has offered an excellent account of the way in which attitudes towards rhetoric replicate the gendered dimension of the public/private dichotomy, noting that "the clear link that would keep women from learning rhetoric as specifically public speech is the long association in which a 'public woman,' and especially one who spoke in public, could only be called a whore," *Literary Fat Ladies* (London: Methuen, 1987): 104; once again, this particular set of prejudices is reflected in Denny's response to Wroth.

[39] Roberts, "Radigund Revisited," 200.

(1.65). Even at the level of writing, as has often been noted, the "mad" overreaching Antissia as female poet is contrasted to the modest, even secretive Pamphilia.[40] Antissia strives beyond her scope, and this is seen in terms that seem to emanate from an Edward Denny rather than a Mary Wroth: "being a dangerous thing att any time for a weake woman to studdy higher matters than their cappasitie can reach to" (2.i.7). Yet this warning stemming from Antissia's experiences is in complete contrast to the role of a woman like Mellissea in the romance. Similarly, the notion of what is truly "masculine" shifts dangerously as well, and menaces the certainty of such gender-based contrasts. Thus the chivalric virtues most evident in the first part of *Urania* are frequently undermined in the second part, when the heroes, having grown old, weaken, sicken, die, grow fat (a fate reserved for Parselius), and become suddenly aware of the precarious nature of the macho ideal: "a dismall fate to all great ones, who neuer so much adored, soe infinitely followed, assur'd, and as Gods on Earthe glorified and magnified, lett their little small winde pipe bee butt stopt, that the body falls, all due respect dyes with that, and the rising sun, is then their only worship" (2.ii.57v).

This is seen most interestingly in relation to that supreme hero Amphilanthus, who in the second part of *Urania* is subjected to a significant reversal of these apparently rigid sexual stereotypes. Amphilanthus's response to the deception practised on him over Pamphilia's apparent marriage is quite unlike her "heroic" stoicism. He behaves "not like Amphilanthus butt a puling lover" (2.i.51v). By book 2 he is behaving "as if hee had bin bred in a ladys chamber" (2.ii.2); he faints at Pamphilia's feet (just before this we are told that he has "hands of that delicasie for pure whiteness, delicate shape, and softnes, as noe lady could compare wth them," ibid.).[41]

It is worth noting that at this moment in the narrative, Wroth offers the reader a quite startling example of a male blazon, as Parselius gazes at Belario:

> hee was of stature tall, and soe proportionably shaped to his moderate stature [height], his lims of that excellent exactnes in

---

[40] See especially the discussion in Lamb, *Gender and Authorship*.

[41] The whole issue of the gaze in *Urania* has been discussed cogently by Helen Hackett, "Yet Tell Me Some Such Fiction," 56 and also in her unpublished paper "Violence in Lady Mary Wroth's *Urania*," delivered at the "Voicing Women" conference in Liverpool, April, 1992. I am grateful to Dr. Hackett for allowing me to consult a copy of her paper.

euen proportion, and singular, as if nature wth art had fained to make him the onely true piece of sweetest excellencie, his haire of a light browne wch did naturally curle, and ly though carelessly (by him uncared for) as to womanish for his more high, and highest thoughts, yett in as due, and compleat order, as if tended wth all curiositie and daintiness could afford, his eyes inclining prettily to blackness, butt nott soe furious as som wch joye in causing perpetuall murder, butt his were of so sweet a commanding power, as to make hearts yt beheld them to confess an nessessitie of admiring them, then liking, then loving, and soe by the stealing inuasions of loue, to be seruants to such perfections, his lips like cherris red, and coule [?], still when shutting seeming to play one wth an other, as young folkes doe wth cherris, sporting wth one another, slender hee was, butt soe adorned wt excellent proportion, and sinewed strength, wch yett the pure whitness, and softnes of his skin, did butt as shew for excellency nott for force; yett was his strength and vallour such as often times itt had bin tried. (2.ii.3v)

This blazon complicates any notion of a male gaze directed solely at the female characters in the narrative, and it is perhaps most appropriate that we find it at this particular moment in *Urania*, when Amphilanthus is being used to unfix gender positions.[42]

This treatment of Amphilanthus forms part of Wroth's examination of a generic intersection with the public/private and male/female dichotomies I have been discussing: the contrast between chivalric and pastoral romance. If Sidney shifted the genre of the *Arcadia* from pastoral towards chivalric during his revisions, Wroth combines both forms in *Urania*.[43] The main chivalric literary influence on *Urania* is *Amadis de Gaule*,

---

[42] Wroth here offers an important counterbalance to the rigid gender divisions reinforced by the blazon as a rhetorical device which have been examined recently by Patricia Parker in *Literary Fat Ladies*, drawing also on the work of Nancy Vickers in "Diana Described: Scattered Woman and Scattered Rhyme," *Critical Inquiry* 8 (1981): 265–79; and " 'The blazon of sweet beauty's best': Shakespeare's Lucrece," in Patricia Parker and Geoffrey Hartman, eds., *Shakespeare and the Question of Theory* (New York: Methuen, 1985).

[43] There have been many attempts to pin down the exact genre of both *Arcadias*; of particular relevance to my argument about the nature of generic interaction in *Urania* is Peter Lindenbaum's thesis about Sidney as an "anti-pastoral" writer in *Changing Landscapes: Anti-Pastoral Sentiment in The English Renaissance* (Athens: Univ. of Georgia Press, 1986), chaps. 2 and 3, and also his essay "Sidney and the Active Life" in M.J.B. Allen at al., eds., *Sir Philip Sidney's Achievements* (New York: AMS Press, 1990).

famously given a backhanded compliment by Sidney in the *Defence of Poetry*: "Truly I have known men that even with reading *Amadis de Gaule* (which God knoweth wanteth much of a perfect poesy) have found their hearts moved to the exercise of courtesy, liberality, and especially courage."[44] Despite the not insignificant fact that *The Mirror of Knighthood* was translated by a woman, Margaret Tyler, who wrote an important defence of her role, *Amadis*, along with the other examples of chivalric romance, was associated with the public persona of the revival of ceremonial chivalry (both Elizabethan and Jacobean), and with the macho image of the questing knight.[45] This could be contrasted with the pastoral as a mode aligned with the private realm of contemplation (and therefore, to some degree, a realm either praised or disparaged for its potentially feminised character).[46] However, as I have noted earlier, Jacobean pastoral is also used as political critique, set against the repetition of the chivalric quest and the potentially tainted nature of what is described in *Urania* as "a painfull court lyfe" (2.i.56) — a phrase that seems to reflect Wroth's experience of that state. The limitations of the chivalric stance and mode are most evident in the manuscript continuation of *Urania*, where Wroth depicts the necessary physical decline of the chivalric hero; but throughout the narrative, set against the undoubted relish with which chivalric encounters are described, is the paucity of any chivalric solution to the major problems which beset the characters.

Therefore, two genres with apparently opposed symbolic implications are used within *Urania* to interrogate each other's assumptions. This process ultimately involves a deferral of any final statement on the rival claims of either genre, just as the allied issues of gender are left undetermined (a situation certainly enhanced by the unfinished state of both the

---

[44] *A Defence of Poetry*, ed. J.A. Van Dorsten (Oxford: Oxford Univ. Press, 1966): 40–41; for a general account of the influence of *Amadis* on Elizabethan literature, see John J. O'Connor, *Amadis de Gaule and Its Influence on Elizabethan Literature* (New Brunswick: Rutgers Univ. Press, 1970); O'Connor makes no mention of *Urania*; the influence of *Amadis* on Wroth is noted in Josephine Roberts, "The Marriage Controversy in Wroth's *Urania*," in Miller and Waller, 126.

[45] For an important analysis of Tyler, see Tina Krontiris, "Breaking the Barriers of Genre and Gender: Margaret Tyler's Translation of The Mirrour of Knighthood," *English Literary Renaissance* 18 (1988): 19–39; see also Hackett, "Yet Tell Me Some Such Fiction," 44–5.

[46] Of the many studies of pastoral, see in particular Helen Cooper, *Pastoral: Medieval Into Renaissance* (Ipswich: D.S.Brewer/Rowman and Littlefield, 1977), chaps. 4–6; Andrew V. Ettin, *Literature and the Pastoral* (New Haven: Yale Univ. Press, 1984).

published *Urania* and the manuscript continuation).⁴⁷ Such a process is recapitulated in the nature of the publication of the *Urania* itself as an intervention in the masculine realm of letters: a shift, in Denny's terms, from the privatized piety of pastoral retreat to the public, political, perhaps even chivalric world of secular literature. The *roman à clef* element in *Urania* ensured that it interacted once again with the realm of the court, so that while Wroth herself had been marginalized (to a degree), *Urania* placed her in a quite different relationship to that particular center, especially given the nature of the political context in 1621, and given her own allegiances within the Sidney/Herbert grouping at court. Wroth's act is interpreted by her as both private (she protests to Buckingham that her book is subject to strange constructions she never intended) and public (she sent Buckingham a presentation copy). While publication is to cease, and "the books left to bee shut up,"⁴⁸ as Wroth reassures Buckingham, the manuscript continuation of *Urania* testifies to a much more complex notion of shutting up than perhaps Buckingham ever imagined, or than any oversimplified dichotomy between public and private might lead us to assume. Ultimately, this is because the strangest constructions are those practised by the narrative, rather than by the supposed impositions of false interpretation. Wroth's own strange constructions are evident if modern readers recognize that her romance has both an investment in heroism and an investment in its decline; an investment in the male quest (as opposed to female confinement) and an affirmation of endless lack at the heart of that quest; a sense of fulfilment within female containment as well as a sense of frustration; and, finally, a sense of female engagement (political and otherwise) as well as female detachment. Now that Wroth's book is moving from being mostly shut up to becoming more generally read and commented upon, it should be seen as a key example of how a woman writer in early modern England was able to question the boundaries between the public and the private, in an example that is of immense relevance to many current literary (and social) debates.

---

⁴⁷ *Urania*'s unfinished state can be viewed as part of Wroth's homage to Sidney, echoing the unfinished *New Arcadia*; but it can also be seen as part of the resistance to closure of the romance form itself; see Patricia Parker, *Inescapable Romance: The Poetics of a Mode* (Princeton: Princeton Univ. Press, 1979).

⁴⁸ Roberts, *Poems of Mary Wroth*, 236.

SUSAN BRUCE

Virgins of the World and Feasts of
the Family: Sex and the Social Order
in Two Renaissance Utopias

> "You shall understand that there is not under the heavens so
> chaste a nation as this of Bensalem; nor so free from all pollu-
> tion or foulness. It is the virgin of the world."
> (Bacon, *New Atlantis*)

> "Utopia ... first consisteth of families."
> (More, *Utopia*)

"OH BRAVE NEW WORLD, THAT HAS SUCH PEOPLE IN IT!" Miranda wonderingly declares on seeing fellow Europeans for the first time; "Had I plantation of this isle, ... I would / By contraries execute all things," Gonzalo meditates earlier in the same play.[1] Shakespeare's treatment of brave new worlds in *The Tempest* is only one of the many examinations of utopian musing that appear in the Renaissance period: Thomas More, who inaugurated the genre and unwittingly bestowed upon it a name with the publication of *Utopia* in 1516, could hardly have guessed how resonant his idea would prove for succeeding generations, both in England and abroad. Gonzalo's own utopian vision, for example, is itself an only slightly modi-

---

[1] William Shakespeare, *The Tempest*, ed. Stephen Orgel (Oxford: Oxford Univ. Press, 1987), 2.1.141–45.

fied version of Montaigne's foray into the genre in his essay "Of the Caniballes": from Andrae's *Christianopolis*, through Burton's *Anatomy of Melancholy* and Campanella's *La Citta del Sole* to Bacon's *New Atlantis* a plethora of writers turned their respective hands to the writing of what Burton called "a utopia of mine own."[2]

Representations of ideal worlds, of course, had been produced before the Renaissance: Plato's *Republic*, for example, lurks in the margins of most instances of Renaissance utopian fiction. But the Renaissance utopia differs, in several ways, from those earlier imaginations of ideal communities. For one thing, it insists on its spatial immediacy. It generally claims an existence in a locatable point on the globe; many indeed, came complete with their own bogus maps, settings whose meaning, Benedict Anderson has acutely remarked, "may be clearer if one considers how unimaginable it would be to place Plato's Republic on any map, sham or real."[3] So too it refuses the temporal displacement common to many other genres of ideal world fiction, presenting itself not as an imagination of how things were (in some past Golden Age,) nor of how they might be (in some future millenium,) but rather as a representation of how things actually are.

In this respect too, then, the Renaissance utopia claims a reality to which earlier (and later) ideal worlds never pretended. And most important of all, for our purposes, is the third facet of the utopia's claim to truth:[4] its insistence on a pragmatic plausibility which, like its spatial and temporal location, distinguishes it from related genres of ideal world fiction both prior to and during the Renaissance. Unlike, for example, the "Land of Cockaygne," the utopia assumes no change in the availability of material goods; unlike the Perfect Moral Commonwealth, the utopia insists that humans are flawed, and not perfect, just as fallible as they are

---

[2] For a brief list of lesser-known examples of the genre, see the bibliography to this book.

[3] Benedict Anderson, *Imagined Communities: Reflections on the Origin and Spread of Nationalism* (London: Verso, 1983), 67–68.

[4] Paradoxically, these claims of truth, whilst marking the utopia's relation to the real world of discoveries and geographical exploration, also mark its fictionality. For a provocative discussion of the epistemological resonance of early fiction's claims to truth, see Michael McKeon, *The Origins of the English Novel 1600-1740* (Baltimore: Johns Hopkins Univ. Press, 1987).

in the real world.⁵ The utopia, in short, refuses to assume either any change in the nature of humankind, or any substantial difference in the availability of material satisfactions. Rather, the utopia assumes the presence of desires subversive to collective well-being, and aims to show how such desires (for commodities, for example, or for power) can be eradicated (by education or persuasion) or, in extreme cases, when education fails, repressed through state intervention.

And it is the treatment of one complex of human desires, by two very different utopian writers, which I want to examine here. Like almost all Renaissance utopias, More's *Utopia* and Bacon's *New Atlantis* center their ideal communities on the family; consequently, both of these texts must find ways of dealing with the potentialities for social disruption which the family entails. How does utopia contain the access of sexual desire in the individual, for example, and confine it into its "proper" place within the family; how does the utopian state ensure that allegiances to one's blood relations do not conflict with allegiance to the larger community; how too do these societies preclude the existence of conflict between the genders? The utopias of both More and Bacon must deal with these problems, because they are utopias. They cannot wish the problems away, cannot, for example, pretend that desire does not exist (as Gabriel de Foigny's *Terra Incognita Australis* was later to do), or simply assume that families will subordinate their interests to those of the state (as do prelapsarian or Millenarian fantasies). Yet although each shares with the other the constraints of their common genre, and although each constitutes the family as its principal social institution, each nevertheless offers a very different picture of the "ideal" family, and a very different representation of the social mechanisms invoked to keep that ideal family in its ideal state. My contention in this essay is that the differences between *Utopia* and the *New Atlantis* in their respective treatments of sexuality and the family are directly (though far from self-evidently) related to a shift in epistemological emphasis between More's earlier text and Bacon's later one. More repeatedly invokes the quality of reason to defend Utopian practices: the customs he depicts in Utopia always rest on a humanist faith in the individual's capacity to subordinate his desires to a reasoned, and reasonable, social

---

⁵ I draw here on J. C. Davis's distinctions between different forms of ideal worlds, in his *Utopia and the Ideal Society: A Study of English Utopian Writing 1516–1700* (Cambridge: Cambridge Univ. Press, 1981), 36.

solution.⁶ Bacon, however, privileges knowledge as the "end of his foundation";⁷ it is the empiricist search for perfect and complete knowledge which his text is designed to further. In other words, between More's text and Bacon's we move from an early Renaissance humanist vision of an ideal world in which the emphasis lies on the twofold qualities of faith and reason, to a late Renaissance utopia whose intent is to illustrate the power of an ideal community based on the scientific principles of experimental observation and the control over nature afforded by more or less complete knowledge of it. It is this shift, I want to argue, which motivates the differences between each text's representation of matters familial, and it is to those matters that I now wish to turn.

1. *Utopia*

Richard Halpern, in his excellent essay on *Utopia*, appears to read More's text as a kind of orgasmic discourse. "Utopia is not merely incoherent; it *explodes*," he maintains, "and this explosion is felt as a pleasurable release."⁸ Quoting one of the prefatory letters to Utopia, where Peter Giles explains that the directions to Utopia were lost as a result of the inopportune cough of one of Morus⁹ servants, Halpern goes on to observe:

> That a cough obscures the way to Utopia is not accidental. If not a positive pleasure, coughing is at least an explosive release of bod-

---

⁶ For some of the many discussions of reason in the *Utopia*, see R. W. Chambers, *Thomas More* (London: Jonathan Cape, 1935); Russell A. Ames, *Citizen Thomas More and his Utopia* (Princeton: Princeton Univ. Press, 1949); Robert C. Elliott, "The Shape of Utopia," *ELH* 30 (Winter 1963). Extracts from all of these are reprinted in R. M. Adams' Norton edition of More's *Utopia* (New York: Norton, 1949). For more recent discussions see T. A. Kenyon, "The Problem of Freedom and Moral Behaviour in Thomas More's *Utopia*," *Journal of the History of Philosophy* 21 (Fall 1983); Patrick Grant, *Literature and the Discourse of Method in the Renaissance* (Hampshire: Macmillan, 1985); George M. Logan, *The Meaning of More's Utopia* (Princeton: Princeton Univ. Press, 1983).

⁷ Francis Bacon, *The Great Instauration and New Atlantis*, ed. J. Weinberger (Arlington Heights, Ill: Harlan Davidson, 1980), 70.

⁸ Richard Halpern, *The Poetics of Primitive Accumulation: English Renaissance Culture and the Genealogy of Capital* (Ithaca: Cornell Univ. Press, 1991), 149.

⁹ I have followed Stephen Greenblatt in referring to the More-within-the-text as "Morus." See his chapter on More in *Renaissance Self-Fashioning: From More to Shakespeare* (Chicago: Chicago Univ. Press, 1980).

ily tension or an irritating pressure. It is therefore the body's revolt against Utopia.[10]

For the Utopians, of course, coughing probably would be a positive pleasure: in Utopia, the first kind of pleasure is

> when delectation is sensibly felt.... This cometh by meat and drink, and sometimes while those things be expulsed... whereof is in the body over-great abundance. This pleasure is felt when we do our natural easement, or when we be doing the act of generation, or when the itching of any part is eased with rubbing or scratching. Sometimes pleasure riseth exhibiting to any member nothing that it desireth, nor taking from it any pain that it feeleth, which nevertheless tickleth and moveth our senses with a certain efficacy, but with a manifest motion turneth them to it; as is that which cometh of music.[11]

The second of Utopia's bodily pleasures is "that which ... resteth in the ... upright state of the body": in other words, perfect health, a condition to which the first or lower kind of pleasure returns the individual. "To be without grief, not having health, that they call insensibility and not pleasure," Hythloday remarks: as Halpern rightly observes, then, the first kind of pleasure is, according to the Utopians, contingent on the body having been in a prior state of displeasure, a displeasure characterized in the text either as a lack or as an excess (91).

But *pace* Halpern, (and Utopia) sexual pleasure is the only pleasure here which cannot be subsumed under the dual categories of excess or lack. Being hungry or thirsty is contingent on a lack; needing to defecate contingent on bodily excess. Sexual desire, however, (or at least, male sexual desire) not only predicates *both* excess and lack simultaneously, thus being overdetermined in its inclusion of both of the categories which the discourse of Utopian pleasure would wish to keep separate and distinct,

---

[10] Halpern, 149.

[11] Thomas More, *Utopia*, ed. Richard Marius (London: Dent, 1985), 90. The standard edition of the text is that edited by J. H. Hexter and Edward J. Surtz in vol. 4 of *The Yale Edition of the Complete Works of St. Thomas More* (New Haven: Yale Univ. Press, 1965). I quote consistently from the Marius edition throughout this essay because it is the only readily available modern edition of the text which prints Ralph Robinson's 1551 translation of More's original Latin. This edition is hereafter cited as *Utopia*.

but it is also, unlike most of the other bodily pleasures, a productive pleasure: it is "the act of generation," the pleasure whose consequence is the renewal of Utopia and its expansion to populate its own country and, when necessary or desirable, those of its neighbors.

At once excess, lack, and productive pleasure, desire is also the pleasure whose absence from or containment in Utopia would undermine the implicit distinction between Utopia and England which More intends to draw in this discourse of Utopian enjoyment. Attempting to ridicule a view which would defend the importance of bodily pleasures, More tells us that

> Like as it is a wise man's part rather to avoid sickness than to wish for medicines, and rather to ... put to flight careful griefs than to call for comfort, so it is much better not to need this kind of pleasure than thereby to be eased of the contrary grief. The which kind of pleasure if any man take for his felicity, that man must needs grant that then he shall be in most felicity, if he live that life which is led in continual hunger, thirst, itching, eating, drinking, scratching, and rubbing. The which life not only foul and unhonest, but also how miserable and wretched it is, who perceiveth not? (92)

"Wretched indeed," Halpern goes on to comment, "and precisely the condition of the English body politic, divided as it is between those whose lives are spent in perpetual hunger and thirst and others whose lives are spent in perpetual eating and drinking."[12] This is true, but the contrast only carries the point insofar as sexual desire has now quietly but completely slipped out of the picture: somehow, a description of a life led in continual sexual desire and fulfilment invokes a picture rather less dystopian — and probably rather more egalitarian — than the one More wishes here to elicit. Worse things, as they say, happen at sea.

Bodily pleasures are for the Utopians necessary pleasures: "wherefore such pleasures they think not greatly to be set by, but in that they be necessary," we are told (92). Sexual pleasure is an eminently necessary pleasure, but it is also one whose containment within the Utopian economy of pleasure threatens to become impossible: its inclusion in the dystopian picture More paints would undermine the distinction between Utopia and the "real world" which More intends here to uphold. Thus whilst

---

[12] Halpern, 171.

Utopia acknowledges the presence of desire within the population which constitutes it, it must simultaneously denude desire of its potentially destabilizing quality. It achieves this first, by inscribing desire in a rational, and plausible, discourse of entirely bodily pleasure: in this manner it removes from desire any of the affective passions (love, jealousy, possessiveness) which motivate its force as a potential source of conflict. Treating of desire insofar as it is an emotion shared by all human beings, it elides the fact that desire (unlike, say, hunger) is, when experienced by individual human beings, an emotion with a specific and individual object. One desires another person, I submit, in a rather different way than one might desire a piece of cake; but this is an objection to the discourse of Utopian pleasure which the text does not allow us to make — or at least tries very hard to prevent us from making.

In its dealings with desire, then, *Utopia*'s first move is to take two general truths about desire (it is "necessary," it is universally felt) and to present these general truths as if they told the whole story about individual instances of desire. Once that is achieved *Utopia*'s second move is quietly and seamlessly to let the problem slip out of the picture. This strategy inhabits More's text not merely insofar as sexual desire is concerned, but much more fundamentally: it is the manifestation on the level of rhetoric of the phenomenon which characterizes Utopia's attitude to individual desires on the level of content. "A crucial characteristic of Utopia," Stephen Greenblatt has argued, is "the steady constriction of an almost limitless freedom ... freedoms are heralded only to shrink in the course of the description."[13] This principle underlies the representation of Utopian gender relations too, whose apparent egalitarianism disintegrates under pressure to reveal a world which often looks uncomfortably familiar. In Utopian eating arrangements, for example, we are at first informed that men and women all eat together, men on one side of the table, women on the other, couples being alternated according to age and served (by the adolescent children) according to seniority (73). But in splendidly Utopian style, there is more to this description of domestic dining bliss than at first meets the eye. Nursing mothers, we are told, sit with their charges in a separate room put aside for the purpose, to which pregnant women can also retire "if any sudden evil should chance to then, as many times happeneth to women with child." Given that Utopian

---

[13] Greenblatt, 40–41.

women presumably reproduced about as frequently as their contemporary English counterparts, conceiving again almost as soon as the previous child was weaned, women of child-bearing age would almost always be suckling children: one suspects, in other words, that there are far fewer women in Utopian dining halls than the text would lead us to envisage.

Utopian eating arrangements, then, offer us a picture poised between an egalitarian principle (men and women eat together) and a rather less egalitarian practice (men eat in the halls, served by the adolescent children; women take care of the kids elsewhere — plus ç'a change, one might wryly interject, plus c'est la même chose). So too with Utopian occupation, where the text initially emphasizes egalitarianism ("of the ... crafts every man learneth one, and not only the men, but also the women" [64]); but then imperceptibly but ineluctably erases women from the discourse which had seemed at first to allow them a relative equality of occupation:

> every man is brought up in his father's craft ... if a man's mind stand to any other, he is by adoption put into a family of that occupation which he doth most fantasy. Whom ... his father, [does] diligently look to that he be put to a discreet and honest householder.[14]

In warfare too, "women that be willing to accompany their husbands in times of war be not prohibited or letted," we at first learn; only to discover shortly afterwards that this is not because Utopian women are valued as particularly good fighters, but rather because their presence will encourage their men to fight the harder in order to protect them: "every man is compassed next about with his own children, kinsfolk, and alliance, that they whom nature chiefly moveth to mutual succour, thus standing together, may help one another" (113).

Characteristically, Utopia recognizes women as equal citizens only immediately to marginalize them, shifting them into a litotic parenthesis: "priests, unless they be women (for that kind is not excluded from priesthood, howbeit few are chosen, and none but widows and old women)" (125);[15] or relegating them to the periphery of a circle whose center is

---

[14] Quite why this search is so necessary in Utopia is never explained.

[15] On the importance of litotes to *Utopia* see Elizabeth McCutcheon, "Denying the Contrary: More's Use of litotes in the *Utopia*," in *Essential Articles for the Study of Thomas More*, ed R. S. Sylvester and G. P. Marc'hadour (Hamden, Conn.: Archon books, 1977).

man ("every man is compassed about"). The most striking example of this pattern occurs in the description Hythloday gives us of Utopian marriage customs. "In choosing wives and husbands," Hythloday informs us,

> [the Utopians] observe ... a custom which seemed to us very ... foolish. For a sad and an honest matron sheweth the woman, be she maid or widow, naked to the wooer. And likewise a sage and discreet man exhibiteth the wooer naked to the woman. (99)

Hythloday explains that the Utopians follow this practice to prevent the post-marital discovery of a partner's physical shortcomings; he then repeats his observation that the custom appeared odd to him:

> At this custom we laughed, and disallowed it as foolish. But they ... do greatly wonder at the folly of all other nations, which, in buying a colt, ... be so chary ... that ... they will not buy him unless ... all the harness be taken off, lest under those coverings be hid some ... sore. And yet in choosing a wife, which shall be either pleasure or displeasure to them all their life after, they be so reckless, that all the residue of the woman's body being covered with clothes, they esteem her scarcely by one handbreadth (for they can see no more but her face), and so to join her to them not without great jeopardy of evil agreeing together, if anything in her body afterward should chance to offend and mislike them. For ... the endowments of the body cause the virtues of the mind to be more esteemed..., even in the marriages of wise men. Verily, so foul deformity may be hid under those coverings, that it may quite alienate ... the man's mind from his wife, when it shall not be lawful for their bodies to be separate again. (99–100)

The initial description of the practice, and the justificatory reference to Utopian monogamy at first emphasize the egalitarianism of the custom. But this equality of discourse disappears as the passage continues. Men and women may alike be shown to their prospective partners, but after the colt analogy it becomes obvious that it is male partners, not female ones, whose interests are at stake here. Indeed, the colt analogy itself begins to anticipate this shift of focus, not simply because men, and not women, would constitute the nations who buy horses, but also because, as Adams points out, More "can hardly have failed to recall that ['Colt' was] the maiden name of his first wife."[16] As the passage continues, the stakes are made quite explicit. Nations buying colts become men choosing wives, the analogy between colts and wives elaborated here through the word "handsbreadth," which describes the woman with the term used for the measuring of horses. The woman's body becomes the gendered locus of potentially hidden deformity; men, and not women, risk being alienated by post-marital revelations and need to be protected against them.[17] An initially egalitarian point of view dissolves into the more familiar scrutiny of the proprietary male gaze: it is women's bodies which are on view in Utopian window-shopping, and male desire only whose ultimate satisfaction is guaranteed.

The rhetorical move which *Utopia* brings to bear on the problem of desire is thus invoked repeatedly in the text's representation of women: initial contemplation of relative egalitarianism is almost invariably replaced by a rhetorical amnesia through which women, their desires and their freedoms are invoked only to disappear into a discourse whose referent is entirely male. This pattern, I want to argue, is fundamental also to the construction of Utopia itself, both as text and as imagined community. In formal terms, the discourse on Utopia proper (the second book) is introduced to us by way of a discussion (the first book) whose participants include only men. Women are referred to in this discussion only once:

> [Peter Giles] is in his talk ... so merry ... that, through his ... delectable communication, in me was greatly abated and diminished the fervent desire that I had to see my native country, my wife, and my children, whom then I did much long and covet to see, because that at that time I had been more than four months from them. (14)

---

[16] Adams, 66.

[17] This Utopian practice can be contextualized by a (possibly apocryphal) anecdote related by Aubrey: William Roper, More's son-in-law to be, "came one morning, pretty early, to my Lord, with a proposall to marry one of his daughters. My Lord's daughters were then both together abed in a truckle-bed in their father's chamber asleep. He carries Sir William into the chamber and takes the Sheete by the corner and suddenly whippes it off. They lay on their Backs, and their smocks up as high as their armepitts. This awakened them, and immediately they turned on their bellies. Quoth Roper, I have seen both sides, and so gave a patt on the buttock he made a choice of, sayeing, Thou art mine. Here was all the trouble of the wooeing." John Aubrey, *Brief Lives*, ed. Oliver Lawson Dick (London: Penguin Classics, 1987), 283.

Women are, then, introduced in book 1 only parenthetically and even then are notable mainly by virtue of their absence, an absence which that parenthesis serves to emphasize, since it stresses not so much that Morus is missing his wife and children as that the company of Peter Giles reduces in him that "longing." We may also note here a paradox: encounters leading to Utopia, — the communal island which "first, consisteth of families," — are also encounters whose effect on the individual is to diminish domestic affect and to abate fervent desire. I shall return to the question of affect shortly; here I want to indicate that the way in which women slip out of the text in book 1 plays out a phenomenon replicated in the ur-moment of Utopian history in book 2. As Louis Marin has observed,[18] the physical construction of *Utopia* is represented in the text as a kind of birth fantasy: Utopus, landing on what was then a peninsula, causes his soldiers to dig up the umbilical-like landlink to the mainland creating thereby the island whose description has induced several readers of the text to observe that the island bears more resemblance to a new womb than it does to the simile the text uses, the new moon (55-56).[19]

In the founding of Utopia, then, a prototypical family is created in which all Utopians become the children of a single father: Utopus himself. The subsequent lack of any other named Utopian individual bolsters our sense of this unified family of compatriots: we perceive them only as Utopians, or in other words, as one and all sons of Utopus, each owning the same patronymic, the name of their universal father. In this ur-family Utopus himself figures as the father, as Marin notes; his paternalistic rule extended over his people who figure as the children he brings up: "Utopus ... also brought the rude and wild people to that excellent perfection in all good fashions, humanity, and civil gentleness, wherein they now go beyond all the people of the world" (56). The island is transformed at one and the same time into both producer (womb/mother) and product (object severed from the main body/child). In other words, father and children are figured in human terms in this description, but motherhood is represented only in terms of an inanimate object. Thus the representation of the is-

---

[18] Louis Marin, *Utopiques, Jeux d'espaces* (Paris: Minuit, 1973), 145-46.

[19] The island's "likeness to the new moon is perhaps less striking ... than its resemblance to a womb." Adams, 34. Earlier, the Manuels note, "the gnostic Simon Magus likened paradise to the womb — an analogy recognized in the map of the island sketched for the Louvain 1516 edition of *Utopia*." Frank E. and Fritzie P. Manuel, *Utopian Thought in the Western World* (Oxford: Basil Blackwell, 1979).

land's generation at once replays and provides the original model for the text's repeated erasure of women from its discourse: the island of Utopia, introduced to us through a conversation which serves to "abate and diminish" the desire for women, is itself created in the text through a discourse which privileges male labor and writes the feminine into the margins of its discourse.

Finally, it should be recognized that this ur-family of Utopians is not merely the symbol of all that a Utopian family should be; it is also the macrocosmic structure into which all microcosmic Utopian families eventually coalesce. For one of the ways that Utopia prevents its inhabitants from saying "this is my child, and as such I want for him more than I would want for your child, or for a stranger" is continually to extend the boundaries of the family beyond its kinship confines. The Utopian family operates on a structure which is the opposite of that of Utopian liberties: if liberties are invoked only to meet with progressive limitation in the text, then the family, limited at first, expands on further attention to become something much greater and more amorphous than it initially appeared to be. But just as affect is always pushed outwards, beyond the bounds of the family, so too affect within the family is always reduced and delimited. Both of these mechanisms can be seen to be at play in Hythloday's final picture of utopian contentment:

> Now I have... described... that commonwealth, which... [is] that which alone... may claim... the name of a... public weal.... Here, where nothing is private, the common affairs be earnestly looked upon... where all things be common to every man, it is not to be doubted that any man shall lack any thing necessary for his private uses.... For there nothing is distributed after a niggish sort, neither is there any poor man or beggar; and though no man have everything, yet every man is rich. For what can be more rich than to live joyfully or merrily, without all grief and pensiveness, not caring for his own living, nor vexed and troubled with his wife's importunate complaints, nor dreading poverty to his son, nor sorrowing for his daughter's dowry? Yea, and they take no care at all for the living and wealth of themselves, and all theirs, of their wives, their children, their nephews, their children's children, and all the succession that ever shall follow in their posterity. (130-31)

Thus Hythloday begins his conclusion of the discourse on Utopia. Emphasizing the Utopian rejection of private property, he argues here that the consequence of its eradication is a happy life: in a world where distribution has undone excess and each man has enough,[20] poverty of the soul, as well as the body, will be banished. This eminently Utopian depiction of the pleasures of the good life (whose happiness is constituted by the absence of reasons to grieve) concludes with a vision of the Utopian — or the utopian — family, a family whose ideality is constituted, like Utopian pleasure, by its absences: of irritations and of sorrows, of worries and of fears.

Thus just as *Utopia* opens with a reference to Morus's family which invokes that family only to emphasize its absence, and the *decrease* in Morus's longing for it, so too it ends with a reference to a Utopian family which is defined not so much by what it is, as by what it is not: it includes no grief, pensiveness, trouble, complaints, dread, poverty, sorrowing, or dowries. In short, the absence of property produces a family without care, a point important enough to bear repeating in the passage twice, and a construct which operates in two senses: without care, certainly, in the sense of being without worries or dread; but also without care in the sense of being devoid of affect and desires. This aspect of carelessness, incidentally, is something which Hythloday himself exemplifies: we learn about him early in the text, not only that "his patrimony that he was born unto he left unto his brethren," (15) but also that this disregard for inheritance produces a diminution of affection: "As concerning my friends and kinsfolk," says Raphael,

> I pass not greatly for them. For I think I have sufficiently done my part towards them already. For these things that other men do not depart from until they be very old and sick, ... those very things did I, being ... in the flower of my youth, divide among my friends and kinsfolk. (19)

Having divested himself of care for his first nuclear family, Hythloday has also kept himself singularly free of any new family ties. The ideal Utopian in so many respects, Hythloday is also the one figure in the text without a family of his own: an atomic being, the original stranger, Hythloday alone in the text maintains bonds with no other individuals.

Utopian representations of the family are always poised between the public and the private, invoking both images but constituted by neither.

---

[20] For a wonderful discussion of the relation between the Utopian discourse on need and the treatment of necessity in *King Lear*, see Halpern's chapter on *Lear* in Halpern, 1991.

Thus in this last vision of the Utopian family Hythloday invokes a picture of a nuclear family, referring to wives, sons, and daughters, only immediately to extend it to include "nephews, their children's children, and all the succession that ever shall follow in their posterity." Within this, so typical, Utopian structure, affect occupies a particularly ambiguous position. On the one hand, it is periodically invoked to bolster Utopian power. Thus for example in warfare "every man is compassed next about with his own children, kinsfolk, and alliance, that they whom nature chiefly moveth to mutual succour, thus standing together, may help one another" (113). But here too, "nature" expands rapidly, to encompass first "kinsfolk" and then "alliance" as well as its more obvious direct descendants: the initially specific and nuclear-family orientated object of affection is extended into one whose bounds are the entirety of Utopians; and the Utopian nation is simultaneously (and again, in this most ubiquitous of Utopian rhetorical strategies, seamlessly) both distinguished from and collapsed into the contained unit which initially justified the invocation of affect. Similarly, although affect may initially seem to motivate this individual Utopian bellicosity, it quickly becomes apparent that should affect fail, shame is waiting in the wings to encourage Utopian valor: "it is a great reproach and dishonesty," we are told, "for the husband to come home without his wife, or the wife without her husband, or the son without his father." Utopians, one suspects, may well end up distinguishing themselves on the battlefield not because they love their kinsfolk, but rather because they fear to show the world that they don't.[21]

In *Utopia* the individual family is written into an extended family, within which each and every one Utopian is bound to each and every other, unhampered and untroubled by the divisory allegiances and competitions attendant on a population whose loyalties are directed first and foremost to their kin. Affective bonds in the Utopian family become modular, easily transferred from the adolescent child of your own loins who leaves your household, to the adolescent child of someone else who may enter it. A familial state without familial loyalties is what Utopia paradoxically tries to offer us; extensible to every other Utopian citizen, affect in the Utopian family is transformed into allegiance, and the family becomes an institution without care. That being the case, it is somehow heartening to end this section of the essay with the exposure of a Utopian

---

[21] See Greenblatt for a provocative discussion of the role of shame in Utopia.

contradiction, of that playful kind with which the text is so wonderfully full. During warfare, that moment of greatest state instability, "every man" we have heard, "is compassed next about with his own children, kinsfolk, and alliance." This concept, designed to impress upon us the cohesion of the Utopian nation, actually reveals its ultimate untenability. Every man cannot be compassed round by his alliance, since to be so he would have to be in two places at once: at the center of his own circle and at the margins of someone else's. But that untenable, unstable place is, of course, where the Utopians always are.

2. New Atlantis

Bacon's New Atlantis may owe several debts to Utopia, but none is more direct than his description of Bensalemite[22] marriage customs. "I have read in a book of one of your men," says Joabin, (the Jew who acts as the Europeans' informant),

> of a Feigned Commonwealth, where the married couple are permitted, before they contract, to see one another naked. This they dislike; for they think it a scorn to give a refusal after so familiar knowledge: but because of many hidden defects in men and women's bodies, they have a more civil way; for they have near every town a couple of pools, (which they call *Adam and Eve's pools*,) where it is permitted to one of the friends of the man and another of the friends of the woman, to see them severally bathe naked.[23]

This allusion constitutes the single direct reference to More in Bacon's text, although there are other similarities between the respective sexual practices of the two imagined communities. In Utopia, Hythloday relates, "there be neither wine-taverns, nor ale-houses, nor stews, nor any occasion of vice of wickedness";[24] in Bensalem, Joabin tells us, "there are no stews, no dissolute houses, no courtesans, nor anything of that kind" (65). Both societies emphasize marriage; both see marriage as a necessary, rather than a pleasurable, institution.

---

[22] Although the text is called *New Atlantis*, the country it describes is never so named in the narrative. For reasons which are never explained, the term used in the narrative to designate the country it describes is "Bensalem."
[23] Bacon, 67.
[24] Utopia, 76.

The evident similarities between the sexual mores of the two societies, however, ought not to blind us to their differences: as Denise Albanese has remarked, the *New Atlantis* characteristically "belies the *Utopia* even as it invites juxtaposition with it."[25] Thus even whilst Bacon emphasizes Utopian influence on "Adam and Eve's Pools" he simultaneously stresses a change in the practice: in Bensalem, the observation is carried out not by the potential spouses but by one of their friends. And to this difference, made explicit by Bacon, we can add another. In the *New Atlantis* there is no reintroduction of the double standard underlying the text's egalitarian surface. "Defects" in Bensalem can exist equally in both bodies; man and woman must alike be examined before marriages can take place.

These changes are odd, and are not explained by the text. Joabin's appeal to the Bensalemite concern for courtesy is patently inadequate as an explanation of the difference: offence would surely result from *any* refusal after one had been surveyed naked, whether it was by one's potential spouse, or his trusted friend. Bensalem's espousal of egalitarianism here is also strange, for it runs counter to the general tenor of Bensalemite society, which is far more overtly patriarchal than Utopia. With the exception of this rejection of the double standard, Bensalem has no truck with any notion of egalitarianism at all, neither in practice, nor (unlike Utopia,) in principle — as the text's description of the Feast of the Family makes clear. This celebration, the ultimate accolade Bensalem offers its citizens, is "granted to any man that shall see thirty persons descended of his body alive together": it consists of an elaborate and highly ritualized honoring of the father, who is given a new title (Tirsan); rewarded with the King's charter which contains "gifts of revenew, and many privileges, exemptions and points of honour"; and feted in various ways (59, 61). The Feast of the Family, in fact, might be better named the Feast of the Father, since it is he whom the ceremony honors. And in addition to honoring him, the occasion also celebrates and confirms his authority. For two days before the Feast itself, the father "sitteth in consultation concerning the good estate of the family": he sees all family members, and resolves their disputes; arranges for the succor of those in distress; reproves and censures any who are subject to "vice" or "ill courses"; directs marriages and arranges for other life decisions (59-63).

---

[25] Denise Albanese, "The *New Atlantis* and the Uses of Utopia," *ELH* 57 (1990): 595.

Bensalemite fathers, then, (at least the most prolific ones) apparently enjoy almost total control over the lives of their descendants. The elaborate rituals of the feast, the sense of spectacle which attends it: all is designed to impress upon Bensalemites, narrator and reader alike the extraordinary regard afforded to paternity in Bensalem. As one might expect, women in this world of fathers get extremely short shrift. They are present in the two day ceremony preceding the Feast itself, (so that, like their brothers, they may be chastized and directed) but thereafter their role is marginalized in the extreme. In the dinner, the Tirsan is "served only by his own children, such as are male ... and the women only stand about him, leaning against the table" (62). And although daughters as well as sons are blessed by the Tirsan after the feast, the mother is relegated throughout the occasion to a kind of closet or attic in the roof (from which vantage point, presumably, the spectacularity of the occasion and the degree of the power which it celebrates is all the more apparent to her):

> if there be a mother, from whose body the whole lineage is descended, there is a traverse placed in a loft above on the right hand of the chair, with a privy door, and a carved window of glass, leaded with gold and blue; where she sitteth, but is not seen. (60-61)

In *Utopia*, we saw, domestic dining arrangements exemplify *Utopia*'s treatment of matters of sexual egalitarianism: an initially egalitarian principle disintegrates on further examination into a rather less egalitarian practice. So too in the *New Atlantis* a feast provides us with a vignette of gender relations within the Bensalemite family, but here no attempt at all is made to present us with anything other than an utterly patriarchal culinary culture. In his Feast of the Family, indeed, Bacon makes literal and explicit an absence which in More functions mainly symbolically or linguistically: in Bensalem, the mother is literally removed from the family celebrations; in Bensalem, male authority in the family is both absolute and unchallenged.

Proportionate to the degree to which Bacon increases the authority of the father in his text is the degree to which he insists that this authority, and the feast which celebrates it, is of a *natural* order. "A most natural, pious and reverend custom it is," states the narrator in introducing the description of the Feast of the Family; "such reverence and obedience they give the order of nature," he maintains shortly after in explaining why the bolstering of paternal authority by the power of the state is so seldom necessary (59, 60). Later the narrator invokes this quality yet again. "I had never heard of a solemnity wherein nature did so much preside," he remarks (somewhat oddly, perhaps, given the accentuation of ritual and artifice in the description of the ceremony [64]). And it is in this recourse to the concept of the natural that the key to Bacon's representation of the family lies. For knowledge of what is natural is the underlying value of the whole of the *New Atlantis*: "this fable my Lord devised," says Rawley, Bacon's secretary, in a prefatory letter to the text, "to the end that he might exhibit therein a model ... of a college instituted for the interpreting of nature and the producing of great and marvellous works for the benefit of man" (37).

That model, Rawley tells us, is Salomon's house, the institution whose experiments are described in exhaustive detail at the end of the *New Atlantis*, and whose purpose is the discovery of "the true nature of all things" (57). But if Salomon's House functions as a model for an ideal scientific community, so too the description of Bensalemite society which constitutes our introduction to Salomon's House is also part of the model which Bacon intended to provide. Everything in the *New Atlantis* serves as the model of ideal *scientific* community, and it is within the context of Bacon's conception of scientific endeavor that we must situate Bacon's representation of the Bensalemite family. What, then, constitutes Bacon's concept of "proper" scientific endeavor? Clearly, that question is too huge to be addressed in any great detail here. What can be pointed out, however, is Bacon's repeated return to the centrality to science not merely of knowledge (which is to be expected) but also of power. "The End of our Foundation," states the dignitary to whom Bacon's narrator is privileged to speak at the close of the *New Atlantis*, "is the knowledge of Causes, and secret Motions of things; and the enlarging of the bounds of Human Empire, to the effecting of all things possible" (70). In this the dignitary speaks very clearly for Bacon: "those twin objects, human Knowledge and human Power," says Bacon in *The Great Instauration*, defining his conception of a science for which we should strive, "really do meet as one" (31).

Knowledge and power, empire and empiricism: these are the ideals which the *New Atlantis* self-consciously and explicitly sets out to illustrate; these too the ideals which the Baconian ideal family was created to further. In other words, although both *Utopia* and the *New Atlantis* privilege the family as a central feature of their respective ideal communities, they do so for very different reasons. In *Utopia*, there is no clear distinction between the family and the state. The one, as we have seen, blends into the other, and the family serves a primarily ideological purpose, producing the (Utopian) subject who chooses, so freely, to serve.[26] In the *New Atlantis* the family exists in a subordinate relation to the state; and one of its principal functions is to provide the commodities from which the state's power emerges. Time and again in the text Joabin or the narrator returns to the importance of the production of children: in the Feast of the Family, for example, the participants repeatedly sing the praises of Adam and Noah, who "peopled the world" (62); the charter offered to the Tirsan is addressed by the King to "*such an one our well-beloved friend and creditor*: which," the Bensalemites say, "is a title proper only to this case. For ... the king is debtor to no man, but for propagation of his subjects" (61).

Thus within the text, ethical discourses surrounding marriage are almost always subordinated to pragmatic concerns with the production of offspring: "Because propagation of families proceedeth from the nuptial copulation," the narrator declares at the beginning of the conversation,

> I desired to know of [Joabin] what laws and customs they had concerning marriage; and whether they kept marriage well; and whether they were tied to one wife? For where population is so much affected, and such as with them it seemed to be, there is commonly plurality of wives. (64)

Similarly, it is primarily a medico-pragmatic concern, rather than an ethical one, which underlies Joabin's critique of European degeneration, a critique, one should note, which once again incorporates a tacit rejection of the double standard. "There are with you infinite men that marry not, but chuse rather a libertine and impure single life, than be yoked in marriage;" Joabin complains, "and many that do marry, marry late," he goes on,

> when the prime and the strength of their years is past.... Neither is it possible that those that have cast away so basely so much of

---

[26] I draw here on Louis Althusser's discussion of ideology and the subject, in his *Lenin and Philosophy and Other Essays*, trans. Ben Brewster (London: New Left Books, 1971).

their strength, should greatly esteem children, (being of the same matter,) as chaste men do. (64)

The Bensalemite rejection of the double standard, then, here as in Adam and Eve's Pools, derives from a medico-scientific insistence on the production of healthy offspring for the power of the state; it is this concern which accounts for the at first sight contradictory insistence on egalitarianism in matters of desire; coupled with a representation of a family so utterly patriarchal.[27] And it is this concern, too, which lies behind the general tone adopted by the *New Atlantis* in its treatment of desire. Like More, Bacon also uses desire to pivot a distinction between England and the ideal, but unlike More, the discourse of sexuality in the *New Atlantis* cannot be contained, even on the surface, under the cool voice of reason, of necessary pleasure. Rather, it is spoken in a tone whose fervor and excess set it apart not only from *Utopia*, but also from the remainder of Bacon's text. "So likewise during marriage, is the case much amended, as it ought to be if those things were tolerated only for necessity?" Joabin asks in speaking to the Europeans about their own sexual customs. "No," he goes on immediately, answering his own question,

> but they remain still as a very affront to marriage. The haunting of those dissolute places, or resort to courtesans, are no more punished in married men than in bachelors.... They hear you defend those things, as done to avoid greater evils; as advoutries, deflouring of virgins, unnatural lust, and the like. But they say this is a preposterous wisdom; and they call it *Lot's offer*, who to save his guests from abusing, offered his daughters; nay they say farther that there is little gained in this; for that the same vices and appetites do still remain and abound; unlawful lust being like a furnace, that if you stop the flames altogether, it will quench; but if you give it any vent, it will rage. (65-66)

It is no coincidence that Joabin introduces his diatribe on European dissoluteness with a condemnation of "necessity," for this word registers

---

[27] On the connection between science and patriarchy see Evelyne Fox Keller, *Reflections on Science and Gender* (New Haven: Yale Univ. Press, 1984); Sandra Harding, *The Science Question in Feminism* (Ithaca: Cornell Univ. Press, 1986); Carolyn Merchant *The Death of Nature: Women, Ecology and the Scientific Revolution* (San Francisco: Harper and Row, 1983).

Bacon's divergence from *Utopia*. What in *Utopia* is acknowledged under the aegis of "necessary" pleasure must in the *New Atlantis* be eradicated completely, its flames quenched lest they consume the whole community. Desire in Bensalem threatens always to become a raging furnace: as the rather frenetic tome of Joabin's discourse on desire makes plain, Bensalem's status as the "virgin of the world" is not merely metaphorical, but bespeaks the urgency of the land's eradication of desire. For like the double standard, the free play of desire would undermine Bensalemite certainty in the production of healthy offspring, a certainty whose value is emphasized not only in the Bensalemite discourse on human sexuality, but also in the description of the experiments undertaken in Salomon's House, where we see manifest a repeated concern with eugenics and selective breeding, both of plants, and of animals:

> we [can make] beasts ... greater or taller than their kind is; and contrariwise dwarf them, ... we make them more fruitful ... than their kind is; and contrariwise ... not generative.... We ... make ... copulations of different kinds; which have produced many new kinds, and them not barren.... We make a number of different kinds of serpents, ... of putrefaction; whereof some are advanced ... to be perfect creatures, like beasts or birds; and have sexes, and do propagate. (72–73)

"Neither do we do this by chance," they go on, "but we know beforehand of what matter and commixture what kind of those creatures will arise."

It is this concern for prior knowledge which motivates the changes which Bacon makes to the Utopian custom which impressed him so much. "So foul deformity may be hid under those coverings," says Hythloday describing the dangers of an o'er hasty marriage; "because of many hidden defects in men and women's bodies," Joabin transcribes the passage. Between "deformity" and "defect" lies a world of difference. In Utopia, I argued, the viewing of the spouse's body prior to marriage guarantees the satisfaction of the desiring male gaze, ensures the fulfillment of subsequent sexual desire. Dissatisfied on seeing, the male subject alone is permitted to request his love back, for this very rational custom is designed to serve the purposes of Utopian marriage, to avoid future strife, to ensure social stability. But in Bensalem, prospective spouses must be replaced by their more disinterested friends, for these, it is (perhaps rashly) assumed, can levy on the spouse's body an "objective" gaze, a gaze not subject to the desire which might lead a spouse to accept a partner *in despite of* his or her bodily shortcomings, and thus to put Bensalemite eugenics at risk.[28] Despite its more overtly patriarchal nature, then, Bensalem must eradicate, as entirely as possible, both male and female desire. It offers us instead an ideal society in which the body is no longer desired, but examined, examined not for its potential to ensure necessary (and subjective) pleasures, but for its threatening capacity to deviate from an objective state of scientific perfection.

---

[28] See Weinberger's excellent discussion of the incident in his introduction to the text. Bacon, xxiii–xxix.

STEPHEN CLUCAS

"A Knowledge Broken": Francis Bacon's Aphoristic Style and the Crisis of Scholastic and Humanist Knowledge-Systems

> "tyrannous aphorisms appear to them the highest points of wisdom; instilling their barren hearts with a conscientious slavery"
> (Milton, *Of Education*)

> "Is not thy common talke sound Aphorismes?"
> (Marlowe, *Doctor Faustus*)

1. Bacon and the anti-Ciceronian debate

FRANCIS BACON'S CONCEPTION OF AN INSTRUMENTAL, operative, and empirical natural philosophy in his *Advancement of Learning* and the *Novum Organum*[1] is wedded to an instrumental conception of rhetoric, whose "duty and office" was "to apply Reason to Imagination for the better moving of the will."[2] Above all Bacon was concerned to develop an instrumental *scientific* rhetoric — his brief, after all, was to "advance"

---

[1] See Antonio Perez-Ramos, *Francis Bacon's Idea of Science and the Maker's Knowledge Tradition* (Oxford: Clarendon Press, 1988), which situates Bacon within the "maker's tradition," i.e., that mode of thought which "postulates an intimate relationship between objects of cognition and objects of construction, and regards knowing as a kind of making." See especially pp. 48–62.

[2] *The Works of Francis Bacon*, ed. J. A. Spedding, R. L. Ellis, and D. D. Heath, (London, 1857–74), 3:409. All references to this edition will hereafter be cited parenthetically by volume and page number within the text.

the various fields of scientific endeavor. The aphoristic style of Bacon's writings on natural philosophy (and his recommendation of the aphoristic *method*), which have in the past been characterized as "Senecan" or "Attic,"[3] can perhaps be more usefully viewed in the context of a tradition of aphoristic scientific writing, and the anti-scholastic side of the English scientific renaissance. Bacon certainly participated in the substantial critique of Ciceronian eloquence which characterized a certain kind of English Protestant humanism from the 1580s onwards.[4] Whilst sympathetic to the reformational impulses of philological humanists who undermined their scholastic opponents by creating "new terms of art to express their own sense and to avoid circuit of speech" (3:283), these endeavours had lapsed (in Bacon's eyes) into the vice of excessive concern with eloquence:

> men began to hunt more after words than matter; more after the choiceness of phrase, and the round clean composition of the sentence, and the sweet falling of the clauses, and the varying and illustration of their works with tropes and figures, than after the weight of matter, worth of subject, soundness of argument, life of invention, or depth of judgement. . . . In sum, the whole inclination and bent of those times was rather towards copie than weight. (3:283-84)

But the thrust of his attack on the linguistic abuses is framed more in terms of its implications for scientific discourse than as a "stoic" humanist response to Ciceronian excess. Although he culls choice quotations from Seneca in the course of the *Advancement*, he could also be critical of the "short and dark sentences" of those who cultivated a sententious Senecan prose-style, which he considered just as much a "character of imposture" as the "great words and high discourse" of the Ciceronian (3:247).

---

[3] See, for example, M. W. Croll, *Style, Rhetoric and Rhythm: Essays*, ed. J. M. Patrick (Princeton: Princeton Univ. Press, 1966), 51–101, and 167–202; George Williamson, "Bacon and Stoic Rhetoric," in *The Senecan Amble : a study in prose-form from Bacon to Collier* (London: Faber, 1951), 150–85. A recent revaluation of the Senecan/Ciceronian opposition has been suggested in Roger Pooley, *English Prose of the Seventeenth-Century 1590–1700* (London: Longman, 1992), 8–10, although he makes no reference to the scientific prose tradition.

[4] On anti-Ciceronianism see J. W. Binns, "Ciceronianism in Sixteenth-Century England: the Latin debate," in *Intellectual Culture in Elizabethan and Jacobean England : the Latin writings of the Age* (Leeds: Francis Cairns, 1990), 270–90, and M. W. Croll, "Juste Lipse et le Mouvement Anticicéronien à la Fin du XVIe et au debut du XVIIe siècle," in Patrick, 7–44.

The communication of scientific knowledge should eschew rhetorical ornamentation (whether Ciceronian or Senecan), Bacon believed, or at least reduce it to a utilitarian minimum. In his *Parasceve, or Preparative towards a Natural and Experimentall History*, Bacon describes the ideal form of recording scientific observations, which has no room for humanist eloquence or sententious accumulation of *auctoritates*. The scientist should dispense with:

> antiquities, and citations or testimonies of authors; also with disputes and controversies and differing opinions; everything in short which is philological. Never cite an author except in a matter of doubtful credit: never introduce a controversy unless in a matter of great moment. And for all that concerns ornaments of speech, similitudes, treasury of eloquence and such like emptinesses, let it utterly be dismissed. Also let those things which are admitted be themselves set down briefly and concisely, so that they may be nothing less than words. (4:254)[5]

This injunction, as Brian Vickers has noted,[6] is not an attack on eloquence *per se*, but its inappropriate place in the collection of data. Using a mercantile or artisanal metaphor, Bacon notes that: "no man who is collecting and storing up materials for ship-building or the like, thinks of arranging them elegantly, as in a shop, and displaying them so as to please the eye; all his care is that they be sound and good, and that they be so arranged as to take up as little room as possible in the warehouse" (4:254-55).[7] Bacon was too much a product of the educational system of his time to reject humanist ideals of eloquence outright: "it is not a thing hastily to be condemned, to clothe and adorn the obscurity even of philosophy itself with sensible and plausible elocution. For hereof we have great examples in Xenophon, Cicero, Seneca, Plutarch, and of Plato." (3:284).

---

[5] Cf. the 1728 statutes of the Royal Society: "In all Reports of Experiments to be brought into the Society, the Matter of Fact shall be barely stated, without any Prefaces, Apologies, or Rhetorical Flourishes, and entered so into the Register-Book, by order of the Society," in R. F. Jones, *The Seventeenth Century: Studies in the History of English Thought and Literature from Bacon to Pope* (Stanford: Stanford Univ. Press, 1951), 84.

[6] "The Royal Society and English Prose-Style: A Reassessment," in B. Vickers and N. S. Struever, *Rhetoric and the Pursuit of Truth: Language Changes in the Seventeenth and Eighteenth Centuries* (Los Angeles: William Andrews Clark Library, 1985), 13.

[7] On the medieval mnemonic use of the "storehouse" image (i.e., the *thesaurus*) see Mary Carruthers, *The Book of Memory: Study of Memory in Mediaeval Culture* (Cambridge: Cambridge Univ. Press, 1992).

He was not averse, for example, to utilizing pagan mythology as a store of "lively images" with which to adorn the *Advancement of Learning* (or as the principal discursive medium of his *Sapientia veterum*), and his prose is studded with a wide variety of apposite sententious quotations culled from classical and contemporary authors. However, he is extremely ambivalent about the place of rhetoric in the prosecution of philosophy. "For surely," he says, "to the severe inquisition of truth and the deep progress into philosophy, it [i.e., *rhetoric*] is some hindrance; because it is too early satisfactory to the mind of man, and quencheth the desire of further search, before we have come to a just period." While it is perfectly acceptable for "civil occasions, of conference, counsel, persuasion, discourse, or the like," nonetheless "the excess of this is ... justly contemptible" especially to "the more severe and laborious sort of inquirers into truth" (3:284). Rhetoric to Bacon is vitiated when employed in a scientific context principally because of its tendency to procure complacency, or acceptance, because it "quencheth the desire of further search," it stifles the *progress* of scientific ideas. I think most of us would now accept Vickers' critique of R. F. Jones, when he argues that "it is not true ... that Bacon had an 'antipathy' to language — but only language in science when it merely reflects and reproduces age-old categories ... which are not tested by reference to reality."[8] Bacon was concerned with language as a tool or instrument for a more direct, operative engagement with "the real" — he sought a new "rhetoric of the real" through which one could break open the "orb or circle" of philological or scholastic procedures and argumentative techniques. Scholastic science is characterized by Bacon as another form of verbal abuse. Aristotle himself is seen as having "made his natural philosophy a mere bond-servant to his logic, thereby rendering it contentious and well-nigh useless" (4:59). The vocabulary of science itself is problematic because of the ossification and inflexibility of accepted usages, which Bacon calls the "Idols of the market Place":

> men believe that their reason governs words; but it is also true that words react on the understanding; and this it is has rendered philosophy and the sciences sophistical and inactive ... words, being commonly framed and applied according to the capacity of the vulgar, follow those lines of division which are most obvious to the vulgar understanding. And whenever an understanding of

---

[8] Vickers and Struever, 12.

greater acuteness or a more diligent observation would alter those lines to suit the true divisions of nature, words stand in the way and resist the change. (4:61).

In fact Bacon says, "There are ... in words certain degrees of distortion and error" (4:62), which are compounded by "The Idols of the Theatre" or "the play-books of philosophical systems" (4:63) which generate, systematize, and compound erroneous vocabularies.

Of the various scholastic techniques, Bacon is particularly critical of the use of *quaestiones* — "the handling of knowledge by ... Questions and their Determinations" (3:405) — whereby various objections to Aristotelian positions are first propounded and then resolved. This method, "if it be immoderately followed," says Bacon, "is as prejudicial to the proceeding of learning, as it is to the proceeding of an army to go about to besiege every little fort or hold" (3:405-6).[9] This "unprofitable subtility or curiosity" affects both the subject of investigation (which can degenerate into "fruitless speculation or controversy") and the method itself, which framed objections to "every particular position or assertion ... and to those objections, solutions; which solutions were for the most part not confutations but distinctions" (3:286). This continual act of distinction and sub-distinction is compared to untying "the bond" which holds together a faggot, and becomes *verborum minutiis* rather than effective discourse. One could "truly say of the schoolmen," he says, that they "fragment the sciences with their over-subtle questions" (*Quaestionum minutiis scientiarium frangunt soliditatem*) (3:286).[10] Just as the humanists fail in their search for truth in "arguments, authorities, similitudes, [and] examples," so the scholastics fail by "particular confutations and solutions of every scruple, cavillation, and objection" which breeds "one question as fast as it solveth another" (3:286). Allegorizing the myth of Scylla, Bacon sees the "generalities of the schoolmen" as "for a while good and proportionable," but "when you descend into their distinctions ... instead of a fruitful womb for the use and benefit of man's life, they end in monstrous altercations and barking questions" (3:286-87). This kind of philosophical discourse descends into "idle words" (*verba ... otiosorum*) and becomes

---

[9] On the role of *quaestiones* in the Aristotelian scientific tradition see Brian Lawn, *The Rise and Decline of the Scholastic 'Quaestio Disputata': with Special Emphasis on its Use in the Teaching of Medicine and Science* (Leiden: E. J. Brill, 1993).

[10] Cf. Montaigne's "De l'Experience" in *Essays*, trans. J. M. Cohen (Harmondsworth: Penguin Books, 1958, repr. 1982), 346-47.

detached from practice and use. As a form of language which was based on "knowledge drawn freshly ... out of particulars" (3:453), the aphorism seemed to Bacon to be the best antidote to the linguistic quibbling of contemporary scientific discourse.

2. Bacon and the Scientific Aphorism

As a response to the perceived linguistic constraints upon contemporary knowledge, Bacon's adoption of the aphorism is an attempt not merely to reform literary expression, but to initiate and effect epistemological and discursive change. Although he does (to some extent) characterize the aphorism in the familiar terms of its sententious plenitude and compression — it is described as presenting the "pith and heart of sciences" (3:405) — he sees the aphorism serving a specific epistemological function, a function which reverses the authority and closure which often attends the aphoristic in the Renaissance.[11] Bacon was certainly not opposed — in the literary sphere — to the conventional role of sententious modes of discourse. In his *Apophthegmes New and Old*, for example, he approves the conventional Ciceronian use of gleaned *sententiae*:

> They are, *Mucrones verborum, Pointed speeches*. *Cicero* prettily cals them, *Salinas, salt pits*; that you may extract salt out of it, and sprinkle it, where you will. They serue, to be interlaced, in continued speech. They serue to be recited, vpon occasion of themselues. They serue, if you take out the kernell of them, and make them your owne.[12]

That is, sententious utterances can be interwoven into one's own compositions, as an ornament, to give one's discourse "savour." Even in this context, however, Bacon is concerned with utility (apophthegmes are "of excellent vse")[13] and, although not a major element of the volume, some of the aphorisms cited relate to his scientific project.[14] He also contrasts

---

[11] On the tension between closure and discursive openness in the seventeenth-century aphorism see Roland Barthes, "La Rochefoucauld: 'Reflections or Sentences and Maxims,'" in *New Critical Essays*, trans. Richard Howard (New York: Farrar, Strauss & Giroux, 1980, repr. Berkeley: Univ. of California Press, 1990), 3–22.

[12] Francis Bacon, *Apophthegmes New and Old — Collected by the right honourable, Francis Lo[rd] Verulam Viscount St Albans* (London, 1625), 3–5.

[13] Ibid., 3.

[14] See, for e.g., aphorism 189, ibid., 45–46.: "Aristippus sayd, *That those that studied*

the utility of aphorisms "chosen with Iudgement and Choice" with modern humanist practice in this area. The collected apophthegmes of Plutarch and Stobaeus, he says, "and much more, the *Moderne* ones, draw much of the dregs."[15] He is certainly not opposed to the use of the aphorism as a hortative and dogmatic device conveying "axioms and advices" and "divers precepts of great caution and direction" (3:440-41) in the moral sphere of "cultivation of the soul" (*cultura animi*).[16] He expends a number of pages of the *Advancement of Learning*, for example, in glossing some of the aphorisms and "sentences politic" of Solomon, whose "profound and excellent cautions, precepts [and] positions" apply to "much variety of occasions" (3:447-52).[17] In this case, Bacon sees the aphorism as authoritative, he is — in his own words — "led by a desire to give authority to this part of knowledge," for "it is allowed in divinity that ... some writings, have more of the Eagle than others" (3:453), and he extends this also to the "wisdom of more ancient times" when moral wisdom was gathered or expressed "in parable or aphorism or fable" (3:453). This desire for aphoristic authority was not extended to natural philosophy. In the scientific domain Bacon had to unmake the aphoristic tradition as it already existed in the humanist tradition, and restore it to what he sees as its pristine scientific character — as a non-dogmatic and initiative form of language, ideally fitted to the requirements of reformulating and advancing *scientific* practice and use:

> the first and most ancient seekers after truth were wont, with better faith and better fortune too, to throw the knowledge which they gathered from the contemplation of things, and which they meant to store up for use, into aphorisms; that is, into short and scattered sentences, not linked together by an artificial method; and did not pretend or profess to embrace the entire art. (4:85)

This view of the aphorism as provisional and unauthoritative, goes against much of the accepted Renaissance understanding of the aphorism, in both the humanist and scientific domain. Humanists viewed the aphorism, in

---

particular sciences, & neglected Philosophie, were like Penelopes Wooers, that made loue to the waiting women."

[15] Ibid., 2-3.

[16] See ibid., 3:432-33, where Bacon uses *sententiae* gleaned from Cicero, Seneca and Hippocrates in support of the textual "husbandry" of the soul.

[17] The perceived rhetorical character of these aphorisms can be gleaned from Bacon's glosses: "Here is taxed...," "Here is commended...," "Here caution is given...," etc.

accordance with post-classical and medieval rhetorical authorities,[18] as a kind of *sententia*, or "concise expression" (*sermo breuis*) in which "the whole meaning of the subject matter of a discourse is written."[19] Julius Rufinianus, for example, characterized the aphorism as "a figure in which something is elucidated by means of very short clauses,"[20] while Coelius Aurelianus, with even more emphasis on the aphorism's plenitude stated that: "Aphorisms are *sententiae*, in which all or at least the most important principles of a science or art are briefly contained."[21]

The use of the term *aphorismus* itself owed a great deal of its currency to the scientific (and specifically the medical) tradition, through the title of Hippocrates' *Aphorisms*. Hippocrates' "Compendious and aphoristic doctrine"[22] did much to formulate the idea of the aphorism as the vehicle for compressed dogmatic wisdom. Its pedagogical associations, and particularly its task of defining the canonical axioms of a discipline, made it a "probative" discourse (in Bacon's terms) of the highest order. The task of aphoristic discourse in this context was to confer expertise on scientific apprentices. The purpose of the Hippocratic aphorism was to inculcate an indisputable corpus of medical wisdom, not to stir students to further inquiry. In the sixteenth century this scientific tradition of "sermo breuis" was accommodated to the sententious *collocatio* of the *studia humanitatis*. Thus in 1590, Hippocrates' aphorisms are presented by Ioannes Lygaeus "elucidated with succinct paraphrases, added briefly to each book, together with the argument of the aphorisms" and "noteworthy *sententiae*

---

[18] For the following (and other) definitions of the aphorism see "aphorismus" in A. Forcellini et al., *Lexicon Totius Latinitatis* (Padua, 1864), 1:276, *Thesaurus Linguae Latinae* (Leipzig, 1900–1906), 2:Col. 230, 9–15, and *Oxford Dictionary of Mediaeval Latin* (Oxford: Oxford Univ. Press, 1975), 1:99.

[19] Isidorus, *Origines* 4,10,1: "integrum sensum propositae rei scribens." Cf. Gregorius Magister, *De mirabilibus Urbis Romae*, 33: "An aphorism is a concise expression which demonstrates perfectly the whole meaning of the matter to be discussed" (Amphorismus est sermo breuis integre rei perfectum sensum demonstrans).

[20] J. Rufinianus, *De figuris sententiarum et elocutionis liber*: "figura, qua aliquid per incisam majore in luce collocatur."

[21] Coelius Aurelianus, *Actuarum seu celerium passionum libri tres*, 3,1,5: "Aphorismi sunt sententiae, quae omnia vel praecipua saltem scientiae vel artis alicujus principia paucis concludunt."

[22] *Hippocrates Aphorismi... cum Guilielmi Plantii Latina interprete et Ioannis Lygaei luculenta Paraphrasi* (Geneva, 1590), 3: "Aphoristicam & compendiosam doctrinam." It is in the medical context which Faustus uses the term "aphorism" in the header quote: "Be a physition Faustus, heape vp golde /... The end of phisicke is our bodies health: / Why Faustus hast thou not attaind the end? / Is not thy common talke sound Aphorismes?"

selected out of the books of Aurelius Cornelius Celsus, one of the most eloquent of Latin physicians."[23] The perceived sententious qualities of Hippocrates[24] are thus augmented by the addition of short expository arguments, and supplemented by equally succinct and brief *lectiones* culled and condensed from Celsus's writings. The exegetical framing of Hippocrates' doctrines stresses the magisterial and dogmatic function of the work in its pedagogical context. In a different pedagogical context, that concerned with the transmission of religious tenets, there is a similar stress on the magisterial and sententious plenitude of the aphorism. Philip Melanchthon in his treatment of the *ars concionandi* had insisted that texts could be reduced to a series of single propositions, or *sententiae* "to which all the arguments of a piece refer, which are expounded and set forth at length in the text as a whole."[25] When reading a text one must reduce it to a "few apt clear and convenient" propositions, drawing out a "clear and certain testimony" of its meaning, which minimizes obscurity and ambiguity (*minimum obscuritatis . . . & minimum ambiguitatis habent*).[26] This was certainly an important criterion for the German pedagogue Johann Piscator, whose methodical reduction of Calvin's *Institutes of Christian Religion* was translated into English by Henry Holland in 1596 as *Aphorismes of Christian Religion*.[27] Piscator considered the aphorism to be coidentical with *sententiae*: "a short sentence selected and set apart, or a definition, distinction, &c."[28]

---

[23] Ibid., title page: "succinctibus paraphrasibus illustrati, adiecto breui in singulos libros & aphorismos argumento" and p. 3: "Insigniores aliquot sententiae selectae ex libris Aurelij Cornelij Celsi medici inter Latinos eloquentissimi." The aphorisms of Celsus are added after the Hippocratic aphorisms, ibid., 347–67.

[24] Many of Hippocrates's aphorisms have the quality of Renaissance *adagia*; see for example aphorism 34, ibid., 351: "Diluted wine is appropriate for the young, undiluted for the old" (Vinum dilutius pueris, meracius senibus conuenit).

[25] I quote here from an anonymous contemporary digest of Melanchthon's ideas, the *Ratio breuis sacrarum concionum Tractandarum, a quodam docto, & pio rhapsodo, Philippi Melanchthonis, similia, congesta*, published by Henry Bynneman, together with Johannes Reuchlin's *Liber congestorum de arte praedicandi* and Johannes Hepini's *De sacris concionibus* with the title *De arte concionandi formulae, ut breues, ita doctae & piae* (London, 1570), sig. C vi^r. Cf. also Robert Dallington's *Aphorismes Civill and Militarie* (London, 1613), sig. A4^v, where he insists that his aphoristic gleanings are not "so loose but that . . . you may ciment them together, and make them con-center into the maine proposition."

[26] Ibid., sig. Eiij^{r-v}.

[27] *Aphorismes of Christian Religion: or, a verie compendious Abridgement of M.I.Caluins Institutions, set forth in short sentences methodically by M.I.Piscator . . . Englished . . . By H. Holland* (London, 1596).

[28] Ibid., 1.

The purpose of culling and reducing Calvin's text in this fashion was, according to Holland, to "giue the willing mind in a uery small time a synopsis or short view of the whole bodie of Gods holy truth."[29] And although its aphoristic style was designed to "excite" and "helpe forwarde" the young "scholers" which were its intended audience, its effect was intended to be unambiguously authoritative. "I rather call these sentences, Aphorismes," Piscator says, "then (as they be called vsually) theames, or questions, for the word *thesis* carieth some signes of doubtfulnesse with it, as may be seene with Aristotle in his Topickes, are said ... to set downe some thing which they do not auouch to be true.... But these sentences contained in these Aphorismes are neither absurde ... nor such as any Christian may lawfully doubt off."[30] They are reduced to unambiguous propositions so that "our auditorie may the better see and know the truth of them, and to be more assured of the same."[31] Piscator renounces the Ciceronian ideal of a "copious style," stressing instead the didactic "solidity" of the aphoristic style, whose "one drift and scope" is "to instruct soundly," significantly allying his stylistic project to a magisterial scientific demonstration:

> these short Aphorismes containe the chiefe points of Christia[n] Religion barely propounded, much like a withered body, or certaine iointes and bones without skinne, flesh or synewes, such as Anatomistes reserue for demonstration sake. So here we have taken away the fulnes and glory of that stile, as the skinne and flesh therof: but the sentences ... are like bare and naked bones knit and jointed one with the other ... firme and solid things indeede, which neither want good synews, nor iuice and marow of heauenly doctrine in them.[32]

Similar pedagogical attitudes to the aphorism can be found in other

---

[29] Ibid., sig. iij*ᵛ.
[30] Ibid., sig. Aiiijᵛ–Avʳ.
[31] Ibid., sig. Avʳ.
[32] Ibid., sig. Avᵛ–Aviʳ. For an earlier example of this pedagogical rhetoric of brevity see Humfrey Lloyd's collection of medical "Aphorismes ... gathered out of ... the most noble and Auncient phisicians," *The Treasury of healthe* (London, 1550), sig. Aiiiᵛ: "I shal most hartly desyre the gentle reader to pardon my audacity & beare wyth my sclender iudgment, and not to despyse this simple worke because it is not garnished wyth colours of rethorick and fyne polished termes, but rather to consyder that Physike is an arte contente only to be playnly and distinctlye taught and nothing desirous to be adourned and decte with eloquence and gay paynted sentences."

scientific writings of Bacon's time. John Dee, for example, in his *Propaedeumata aphoristica*,[33] in which he outlines a new astrological technique based on the conic propagation of astral influences, presents his work within a context of humanist reading-practices. His work, he stresses, has been gleaned carefully: "whatever parts are choicest collected 'harmoniously' into one solid frame."[34] Like Lygaeus's selections from Celsus, these brief expressions are "selectissima" and (unlike Bacon's "knowledge broken") form a "solid body" of doctrine. Dee's advice about using his aphoristic text also stresses a humanist model of reading: "if you will search diligently in repeated readings, by weighing everything with great care you will assuredly observe, besides the most excellent discoveries of all our ancestors, with what wonderful and honourable ornaments the composition is packed."[35] Knowledge is to be accessed through "repeated readings" (*frequenti . . . lectione*), and consists in appreciation of both inventions (*inventa*) and ornaments (*ornamentis*). Which is to say, through the search for both *sententia* and *elocutio*. Nonetheless, this is a scientific text, and it does anticipate a reader essentially in search of *scientia*, rather than *eloquentia*. He sees his aphorisms, like those of Hippocrates, as compendiously laying out the axiomatic foundations of his science ("the main principles of the science have been laid down and established here").[36] However, unlike the pedagogical Hippocratic *gradatim* structure, Dee's aphorisms assume a prior expertise on the part of the reader: "The aphorisms are for the more advanced, the books will certainly be rather long and difficult for those who have made less progress in the understanding of the many and great sciences."[37] This is because Dee's aphorisms are produced as part of an occult discourse, where the very opacity of the aphoristic pronouncement is seen as a necessary defense against the vulgar and impious reader, and as an insurance of an elite audience: "You must not reveal openly to unworthy and profane persons what — driven by a yearning to illuminate and broaden the truth so that it might be fully apparent only to you — I have stretched the sinews of my poor wit to provide."[38]

---

[33] John Dee, *Propaedeumata aphoristica* (London, 1558, repr., 1568), repr. and trans. W. Shumaker and J. L. Heilbron, *John Dee on Astronomy, Propaedeumata Aphoristica (1558 and 1568), Latin and English* (Berkeley: Univ. of California Press, 1978).

[34] Ibid., 120: "Omne, vel SELECTISSIMA QUAEQUE potius IN CORPUS UNUM SOLIDUM *apmonikos* CONGLOBATA."

[35] Ibid., 121.
[36] Ibid., 113.
[37] Ibid., 120–21.
[38] Ibid., 121. Cf. also ibid., 113: "I request you publicly that no 'incautious person'

These aphorisms are not for students, but are things "credible to a few wise men, but known only to a very few" (*paucis vix credibiles Sapientibus, paucissimis notas*), and not fitted for the "incautious person"[39] and for someone more used to scholastic philosophy (*ex communi, tritave philosophia via*).[40] Paradoxically, this exclusive and expert discourse is held to possess an axiomatic clarity. In a letter to William Camden, for example, Dee held that the first aphorism of his *Propaedeumata* was a canonical foundation for his whole art: "Immediately in the first aphorism (not to speak of the others) the firm foundation of a certain great art is displayed, which (very concisely) is explained by me."[41] This aphorism is, in fact, merely a general statement — a declaration of theurgical intent — that it is not possible to perform operations which contravene the laws of nature without God's aid.[42] This uneasy coexistence of canonical clarity and occult figuration is characteristic of the work as a whole. His aphorism 92, for example:

> Any two stars, when positioned on opposite sides of the earth in equal declinations over the same part of the earth, stay equal distances from the same meridian, all the impingements of the rays will make equal angles. Accordingly, through the diurnal motion of the whole, those stars, by their rays, enwrap and embrace any terrestrial bodies by turns, as if a similar care had been committed to them.[43]

Beginning with the geometrical rhetoric of the Euclidian proposition with its equal declinations (*aequales ... declinatione*) and angles (*angulos ... aequales*), the aphorism veers into analogical and metaphoric language of alchemical discourse: stars enwrapping, embracing, and caring for their

---

should strive to fish out and draw forth from them, to his harm, things that are not written for him."

[39] Ibid., 112–13.

[40] Ibid., 121.

[41] John Dee to William Camden, 7 August 1574, Bodleian Library, MS. Ashmole 1788, fol. 72: "At in primo statim aphorismo meo (ut caetera taceam) artis cuiusdam magnae jactum est fundamentum firmum, quae (breuissime) ... explicata est."

[42] Shumaker and Heilbron, *John Dee on Astronomy*, 122–23: "As God created all things from nothing against the laws of reason and nature, so anything created can never be reduced to nothing unless this is done through the supernatural power of God and against the laws of reason and nature" (Ut deus, ex nihilo, contra rationis & naturae leges, cuncta creauit : ita in Nihilum abire, rerum creaturam aliqua nunquam potest, nisi contra rationis Naturaeque leges, per Supernaturalem Dei potentiam fiat).

[43] Ibid., 177–78.

terrestrial charges (*per mutuas vices ita involvunt, implicantque, ac si, eiusdem, illis esset similis commissa cura*). This mixing of argumentative registers is also found in the aphoristic "theorems" of Dee's *Monas Hieroglyphica*.[44]

Dee's use of the aphorism was not without its precedents in the magical tradition. Arbatel's *De Magia* was also written in the form of aphorisms, comprising "nine Tomes, and seven septenaries of APHORISMS." Like Dee, Arbatel stresses both the pedagogical function of the aphorism (each of the septenaries "teacheth the operations" of a particular branch of magic) and the precautionary opacity of its compression, which protects the magical knowledge from the impious, as the prefatory quotation from Prov. 11 makes clear: "He that walketh fraudulently, revealeth secrets, but he that is of a faithful spirit, concealeth the matter." As in Dee's work, the interpretative circularity of the statements is not seen as a barrier to their function as axiomatic propositions. The volume begins with a set of aphorisms which "is called *Isagoge* or, A Book of the Institutions of Magick ... which in fourty and nine Aphorisms comprehendeth the most general Precepts of the whole Art," but like Dee's, these consist mostly of the statement of a theurgic "code of practice."[45] Nicholas Hill's unusual and eclectic volume of aphorisms, the *Philosophia Epicurea*, while it insists on its freedom from dogmatic authority ("I do not propound anything dogmatically, but leave each to judge for himself"),[46] nonetheless uses the aphoristic method in a largely iterative, propositional and probative manner. There are definitions (e.g., "The primary seed is atomic matter, which is combined into figures by divine power")[47] and proofs (e.g., aphorism 434, in which "The motion of the earth is sufficiently proven"),[48] which are sometimes accompanied by the marginal citations of *auctoritates*.[49] Like Bacon, Hill seems to be positing the aphorism as a

---

[44] John Dee, *Monas Hieroglyphica Ioannis Dee, Londinensis, ad maximilianum, Dei Gratia Romanorum Bohemiae et Hungariae regem sapientissimum* (Antwerp, 1564). In a list of his "vnprinted Bookes and Treatises" appended to *A Letter containing a most briefe discourse Apologeticall* (London, 1599), sig. A4ᵛ, Dee refers to a collection of three hundred aphorisms written in 1553 entitled *Aphorismi Astrologici*.

[45] *Arbatel of Magick, or the Spiritual Wisdom of the Ancients*, in *Henry Cornelius Agrippa his Fourth Book of Occult Philosophy*, trans. Robert Turner (London, 1655), 177–78.

[46] Nicholas Hill, *Philosophia Epicurea, Democritiana, Theophrastica proposita simpliciter, non edocta, per Nicolaum Hill Anglum, Londinensum* (Paris, 1601), sig. Aiiiᵛ: "me nihil proponere dogmatice, sed suum vnicuique permittere arbitrium."

[47] Ibid., aphorism 4, sig. Aʳ: "Semen primarium est materiae atomicae, figurae virtutisque diuinae prima complexio."

[48] Ibid., 92: "Terrae Motum sufficienter probant."

[49] Aphorism 434, for example, refers the reader to Hermes Trismegistus, Cusanus,

practical discursive alternative to the linguistic redundancy of scholasticism, which he criticizes as: "the incongruous forms of an immoderate and argumentative wit, consisting of disadvantageous inventions, and matter which could be composed in precepts using clear and simple words wrapped up in a multitude of impertinences."[50] Another tradition of aphoristic scientific writing which opposed scholastic forms of discourse is represented by the Aristotelian university tradition, which sometimes presented Aristotle's teachings in a condensed, sententious form. Johannes Magirius, for example, in his *Physiologiae Peripateticae* presents Aristotle's teachings in aphorisms (e.g., "Heat is a primary active quality, which brings together homogenous things, and dissipates heterogenous things. See Book Two, Section 8 of Aristotle, *De generatione et corruptione* and Book Three, section 74 of *De Caelo*").[51] These are good examples of the "tyrannous aphorism": brevity as fixity, closure, and authority.[52] Magirius's editor, Conrad Nebenius, is in no doubt about the virtues of this aphoristic brevity:

> He has collected together accurately and clearly, briefly, methodically and compendiously, in a manner fitted to the nature of study, things scattered far and wide in Aristotle's books on physics, and in the most outstanding writings of the philosophers, omitting the obscure and thorny disputations.... He does not elucidate by means of commentary and *quaestiones*, but corrects, picks out and edits [the texts], putting them into the form of little precepts [*praeceptiunculas*], which seem to disagree with the common norms of the art.[53]

Nicetas, Copernicus, Bruno, Gilbert, and Patrizzi.

[50] Ibid., aphorism 219, 32 : "forma argumentoso & luxurianti ingenio incongrua, inuentioni aduersissima & res per se satis manifestas simplici verborum textura praeceptorum impertinentium multitudine inuoluit." Hill also shares a number of other of Bacon's scientific ideals, such as the need for scientific cooperation – see ibid., Aphorism 227, 33: "The rocky and wave-tossed ocean of the arts cannot be navigated by one hand alone, but needs the co-operation of many individuals" (Scopuloso fluctuosque artium oceano non una manu nauagibili, sed multos cooperarios exigente).

[51] Johannes Magirius, *Ioannis Magiri Physiologiae Peripateticae libri sex cum commentariis ... Editio Quinta* (Leipzig, 1611): "Calor est qualitas prima actiua, Congregans homogenea & disgregans heterogenea. Arist. Lib.2 de ortu & c.2 tex. 8 & Lib. 3 de Caelo, c. 8, tex. 74."

[52] Closure is completed by adding recent Aristotelian authors – such as Jakob Schegk or Giacomo Zabarella – as corroborative *auctoritates*. For another example of the "aphoristic Aristotle" see Felix Accorombonius, *Interpretatio Obscuriorum locorum & sententiarum omnium operum Aristotelis* (Rome, 1590).

[53] Ibid., 9: "ex omnibus Aristotelis libris Physicis longe lateque diffusis, necnon ex

Brief, methodical, compendious — the aphorism by its compression excludes the "thorny and obscure disputations" prompted by the more "diffuse" style of the schoolmen. It is "useful," especially in educational terms.[54] This stress on a brief and utilitarian discourse was fast becoming a normative value in late sixteenth-century Europe, at least in educational circles (largely as a result of the teachings of Sturm, Melanchthon, and Ramus).[55] Considerations of the benefits of "methodical" writing or *via compendiaria* were becoming an intrinsic part of logical and rhetorical treatises, and these evidently had an influence on Bacon (although he doesn't cite any of the more obvious of his predecessors).[56] Giacomo Aconzio, or Acontius, for example, an influential emigree voice in Elizabethan and Jacobean England,[57] in his *De Methodo* (Basel, 1558) — which claims to treat "the correct method for communicating and investigating in the sciences"[58] — emphasizes the need for a departure from the "obscure and thorny style" of the scholastics, which is useful for disputation, but does not *invent* new objects of thought.[59] The Acontian method aimed at aphoristic qualities: "the maximum of brevity combined with the maximum of perspicuity,"[60]

---

praestantissimorum Philosophorum scriptis, omissis obscurioribus ac spinosis disputationibus, accurata & dilucida, breuique Methodo compendium de nature studio collegisset ... non Commentariis modo & quaestionibus valde utilitas ac necessariis illustrauit, sed praeceptiunculas etiam alicubi in eo positas, quae as communis artium normas dissentaneae videbantur, correxit, expunxit sustulit."

[54] Nebenius particularly praises the collection's "singular use and convenience" for teaching in the German academies (singularem vsum atque commoditatem omnibus fere in Germania Academis).

[55] See for example the attack on the books of the scholastics "entangled with thorny and intricate questions and quiddities" (spinosis et intricatio quaestionibus et quidditatibus involutur) by the Christ Church dialectician John Argall, in his *Ad artem dialecticam introductio* (London, 1605), cit. in B. Lawn, *Rise and Decline*, 132. See also I. Thomas, "Mediaeval Aftermath: Oxford Logic and Logicians of the Seventeenth-Century," in *Oxford Studies Presented to Daniel Callus* (Oxford: Clarendon Press for the Oxford Historical Society, 1964), 297–311.

[56] See Walter J. Ong, *Ramus, Method and the Decay of Dialogue* (Cambridge: Harvard Univ. Press, 1958, repr. 1983), 226: 'Bacon's interest in method and his interest in aphorisms go together.'

[57] See Charles D. O'Malley, *Jacopo Aconcio*, trans. Delio Cantimori, (Rome: Edizioni de Storia e Letteratura, 1955), Paolo Rossi, *Giacomo Aconcio* (Milan: Storia Universale della Filosofia, 1952), and F. Meli, *Spinoza e due antecedenti italiani dello spinozismo* (Florence, 1934).

[58] J. Acontius, *De Methodo* (Basel, 1558), titlepage: "de recta inuestigandarum tradendarumque scientarium ratione."

[59] Ibid., 7–8: "obscuro ... ac spinoso dicendi genere."

[60] Ibid., 15: "maximam breuitatem cum pari perspicuitate coniungeremus." Cf. also

and — like Bacon — links utility and lack of verbosity: "In the arts, usefulness does not consist in cognition, but in use: it is necessary if you want to extract the use out of any art, that its precepts be ready to hand... and all verbosity is avoided"[61] But if Bacon shared Acontius's goals in so far as he wished to promote an unambiguous and utilitarian scientific discourse, he did not see the aphoristic method as merely a compendious transmission of ready-formed truths in the shape of "absolute and perspicuous precepts" (*absoluta ac perspicua ... praecepta*).[62] In this Acontius is closer to Ramus and the Aristotelian pedagogic tradition. The Ramist conception of method, "which locates the universal and general things first, then the special and secondary afterwards,"[63] is the opposite of Baconian induction, which starts with particulars, before constructing general statements. Ramus was, as Ong has rightly pointed out,[64] "curiously unscientific" as regards the field of empirical investigation which was Bacon's province: "logic has nothing to do with it, for it is a matter of mechanics and action, that is, of dealing with the thing itself and effecting it, and it is thus managed not by means of argument but by means of hands and feet and other bodily instruments."[65] To the extent that Ramus's conception of the scientific field was a pre-existent corpus of essential truths to be ordered, disposed, and arranged in an effective pedagogical order, his concept of "method" is at variance with Bacon's, which stresses

---

ibid., 51 where the ideal style is described as being "above all plain and perspicuous, that is, composed of literal words in common usage, with nothing obscure, ambiguous or translated at too great length" (insuper plana & perspicua, hoc est, si constet uerbis proprijs & usitatis, non autem obscuris, ambiguius, aut ex longinquo translatis).

[61] Ibid., 15: "Nam cum artium utilitas non ex earum cognitione, sed usu constet: necesseque fit, si quidem arte aliqua uti uelis, eius tibi praecepta esse in promptu... verbositas omnis fugienda." Cf. ibid., 59: "It is is necessary that this is all expressed clearly and perspicuously, in as few words as possible, so that nothing is redundant and nothing left out" (necesse est ut haec omnia exprimantur uerbis claris, ac perspicuis & quoad eius fieri poterit paucissimus, ita ut nihil desit, nihil redundet). Acontius' *De Methodo*, and the "sentential" tradition of Hippocratic and Aristotelian translation represent a neglected source in considerations of "plain style" in England, which has traditionally been related more readily (if not more accurately) to the literary Ciceronian/Senecan debate.

[62] Ibid., 5.

[63] Pierre Ramus, *Dialectici commentarii tres authore Audomaro Talaeo editi* (Paris, 1546), 84: "Methodus igitur et certa dispositionis via sola requiritur, quam unam simplicem doctrina nobis ostendit universa primum generaliaque, deinde specialia et secondaria collocantem."

[64] Ong, *Ramus*, 269.

[65] P. Ramus, *Dialectica A. Talaei praelectionibus illustrata* (Basel, 1569), 520.

the need to stimulate fresh inquiry, not rearrange extant knowledge:

> There are and can be only two ways of searching into and discovering truth. The one flies from the senses and particulars to the most general axioms, and from these principles, the truth of which it takes for settled and immoveable, proceeds to judgement and to the discovery of middle axioms. And this way is now in fashion. The other derives axioms from the senses and particulars, rising by a gradual and unbroken ascent, so that it arrives at the most general axioms last of all. This is the true way, but as yet untried. (4:50)

Bacon seeks to use the aphorism not to compendiate the axioms of an alternative natural philosophy (he does not yet have a system to replace the Aristotelian corpus), but to promote and invigorate dissatisfaction with contemporary philosophical discourse and its concepts and create new epistemological grounds from which to interrogate the particulars or *specialia* which Ramus rejects as merely artisanal products "beneath the attention of an educated man."[66] Whereas Ramus is still caught up in the humanist belief that the ancients possess the height of human knowledge, and consequently sees knowledge as essentially the intelligent manipulation of (preferably classical) texts, Bacon was much closer to a new current of experimental (or experiential) science in continental Europe.[67] Robert Ashley's translation of Louis le Roy's *De la Vicissitude ou variété des choses en l'univers* (Paris, 1575), for example, breathes the atmosphere of Bacon's *Advancement*, and it is difficult not to see it as an influence on his work:[68]

> let vs not be so simple, as to attribute so much vnto the Auncients, that wee beleeue that they haue knowen all, and said all; without leaving anything to be said... considering the difficultie of knowledge, and the weaknes of mans understanding, they haue exhorted others to trauaile therein; speaking rather to stir them up,

---

[66] Ong, *Ramus*, 268.

[67] On the problematic definition of "experiment" in the early-modern period see Nicholas Clulee, *John Dee's Natural Philosophy — Between Science and Religion* (London: Routledge, 1988), 170–74, and D. Deleule, "Experientia-Experimentum ou le mythe d'expérience chez Francis Bacon" in M. Fattori, ed. *Francis Bacon, Terminologia e Fortuna nel XVII Secolo* (Rome: Ateneo, 1984), 59–72.

[68] See F. R. Johnson, *Astronomical Thought in Renaissance England* (Baltimore: Johns Hopkins Univ. Press, 1937), 297: "It was undoubtedly known to Bacon, although, as was often his custom, he made no specific acknowledgement of his indebtedness."

and prouoke them therevnto, then to keepe them back, or stay them from writing.⁶⁹

Like Bacon, Le Roy values "long experience" and "diligent observation" in scientific matters, and felt that "there was never [an] age more happie for the aduancement of learning."⁷⁰ Bacon's aphoristic method has much in common with Le Roy's conception of classical philosophy. The Baconian "method of aphorisms" was to "stir" and "prouoke" men to knowledge, not to "keepe them back" with tyrannous axioms. If the humanist, the occult-scientific, and the pedagogical traditions stressed the aphorism's ability to contain the "integrum sensum" of a science, communicating essential truths with a miraculous brevity and concision, Bacon thus radically resituated it. Instead of viewing it as an ornamental figure in rhetoric (which he sees as a performative "illustration of tradition"), he sees it as a "method of tradition" (3:403, 408-9) – "method" in the logical sense of that word in the Renaissance as something which "precedeth delivery" which is "material ... to the use of knowledge" (3:403),⁷¹ which not only enhances the "use" of knowledge, but also contributes to its "progression," because it "inspireth the felicity of continuing and proceeding." These two parts of method he calls the "magistral" (the part of method which is "referred to Use") and the "probative" (that which is "referred to Progression," 3:403). The aphoristic, then, is not merely a stylistic or rhetorical feature, but inextricably linked to the use and progression of knowledge. As a "scientific" method, the aphorism had for Bacon one great advantage: it was especially fitted to stimulate men's curiosity, and spur them on to inquire further: "Aphorisms, representing a knowledge broken, do invite men to enquire farther; whereas [other] Methods, carrying the shew of a total, do secure men, as if they were at furthest" (3:405). One of the major flaws of the "probative" aspect of contemporary method, Bacon thought, was that philosophers were over-

---

⁶⁹ Robert Ashley, *Of the Interchangeable Course, or Variety of Things in the Whole World* (London, 1594), fol. 127ʳ.

⁷⁰ Ibid.

⁷¹ Bacon says, for example, that "Method hath been placed and not amiss, in logic, as a part of judgement." For various perspectives on Renaissance concepts of "method" see Ong, *Ramus*, 225-69 et passim, Neil W. Gilbert, *Renaissance Concepts of Method* (New York: Columbia University Press, 1960), Wolfgang Schmidt-Biggemann, *Topica Universalis, eine Modellgeschichte humanistischer und barocker Wissenschaft* (Hamburg: Felix Meiner Verlag, 1983) and Nelly Bruyère, *Mèthode et Dialectique dans l'Oeuvre de la Rameé, Renaissance et age classique* (Paris: Vrin, 1984), 41-201.

sedulous to convince their readers that their theories were correct: "for he that deliuereth knowledge desireth to deliver it in such a form as may be best believed, and not as may be best examined" (3:404).[72] Contemporary thinkers, and their humanist and scholastic precursors, were guilty of *rhetorical over-functioning*. A scientific rhetoric which leads through over-effective persuasion to a consensual stasis will not advance learning, or stimulate progress.[73]

It is precisely this consensual humanistic closure of the aphorism which Bacon eschews. He does not approve of the sententious, monologic use of aphorism, which "hath been too much taken into custom, out of a few Axioms or observations upon any subject to make a solemn and formal art; filling it with some discourses and illustrating it with examples, and digesting it into a sensible Method" (3:405). Rather he sees the aphorism as an antidote to the totalizing impulse of methods which give a "show of a total," by a self-referential and closed discourse of mutually-supportive demonstrations and definitions (as scholasticism has sometimes been characterized):[74] "they carry a kind of demonstration in orb or circle, one part illuminating another, and therefore satisfy" (3:405). Bacon's aphoristic method does not seek to satisfy, but carries the reader outside of the vicious "orb or circle" into new insatiable modes of inquiry, by displaying the "dispersed directions" offered by "particulars" and "some good quantity of observation" (3:405). Knowledge "broken" or "dispersed" into the particulars of empirical observation will transcend the quiescent assent of totalization, and instead act as a progressive spur to action. Other methods, Bacon argues, "are more fit to win consent or belief, but *less fit to point to action*" (3:405, my emphasis). It is in the context of his *will to*

---

[72] Cf. also ibid., 293, on the "error ... in the manner of the tradition and delivery of knowledge," which is "for the most part magistral and peremptory ... in a sort as may be soonest believed, and not easiliest examined."

[73] See *Works*, 3:284, where Bacon sees rhetoric as a "hinderance" to "the severe inquisition of truth, and the deep progress into philosophy" because "it is too early satisfactory to the mind of man, and quencheth the desire of further search, before we come to a just period."

[74] See Peter Dear, "Narratives, Anecdotes, Experiments: Turning Experience into Science in the Seventeenth-Century" in Peter Dear, ed., *The Literary Structure of Scientific Arguments* (Philadelphia: Univ. of Pennsylvania Press, 1991), 135–63. See esp. p. 143: "The point of Aristotelian scientific demonstration was to define conclusions deductively from premises that were already accepted as certain ... there was no question of testing the conclusions against experience. The proper place for experience was in grounding the inductive generalizations contained in the original premises ... once they had been established, so too, in effect, had the conclusions deduced from them."

agency, or "instrumentalism" that Bacon's aphoristic style is best situated,[75] although Bacon himself balked at the idea of a discourse which was grounded solely on manual operation, which he saw as artisanal, the domain of the "mere empiric."[76] Instead he saw his inductive method as a rapprochement between the instruments of the hand and the instruments of the mind:

> Neither the naked hand nor the understanding left to itself can effect much. It is by instruments and helps that the work is done, which are as much wanted for the understanding as for the hand. And as the instruments of the hand either give motion or guide it, so the instruments of the mind supply either suggestions for the understanding or cautions. (4:47)

Bacon's scientific aphorisms are to be seen as such "instruments of the mind" which provide "suggestions" for the understanding to act upon.

3. Bacon and "particulars": an initiative rhetoric of the real

Having fully examined the "diseases" of contemporary knowledge production in the *Advancement*, in the *Novum Organum* Bacon set out the desiderata for a new philosophy in a series of such instrumental aphorisms: "One method of delivery alone remains to us; which is simply this: we must lead men to the particulars themselves, and their series and order; while men on their side must force themselves for awhile to lay their notions by and begin to familiarize themselves with facts" (4:53). Previous "notions" of science, he felt, had dealt too much in abstractions and ungrounded suppositions. The syllogism, for example, by accepting unproven principles for its axioms, and manipulating only "intermediate" axioms, "commands assent... to the proposition, but does not take hold of

---

[75] Bacon's hortative, instrumental rhetoric can be usefully compared to Jardine and Grafton's concept of "goal-orientated" humanist reading, which they characterize as "reading ... intended to *give rise to something else*," Lisa Jardine and Anthony Grafton, "Studied for Action: How Gabriel Harvey Read his Livy," *Past & Present* 129 (1991): 30–78; 30 (my emphasis). Bacon's aphoristic style is *writing* "to give rise to something else," in an epistemological sense.

[76] See his attack on the system of the "Empirical" which is "based on too narrow a foundation of experiment" in *Works*, 4:63, and see also his criticism of medicinal practice when unaccompanied by theory, *Works*, 3:367: "we see also that the science of medicine, if it be destituted and forsaken by natural philosophy, it is not much better than an empirical practice."

the thing" (4:49). What he proposed instead was a "study of nature with a view to works" (albeit not as a "mechanic," a "mathematician" or a "physician," 4:48), to once more "take hold" of things and facts themselves. For the "fantastical" notions of scholastic science, he wishes to substitute the "soundness" of observed phenomena (4:49), and so "render sciences active" (4:51). While Bacon does not propose (in any detail) a methodology, or repertoire of techniques for the observation or manipulation of natural phenomena, he does initiate a *vocabulary of the real* which functions rhetorically as a spur to engage in a natural philosophy which is more properly engaged with the material world (i.e., solid, real, particulars, substantial, experience, etc.), and it is this initiative role which the aphorism plays in the *Novum Organum*; his aphorisms here aren't full of "things," but instead articulate a will towards unmediated observation.

In his six-part scheme for the restauration of knowledge (the *instauratio magna*),[77] Bacon sees the aphorisms of the *Novum Organum* as providing both the stylistic and methodological template for scientific investigation. That is to say, it enacts at a stylistic level the kind of discourse to be employed in the science of observation and particulars for which the *Organum* is a polemical manifesto. Once the methodological recommendations of the *Organum* had been taken on board, they were envisaged by Bacon as being applied to the world of particulars — both in the "real world" and in the textual records of past encounters with the real (i.e., he envisages the judicious "fanning" of all past empirical findings in arts, sciences, and trades, in order to extract from them what is pertinent and usable).[78] This is set out in his *Sylva sylvarum*, posthumously published by his colloborator Walter Rawley in 1627.[79] Rawley's preface to the reader provides us with useful insights into the rhetorical intentions behind Bacon's production of this "Naturall Historie," as well as signalling some of the obstacles to the fulfillment of Bacon's ideals. The *Sylva* was to be viewed as a collection of "Materialls for the Building [of a true Philosophy]" while the *Organum* provided "the Instruments and Directions for the Worke."[80] According to Rawley, the publication of the *Sylva* was an

---

[77] See James Stephens, *Francis Bacon and the Style of Science* (Chicago: Univ. of Chicago Press, 1975), 112.

[78] See *Works*, 4:265–70 where Bacon lists one hundred and thirty "Particular histories" which would have to be written in order to achieve the *instauratio magna*.

[79] Francis Bacon, *Sylva sylvarum or a Naturall Historie in Ten Centuries* (London, 1627).

[80] Ibid., sig. A^v–A2^r.

altruistic act on Bacon's part, as it is not calculated to enhance "the glorie of his owne Name," but rather to incite men to labor:

> For it may seeme an Indigested Heap of Particulars; and cannot haue that lustre, which Bookes cast into Methods haue: But that he resolued to preferre the good of Men, and that which might best secure it ... he knew well, that ther was no other way open, to vnloose Mens mindes, being bound; and as it were Maleficiate, by the Charmes of deceiuing Notions, and Theories; and thereby made Impotent for Generation of Workes.[81]

But if one is determined "no wher to depart from ... cleare experience," in the relation of observations, and eschew theoretical explanation (which might foreclose and rhetorically "enchant" the minds of the reader to assent), one runs the risk of one's work appearing "indigested." Ultimately Bacon's ideals of theoretical disinterest had to be compromised — he had to address the problem of how to arrange particulars usefully, so that the reader did not "think themselues utterly lost, in a Vast Wood of Experience."[82] To this end, *some* theoretical direction had to be deemed appropriate: "his lordship thought good ... to add vnto many of the *Experiments* themselves, some *Glosse* of the *Causes*; that in the succeedinge work of *Interpreting Nature* and *Framing Axiomes*, all things may be in more Readines."[83] Not only do Bacon's glosses thereby compromise the ideal of unmediated "cleare experience," but the materials themselves compiled exacerbate this problem. In compiling a collection of unattributed quotations from previous works on natural philosophy by Girolamo Cardano, Giovanni-Battista della Porta, and others, Bacon risks (and sometimes incurs) the importation of those very theoretical prejudices which the collection of particulars is designed to avoid. In the "Experiments in consort touching the inducing and accelerating of putrefaction," for example, Bacon stresses the need for "universal inquiry," but chooses to preempt the possible outcome of such observational inquiries by stating that "Putrefaction is the work of the spirits of bodies, which are ever unquiet to get forth in the air, and to enjoy the sunbeams."[84] While

---

[81] Ibid., sig. A^{r-v}.
[82] Ibid., sig. A2^v.
[83] Ibid., sig. A2^v.
[84] Ibid., 88–89. Cf. also ibid., 185: "As for tears, they are the effects of compression of the moisture of the brain, upon dilatation of the spirits."

some of Bacon's "experiments" seem designed to stimulate notions of rigor and control into observations of natural phenomena,[85] there are other narratives which seem closer to the "natural histories" criticized by Rawley in his preface, "being gathered for Delight ... full of pleasant Descriptions and Pictures ... [which] affect and seeke after Admiration, Rarities and Secrets"[86] or the "superstitious stories" rejected by Bacon in his *Parasceve* (4:255). The "Experiments in consort touching the magnitude and exility and damps of sounds," for example, which concern the alteration of the human voice in a "cassion" produced by a bucket inverted in water, stresses the novelty of the sounds thus produced "like the voice of puppets," and presents the experiment as a trick or diversion: "Note that it may be much more handsomely done, if the pail be put over the man's head above water, and he cowers down, and the pail be pressed down with him."[87] Over half of the narrative is also given over to a "delightful" retelling of the mythological story of Hylas and Hercules from the thirteenth of Theocritus's *Idylls*. As such it is much nearer to what William Ashworth has recently called "humanist natural history"[88] than to a new experimental method. Nonetheless, there are many descriptions in the *Sylva* of actions, practices, and operations on natural objects. As has recently been emphasized by historians of science, much of the efficacy of experimental science and the grounds of its truth claims have a narrative character.[89] Peter Dear, for example, notes that:

---

[85] See for example, ibid., 236: "Experiment solitary touching the rise of water by means of flame" where by varying the components (e.g., oil, flour, or sand substituted for water) of an experiment he employs a rudimentary set of limits or controls. Cf. also ibid., 264, where he describes a "magical" wart cure, which he suggests be given a variety of experimental trials: "It would be tried with corns and wens, and other such excrescences. I would have it also tried with some parts of living creatures that are nearest the nature of the excrescences ... I would have it tried both ways; both by rubbing those parts ... and by cutting off some piece of those parts, and laying it to consume."

[86] Ibid., sig. A^v.

[87] *Sylva Sylvarum*, 47–48. The *Sylva* also includes the description of at least one mountebank's trick as part of its programme, see ibid., 126–27: "Experiments in consort touching the sympathy and antipathy of plants" where the apparent autokinesis of "oat-beards" is explained by their reaction to moisture. Bacon proposed a "History of Jugglers and Mountebanks" as a *desideratum* in his "Catalogue of Particular Histories," *Works*, 4:270.

[88] William B. Ashworth, Jr., "Natural History and the emblematic world view," in D. C. Lindberg and R. S. Westman, eds., *Reappraisals of the Scientific Revolution* (Cambridge: Cambridge Univ. Press, 1990), 303–32.

[89] See, for example, G. Cantor, "The Rhetoric of Experiment," in P. Gooding, T. Pinch and S. Schaffer, eds., *The Uses of Experiment* (Cambridge: Cambridge Univ. Press,

> The meaning of an account of an experimental event — that which makes it an account of an experimental event rather than a series of marks on paper — is provided by its implicit reference to a spatio-temporally defined region of clinking glassware or grooved pieces of wood being manipulated by a human agent. The meaning of that spatiotemporal region itself — what makes it discernible as an experimental event — is conferred, reciprocally, by the *account* of an experimental event.[90]

To the extent that the *Sylua syluarum* does try to institute a series of "discrete, contrived and reported events" it is fulfilling the dicta of the *Advancement* and the *Novum Organum*, insofar as they exert a rhetorical pressure to confront (and narrate) nature in an unmediated form. That the extent to which it does so varies markedly is perhaps a testament to the liminal placement of Bacon's project: caught up in the "cultural matrix" of humanist knowledge production,[91] and without a recognizable or systematic programme of mechanical experimentalism or mathematical physics,[92] Bacon could not hope to do more than spur men to follow his example. According to Rawley, Bacon had neglected to "methodize" the particulars included in the volume, because he did not wish to procure assent but imitation: "because hee conceiued that other men would now thinke, that they could doe the like; And soe goe on with a further collection: which if the Method had been Exact, many would have despaired to attaine by Imitation."[93] As a rhetorical strategy, this supposed aim of the *Sylva sylvarum* was doubtless a success. The British Library copy[94] — owned successively by Sylvester Browne[95] and James Clitherow (who, ac-

---

1989), 159–80, and Steven Shapin and Simon Schaffer, *Leviathan and the Air-Pump: Hobbes, Boyle and the Experimental Life* (Princeton: Princeton Univ. Press, 1985).

[90] Dear, "Narratives, Anecdotes, Experiments," 136–37.

[91] See Ashworth "Natural History," 307.

[92] Bacon, unlike some of his contemporaries (such as Thomas Harriot, or John Dee), was not sympathetic to the idea of applying mathematics to physical phenomena. In the *Advancement*, for example, he says: "For it being the nature of the mind of man (to the extreme prejudice of knowledge) to delight in the spacious liberty of generalities, as in a champion region, and not in the inclosures of particularity; the Mathematics of all other knowledge were the goodliest fields to satisfy that appetite," *Works*, 3:359–360. Bacon's problem, of course, is to find a way to stimulate the "appetite" for "particularities."

[93] *Sylva sylvarum*, sig. A2^v.

[94] British Library 982.f.14.

[95] See inscription: "Si cupis dominum cognosce liber cir[cum]flecte occellos et nomen habebis ibi Siluester Br[owne]."

cording to the title-page inscription, purchased the book in 1637) — bears signs, in its annotations, of the observational stimulus which the work provoked. In the third "century" of the *Sylva*, for example, Bacon notes: "I haue knowne a Dog, that if one howled in his Eare, he would fall a howling a great while." To which Browne responds, in apparent earnest, in the margin: "I have tried this true, but ye dogg must love him who doth it."[96] But this ostensibly ludicrous experimental trial also highlights the epistemological constraints of Bacon's project. There is in 1625 no consensus on what constitutes a "valid" scientific experience, no methodology for designating which particulars are to be gathered, or what the possible reasons might be for gathering them. Bacon's initiative was being made into what was, as yet, an epistemological void — if Bacon pointed to new horizons, he could not himself see what lay on those horizons. If many Renaissance sciences, like alchemy, practical cabala, theurgy or occult mnemonics depended on what Jung called a "participation mystique"[97] in which the scientific actors believed themselves to be unified with the object of their discourse, Bacon's instauration seems to be moving toward an "*operation* mystique," founded on an ontological division between observing scientist and observed experience.[98] The movement towards this operative conception of science in Bacon's work is twofold — first there is the forensic rhetorical investigation of the scientific field of knowledge, which in many respects reiterates (or reinscribes) itself within the humanist discourse which it is designed to overturn. Then there is the adoption of the experiential field, towards which the rhetorical project of the *Advancement* and the *Novum Organum* is orientated, which is the concern of the *Sylva sylvarum*. The limitations of experiential science soon became apparent, and were only gradually overcome during the course of the seventeenth century. The discourse initiated by Bacon was constantly rehearsed and reiterated by the mid-century "Baconian reformers" who were, like Bacon, trapped between an experiential rhetoric of the "real" and the older humanistic and scholastic-methodological practices which had not yet lost their appeal and usefulness.[99] The anxiety about "verbo-

---

[96] Ibid., 65. Cf. also other observations by Browne in the margins, ibid., 2, 69.

[97] *The Collected Works of C. G. Jung*, ed. Herbert Read et al., (London: Routledge and Kegan Paul, 1953), 12:242–87.

[98] This "operation mystique" is not to be seen as part of a disjunctive, revolutionary scientific moment, but as part of a chronic praxiological shift which began in the late middle ages, in the scientific-philosophical, technological, and the religious spheres. The Baconian project arrives on the cusp of this cultural synthesis.

[99] See Stephen Clucas, "In Search of 'The True Logick': Methodological Eclecticism

sity" and "mere words" persisted, but were ironically accompanied — in the absence of a set of experimental practices — by an array of *verbalized desires*. What Bacon bequeathed to the seventeenth century was truly a "knowledge broken" — a rhetorical spur to inquiry, an invitation to seek progression, without a programme of specific, implementable reforms. The Baconian aphorism is the lynch-pin of an epistemological reform — a knowledge broken from *within* the current systems of knowledge. It promises to be a means or instrument, for overcoming the suffocating enslavement to words instead of things by providing a vocabulary of experience, operation, and utility, and a method for communicating practical and empirical observations in such a way that it will stir men to progressive action. Bacon saw the aphorism as a way of pressing *verba* into the service of *res*. But if the Baconian project clearly formulated and identified the barriers and obstacles to discursive change within the current systems of knowledge, it did not necessarily have the conceptual wherewithal to replace those obsolescent discursive modes which it sought to undermine. Many of Bacon's own writings and conceptions are predicated on the old systems of knowledge. The *Advancement of Learning* may bring scholastic and humanistic discourses to their knees, or to the point of collapse, but its attempts to provide an operative discourse to replace them seem helplessly entangled in those same discourses. Confronted with the seemingly insoluble problem of instituting a scientific discourse which did not lay rhetorical claims to authority, Bacon took the unprecedented course of replacing a dogmatic discourse with a discourse about the desirability of undogmatic discourse. That such a discourse could only be a temporary measure, and that the fulfillment of the *instauratio magna* was not imminent quickly became apparent, but the initiative character of his aphoristic method — and its unique inversion of the aphorism's ideal of "perfectum sensum" bore out his own firm belief in the sententious wisdom of Solomon, who had written "The words of the wise are as goads and nails fixed deep in" (*Verba sapientum tanquam aculei, et tanquam clavi in altum defixi*) (3:311-12). For Bacon, the desired figure of contemporary scientific discourse was the goad. "I have made a beginning of the work," he told his audience, "the fortune of the human race will give the issue."[100]

---

among the 'Baconian Reformers,'" in Mark Greengrass, Michael P. Leslie, and Timothy J. Raylor, eds., *Samuel Hartlib and Universal Reformation: Studies in Intellectual Communication in the Seventeenth-Century* (Cambridge: Cambridge Univ. Press, 1994), 51-74.

[100] See Stephens, *Style of Science*, 121.

JONATHAN SAWDAY

Shapeless Elegance: Robert Burton's Anatomy of Knowledge

I. The Cathedral

HAS ROBERT BURTON'S THE ANATOMY OF MELANCHOLY always been a historical and critical puzzle? In 1945, when Douglas Bush published his influential survey of English literature in the seventeenth century, *The Anatomy of Melancholy* represented the latent "intellectual confusion" of its age. Bush chose to understand Burton as a scientist *manqué*. So, although the *Anatomy* was a "traditional bedside book" which "we read for fun," it nevertheless appeared in the chapter of *English Literature in the Earlier Seventeenth Century* devoted to the "evolution" of seventeenth-century science — the moment which "gave birth to the modern world."[1] But Burton was not quite of that world. In his "loose and eccentric fashion" Burton embodied the "religious and ethical assumptions of Renaissance humanism" rather than the empirical world of Bacon and Hobbes. Burton was, therefore, a continental writer rather than a specifically English thinker working within the native tradition. Whether such a tradition ever existed is open to debate; but, in Bush's telling simile, it was Bacon and Hobbes who established just how antique and unfamiliar Burton was supposed to appear even to his contemporaries: "sitting between Bacon and Hobbes, he appears as a kind of gargoyle between the

---

[1] Douglas Bush, *English Literature in the Earlier Seventeenth Century* (1945; repr., London: Oxford Univ. Press, 1973), 296, 272.

two spires of the cathedral of English scientific thought."[2] As a gargoyle squatting between the two spires of empiricism, Burton belonged on the facade of Nôtre Dame, rather than Westminster or Old St. Pauls.

Bush's view of Burton as a literary gargoyle (grotesque, quaint, entirely non-functional) still predominates. A more recent account of Burton concludes that the *Anatomy* is "digressive, an accumulation of facts, opinions, misinformation, absurdities, and sensational stories" — evidence of a Jacobean love of "obscure learning" which can have little to do with an emergent scientific rationalism.[3] In the 1960s however, the author of the *Anatomy* seemed about to be rescued from his uncomfortable perch by the advent of literary theory. The appearance of an essay on Burton in 1962 by Jean Starobinski in the avant-garde theoretical journal *Tel Quel* probably marks the first reappearance of the *Anatomy* in the garb of literary theory rather than antiquarianism.[4] But the makeover could not be considered complete until the publication of Stanley Fish's *Self-Consuming Artifacts* (1972) where Burton was located, alongside Bacon, Herbert, Bunyan, and Hooker, as the author of a text which "undermines the reader's ability to make judgments and determine value."[5] Suddenly, the *Anatomy* was revealed as an example of postmodernism *avant la lettre* — a mocking, self-parodic exploration of the disorganized and fragmentary nature of the world in which it refused to be located. Though Fish's exercise in re-creating Burton as a reader of his own text was enormously influential (not least on this present essay), it never quite dislodged the *Anatomy* from its preeminent position within a more traditional, source-based scholarship.[6] Burton, it was true, had become the great ironist, but even behind the mask of irony, he could still be considered the patron saint of that quintessentially Burtonian journal *Notes and Queries*.[7]

---

[2] Bush, 296.

[3] Bruce King, *Seventeenth-Century English Literature* (London: Macmillan, 1982), 81.

[4] See Jean Starobinski, "La Melancholie de L'Anatomiste," *Tel Quel* 10 (1962): 21–29.

[5] Stanley E. Fish, *Self-Consuming Artifacts: The Experience of Seventeenth-Century Literature* (Berkeley: Univ. of California Press, 1972), 351.

[6] See, in particular: Richard L. Nochimson, "Burton's *Anatomy*: The Author's Purposes and the Reader's Response," *Forum for Modern Language Studies* 13 (1977): 256–84; James S. Tillman, "The Satirist Satirized: Burton's Democritus Jr.," *Studies in the Literary Imagination* 10 (1977): 86–96; Cynthia W. Sulfridge, "Intimate Narratives: Narrator-Reader Relationships in Three Renaissance Precursors of *Tristram Shandy*" (Ph.D. diss., Johns Hopkins University, 1978).

[7] See Joey Conn, *Robert Burton and the Anatomy of Melancholy: An Annotated*

In this essay, rather than approach the *Anatomy* as either a source text, or as a pure exercise in fictive self-creation, I want to account for the evolution of Burton's text, and for the very different fortunes it has enjoyed since its first appearance in 1621. Central to my argument, therefore, is the "fact" of literary history — that in the eighteenth century, the *Anatomy* became virtually unreadable. In what follows, I shall argue that the reasons for this "unreadability" (against which latter-day readers of Burton are still struggling) are derived from the theory of speech and language which Burton shared with his seventeenth-century contemporaries. That theory (itself central to our understanding of seventeenth-century writing) was displaced by the advent of Locke's influential account of language in his *Essay Concerning Human Understanding* (1689). At the same time, as I hope the conclusion to this essay will demonstrate, Burton was by no means "unscientific." Rather, he worked within the paradigms of natural science which were available to him prior to the 1640s. From this follows the larger claim of the essay: that, in many ways, Burton was actually in the vanguard of the scientific movement of the *earlier* seventeenth century, the period before Harvey and the advent of the Royal Society. This is the age associated with the French sixteenth-century "encylopaediasts" and their English counter-parts: John Norden, Henoch Clapham, John Hagthorpe, the mysterious "Ro. Un.," and John Davies of Hereford.[8] The *Anatomy* represented just the first stage of a vast intellectual project which was never completed. Why it should never have been completed will, I hope, be self evident in the essay's conclusion. My intention, then, is to show that, far from being a gargoyle, Burton's *Anatomy* was one of the foundation stones of a "cathedral" of scientific thought. But this great edifice was never to be built. In common with other encyclopedic projects of the age, the *Anatomy* represented what was eventually to become a blind alley. But in order to substantiate this claim we must return to 1640/41, the year in which Robert Burton died, and to the work of a contemporary of Burton's, Ben Jonson, with whom the author of the *Anatomy* would appear, at first glance, to share very little.

Bibliography of Primary and Secondary Sources (New York: Greenwood Press, 1988), 102.

[8] John Norden, *Vicissitudo rerum* (London, 1600) and *The Labyrinth of Mans Life* (London, 1614); Henoch Clapham, *Aelohim-triune* (London, 1601); "Ro. Un." has been identified as Robert Underwood whose *The Little World* was published c. 1605. John Davies of Hereford (?1565–1618) was the author of three poetic-scientific treatises: *Mirum in Modum* (1602), *Microcosmos* (1603), and *Summa totalis* (1607). On these "scientific" poets see Jonathan Sawday, *The Body Emblazoned: Dissection and the Human Body in Renaissance Culture* (London: Routledge, 1995), 142–45, 295 (note).

II. Morphology

Ben Jonson's commonplace book, *Discoveries*, was published in the same year in which Burton died. Jonson provides us with the Renaissance paradigms by which the vast lifework which was Burton's *Anatomy* may begin to be understood. As a dramatist, Jonson was concerned with the morphology — the shape and structure — of his art. And it was with an account of structure that Jonson concluded his brief treatise on poetry to be found at the end of *Discoveries*. "For the whole," Jonson observed:

> ...as it consisteth of parts, so without all the parts it is not the whole; and to make it absolute is required not only the parts, but such parts as are true. For a part of the whole was true, which, if you take away, you either change the whole, or it is not the whole. For if it be such a part, as being present or absent, nothing concerns the whole, it cannot be called the part of a whole.[9]

Had Burton known Jonson's definition, he would undoubtedly have quoted it, not just because he seemed to quote everything that drifted past him in his copious reading, but because his own project was so entirely concerned with the relationship between wholeness and partition; a concern we might expect in a text which announces itself as an "anatomy" of its subject.[10] But would he have quoted Jonson's words approvingly? Behind Jonson's definition of the relationship between wholeness and segmentation lay the Renaissance and medieval tradition of Aristotelian interpretation — a tradition in which Burton was well versed. What is a whole, asks Jonson. It is made up of parts. How do we know whether or not a part forms part of the whole? Because if we were to take that part away from the whole, and the whole remained unchanged, then the removed part could never have formed a part of that whole from which it had appeared to have been removed. Either the whole is altered by the removal of a part, or it remains the same, in which case the removed segment is superfluous to the organic unity of the larger structure. And the proof (though Jonson does not enlarge on his syllogism, since it was presumably too obvious) must lie in the corollary: that to add a part to a

---

[9] Ian Donaldson, ed., *Ben Jonson* (Oxford: Oxford Univ. Press, 1985), 594.
[10] Sections of *Discoveries*, as Donaldson points out (735) were in circulation by 1623, when Jonson may have used the gatherings of his commonplace book as the basis of lectures at Gresham College.

whole is to establish that the original whole was incomplete, and not, therefore, truly whole.

What was Burton's sense of morphology? "Burton's genius lay in expanding rather than contracting," James Roy King has observed, implying that Burton had no sense of morphology whatsoever. It was this delight in expansion, in King's view, which led to the conclusion that Burton possessed:

> an almost comic inability to manage the most fundamental problems involved in writing a book: an unwillingness to decide once and for all what was significant and what had to be eliminated.[11]

The print history of the *Anatomy* seems to substantiate this view.[12] In 1628 the third edition of the *Anatomy* appeared in a folio volume of 762 pages and something over 470,000 words. Burton seems to have believed that, with the publication of this edition, the gigantic work was complete. His enquiry into "Melancholy, what it is, with all the kinds, causes, symptomes, prognostickes and severall cures of it" (titlepage, 1628 ed.) was, at last, at an end:

> But I am now resolved never to put this Treatise out againe, *Ne quid nimis*, I will not hereafter adde, alter, or retract, I have done.[13]

The whole needed no further addition. But here was the first of that "series of false promises" which Stanley Fish has claimed as being the end of the complete *Anatomy*.[14] For the resolve "never to put this Treatise out againe" was to be made again and again (this statement was retained in each subsequent edition), and its terms were to be just as comprehen-

---

[11] James Roy King, *Studies in Six Seventeenth Century Writers* (Athens: Ohio Univ. Press, 1966), 77, 83.

[12] In tracing the "morphology" of Burton's *Anatomy*, I am entirely indebted to the bibliographical scholarship to be found in the three volume Clarendon edition of Burton's work. See Thomas C. Faulkner, Nicholas K. Kiessling, Rhonda L. Blair, eds., "Textual Introduction. Publishing History: The Growth of the *Anatomy*," in Robert Burton, *The Anatomy of Melancholy*, ed. Faulkner, Kiessling, and Blair (Oxford: Clarendon Press, 1989) 1:xxxvii–lx. This edition will hereafter be cited as Faulkner et. al. On the general question of the "structure" of the *Anatomy* see: Ruth A. Fox, *The Tangled Chain: The Structure of Disorder in the Anatomy of Melancholy* (Berkeley: Univ. of California Press, 1976), passim.

[13] Robert Burton, *The Anatomy of Melancholy* (London: Chatto & Windus, 1907), 13. All references to the text of the *Anatomy* are to this edition.

[14] Fish, 304.

sively ignored. The 1628 edition was followed by a fourth edition (1632) containing a further 28,000 words, a fifth edition (1638) which added over 8,000 words, and a sixth (posthumous) edition (1651) which included yet more words — 2,200 more. Words were piled upon words, in a promiscuous heap. If Jonson was correct in his description of the relationship between parts and wholes, then the *Anatomy* was either unfinished before 1651, or it existed in six entirely different versions. In any event, from its first appearance in 1620/21, the *Anatomy* had grown by over 160,000 words, so that, over a thirty year period, it had increased in size by just over thirty per cent.

The numerical symmetry would have appealed to Burton, the "learned mathematician," who, so it was rumoured by the students of Christ Church College Oxford, having calculated from his birth-date the date of his death, "rather than there should be a mistake in the calculation... sent up his soul to heaven through a slip about his neck."[15] It is just the kind of seemingly pointless correspondence that Burton delighted in teasing out of the world around him, and would certainly have been worthy of a Burtonian footnote, or, perhaps, the dignity of a digression. In the case of the *Anatomy* our awareness of its vegetative growth is fundamental to our attempts at interpretation. The *Anatomy* is the nearest we can come, in the world of texts, to a *process*. To read it is not to move through narrative time and space from a point of (supposed) origin to a point of (supposed) finality, but to be aware of something potentially limitless. In this sense, the *Anatomy* itself may be thought of as a cathedral, but gothic rather than baroque — a vast creation continually evolving as new architectural forms come into vogue and are incorporated into the larger structure. It is this (potentially) limitless quality which is suggested (with all the flourishes characteristic of the Burtonian *persona* — Democritus Junior) by the last phrase of the preface to the *Anatomy*, "Democritus to the Reader": "I will begin." This beginning is announced only at the end (in the 1628 edition) of nearly 52,000 words. In similar measure, the end of the *Anatomy* is a desperately provisional affair. There is no grand conclusion to the whole, no summation, no peroration, no word of final advice to the reader. Instead, the *Anatomy* simply stops speaking: "I can say no more, or give better advice ... than what I have given and said" (739). A precursor to *Finnegans Wake*, the *Anatomy* turns the reader back to the beginning by

---

[15] Anthony à Wood, *Athenæ Oxoniensis* (London, 1721) 1:627. See also John Aubrey, *Brief Lives*, ed. Oliver Lawson Dick (Harmondsworth: Penguin Books, 1972), 326.

way of concluding. A further quotation follows (from St. Augustine), and the work is at an end. Thus the *Anatomy* appears to establish a pattern, an order, a symmetry; but the symmetry may be an illusion. The equation, once it has been run, guarantees nothing more than a dizzying *mise en abime*: a prospect of infinite regression and thus infinite production.

"The beginning of a narrative, of a discourse, of a text, is an extremely sensitive point," Roland Barthes has (famously) observed by way of a preface to his own analysis of narrative. "The *said* must be torn from the *not-said*, whence a whole rhetoric of beginning *markers*."[16] Robert Burton found the separation of the "said" from the "not-said" an all but impossible struggle, and his *Anatomy* is everywhere scarred by "markers" of commencement. The establishment of a deferred beginning, and a simple cessation in lieu of an ending was not, however, how the *Anatomy* first began its sequence of public appearances. In 1620/21, the *Anatomy* ended with a "conclusion of the Author to the Reader" dated "From my Studie in Christ-Church Oxon. Decemb 5. 1620." With the second edition of 1624, however, this conclusion was reworked so that it could become the bulk of the material in "Democritus Junior to the Reader." As bibliographic evidence further suggests, the new introduction was printed last, and was probably still being written whilst the rest of the book was being printed. Thus, between the 1620/21 (first) and the 1624 (second) editions the morphology of the *Anatomy* underwent a fundamental revision. Its ending became its beginning, and that beginning was printed only after the larger whole had been finished.

Burton must have represented a print-shop nightmare, the personification of a compositor's worst fears, and a distant ancestor of James Joyce in his ability to forward copy and still demand revision beyond the normal stages of print production. Once he had found a way to begin, moreover, it was as though this obsessive author could not, somehow, stop talking. The delivery of manuscript copy to the printer usually represents the (albeit often temporary) silence of the author. Speaking (to explore a metaphor that is vital to the *Anatomy*) has stopped, and the process of transforming words from the transient and semi-private world of the manuscript into the more rigidly determined, and public, arena of print has begun. But in the seventeenth century such a relationship was still in its infancy. And Burton either did not know the rules, or (more likely)

---

[16] Roland Barthes, "The Struggle with the Angel," in Roland Barthes, *Image-Music-Text*, ed. Stephen Heath (London: Fontana/ Collins, 1977), 129.

decided to bend the rules to his own peculiar advantage. Contemporary practice was to deliver proof sheets of a text to the author for correction as they came off the press. Often, indeed, the author was expected to be physically in proximity to the machines.[17] Such a system, it might be thought, allowed little enough time for the author to attempt to incorporate second thoughts into the text. But Burton was an adept at the process of revisionary rewriting, and he rebelled against the emerging system of print production. In 1621, in the "Conclusion of the Author to the Reader," Burton complained that he had been unable to attend the press in order to correct the proofs of the first edition of the *Anatomy*. By 1638, and the fifth edition of the *Anatomy*, the *mechanics* of print production — the very process which Burton had claimed was so uncongenial to him — had been incorporated into the structure of the whole work, to the extent that it was now possible for Burton to argue with the very idea of authorship. In 1638, Burton wrote yet another form of opening (which was also a closing): the latin address to the reader placed (how typical of Burton!) over the errata list, on the last leaf of the text. The address begins with the admonition to "listen":

> Listen, good friend! This edition was begun not very long ago at Edinburgh, but was suppressed on the spot by our Printers. Subsequently, it was continued at London with their permission, and last it was completed at Oxford; now for the fifth time it comes into the light as whatever kind of an edition it is. In truth, if the first part does not indeed fit, nor the middle part with either the beginning or the end, on account of the frequent mistakes and omissions, whom do you blame?[18]

Here is an answer to Jonson's argument over wholeness and division. How can such antique distinctions hold good in the age of mechanical reproduction? Wherein lies the authenticity of the text? Aristotle, of course, had observed that an epic poem should have a "beginning, a middle, and an end, so that like a single complete organism the poem may produce its own special kind of pleasure."[19] Burton, it is true, was not writing a

---

[17] See H. S. Bennett, *English Books and Readers* (Cambridge: Cambridge Univ. Press, 1970), 3:211–12.

[18] Faulkner et al., "Textual Introduction," 1:xl.

[19] Aristotle, "On the Art of Poetry" in *Classical Literary Criticism* ed. T. S. Dorsch (Harmondsworth: Penguin Books, 1965), 65.

poem, but sensitive to classical authority, he shrugged off his violation of Aristotle's *dictum* by refusing the responsibility of authorship. The *Anatomy* has a beginning, a middle, and an end (he seemed to say), but not necessarily in that order, and in that lay its "special kind of pleasure." This was the pleasure of the manipulation of print — the *jouissance* of technology. It was the *technology* of print which enabled Burton to revise his text so continuously, and, in this, Burton — the closeted Oxford scholar — discovered a truth which Walter Benjamin was to display over three hundred years later: "the presence of the original is the prerequisite to the concept of authenticity."[20] But there was to be no "original" *Anatomy*, and hence no truly "authentic" text. All was to be provisional.

Burton, then, had become adept at evading the prescriptive role of author. Not only was this to be a text which never quite entered the world as the author claimed he wished it to emerge, it was to straddle geography as well as time. The *imprimatur* "From my Studie in Christ-Church Oxon. Decemb 5. 1620" seems to mark a point in time and a place, a means of locating, for the reader, the speaking voice of the text. This was the *locus* of the words which comprise the whole. But such fixity (as we would expect) was entirely alien to the Burton persona. Burton was, notoriously, an author bound to a narrow circuit: "I never travelled but in map or card" (3), he writes, before affirming that his imagination, like his text, expatiates as widely as the long-winged hawk which soars aloft at the beginning of the "Digression of the Air." But for all his fixity, Burton's text could trace its origins (in a mechanical sense, once more) to a mobile geography. Thus, the 1651/52 (posthumous) edition of the text began life in the print shop of Robert Young, the King's printer for Scotland. Some 346 pages were printed in Edinburgh, before the task was transferred to Young's partner in London, Miles Flesher, who printed a further sixty-eight leaves. Still incomplete, the work was sent down to Oxford, where it was completed by two printers — Leonard Lichfield and William Turner. Like Joyce's codicil to *Ulysses* "Trieste-Zurich-Paris, 1914–1921," the 1651/52 edition of the *Anatomy* was re-compacted, over a period of time, from fragments scattered over the kingdom: Edinburgh-London-Oxford, 1620–1652.

With the death of Burton in 1640, the author's voice might, at last, have been supposed to have been stilled. Inevitably, such was not the

---

[20] Walter Benjamin, "The Work of Art in the Age of Mechanical Reproduction," (1936) in Walter Benjamin, *Illuminations*, ed. Hannah Arendt, trans. Harry Zohn (London: Fontana/Collins, 1973), 222.

case. Though Burton was dead, he had not quite stopped talking, and the *Anatomy* was still growing. The posthumous sixth edition of the work contained an address from the publisher to the reader, in which Burton's ghostly voice could still be heard:

> Be pleased to know (Courteous Reader) that since the last Impression of this Book, the ingenious author of it is deceased, leaving a copy of it exactly corrected, with several considerable Additions by his own hand; This Copy he committed to my care and custody, with directions to have those Additions inserted in the next edition; which in order to his command, and the Publicke Good, is faithfully performed in this last Impression.[21]

Now, at last, the *Anatomy* appeared to have ended. Thirty years in the making, it had straddled the realm, the reigns of James I and Charles I, the cataclysm of a civil war, the advent of a republic, and the author's own death.

These bibliographical data, unusual as they are even for a seventeenth-century text, underline one of the chief formal characteristics of the *Anatomy*: the fact that it appears to be random in its development. To return to Jonson's part/whole distinction, the parts of the *Anatomy* could, it seems, be re-arranged, or reordered, and the whole would remain the same. In other words, the *Anatomy* does not appear to possess "linearity." Instead, it seems to merely move forward, "heaping" (a word Burton liked enormously) *exempla* on *exempla*, illustration on illustration, words upon words. The reasons for this structure will become clearer later in this essay, but for the moment it is enough to note that Burton was self-consciously aware of this quality. Writing in the *persona* of Democritus Junior, he explained the genesis of the *Anatomy* as follows:

> enforced, as a Beare doth her whelps, to bring forth this confused lumpe, I had not time to licke it into forme, as shee doth her young ones, but even so to publish it, as it was first written *quicquid in buccam venit*, in an extemporean stile, as I doe commonly all other exercises, *effudi quicquid dictavit Genius meus*, out of a confused company of notes, and writ with as small deliberation as I doe ordinarily speake, without all affectation of big words, fustian phrases, jingling termes, tropes, strong lines, that like *Acesta's* ar-

---

[21] Faulkner et al., "Textual Introduction," 1:xliii.

rowes cought fire as they flew; straines of wit, brave heats, elogies, hyperbolicall exornations, elegancies, &c. which many so much affect. (11)

Here is the classic Burtonian formulation: a grumpy sentence which winds compulsively back on itself to deny, through its own rhetorical strategies, what it had set out to enunciate. Born like a bear-cub, half-formed, the *Anatomy* is, nevertheless, "extemporean" or out of time.

To claim that a text that was thirty years in its fashioning is "extemporean" is, it might be thought, stretching the boundaries of a reader's credulity. But the "extemporean" quality of the *Anatomy* is not only a function of its development over time. It is also a function of the careful manipulation of the illusion of a speaking voice. Here, Burton drew on classical precedent.[22] But Burton also claimed a different form of authority for his text. If the work refused authenticity in one guise, then it gleefully claimed a different kind of authenticity: that of speech over writing. The *Anatomy* was written, Burton tells us, "as I doe ordinarily speake," and Burton was a great speaker. Anthony à Wood recorded hearing the "ancients of Christ Church" describe Burton as:

> very merry, facete, juvenile; and no man in his time did surpass him for his ready and dexterous interlarding his common discourses among them with verses from the poets, or sentences from classic authors.[23]

If we are to trust Wood (a risky prospect) Burton appears to have spoken as he wrote. And if we are to trust the Burton of the *Anatomy* (even more risky), he wrote as he spoke. His speech was a palimpsest, an inter-weaving of memories of written texts with his own observation. This was the speech of the commonplace book, a collection of parts and fragments, ordered only by the writer's (or speaker's) memory of the significance of the components. To the outward observer (or listener) it was the Burtonian *persona* — itself a fictive creation — which endowed the whole with coherence, a semblance of rational progression. Yet, to the modern reader, there is something shifty in this "interlarding" distributer of the words of others. The "Burton" who spoke in the common room of Christ church,

---

[22] See George Williamson, *The Senecan Amble: A Study in Prose Form from Bacon to Collier* (Chicago: Univ. of Chicago Press, 1951), 193-95, 198-200.

[23] Wood, *Athenæ Oxoniensis*, 1:627.

as Wood recalls hearing others recollect, was remembered for his evasive habit of sheltering behind memories of words other than his own. When did "Burton" stop talking, and start remembering? Who was speaking, and what ontological status did the speaking voice possess?

Burton was trained (as were his listeners and his contemporary readers) as a rhetorician. As such, Burton was versed in the arts of imitation, and imitation theory (as Terence Cave reminds us) offered a complex account of the process of the generation of discourse, particularly literary discourse. If we set about "subtracting" (as Cave describes the process) the source materials from Burton's text, reversing the "interlarding" technique for which Burton was famous, then, to a literary historian, the "residue" which remains might be thought of as the authentically Burtonian word, with its "source or origin in the author's mind ... produced by an act of creation." But such a theory of origin (and hence authenticity) was entirely alien to a rhetorician such as Burton. In Renaissance imitation theory, (as Cave goes on to demonstrate) "the writer is always a re-writer":

> the problem then being to differentiate and authenticate the re-writing. This is executed not by the addition of something wholly new, but by the dismembering and reconstruction of what has already been written.[24]

The figure of dismemberment is entirely appropriate to a text which was ordered into a system of partitions, sections, members, and subsections. Indeed, the "dismembering and reconstruction of what has already been written" fairly accurately represents the growth of the *Anatomy* over its thirty-year period of composition. The *Anatomy* was, after all, a feat of memory, an incorporation of remembered fragments into a larger whole. But this reconstructive process is not (paradoxically) evidence of a writer with more and more things to say. On the contrary, Burton had less and less to say, but more and more to digest. Jonson's part/whole distinction is again relevant. Each text encountered in the author's copious reading had to find its proper place in the digest of the whole, an endeavor which would either have necessitated the continuing reconstruction of the text, or the creation of a structure architecturally fluid enough to accommodate the never-ending process of accretion which, as the genesis of the *Anatomy* indicates, was the reality of the text's growth.

---

[24] Terence Cave, *The Cornucopian Text: Problems of Writing in the French Renaissance* (Oxford: Clarendon Press, 1979), 76.

III. Thinking and Speaking

By concentrating on the properties of speech as opposed to writing, we can begin to understand the formal structures of the *Anatomy*. Speech was what Burton was famous for amongst his contemporaries, and speech was a quality in the *Anatomy* that his readers have often noted. But speech (speaking historically) has often been seen as the poor cousin of writing. If it is true, as Bush claimed, that the "popularity of the *Anatomy* lapsed during the eighteenth century," then that lapse into desuetude had much to do with the *Anatomy*'s status as a spoken as opposed to written artifact.[25] It was Burton's determination to prioritize speech over and above writing which caused eighteenth-century readers such difficulty. Thus, Thomas Warton, the historian of English poetry, in his edition of Milton's poetry (1785), termed Burton's *Anatomy* a work of "shapeless elegance."[26] Warton's epithet is worth pausing over for a moment. How could a work be pronounced both "elegant" and "shapeless" at the same moment, particularly within the paradigms of late eighteenth-century attention to neo-classical form? The critical oxymoron is only explicable if we understand that what Warton was describing was not so much the *Anatomy* as an artistic work, but the effect that it had on later readers.[27] That effect was one which is best characterized as being the product of attending to the spoken as opposed to the written word. To an eighteenth-century reader Burton's text possessed some of the characteristics of speech — a certain elegance of phrasing could be admired, but it existed in a world in which writing and speech should be divorced from one another. Writing presupposed order or shape, while speech was evanescent, transient, a fading medium. The very essence of speech was that its "shape" was provisional, relying on the interplay of conversation, rather than (as in writing) the formal organization of a mind in a different form of conversation with itself.

To a seventeenth-century audience, however, the relationship between speech and thought was of a different order. The puritan divine, Thomas

---

[25] Bush, 295.

[26] Thomas Warton, ed., *Poems upon Several Occasions, English, Italian, and Latin, with Translations, by John Milton* (London, 1785), 93.

[27] Warton's discussion of Burton takes place within the context of an account of the effect of the *Anatomy* on Milton as a reader. In Warton's words, the *Anatomy* (and particularly the prefatory verses with which it began in the 1628 and subsequent editions) had "taken possession of Milton's mind" when he came to write "L'Allegro" and "Il Penseroso." See Warton, 93–96.

Goodwin, for example, offered the following definition of "thoughts" in 1643. Thoughts, he wrote, are "those talkings of our mindes with the things wee know ... those same parleys, enterviews, chattings, the mind hath with the things let into it."[28] A thinking mind, then, was a mind in conversation. If, as Descartes was to claim, the mind was a thinking thing, then the mind was in perpetual dialogue not only with itself but with the "things" that it encountered. But the important element in this theory of speech and thinking, and one that informed Burton's work (and foreshadowed Descartes), was that there was no distinction between the two activities. "*Oratio imago animi*" — "speech, the image of the mind" was Jonson's pre-Cartesian view of the matter in *Discoveries*, and he continued:

> Language most shows a man: speak, that I may see thee. It springs out of the most retired and inmost parts of us, and is the image of the parent of it, the mind. No glass renders a man's form or likeness so as his speech.[29]

This mode of understanding was fundamental to any view of speech and thought current in the seventeenth century prior to Descartes. For Descartes, *thought* was what determined the knowledge of existence. For Jonson, speech provided the necessary reflective medium by which thought could be held to exist. Moreover, speech was considered to be *more* authentic than written discourse for two reasons. First, it appeared to be engendered directly by the mind. If the mind was the true source of all authority, then speech was the medium by which the mind was to be known. Secondly, as Hobbes was to argue in *Leviathan* (1651), speech was "the most noble and profitable invention of all other ... whereby men register their Thoughts" since not only could there be no human society without speech, but speech was divine in its origin:

> The first author of Speech was *God* himself, that instructed *Adam* how to name such creatures as he presented to his sight; For the Scripture goeth no further in this matter. But this was sufficient to direct him to adde more names, as the experience and use of the creature should give him occasion.[30]

---

[28] Thomas Goodwin, *The Vanity of Thoughts Discovered with their Danger and Cure* (London, 1646), 5.

[29] Donaldson, 574.

[30] Thomas Hobbes, *Leviathan* (1651), ed. Richard Tuck (Cambridge: Cambridge Univ. Press, 1991), 24.

God, according to Hobbes's formulation, was the author not so much of language *per se* but of the language-creating facility. The exercise of this facility, indeed, the very copiousness of discourse, could (despite the linguistic disaster of Babel) be understood as the realization of God's intention. Within these paradigms, of course, Burton's renowned copiousness, as well as his deployment of the illusion of a speaking voice in the *Anatomy*, was a fundamentally fideistic exercise. We can even understand Burton's deliberate manipulation of print technology as an anticipation of Hobbes's view of the relationship between speech, printing, and writing. "The Invention of *Printing*," Hobbes observed, "though ingenious, compared with the invention of Letters, is no great matter." And both paled into insignificance beside the divine origin of speech. The evolutionary descent was clear: speech, then writing, then print.

Such a direct, causal relationship was to be overturned by the theory of language inherited in the eighteenth century from Locke. For Locke, as he explored the problem of language in book 3 of his *Essay Concerning Human Understanding* (1689), the relationship between language and thought was neither direct, nor (as it was for Jonson) an easy reflection of the mind of the speaker. Instead, words were conceived of as standing "*for nothing, but the* IDEAS *in the mind of him that uses them.*"[31] For Locke, the unmediated link between ideas and words, so self-evidently the case for Jonson, was not the reality of how language worked. Instead, Locke posited "a double use of words" in which language served two functions. The first function of language is the "recording of our own thoughts":

> whereby, as it were, we talk to ourselves, any words will serve the turn. For since sounds are voluntary and indifferent signs of any *Ideas*, a Man may use what Words he pleases, to signify his own *Ideas* to himself.[32]

The second function of language is communication with others, specifically, the communication of ideas. But the relationship between words and ideas is arbitrary, as the example of someone thinking to themselves using "what words he pleases" illustrates. For communication (as opposed to thinking) to take place, both the hearer and the speaker must agree on the precise idea signified by a given word. This level of agreement is not innate within language, but it is a prerequisite for any communicative act.

---

[31] John Locke, *An Essay Concerning Human Understanding*, ed. Peter H. Nidditch (1975; rev. ed. Oxford: Clarendon Press, 1979), 405.

[32] Locke, 476.

By contrast, writing some forty years earlier than Locke, Jonson observed that "the conceits of the mind are pictures of things, and the tongue is the interpreter of those pictures" — an observation which not only presupposes a commonality of both thought and speech, but was essentially a commonplace of Renaissance thought.[33] For Jonson, then, we think as we speak. For Locke, thinking and speaking are distinct and (often) different undertakings.

Locke's post-Cartesian skepticism, against which, as Tony Crowley observes, he fought "a rearguard action" throughout the *Essay*, came to inform eighteenth-century views on language.[34] Such skepticism, too, had the effect of making Burton's *Anatomy* a rogue text. Sterne, it is true, was indebted to Burton in composing *Tristram Shandy*, but such admiration was not the rule.[35] To Warton, in a post-Lockean world, Burton's interweaving of thinking and speaking was entirely alien. Hence the "shapelessness" of Burton's work. Even amongst Burton's admirers, the speech-like quality of the *Anatomy* was a matter of concern. Famously, the *Anatomy* was said to be the only book that forced Dr. Johnson to rise from his bed "two hours sooner than he wished."[36] Like a latter-day alarm clock, it was as if Johnson had been roused by sound, a speaking voice. For Johnson, that quality was connected to the apparently unmediated nature of Burton's text, as though it possessed the characteristics of speech rather than writing: "there is great spirit and great power in what Burton *says* when he *writes* from his own mind" (my emphasis), Johnson is recorded as saying.[37] Here, though, was an uneasy relationship. In Johnson's (historical) view, Burton's text could be separated into two segments: the authentic record of the mind possessing "spirit and great power," and the unau-

---

[33] Donaldson, 577. Donaldson notes (753) that Jonson was following John Hoskyns's unpublished *Directions for Speech and Style* (c. 1599), and interweaving observations culled from Lipsius and Horace.

[34] See Tony Crowley, *Proper English? Readings in Language, History, and Cultural Identity* (London: Routledge, 1991), 14.

[35] Sterne's "borrowings" from the *Anatomy* were first noted in 1792 by "H.H." in *The European Magazine* and (later) by John Ferriar in the *Analytical Review* (1794). The identification of Sterne's debt to Burton in the 1790s may have much to do with the Romantic "re-discovery" of Burton in the later eighteenth century. See Max Byrd, *Visits to Bedlam: Madness and Literature in the Eighteenth Century* (Columbia: Univ. of South Carolina Press, 1974), 119–27.

[36] James Boswell, *The Life of Samuel Johnson* ed. George B. Hill (Oxford: Clarendon Press, 1934–50) 2:121.

[37] Boswell, 2:440.

thentic accretion of the words of others. Heard as spoken word, Burton's text was the trace of a mind thinking. Interference in this mental process was a function of the written texts — the authorities, quotations, and references — jostling over the pages of Burton's record of a thinking mind. Thus the Anatomy was also a source of irritation to the lexicographer. Was it speech or was it writing? As a spoken text, the Anatomy, in Johnson's view, was "overloaded" with quotation, a key shift if we compare this description to Wood's notion of the Anatomy's "interlarded" quality. The Anatomy hinted at direct access to mental processes, but denied that access through its reliance on the words of others. To a gatherer of words such as Johnson, Burton's project must have seemed disturbing, even if it was also endlessly fascinating. The Anatomy represented a vast storehouse of definition, etymology, quotation, allusion, and *memorabilia* of the written word.[38] But the Anatomy was also a terrible warning. It appeared to be the result of a mind no longer in control of words, a mind which did not, any longer, know itself, because it could no longer sift the authentic from the unauthentic. It could no longer hear itself, and had confused (in Lockean terms) the private space of the thinking mind and the public space of communicative speech. To Johnson, such a situation was intolerable. Though Johnson drew on the Anatomy over a dozen times for *exempla* and illustrations in his Dictionary of the English Language, the Dictionary was aimed precisely at remedying such a state of affairs, as the 1747 Plan made quite clear:

> By tracing in this manner every word to its original, and not admitting, but with great caution, any of which no original can be found, we shall secure our language from being over-run with *cant*, from being crouded with low terms, the spawn of folly or affectation, which arise from no just principles of speech.[39]

---

[38] Johnson drew on the Anatomy over a dozen times for *exempla* and illustrations in his Dictionary. But, as H. J. Jackson has noted, the demands of lexicography were such that Johnson was not averse to altering those passages of the Anatomy which provided the context for the words whose use he wished to illustrate. See H. J. Jackson, "Johnson and Burton: The Anatomy of Melancholy and The Dictionary of the English Language," English Studies in Canada 5 (1979): 36–48. Johnson owned copies of both the sixth (1651–52) and eighth (1676) editions of the Anatomy. See Edward Bensly, "Dr Johnson's Copies of Burton's Anatomy of Melancholy," Notes and Queries ser. 11, no. 6 (1912): 390 and Notes and Queries ser. 11, no. 10 (1914): 117.

[39] Samuel Johnson, "The Plan of a Dictionary of the English Language" (1747) in Samuel Johnson, Poetry and Prose, ed. Mona Wilson (London: Rupert Hart-Davis, 1979), 129.

The *Anatomy*, of course, announced itself as the "spawn of folly," which was also the child of speech. But Burtonian (as opposed to Johnsonian) "speech" contained no such "just principles." Or so Burton/Democritus (facetiously) claimed: "I have spoken foolishly, rashly, inadvisedly, absurdly, I have anatomized mine own folly" (73).

IV. Speech as Symptom and Cure

We can account for Burton's fascination with speech, in part, to the Renaissance idea, as we have seen it displayed by Ben Jonson, of speech as the mirror of the mind. Similarly, the divine origin of speech is, clearly, of importance to Burton's project. But neither of these reasons can represent the entire case of the *Anatomy*, since we also have to acknowledge that no author could, in such a self-contradictory fashion, promise such access to his mind, and then deny access by sheltering so comprehensively behind a mask of facetious parody. If speech was a mirror, then Burton was a master at hiding within the pallid and shimmering reflective surface of spoken language. To say (as Burton says in his nevertheless written text) "I have spoken foolishly" is to deny the authority of speech, even whilst the utterance relies on that authority for any claim on our attention. In other words, is Burton/Democritus speaking foolishly when he says he is speaking foolishly? Whom do we trust? The speech which may be foolish, or the speaker who claims to be a fool?

But what of Johnson, unwillingly rising from his bed to attend to this voice of folly? For contemporary literary theorists, what awoke Johnson (had he but known it) was the tocsin of intertextuality. In its plenitude, its resistance to closure, its copiousness, its interrelationship of body and text, and the alarming presence of an author who, grinning facetiously behind the mask of "Democritus Junior," warns us of ever taking anything at face value, the *Anatomy* can easily be understood as a proto-theoretical text. Contemporary theory has reversed the eighteenth-century view of the *Anatomy* as a "quaint" literary curiosity, and given us, instead, an *Anatomy* which, self-reflexively, is a fragmented product of a fragmented world.[40] Nothing, indeed, appears to be more contemporary than the

---

[40] Or, in Stanley Fish's words, the *Anatomy* operates by a "strategy of inclusion, which collapses speaker, reader, and a thousand or more 'authorities' into a single category of unreliability, [which] extends also to every aspect of what we think of as 'objective reality.'" See Fish, 314.

problem which the *Anatomy* poses in the realm of speech and writing.⁴¹ But speech had a particular quality for Burton which carried him beyond the Jonsonian formulation of speech as a mirror, and beyond the view which was eventually to be developed by Hobbes (and reformulated by Locke) of speech as the medium of social communication. Rather, for Burton, speech was both symptomatic and palliative. Speech, or rather its absence, was one of the symptoms of the burden of melancholy, which it was the task of the *Anatomy* to unravel.⁴² The *Anatomy* was a text which, like a mirror, reflected precisely those sentiments which were the reason for its composition. A text born out of melancholy, it rehearsed, in its extraordinary length, the symptoms of melancholy, hinting at (but always deferring) the promised cure.

The promised cure was speech. Quoting Lucian, Burton/Democritus claims that he wrote only because he had nobody with whom to speak. The alternative was to "recite to trees, and declaim to pillars for want of auditors" (5). Thus the *Anatomy* is already a substitute text, a trace of what should have been spoken rather than written. But later, we learn that melancholics are *pauciloqui* "of few words, and oftentimes wholly silent" (258), their friends cannot make them speak, and, tellingly, "they had rather write their mindes than speake" (259). It was not that the *pauciloqui* had little to say. On the contrary, they were over-stored with words, suffering from an excess which demanded relief. Speech was the remedy. Speech was the opening up of the mind to another. "As a bull

---

⁴¹ See Derrida's remarks on the "supplement" in his account of speech and writing in Rousseau, to be found in *Of Grammatology*, trans. Gayatri Chakravorty Spivak (Baltimore: Johns Hopkins Univ. Press, 1976), 141–64.

⁴² The importance of speech to the pathology of the *Anatomy* was recognized in Joseph L. Blau, "Robert Burton on Voice and Speech," *The Quarterly Journal of Speech* 28 (1942): 461–64. There is, of course, no precise modern equivalent to the term "melancholy." In the seventeenth century the idea of melancholy could signify a vast range of human conditions, a range which goes some way to justifying the enormous scope of Burton's treatise. Modern terms cognate with Burtonian melancholy would have to include: *ennui*, sadness, *triste*, moodiness, depression, anger, sullenness, mournfulness, and even *dementia*. The most comprehensive modern survey of the topic remains Lawrence Babb, *The Elizabethan Malady: A Study of Melancholia in English Literature from 1580 to 1642* (East Lansing: Michigan State College, 1951). But see also: L. C. Knights, *Drama and Society in the Age of Johnson* (1937; repr., New York: W. W. Norton, 1968), 315–32; Andria Beacock, "Notes on Melancholia / Schizophrenia as a Social Disease: Robert Burton, R. D. Laing, and *Hamlet*," *Massachusetts Studies in English* 6 (1979): 1–14. On the distinction between "mania" and "melancholia" see Roy Porter, *A Social History of Madness* (London: Weidenfeld and Nicholson, 1987), 104.

that is tied to a fig-tree," Burton wrote, "becomes gentle on a sudden (which some, saith Plutarch, interpret of good words), so is a savage, obdurate heart mollified by fair speeches" (362). Words, Burton observed, "are cheerful and powerful of themselves" (362), as though words carried within themselves some particular redeeming force — an observation which Locke, of course, was to deny. Words structured into narrative, moreover, offered the prospect of relief. "Simple narration many times easeth the distressed mind" (362), Burton claimed, and in that formulation it is possible to see the emergence of a kind of primitive psychoanalysis — the beginnings of "the talking cure." This "cure" was to be understood as the alleviation of symptoms which were disturbingly physical in their nature. To "ease" the mind is suggestive (in the seventeenth-century sense) of bodily purgation, a connection which Burton/Democritus makes when he observes that he had "a kind of imposthume in my head, which I was very desirous to be unladen of, and could imagine no fitter evacuation than this" (5). So, the speaker-writer relieves himself against trees and pillars (or readers), or eases himself in the solitude of his study, and the result is the *Anatomy* — a waste product which is a substitute for speech.

This language of physicality runs deep in the *Anatomy*, and in this the text alludes to older, Renaissance, views on the art of imitation. What has been voided in retiring solitude can be gleaned by another solitary and incorporated into a new product. It was Erasmus, building on Quintillian, who offered in the *Ciceronianus* (1528) a digestive metaphor for understanding the process of generating discourse:

> You must digest what you have consumed in varied and prolonged reading, and transfer it by reflection into the veins of the mind, rather than into your memory or into your notebook. Thus your natural talent, gorged on all kinds of foods, will of itself beget a discourse ... redolent ... of your own heart.[43]

Burton/Democritus, however, transforms this *topos* into the scatological. Like Plutarch's bull, passified beneath a fig tree where he is occupied with consumption and evacuation, so the writer must become a coprophagist. Dung-hills are scraped in order to "lard" otherwise "lean" books with the "fat of others Workes" (6). The result is that "not only Libraries and Shops are full of our putid [sic] Papers, but every close-stoole and Jakes" (6). The psychoanalytic concept of the "corporeality of language" has been fore-

---

[43] Quoted and translated in Cave, 45.

shadowed in a metaphor for communication which announces a cyclical process of consumption, digestion, and evacuation.[44] Nor was this image of speech as a form of evacuation unique to Burton. Francis Bacon, in his essay "Of Friendship" (itself part of a collection which grew in a Burtonian fashion throughout the early part of the seventeenth century) understood with Burton the somatic relief that speech could provide. Speech was not merely the mark of friendship. It allowed for the "ease and discharge of the fulness and swellings of the heart, which passions of all kinds do induce." Speech was a kind of self-directed mental scalpel, since, as Bacon wrote:

> We know diseases of stoppings and suffocations are the most dangerous to the body; and it is not much otherwise in the mind: you may take sarza to open the liver, steel to open the spleen, flowers of sulphur for the lungs, castoreum for the brain; but no receit openeth the heart, but a true friend, to whom you may impart . . . whatsoever lieth upon the heart to oppress it, in a kind of civil shrift or confession.[45]

Needless to say, such public confession (in which the *Anatomy* and Bacon's *Essays* seem to share in the urge to make "civil shrift") would have horrified Johnson the lexicographer, dedicated to scouring the language: ransacking it and tidying it of its waste products at the same time. Against that eighteenth-century view of conversation as a civilized encounter between individuals in the social sphere, Burton's and Bacon's view of speech as the release of an interior blockage would have appeared not merely prolix but somehow undignified, even uncivilized. But Burton's project was closer to Johnson's heart than the lexicographer might have cared to admit, since what more "interlarded" text could there be than a dictionary which sought to impart order to a language which was described as a "confused heap of words without dependence and without relation"?[46] The "confused lumpe" of the *Anatomy*, then, had become like the "confused heap" of language itself prior to Johnson's imposition of order.

---

[44] See Paul Henry, "On Language and the Body," trans. Ben Brewster, in Colin MacCabe, ed., *The Talking Cure: Essays in Psychoanalysis and Language* (Basingstoke: Macmillan, 1981), 70–74.

[45] Francis Bacon, *Essays*, ed. Michael J. Hawkins (1915 repr., London: Everyman, 1994), 68.

[46] Johnson, 128.

V. Speaking of the Body

But of course the *Anatomy* was obsessed with order. Indeed, order was its true subject. To understand the order of the *Anatomy*, we need to pursue the link between writing, speech, and the body. Ben Jonson's account in *Discoveries* provides us with both the vocabulary with which Burton was familiar, and the underlying stylistic principles which informed the *Anatomy*. Jonson observed that language, if it was to be used harmoniously, should conform to the most harmonious object in the world. And what was more harmonious than the human body? Language was thus like a building constructed according to Vitruvian principles — constructed, that is, with the proportions of the human body as its pattern.[47] For Jonson, this analogy structured his account of language at every turn: "as we consider feature and composition in a man, so words in language: in the greatness, aptness, sound, structure, and harmony of it." The human form, of course, was infinitely variable in its realization, but nevertheless conformed to the divine pattern in its underlying structure, and so with language. Having marked the degree of variation to be observed in different linguistic registers, Jonson continued: "After these, the flesh, blood, and bones come in question." The flesh, blood, and bones of language are its stylistic qualities:

> We say it is a fleshly style, when there is much periphrasis, and circuit of words; and then with more than enough, it grows fat and corpulent ... full of suet and tallow. It hath blood and juice, when the words are proper and apt, their sound sweet, and the phrase neat and picked. But where there is redundancy, both the blood and juice are faulty and vicious.[48]

By this definition, of course, the *Anatomy* — with all its periphrastic circulation of discourse — was not merely corpulent but obese. To a modern reader, Jonson would appear to be deploying nothing more than a fairly strained species of metaphor to describe language. But, to a seventeenth-century reader, this account replicated the inherent structure of

---

[47] This insistence on the correspondence between harmonious form and language concealed, for Jonson, an important moral truth. In the preface to *Cynthia's Revels* (addressed to the Court), Jonson wrote: "Beware then thou render men's figures truly, and teach them no less to hate their deformities, than to love their forms." See Ben Jonson, *The Complete Plays*, ed. Felix Schelling (1910, repr., London: Dent, 1967) 1:149.

[48] Donaldson, 575.

language. Moreover, the belief that language and the body intersected in some way ran deep into the heart of the literary culture of the sixteenth and early seventeenth centuries.[49] Language, like the physical form of the human body, was not only a divine donation, but the very mark of humanity. "Speech is the only benefit man hath to express his excellency of mind above other creatures.... In all speech, words and sense are as the body and the soul," Jonson wrote.[50] Or as Hobbes expressed it, without speech there could be "neither Common-wealth, nor Society, nor Contract, nor Peace, no more than amongst Lyons, Bears, and Wolves."[51]

The language of physicality which we encounter in Burton's *Anatomy*, then, is allied to a complex amalgam of Renaissance beliefs concerning the nature of speech, writing, and language. Writing is a process of digesting and then reproducing the thoughts of others within the discourse which is being generated. Speech is a means of evacuating the mind, easing it of its distressing burden of thought. Language, like the human body, is a divine donation and one of the distinguishing features of humanity. With these three somatic principles in mind, we can begin to see how the *Anatomy* came into being.

But there is a paradox inherent within Burton's development of the term "anatomy," which has to be traced in some detail in order to appreciate the true morphology of Burton's text. Why did Burton entitle his text the "Anatomy" of Melancholy? Why not (and perhaps more appropriately) the "compendium," the "encyclopedia," or (ironically) the "epitome" or "digest"? Burton/Democritus (predictably) offers a plethora of reasons for his choice. Commerce, he claims, is one motive since "it is a kind of policy in these days, to prefix a fantastical title to a book which is to be sold" (4). Fashion is another, and Burton/Democritus reels off the titles he is aping in a footnote: "Anatomy of Popery. Anatomy of Immortality. *Angelus Salas*, Anatomy of *Antimony*, &c." as well as "Anthony Zara, Pap. Episc., his Anatomy of Wit in four sections, members, subsections, &c.," (4). But the example of Democritus himself is the chief reason for the work's being an "anatomy." Hippocrates, Burton writes, encountering Democritus the satirical philosopher surrounded by the viscera of dissected animals, was told that these anatomical explorations were aimed

---

[49] On the intersection of language and the body in the realm of the grotesque see Neil Rhodes, *Elizabethan Grotesque* (London: Routledge and Kegan Paul, 1980), 11–13.

[50] Donaldson, 570–71.

[51] Hobbes, 24.

at discovering the "seat of this *atra bilis*, or melancholy, whence it proceeds, and how it was engendered in men's bodies" (4). The psychological and the somatic are thus re-united in the endeavors of Burton/Democritus. But there were other (unstated) reasons for Burton's choice of title, and these return us to the question of morphology.

The period of composition of Burton's work is also the period during which, in a medical sense, the art of anatomy — the scientific reduction of the human body into its composite members — reached its zenith in England. It was precisely during the period of the continual re-composition of Burton's *Anatomy* that England began to rival the great continental medical schools for proficiency in both anatomical teaching and discovery. The third edition (1628) of the *Anatomy*, indeed, appeared in the same year that the greatest anatomical discovery of the age was announced with the publication of William Harvey's work on blood circulation in his *De Motu Cordis*. Thus the public announcement of the discovery of a complex mechanical system of circulation, regulated by cardiac valves operating according to hydraulic principles, was echoed by the re-publication of Burton's text which relied on the mechanics of print production in order to present itself as a circulating text whose end had become its beginning. But such a Burtonian awareness of textual correspondence, striking as it may appear, is deceptive. Harvey is never mentioned in Burton's text, and, as J. M. Bamborough has noted, Burton mentions Vesalius — the founder of "modern" anatomy — only three times, and refers only cursorily to modern, continental anatomists.[52]

There appears, then, to be a curious silence on the part of the text which could be taken as representative of the Renaissance "culture of dissection" — that obsessive delight in partition and distinction which informed so many areas of intellectual enquiry in Europe in the sixteenth and seventeenth centuries.[53] Why was Burton the anatomist so ill-read in anatomy? That he was learned in medicine is evident from the contents of his library, but the works of the great continental anatomists of the age, whose observations were now being published throughout Europe, were entirely absent from Burton's collections.[54] In fact, this appearance of

---

[52] See J. M. Bamborough, "Introduction" in Faulkner et al., 1:xxi.

[53] For an outline of this culture, see Sawday, *The Body Emblazoned*, passim.

[54] For an account of Burton's library, the meticulous work of Kiessling is invaluable. See Nicholas K. Kiessling, *The Library of Robert Burton*, Publications of the Oxford Bibliographical Society, n. s., 22 (Oxford: Oxford Bibliographical Society, 1988). Of course, many of the works cited in the *Anatomy* were not owned by Burton, since

silence is deceptive. Anatomical knowledge, in itself, was of little interest to Burton, so that the "Digression of Anatomy" (member 2, subsections 1-4 of the first partition of the *Anatomy*) is, indeed, a somewhat cursory survey of knowledge in this area, which cites the syncretic texts of Laurentius and Helkiah Crooke as the chief authorities on the structure of the human body.[55] But what Burton did take from the anatomists was something more important than anatomical information, and that was a compositional method. When, in 1543, Vesalius published his *De corporis humani fabrica* together with an *Epitome* of the main text — the founding work of modern anatomy by virtue of its superior illustrations rather than its more detailed observations — he also offered a radically new means of understanding the body as a structure. Vesalius's method of understanding the body, in fact, was far in advance of the available technology. Vesalius proposed that the body should be *constructed* by the student of anatomy, rather than fractured into its isolated regions, sections, organs, and features. The student who, with the illustrations in front of them to be found in the *Epitome*, was encouraged to cut out the various organs from the pages and glue them to the male and female forms which the *Epitome* also, helpfully, provided, was entering into a theoretical engagement with the body of a totally new order. This was the programme, hinted at in Leonardo's anatomical notebooks, of *cresciere l'uomo* — literally building a human being.[56]

Of course, such a procedure could not be replicated in the anatomy theaters of London, Padua, Paris, Leiden, and (later) Amsterdam which, at the time during which the *Anatomy* of Burton was being issued and reissued, were drawing crowds of admirers to witness this newest of sciences in the flesh. So, as the print-history of the English editions of Vesalius illustrates, the tendency was to publish the all-important Vesalian illustrations, but accompany these with an older, more traditional text.[57] These composite texts offered a guide to the received method of dissection

---

Democritus was a great scourer of Oxford libraries. For citations of works not in Burton's library, see Kiessling, 372.

[55] The citations are to Laurentius (André Du Laurens), *Historia Anatomica* (1595), and Helkiah Crooke, *Microcosmographia* (London, 1615). Burton owned neither of these texts.

[56] For a detailed account of the Vesalian text and its intersection with the practicalities of dissection in the Renaissance, see Sawday, *The Body Emblazoned*, 100-102.

[57] On the English "re-composition" of the Vesalian text, see: S. V. Larkey, *The Vesalian Compendium of Geminus, and Nicholas Udall's Translation. Their Relation to Vesalius, Caius, Vicary, and De Mondeville* (London: Bibliographical Society, 1933), passim.

whereby the body was investigated according to its rate of decay: first the abdomen, then the thorax, finally, the head and the peripheral members. Burton's actual anatomical knowledge was, then, entirely traditional. His notion of the body was Galenic: a hierarchical structure which was informed by a belief in correspondence between the microcosm and the macrocosm.[58]

But, in another sense, the *Anatomy* was a radical experiment in the possibilities of adopting the new *form* of anatomical investigation to a compendious topic such as melancholy. We have already seen how the *Anatomy* is a text which, in its morphology, can be understood as an organic entity. In quite the opposite sense to our modern understanding of the term "anatomization," the *Anatomy* simply grew and grew. What Burton had realized was that the theoretical ideal of an intellectual *construction* of the human frame, an anatomy in the intellectual sense proposed by Vesalius, could be adapted to his own endeavor. It was one of Burton's few anatomical sources, Helkiah Crooke's *Microcosmographia*, that made the distinction between practical and theoretical anatomy. The study of anatomy, Crooke wrote in 1615, "either ... signifieth the action that is done with the hand, or the habit of the minde, that is the most perfect action of the intellect." This "perfect action of the intellect," Crooke continued, was only to be gained "by reason and discourse."[59] Within a very few years (and again the period of time mirrors the republication of Burton's text) the study of anatomy had become iconic of the pursuit of reason in general. In 1649, for example, John Hall in *The Advancement of Learning* was arguing that the practice of anatomy was akin to the very exercise of reason itself, since reason was "no better way attempted, then if the veynes of things were rightly and naturally cut

---

[58] For all Burton's traditionalism, this did not mean that his conception of the body was significantly different from his contemporaries. When, for example, Burton described the heart as "the sun of our body, the king and sole commander of it ... *primum vivens, ultimum moriens*" (97), he was making an observation undoubtedly derived from the Paracelsian works which featured so prominently in his collections, and which were still circulating in the late 1650s. But this was also an observation with which Harvey would not have disagreed in 1628, since these were the Aristotelian terms in which he addressed the king in the dedicatory preface to *De motu cordis*. Neither is it entirely fair to charge Burton with ignorance of the theory of blood circulation (as does Bamborough in Faulkner et al. 1:xxi). Harvey's theories were *not* announced in 1616, but interpolated into the MS of his *Praelectiones* at a later date. On this question see Geoffrey Keynes (following Gweneth Whitteridge), *The Life of William Harvey* (Oxford: Clarendon Press, 1978), 92–93.

[59] Crooke, 26.

up."⁶⁰ This theoretical application of the practical explorations of the anatomists was, clearly, very different from the reduction of the body into a fragmented entity. In essence, theoretical anatomy reversed the procedures of the dissection slab. Theoretically, anatomical reasoning offered a compendious, and ever-growing, fabric of knowledge in place of a scattered corpse. We can understand this morphology as analogous to the familiar Ramist device of creating bracketed tables of dichotomies — the familiar telescopic diagrams ("synopses") which Burton deployed in the *Anatomy* at the beginning of each partition of his text. Here, the subject is shown to be progressively divided, resulting in an ever-increasing flow of information over the page which is, strictly speaking, limitless. Just like the *Anatomy* itself, a branching structure whose fractile possibilities involved Burton in a never-ending attempt at revision, there was no end to the production of knowledge in these spatial diagrams, once the process of anatomization had begun. But, crucially, there was no need to reorder the whole to incorporate new information. Jonson's Aristotelian part/whole distinction had, simply, been collapsed into a structure which could branch, panoptically, forever. This organization of knowledge, in turn, had evolved from earlier attempts at representing knowledge, and even the mind itself, in terms of spatial diagrams. Print culture (as Walter Ong has observed) encouraged the reproduction of such elaborate *schema* in a way that was not possible under the conditions of manuscript production.⁶¹

If intellectual anatomy relied on print, the new forms of practical anatomy looked to speech, and endeavored to displace the primacy of written texts. For the older, traditional method of understanding the morphology of the human body (inherited from Galen, but eventually challenged by Vesalius and the modern anatomists) relied on the authority of written texts — Galen and commentaries upon Galen — which were themselves

---

⁶⁰ John Hall, *The Advancement of Learning* (1649), ed. A. K. Croston (Liverpool: Liverpool Univ. Press, 1953), 38.

⁶¹ Burton's familiarity with Ramism, indicated by the Ramist works which he bequeathed to the Bodleian and Christ Church College Libraries, has been traced by David Renaker, "Robert Burton and Ramist Method," *Renaissance Quarterly* 24 (1971): 210–20. Perhaps because Walter Ong, in his otherwise masterful study of Ramus and Ramism, dismisses the "intellectual" anatomy as a "fad," investigation of the Ramist influence on Burton has been somewhat neglected. See Walter Ong, *Ramus, Method, and the Decay of Dialogue* (1958 repr., Cambridge, Mass.: Harvard Univ. Press, 1983), 315. An exception to this neglect (besides the work of Renaker) is Karl J. Höltgen, "Robert Burton's *Anatomy of Melancholy*: Struktur und Gattungsproblematik im Licht der ramistischen Logick" *Anglia* 94 (1976): 388–403.

mapped onto the body. The body was thus the receptacle, or the blank canvas, upon which the authority of the past was reinscribed within the anatomy theater.[62] The seventeenth-century anatomist, however, struggled to break free of this burden of past authority. Turning to the body, the anatomist's project was to *speak*, directly, of the body. His listeners crowded into the anatomy theater to hear the spoken word whose authority was no longer dependent upon a prior written text, but upon the scattered and fragmented criminal body which was stretched out on the dissection slab. Within the ornate, baroque structures of the seventeenth-century anatomy theater, anatomy had emerged as a speaking science. What this science spoke of was a new order of knowledge. The base of this knowledge was the corporeal body, investigated, empirically, by the anatomists' scalpels. But the superstructure — the complex process of ordering knowledge into a scheme whereby what was being uncovered could be recorded and preserved — had to be fashioned into a flexible morphology so that new information could be reincorporated into the whole without the necessity of dismantling the entire structure, and starting out on the laborious business of reconstruction *ab intitio*. And what more flexible architecture was there than the form of a theoretical anatomy as proposed by Vesalius? Anatomy, then, served three distinct functions. First, it prioritized the spoken word over the written, a priority which appealed to Burton for the reasons we have been exploring throughout this essay. Secondly, the anatomy (in a practical rather than theoretical sense) enabled Burton to appear in the guise of universal satirist, with the scalpel of reason in his hand.[63] Thirdly, the emergence of theoretical anatomy, in which the body was *constructed* out of fragments, offered Burton the perfect model for his own project — which was nothing less than the reconstruction of the complete human being: divine in nature though fallen, an amalgam of reason and madness, the corporeal and the spiritual.

---

[62] For an account of the emergence of new forms of anatomical teaching and their symbolic significance see: Jonathan Sawday, "The Fate of Marsyas: Dissecting the Renaissance Body," in Lucy Gent and Nigel Llewellyn, eds., *Renaissance Bodies: The Human Figure in English Culture c. 1540–1660* (London: Reaktion Books, 1990), 111–35.

[63] On the *Anatomy* as a satire, see: William R. Mueller, "Robert Burton's 'Satyricall Preface,'" *Modern Language Quarterly* 15 (1954): 28–35; Bud Korkowski, "Genre and Satiric Strategy in Burton's *Anatomy of Melancholy*," *Genre* 7 (1975): 74–85. On the more general question of the intersection of medical science and satire, see: M. C. Randolph, "The Medical Concept in English Renaissance Satiric Theory: Its Possible Relations and Implications," *Studies in Philology* 38 (1941): 125–57.

VI. The Book of Books

Robert Burton's *The Anatomy of Melancholy*, despite its continual reemergence throughout the first half of the seventeenth century, was doomed to an anachronistic half-life within a relatively short period of its first appearance. In the year of the Restoration, the seventh (1660) edition of the *Anatomy* appeared. There was to be one more edition (1676) and, significantly, the 1679 "edition" of extracts, before Burton's text disappeared for over one hundred years from the print shops which had been kept busy throughout the seventeenth century with the enormous work. No further edition was published until 1800, so that, throughout the eighteenth century, Burtonians found their text only by scouring the second-hand booksellers. The 1679 edition of extracts, however, was significant in that it foreshadowed the reappearance of a new Burton — the author who (in the words of the 1679 titlepage) was to become the "wittie companion," and compiler of "jests of all sorts."[64] The Romantic movement was to rediscover Burton, true, and Keats in particular was to be indebted to the *Anatomy*, but henceforth Burton's fate was to be remembered more for his "quaintness" than his importance as a philosophical writer.[65]

Thus Burton emerged as a gargoyle. What placed him in his peculiar niche was nothing intrinsic to the work itself, for it was (as Burton himself pointed out in explaining why he had chosen to write an "anatomy") the fashion of the times to produce such vast syncretic enterprises. What ensured his silence as a philosopher but, ironically, his emergence as a "talker," was not just the shift in taste associated with eighteenth-century neo-classicism, with all its Lockeian attention to a reformulated theory of language. Rather, in 1660, the year of the seventh edition of the *Anatomy*, a new enterprise began which was to force Burton's view of endlessly recycled discourse into redundancy. That new enterprise was the formation of The Royal Society, and with it the prospect of a different kind of interrogation of nature. The Royal Society (together with the essentially

---

[64] The 1679 edition (*Versatile Ingenium*) was the precursor of Burton's most popular manifestation throughout the nineteenth and through much of the twentieth century: as the author of "witty extracts" from the larger work. For an anatomy of these anatomies of the *Anatomy* see Conn, 2–13.

[65] For Burton's influence on Keats (who owned and annotated a copy of the *Anatomy*), see: Claude L. Finney, *The Evolution of Keats' Poetry* (New York: Russell and Russell, 1963) 2: 562–64, 634–36; Janice C. Sinson, *John Keats and the Anatomy of Melancholy* (London: Keats-Shelley Memorial Association, 1971).

Lockeian view of scientific language developed by Sprat, Glanvill, Wilkins, and the *virtuosi*) promised an end to the Burtonian universe in which everything, somehow, was linked to everything else. Abraham Cowley's "Ode to the Royal Society" pronounced the epitaph on Burton's project. To the new empiricism, the *Anatomy* could be nothing more than a labyrinth "of ever fresh discourse" whose delight in "words, which are but pictures of the thought," had to be replaced by an attention to "things, the Minds right object."[66]

In that familiar, self-mocking tone in which he luxuriated, Burton described the *Anatomy* as no more than a "confused lumpe." Historians of ideas and of literature, confronting this sprawling work, have often echoed this (nevertheless) self-parodic assessment. But, in reality, Burton's project was a daring one. His holistic enterprise aimed at traversing a divide which, now, appears utterly unbridgeable. The *Anatomy* looked to one of the newest sciences — the empirical study of the body which was to become the center of post-Cartesian human science — in order to develop a methodology which would unite the centuries of scriptural and classical interpretation which culminated in the humanist undertaking of the Renaissance. In this sense, the claim that Burton looked back to humanism is undoubtedly true. But that is to tell just one half of the story, for the *Anatomy* looked forwards as well. Burton's aim was nothing less than to produce a syncresis of knowledge, handled in a form which was being developed by a series of interlocking intellectual enterprises in the sixteenth and early seventeenth centuries: the "new" observations and theoretical models of the Vesalian and post-Vesalian anatomists, together with the rhetorical and grammatical innovations of Ramism in the realm of dialectic. The logic of Burton's project (which he followed through with such single-minded determination throughout his life) might remind the twentieth-century reader of a Borgesian fable. For, henceforth, there would only need to be one book, one endlessly redivided and ever-growing anatomy of knowledge. If Burton's telescopically self-generating organization of human knowledge had been carried forward, undoubtedly it would have eventually consumed all other texts which might have existed, for there was room for them all within the fractile structure he had devised. In writing *The Anatomy of Melancholy*, Burton had embarked upon the first chapter of this book which was never to be written — this "extemporean" book which would contain all books.

---

[66] Abraham Cowley, *Works*, 7th ed. (London, 1681), 38–39.

MARTIN DZELZAINIS

Milton and the Limits of Ciceronian Rhetoric

I

WITH THE PUBLICATION OF *PRO SE DEFENSIO* in August 1655 Milton brought to a close a sequence of works — *Observations upon the Articles of Peace* (1649), *Eikonoklastes* (1649), *Pro Populo Anglicano Defensio* (1651), and *Pro Populo Anglicano Defensio Secunda* (1654) — written on behalf of the successive regimes which he served as Secretary for Foreign Tongues. In executing these various commissions, and in discharging his other duties, Milton was self-consciously complying with the humanist dictum that no truly wise or virtuous man would ever prefer a life of leisure and contemplation (*otium*) to one of active involvement in public affairs (*negotium*). Admittedly when humanists, following in the footsteps of their classical predecessors, debated the rival claims of these two ways of life they were often prepared to admit to doubts about what a commitment to *negotium* might entail. But usually this was a prelude to declaring themselves in favor of active participation.[1] Indeed, so highly was *negotium* valued during the Renaissance that, as Richard Tuck has recently observed, "all over Europe, the anterooms of princes and the council-cham-

---

I would like to thank John Creaser, Nicholas von Maltzahn, Jeremy Maule, Adam Roberts, and Quentin Skinner for reading a draft of this essay. I am also indebted to the students taking the Milton MA at Royal Holloway, especially Markus Klinge, for making me think more carefully about the issues it addresses.
    [1] For these debates see, respectively, M. T. Griffin, *Seneca: A Philosopher in Politics* (Oxford: Clarendon Press, 1976), 339–46, and Q.R.D. Skinner, *The Foundations of Modern Political Thought*, 2 vols. (Cambridge: Cambridge Univ. Press, 1978), 1:108, 115–16.

bers of republics had been filled with young men educated in the humanist manner who saw their role (whether as loyal servants of their government, or its radical critics) as in some way implementing the ideals of humanist culture."[2] Milton was no longer a young man when summoned by the Council of State in March 1649, and the loyal servant was sometimes to prove indistinguishable from the radical critic, but in almost every other respect he seems to have exemplified the type.

It is true that Hugh Trevor-Roper takes a somewhat less charitable view of what a life of *negotium* meant for Milton. He alleges that office, rather than providing an opportunity for Milton to implement humanist ideals, merely reduced him to "the shrill and blinkered scribe of a revolutionary party."[3] As we shall see, Trevor-Roper is right to the extent that Milton did accommodate himself to the new regime (albeit one anxious to shed its revolutionary aura). But irrespective of whether one takes an exalted or a jaundiced view of Milton's writings between 1649 and 1655, the underlying assumption must be that they differed in kind from what he produced either before or after. Quite how they differed is less readily apparent. However, such studies as there are which address the question of why Milton wrote as he did when he did — those of W. E. Gilman, Irene Samuel, and, most recently and extensively, Elizabeth Skerpan — concur in stressing the overwhelming importance of rhetorical models.[4] This essay will follow their example in bringing to bear on Milton's prose the generic classifications developed by classical writers on rhetoric, the most important of whom, both as theorist and practitioner, was of course Cicero. My aim in doing so, and in seeking in particular to recapture some of the significance which Cicero's *De officiis* and *Verrines* had for Milton, is that it should help to clarify what was distinctive about his published performances as a servant of the Commonwealth and the Protectorate.

---

[2] Richard Tuck, *Philosophy and Government 1572–1651*, Ideas in Context (Cambridge: Cambridge Univ. Press, 1993), 4. One of Tuck's main themes is the emergence of a major division between an "old" and a "new" humanism, with the former "dominated by the ideas and the style of Cicero" and the latter "by those of Tacitus;" Milton, he claims, was an exponent of the "new," Tacitean humanism (5, 252–53). I see Milton's allegiances as markedly Ciceronian, for reasons which I hope will become clear.

[3] H. Trevor-Roper, *Catholics, Anglicans and Puritans* (London: Collins, 1989), 233.

[4] See W. E. Gilman, *Milton's Rhetoric: Studies in His Defense of Liberty* (Columbia: Univ. of Missouri Press, 1939); Irene Samuel, "Milton on the Province of Rhetoric," *Milton Studies* 10 (1977): 177–93; Elizabeth Skerpan, *The Rhetoric of Politics in the English Revolution 1642–1660* (Columbia: Univ. of Missouri Press, 1992).

II

The author of the pseudo-Ciceronian *Rhetorica ad Herennium*, Cicero himself in his various rhetorical treatises and Quintilian in his *Institutio oratoria* all agreed that the simplest way of differentiating between the various types of oratory was to adopt the tripartite scheme of Aristotle.[5] According to this, all speeches belonged to one of three *genera*; the judicial (or forensic), which involved speaking for the prosecution or the defence; the deliberative, in which advice was offered about the best course of action to take or that most to be avoided; and demonstrative (or epideictic), the special province of which was the bestowing of praise (*laus*) and blame (*vituperatio*). But whereas Greek orators like Isocrates had specialized in epideictic (Plato we should note specifically exempts encomiasts from his ban on poets), the Romans were in practice principally concerned with forensic oratory.[6] This emphasis is duly reflected in their rhetorical treatises where most attention is given to forensic matters while epideictic in particular tends to be treated in a perfunctory and even dismissive way.[7]

Irene Samuel observes that Milton himself showed "a consistent preference for deliberative over epideictic and forensic oratory." The problem for him, she suggests, was that "human affairs with their habitual muddle" made it hard to keep to this generic preference since "to persuade others almost inevitably involves contending with opponents."[8] It is arguable, however, that Samuel has underestimated the degree to which such a mixture of genres was conventional. The ancient rhetoricians themselves were the first to admit that these categories were misleadingly

---

[5] See Aristotle, *The "Art" of Rhetoric*, trans. J. H. Freese, Loeb Classical Library (London: Heinemann, 1959), 32–39 (1358b–1359a); [Cicero], *Ad C. Herennium de ratione dicendi [Rhetorica ad Herennium]*, trans. H. Caplan, Loeb Classical Library (London: Heinemann, 1964), 4–5 (1.2.2); Cicero, *De inventione*, trans. H. M. Hubbell, Loeb Classical Library (London: Heinemann, 1960), 17 (1.5.7); Cicero, *De partitione oratoria*, trans. H. Rackham, Loeb Classical Library (London: Heinemann, 1960), 362–6 (20.70); Quintilian, *Institutio oratoria*, trans. H. M. Hubbell, Loeb Classical Library, 4 vols. (London: Heinemann, 1949), 1:390–91 (3.3.14–15; 3.4.1).

[6] See Plato, *Republic*, 10:607d.

[7] See Quentin Skinner, "'*Scientia civilis*' in Classical Rhetoric and in the Early Hobbes," in Nicholas Phillipson and Quentin Skinner eds., *Political Discourse in Early Modern Britain* (Cambridge: Cambridge Univ. Press, 1993), 75.

[8] Samuel, "Milton on the Province of Rhetoric," 182.

arbitrary. Thus Aristotle allows that epideictic can perform some of the functions of deliberative oratory since "to praise a man is in one respect akin to urging a course of action."[9] The *Ad Herennium* notes that although epideictic is "rarely employed by itself" it is frequently seen that "in judicial and deliberative causes extensive sections are devoted to praise or censure."[10] Even Cicero, who at times makes some disparaging remarks about epideictic as we shall see, has one of the speakers in his *De oratore* admit that "these topics of praise and blame" are employed "in every class of law-suit" while another speaker in his *De partitione oratore* even claims that "there is no class of oratory capable of producing more copious rhetoric or of doing more service to the state" than epideictic.[11] Nor were these merely theoretical concessions. When Cicero, in the *Orator*, seeks to illustrate the adaptability of epideictic style he needs to look no further than his own forensic speeches, the *Verrines*, for examples.[12] His *Pro Archia* includes a famous and influential panegyric on poetry. And, as Quintilian points out, "the published speeches of Cicero directed against his rivals in the election to the consulship, and against Lucius Piso, Clodius and Curio, are full of denunciation, and were notwithstanding delivered in the senate as formal expressions of opinion in the course of debate." This willingness to complicate both the theory and practice of rhetoric is summed up by Quintilian's remark that the division into three *genera* "is easy and neat rather than true: for all three kinds rely on the mutual assistance of the other."[13]

Although Cicero often commented on the decay of eloquence in his own time, he could not have foreseen the changes that were to occur as a result of social and political developments under the principate.[14] The reduced role of the senate, the increase in treason trials, and the activities of the informers meant that deliberative and forensic oratory went into de-

---

[9] Aristotle, *Rhetoric*, 191 (1367b). See B. Vickers, *In Defence of Rhetoric* (Oxford: Clarendon Press, 1988), 55–56.

[10] *Ad Herennium*, 183–85 (3.7.7).

[11] Cicero, *De oratore*, trans. E. W. Sutton and H. Rackham, Loeb Classical Library, 2 vols. (London: Heinemann, 1959–60), 1:462–63 (2.85.349); *De partitione*, 362–63 (20.69).

[12] Cicero, *Orator*, trans. H. M. Hubbell, Loeb Classical Library (London: Heinemann, 1962), 480–83 (62.210).

[13] Quintilian, *Institutio*, 1:396–97, 464–65 (3.4.15; 3.7.2).

[14] For example, see Cicero, *Brutus*, 2.7; *De officiis*, 2.67.

cline.[15] Conversely, panegyric came into vogue; as Winterbottom points out, "it is no coincidence that this is the only sort of speech preserved for us other than fragmentarily after the death of Cicero."[16] In fact, epideictic oratory never lost its new-found status. It survived the classical period intact, and, as has often been remarked, prospered to the extent of becoming the central genre in medieval and Renaissance literature.[17] But the triumph of epideictic discourse poses an obvious problem for the student of Renaissance oratory: if it is literally true that "all literature became subsumed under epideictic, and all writing was perceived as occupying the related spheres of praise and blame," then more elaborate criteria are needed to differentiate one work from another.[18] For example, Vickers cannot but be right to classify Sir Philip Sidney's *Defence of Poesy* as "a work of epideictic rhetoric, praising poetry and downgrading other verbal arts."[19] But Imbrie seems no less correct when she identifies it as a forensic oration.[20] This being so, I can see no real objection to calling it epideictic-forensic since this seems to capture what Sidney was actually trying to achieve. The same liberty has been taken here with Milton.[21] To do otherwise would be to strive after a generic purity disavowed by the ancient rhetoricians, and to impose limits which Cicero himself did not observe in practice.

Milton's pamphlet *Of Education*, addressed to Samuel Hartlib and published in June 1644, is a case in point. It is cast in the form of a letter, a

---

[15] See G. Kennedy, *The Art of Rhetoric in the Roman World, 300 B.C.-A.D.300* (Princeton: Princeton Univ. Press, 1972), 446-64.

[16] M. Winterbottom, "Quintilian and Rhetoric," in *Empire and Aftermath: Silver Latin 2*, ed. T. A. Dorey (London: Routledge, 1975), 89.

[17] See E. R. Curtius, *European Latin Literature and the Latin Middle Ages*, trans. W. R. Trask (London: Routledge, 1953), 155-66; O. B. Hardison, *The Enduring Monument: A Study of the Idea of Praise in Renaissance Literary Theory and Practice* (Chapel Hill: Univ. of North Carolina Press, 1962), 24-42; B. Vickers, "Epideictic and Epic in the Renaissance," *New Literary History* 14 (1982): 500-502, 505-13.

[18] Vickers, *Defence*, 54.

[19] Vickers, *Defence*, 292.

[20] A. E. Imbrie, "Defining Nonfiction Genres," in *Renaissance Genres: Essays on Theory, History and Interpretation*, ed. B. K. Lewalski (Cambridge, Mass.: Harvard Univ. Press, 1986), 63.

[21] John Creaser and Jeremy Maule both advised that it might be better to avoid talking of genres at all and to adopt instead the terminology used by Alastair Fowler in chap. 7 of his *Kinds of Literature* (Oxford: Clarendon Press, 1982). But see Fowler's own cautionary note, p. 114.

genre which, like the sermon, only came fully into its own in the Renaissance. Initially, Erasmus sought to assimilate letters to the classical *genera*, arguing that they were either deliberative, forensic, or epideictic, but he later added a fourth *genus*, the "familiar" letter which also had a classical precursor in Cicero's *Epistulae ad familiares*.[22] But when Milton arranged for his own *Epistolarum Familiarium Liber Unus* to be published in 1674, the volume did not include *Of Education*. Its absence is explained easily enough by the fact that it had already been republished as an appendix to the *Poems* in 1673, but it is clear that it would not have fitted the volume's categories in any case. For although Milton's relationship with Hartlib dominates the exordium it is not a familiar letter as such, but deliberative, in that it urges the merits of a new model of education, and epideictic, in that it praises that model while censuring existing practices. At the same time, however, *Of Education* is also the closest Milton came to composing an essay in the classical manner on the function and importance of oratory itself; indeed, the title of one of Cicero's unfinished works, *De optimo genere oratorum* (The Best Kind of Orator), would serve it almost as well.

This may not be quite what readers are led to expect by Milton's much-quoted assertion, placed prominently after the exordium, that the "end then of learning is to repair the ruins of our first parents by regaining to know God aright."[23] In fact, he pays relatively scant attention to religion in the work, the actual theme of which is held back until he has finished his narrative "demonstration of what we should not doe." Only then, on the third of the text's eight pages, does he show his hand: "I call therefore a compleate and generous Education that which fits a man to perform justly, skilfully and magnanimously all the offices both private and publike of peace and war" (2:376-79). The term "offices" instantly calls to mind the most influential of all classical works of moral philosophy, Cicero's *De officiis*, ostensibly a letter of guidance addressed to his son who

---

[22] For these developments, see C. Guillén, "Notes towards the Study of the Renaissance Letter," in Lewalski, *Renaissance Genres*, 70-101, and J. R. Henderson, "Erasmus on the Art of Letter-Writing," in J. J. Murphy (ed.), *Renaissance Eloquence*, (Berkeley: Univ. of California Press, 1981), 331-55. For Milton, see N. Wright, "Milton's Use of Latin Formularies," *Studies in Philology* 40 (1943): 390-98.

[23] *The Complete Prose Works of John Milton*, ed. D. M. Wolfe et al., 8 vols. (New Haven: Yale Univ. Press, 1953-82), 2:366-67. Where possible, further reference to this, cited as the Yale Prose, will be included in the text by volume and page number.

was studying in Athens. Cicero sets out his main precepts in book 1, where he weighs *otium* against *negotium*, deciding that "all the praise that belongs to virtue lies in action" (1:19); considers which occupations "should be thought fit for a free man [*liberales*], and which demeaning [*sordidi*]" (1:150); questions the prevailing assumption that, of the highest forms of office, the military is superior to the civil (1:74–76); and concludes that the triumphs of oratory, his own amongst them, represent the apogee of civil achievement (1:77–78).[24] Milton's curriculum is informed by the same values, being designed to promote a "delight in manly, and liberall exercises," and to supply the commonwealth with those who will proved "renowned and perfect Commanders in the service of their Country" and "stedfast pillars of the State" (2:385, 398, 412).

We need to ask, however, why Milton thought it necessary to reiterate these precepts at this time. Admittedly, this is a question which some commentators would think it not worth posing. One sees *Of Education* as "devoid of rhetoric" and with a "thesis" which is "self-evident."[25] Others regard it as a somewhat unrealistic, idealized project which can be compared to others then in circulation but which otherwise flies in the face of realities rather than engaging with them.[26] But this is to overlook the impatience with which Milton himself dismissed such impractical schemes only months later in *Areopagitica*: "To sequester out of the world into *Atlantick* and *Eutopian* polities, which can never be drawn into use, will not mend our condition" (2:526). And it is also to ignore the beleaguered state of the parliamentary cause which, having come close to defeat in 1643, saw its armies decimated in 1644. A major victory was won at

---

[24] The English translation of *De officiis* used throughout is that by Margaret Atkins in Cicero, *On Duties*, ed. M. T. Griffin and M. Atkins, Cambridge Texts in the History of Political Thought (Cambridge: Cambridge Univ. Press, 1991). Quotations may be located by using the divisions of the work; this applies also to incidental references to the Latin original, taken from Cicero, *De officiis*, ed. W. Miller, Loeb Classical Library (London: Heinemann, 1975).

[25] John Milton, *Selected Prose*, ed. C. A. Patrides (Harmondsworth: Penguin, 1974), 29.

[26] See Yale Prose, 2:206–12; Perez Zagorin, *Milton: Aristocrat & Rebel: the Poet and his Politics* (Rochester, N.Y.: D. S. Brewer, 1992), 61. The account offered in R. T. Fallon, *Captain or Colonel: The Soldier in Milton's Life and Art* (Columbia: Univ. of Missouri Press, 1984), 64–67, is a striking exception. For a fuller treatment of the tract, especially its Ciceronian aspect, see my "Milton's Classical Republicanism," in David Armitage, Armand Himy and Quentin Skinner eds., *Milton and Republicanism* (Cambridge: Cambridge Univ. Press, 1995), 9–15.

Marston Moor in July (a month after *Of Education* appeared), but this was only for its fruits to be squandered, politically at London and on the field at Lostwithiel and Newbury.[27] Looked at in this light, Milton's attention to the ills afflicting the army and his insistence on the benefits which the training he prescribes will bring, appear very much to the point.

But Milton was no less concerned by the fact that in this "dangerous fit of the common-wealth," as he calls it, many "great counsellors" had turned out to be but "poor, shaken, uncertain reeds" (2:398). Once again, the diagnosis prompts the remedy: his curriculum will also ensure that the commonwealth is supplied with leaders of greater resolve and enhanced ability to influence the course of events. For Milton, the reason why education was failing to achieve these ends was summed up by its liking for "preposterous exaction" (literally "back to front," as in the Latin *praeposterus*) which forced "the empty wits of children to compose Theams, verses, and Orations" which should really be "acts of ripest judgement and the finall work of a head fill'd by long reading, and observing." Milton's solution is simply to insist that things be done in the right order and at the right time. Before composing anything, students must complete a comprehensive, even heroic course of reading: "From hence and not till now will be the right season of forming them to be able writers and composers in every excellent matter, when they shall be thus fraught with an universall insight into things." The outcome of proceeding in this fashion was sure to be that "honour and attention would be waiting on their lips" whenever they spoke in parliament or from the pulpit (2:372, 406).

Perhaps the best example of the kind of thing Milton had in mind is furnished by his own *Areopagitica* (November 1644) which urged parliament to repeal its licensing order of June 1643. Much has been made, rightly, of the title page (2:485) as an "entry code" to interpretation which encapsulates the issues at stake.[28] Thus the full title, *Areopagitica, A Speech of M^r. John Milton for the Liberty of Vnlicenc'd Printing, To the Parlament of England*, identifies it as a deliberative oration, while the fact of its existing only in print identifies it as an example of secondary rather than primary (that is, written rather than spoken) rhetoric. However, the

---

[27] See A. Woolrych, "Cromwell as Soldier," in *Oliver Cromwell and the English Revolution*, ed. J. Morrill (London: Longman, 1990), 100–101.

[28] A. Patterson, *Censorship and Interpretation: the Conditions of Writing and Reading in Early Modern England* (Madison: Univ. of Wisconsin Press, 1985), 115.

distinction between the two was far from absolute. Parliamentary speeches, for example, were often printed, though not always exactly as delivered, and some were printed though never given, as were a number of complete fabrications.[29] Nor was this only a phenomenon of print culture. Cicero published both the speeches he gave and some which he did not.[30] Attentive to these ambiguities, Milton seeks to differentiate between his own not-to-be-delivered oration and such as could or would have been delivered but for some contingency by alluding to the Athenian orator who *never* delivered the speeches he wrote: Isocrates. The point, I take it, is that Milton would rather appear an outsider exercising a known if restricted right of access than cut the figure of a would-be insider reduced to publishing the speech he would have given if only he were a member; paradoxically, keeping a distance secured entry, not exclusion. In lighting on Isocrates' *Areopagiticus*, however, Milton resolves one ambiguity only to introduce another; for, as has often been noted, Isocrates was actually urging his audience, the Ekklesia, to accept that the Areopagus should resume its lapsed powers of social control and censorship.[31]

Pitted against this is the epigraph, Milton's translation of lines from Euripides' *Supplices*:

> *This is true Liberty when free born men*
> *Having to advise the public may speak free,*
> *Which he who can, and will, deserv's high praise,*
> *Who neither can, nor will, may hold his peace;*
> *What can be juster in a State then this?*

Since, as Patterson notes, this was "the formula with which, after the democratic reforms of 436 BC, the herald opened the proceedings of the democratic assembly in Athens, the Ekklesia," Milton could be said to be

---

[29] See A. D. T. Cromartie, "The Printing of Parliamentary Speeches, November 1640–July 1642," *Historical Journal* 33 (1990): 23–44. I am grateful to Jeremy Maule for this reference.

[30] See R. G. M. Nisbet, "The Speeches," in *Cicero*, ed. T. A. Dorey (London: Routledge, 1964), 62.

[31] See R. C. Jebb, *The Attic Orators from Antiphon to Isaeus*, 2 vols. (London, 1893), 2:5, 212–13; J. A. Wittreich, "Milton's *Areopagitica*: Its Isocratic and Ironic Contexts," *Milton Studies* 4 (1972): 101–15; P. M. Dowling, "*Areopagitica* and *Areopagiticus*: the Significance of the Isocratic Precedent," *Milton Studies* 21 (1985): 46–69.

offering parliament a choice "between different versions and phases of Athenian democracy."[32] The implication is that parliament's decision to accept or reject Milton's deliberations on the licensing order will be tantamount to choosing one or other of these paths for itself.

However, there is one allusion in the body of the text itself which is no less significant. Towards the end of the digression, in which he rehearses the complaints of Italian intellectuals about the stifling effects of the Inquisition, Milton recounts his astonishment at hearing the same protests

> by as lerned men at home utterd in time of Parliament against an order of licencing; and that so generally, that when I had disclos'd my self a companion of their discontent, I might say, if without envy, that he whom an honest *quaestorship* had indear'd to the *Sicilians*, was not more by them importun'd against *Verres*, then the favourable opinion which I had among many who honour ye, and are known and respected by ye, loaded me with entreaties and perswasions; that I would not despair to lay together that which just reason should bring into my mind, toward the removal of an undeserved thraldom upon lerning. (2:539)

This refers to Cicero's sole appearance as prosecutor when he reluctantly agreed to act on behalf of the Sicilians, as their former quaestor, against their former governor, Gaius Verres in 70 BC. Cicero's performance in the extortion court was so effective that Verres fled before he had completed his case. Not to be baulked, Cicero published the speeches he would have delivered together with (and in many respects indistinguishable from) the ones he had given.[33] Milton draws upon these circumstances to present himself as one who has been prevailed upon to speak, and to establish that this is not the "disburdning of a particular fancie" but the voicing of a "common grievance" (2:539). But they also permit Milton to cast himself in the part of a public prosecutor seeking, as it were, to convict the licensing order. What all this points to, in short, is the forensic as distinct from the deliberative aspect of *Areopagitica*.

Precisely because the *Verrines* were in part simulacra of court proceedings, they provided an especially suitable model for the conduct of a no-

---

[32] Patterson, *Censorship*, 115–16.

[33] See R. E. Smith, *Cicero the Statesman* (Cambridge: Cambridge Univ. Press, 1966), 63–71.

tional prosecution. For example, Cicero frequently apostrophizes the extortion court, and also employs the figure of *communicatio* (in which the speaker appears to address, or confer with, members of the audience). Milton avails himself of the same devices, apostrophizing the "High Court of Parliament" (a significant reminder of its technical claim to powers of jurisdication as well as legislation) in his opening sentence, and referring throughout to "Lords and Commons" or more simply, as above, "ye." Speaking communicatively, he gestures towards the figure of "one of your own now sitting in Parliament, the chief of learned men reputed in this Land, Mr. *Selden*" (2:486, 513). Cicero also makes great play with physical evidence, often producing with a dramatic flourish the letters, testimonies, transcripts, and forged tablets he had gathered in his investigations. And Milton follows suit, handing over as if for scrutiny ("Voutsafe to see") the imprimaturs transcribed from actual volumes by Bernado Davanzati Bostichi and George Conn (2:503-4).[34]

But the congruence between the *Verrines* and *Areopagitica* may run deeper still. At the very moment that Cicero was prosecuting Verres in the extortion court, the court itself, a patrician stronghold, was under threat of reform from outside. Cicero exploits this by reminding the court repeatedly that it is on trial as much as Verres, going on to suggest that the only way in which it can reestablish its credentials, appease the reformers and so save itself, is by finding Verres guilty.[35] Milton seeks to pressurize the two Houses in exactly the same way: at this juncture, he warns, the only way they can avoid alienating the support without which their existence will be imperilled is by repealing the order. By the time he approaches his peroration, the threat to those who support licensing is hardly veiled: "Beleeve it, Lords and Commons, they who counsell ye to such a suppressing, doe as good as bid ye suppress your selves" (2:559).

---

[34] For examples of Cicero's use of the "recita" formula imitated here by Milton, see *The Verrine Orations* [*In C. Verrem*], trans. L. Greenwood, 2 vols. (London: Heinemann, 1959), 1:204, 210, 222, 224, 260, 274, 284 ("Actionis secundae in C. Verrem liber primus"). For the imprimaturs, see L. Miller, "Italian Imprimaturs in Milton's *Areopagitica*," *Papers of the Bibliographical Society of America* 65 (1971): 345-55.

[35] This is the usual view, based largely on Cicero's testimony. But for a deeply skeptical account, questioning whether Cicero was actually participating in a popular assault on the Sullan constitution, and even casting doubt on the political significance as such of the case, see T. N. Mitchell, *Cicero: the Ascending Years* (New Haven: Yale Univ. Press, 1979), 107-9, 133-49.

The Long Parliament finally succumbed to outside forces when it was purged by the army on 6 December 1648 — the *putsch* which led to the king's trial and execution the following month. Milton's response to these events was embodied in *The Tenure of Kings and Magistrates* (February 1649), rhetorically perhaps the most complex of his English prose works. Since it takes the five-part form specifically recommended by Quintilian for judicial oratory there can be little doubt about its forensic character.[36] This is so despite its often-noted failure to mention Charles I by name and despite Milton's apparent disclaimer in the exordium: "who in particular is a Tyrant cannot be determin'd in a general discours, otherwise then by supposition; his particular charge, and the sufficient proof of it must determin that: which I leave to Magistrates" (3:197). The fact that *The Tenure* is to avoid the "particular charge" against Charles and identifies itself instead as "a general discours" should not be taken to mean that it is not forensic but rather as indicating that it will concern itself with one of the four *constitutiones* ("issues") typically dealt with in forensic speeches, as laid down by Cicero in *De inventione* (1:10; 2:62–71): the *constitutio generalis* or qualitative issue concerning fundamental issues of right and wrong.[37]

This is moreover only part of what Milton is seeking to accomplish, as the statement of his intentions on the title page (3:189) makes clear:

> PROVING, That it is Lawfull, and hath been held so through all Ages, for any, who have the Power, to call to account a Tyrant, or wicked KING, and after due conviction, to depose, and put him to death; if the ordinary MAGISTRATE have neglected, or deny'd to doe it.
> And that they, who of late so much blame Deposing, are the Men that did it themselves.

We should note the care with which Milton circumscribes the topic he is about to address; not whether Charles is a tyrant, and not if a tyrant may be proceeded against, but *who* is to proceed against one when those usually charged with the duty have defaulted. The answer he arrives at and urges his audience to accept in the more deliberative parts of the oration is that literally anyone may, if they have the power. On this view of the matter, the army was fully justified in intervening to ensure that the king was

---

[36] See Quintilian, *Institutio*, 1:515 (3.9.1).
[37] See Cicero, *De inventione*, 21–33, 225–37.

brought to trial, given the scandalous neglect of its duty by parliament, the "Magistrates" of the work's title. But it is obvious that to present the issue in this way is at one and the same time to praise the army and those who invited it to act, and to censure the Presbyterian majority in parliament which, urged on by its claque of divines outside, had favored a negotiated settlement with Charles. As a result, epideictic, in the form of *laus* and *vituperatio*, takes up much of the work, and especially the exordium and peroration where Milton labors to expose the hypocrisy of the Presbyterians who now opposed the purge and trial ("who of late so much blame Deposing") even though they had at one time done everything in their power to bring Charles down.

In developing these arguments, Milton turned to Cicero and, above all, to *De officiis*. After all, the assassination of Julius Caesar — or rather the tyrannicide, as Cicero insists — overshadows *De officiis* as much as the action against Charles does *The Tenure*.[38] What Milton took from *De officiis*, however, was not so much the example of one tyrant's fate as its analysis of tyranny. This analysis derives in large part from the stoic view that duties relate not only to family, friends, and country but extend to mankind as a whole. As Cicero puts it, "men are born for the sake of men," and thus form a "fellowship" bound together "by the exchange of dutiful services [*officiorum*]" (1:22). The antithesis to these peaceful exchanges is hostility, which leads to exclusion from society. The tyrant is the prime example of one who loses human status by behaving like a wild beast (*belua*) and, like a wild beast, may be killed by anyone (3:32). Each of these steps is reproduced in *The Tenure*. Given that there is a "mutual bond of amity and brother-hood between man and man over all the World," Milton says, it follows that whoever "keeps peace with me, neer or remote, of whatsoever Nation, is to mee as farr as all civil and human offices an Englishman and a neighbour." It is not therefore "distance of place that makes enmitie, but enmity that makes distance." And the conclusion he draws from this, like Cicero, is that a tyrant is to be regarded as "a savage Beast" and "common pest" to be slain by anyone (3.206, 212, 214, 215).

The real value of this argument lay in its radical simplicity. For what it enabled Milton to do was to obliterate the complex set of distinctions — between private persons and inferior magistrates, foreign and domestic

---

[38] See Cicero, *On Duties*, xii–xiii.

tyrants, and tyrants with and without title — upon which the constitutional theory of resistance depended. And this mattered in turn because the theory had been invoked by the Presbyterians in their attempts to denounce the purge as illegitimate.[39] To them, the army consisted of mere private persons who had usurped the authority due only to the inferior magistrate. But from a stoic perspective, of course, these were distinctions which made very little sense.

III

The Tenure proved to be Milton's entrée to government service. However, the fact that his efforts were rewarded in this way can be seen as issuing in a paradox. For while it was in part a display of deliberative powers which led to the invitation from the council of state, the outcome of accepting it was that he found himself almost invariably writing to a brief which called on every part of his rhetorical repertoire other than the deliberative. Samuel is certainly right to distinguish between works which "were in a sense imposed tasks" and the earlier ones which Milton "wrote wholly of his own choice." Where she errs is not much in maintaining that the latter were "consistently in the deliberative vein, advising on a course of action, not attacking or defending" (which, as we have seen, was not the case) as in failing to note the degree to which those which were commissioned lacked deliberative edge.[40] The fact is that office constrains the office-holder, and if this explains why governments often sought to manage opposition by recruiting its leading lights (witness the careers of Edward Lyttleton, William Noy, and John Selden in the 1630s), it is easy to see how it could also shackle the more zealous supporters of a regime. Once in post, Milton rapidly adjusted himself to the new realities.

One such accommodation is inscribed in the second edition of *The Tenure* itself, perhaps published by October 1649. The title page advertises the "*many Testimonies also added out of the best & learnedest among Protestant Divines asserting the position of this book*," a reference to the dozen or

---

[39] For this aspect of the work, see John Milton, *Political Writings*, ed. M. Dzelzainis, Cambridge Texts in the History of Political Thought (Cambridge: Cambridge Univ. Press, 1991), xii–xv. For other aspects of Milton's attack on the Presbyterians, see my "Milton, *Macbeth*, and Buchanan," *The Seventeenth Century* 4 (1989): 55–66.

[40] Samuel, "Milton on the Province of Rhetoric," 182.

so pages of new material tacked on at the end of the peroration. However, this testimony not only mars the five-part *dispositio* of the original text, but also contradicts rather than supports its argument. Whereas Milton had maintained in the first edition that private persons could legitimately seize the initiative from the inferior magistrate in calling a tyrant or wicked king to account, he now finds that it is the "cleere and positive determination" of these divines "that to doe justice on a lawless King, is to a privat man unlawful, to an inferior Magistrate lawfull" (3.257).[41] It would be hard to improve upon this as a summary of orthodox Calvinist teaching on resistance.

Milton in fact signalled his flexibility on this point within weeks rather than months of taking office. Commissioned on 28 March 1649 and published in mid-May, *Observations upon the Articles of Peace* was in part a reply to what Milton styled "an Insolent and seditious Representation from the Scotch Presbytery at *Belfast*." The Belfast Presbyterians had again denounced the "Sectaries in *England*" as "but private men," repeating the charge levelled by their London colleagues against the army at the time of the purge. Significantly, Milton chose not to rehearse his earlier arguments about the lawfulness of individual political action, but contented himself with accusing the Presbyterians of "Despising Dominion," "speaking ill of Dignities," and "not fearing the due correction of their Superiors." Indeed, he loftily instructs them that "as Members of the Common Wealth they ought to mix with other Commoners, and in that temporall Body to assume nothing above other Private persons." Now that the boot was on the other foot, Milton switched with due facility from legitimating individual action against the Long Parliament to defending the Rump, the "sovran Magistracy of *England*," against its individual detractors (3:296–97, 300, 320, 321, 333).

The Rump's religious policies elicited a different but no less revealing response early in 1652 when a concerted effort was made to turn back the tide of radicalism. A leading Independent divine, John Owen, together with fourteen others, complained to parliament on 10 February about the recently published Racovian Catechism, a complaint which led to the setting up of one committee which eventually examined Milton for having apparently approved publication of the Catechism in August 1650, and to

---

[41] On changes to the second edition of *The Tenure*, see Milton, *Political Writings*, xviii–xix.

the setting up of another to receive proposals for establishing a state church. Owen's proposals, submitted on 18 February, later turned out to include a set of fifteen "fundamentals," framed with an eye to rooting out antitrinitarianism. They were to be used to test ministers' doctrinal orthodoxy and hence their eligibility for state maintenance. Although the scheme was referred back to the Committee for the Propagation of the Gospel on 29 April, this was with the proviso that tithes would continue to be paid until a suitable alternative could be found.[42]

Given that Milton wanted to see the complete separation of church and state, wished ministers to be maintained (if at all) on a voluntary basis, and thought that attempts to define heresy were vitiated by a fundamental misunderstanding of what the term "heresy" meant, there was much here to alarm him. It is striking therefore that he chose not to voice his concerns to a wider public in deliberative form (though it has been speculated that he influenced Marchamont Nedham's editorials in *Mercurius Politicus* attacking trends in religious policy).[43] Instead, he privately addressed laudatory sonnets to Cromwell (in May) and to Sir Henry Vane the Younger (in July).[44] It is true that the poems are deliberative in the sense that Milton projects a vision of Ciceronian statesmanship upon Cromwell and Vane which he hopes they will then display in the forum of ecclesiastical debate. Thus Cromwell is reminded that "peace hath her victories / No less renowned than war" (lines 10–11), echoing Cicero's claim (*De officiis*, 1:74) that "many achievements of civic life have proved greater and more famous than those of war." The "new foes" (line 11) Cromwell must defeat are the would-be architects of a state church. Similarly, his praise of Vane, "Than whom a better senator ne'er held / The helm of Rome, when gowns not arms repelled" her enemies (lines 2–3), is borrowed from Cicero's boast about his defeat of Catiline:

---

[42] See *Commons Journals*, 7:111, 113–14, 128; W. A. Shaw, *A History of the English Church during the Civil Wars and under the Commonwealth 1640–1660*, 2 vols. (1900), 1:80n; S. R. Gardiner, *History of the Commonwealth and the Protectorate*, 4 vols. (1903), 2:98–105; B. Worden, "Toleration and the Cromwellian Protectorate," in *Persecution and Toleration: Studies in Church History*, vol. 21, ed. W. J. Sheils (Oxford: 1984), 203, 215; W. R. Parker, *Milton: A Biography*, 2 vols. (Oxford: Clarendon Press, 1968), 1:395; 2:994.

[43] See *Mercurius Politicus*, no. 101, 6–13 May 1652, 1585–89; no. 114, 5–12 August 1652, 1785–89; C. Hill, *Milton and the English Revolution* (London: Faber, 1977), 184.

[44] References are to the texts in John Milton, *Complete Shorter Poems*, ed. J. Carey (London: Longman, 1971), 323–27.

"when I held the helm of the republic, did not arms then yield to the toga?" (*De officiis*, 1:77). And the fact that Vane has also learned to draw the bounds between "spiritual power and civil," makes him uniquely qualified as a guide: "on thy firm hand Religion leans" (lines 10, 13). But undeniably austere and elevated though the sonnets are, they are still flattering — indeed, all the more so *because* austere and elevated. At this juncture, it seems that Milton (to borrow a phrase from Marc Fumaroli) only "had recourse to the deliberative through the epideictic."[45]

There may be one exception to this apparent abstinence from deliberative writing; namely, the suggestion that Milton "planned and in part composed" his *Considerations Touching the Likeliest Means to Remove Hirelings out of the Church* when the question of tithes was again being debated in the Nominated Assembly of July to December 1653.[46] If this was the case, however, then it is significant that it was only published in August 1659; that is, some three months after the fall of Richard's Protectorate. It was also the work in which he seized the opportunity explicitly to repudiate the whole of the Protectorate as "a short but scandalous night of interruption" (7:274).[47] For a period of some ten years, therefore, between *The Tenure* in 1649 and the twin-treatises, *A Treatise of Civil Power in Ecclesiastical Causes* and *Considerations*, in 1659, Milton refrained from publishing anything which was openly deliberative. His awareness that this hiatus had come to an end, and that he was free once more "*to advise the public*" as he had in *Areopagitica*, is underscored by the epigraph, adapted from Juvenal, on the title page of the second edition of *The Readie and Easie Way to Establish a Free Commonwealth* (1660): "*et nos / consilium dedimus Syllæ, demus populo nunc*" (We have advised Sulla [i.e., Oliver Cromwell] himself, advise we now the People) (7:405).[48] To put it another way: while it has been customary to think of the twenty years Milton

---

[45] M. Fumaroli, "Rhetoric, Politics, and Society: From Italian Ciceronianism to French Classicism," in Murphy, *Renaissance Eloquence*, 258.

[46] The suggestion is W. B. Hunter's: see Yale Prose, 7:230n.

[47] See A. Woolrych, "Milton and Cromwell: 'A Short But Scandalous Night of Interruption?'" in *Achievements of the Left Hand: Essays on the Prose of John Milton*, ed. M. Lieb and J. T. Shawcross (Amherst: Univ. of Massachusetts Press, 1974), 185–218.

[48] For doubts about the identification of Cromwell as Sulla, see Austin Woolrych's remarks, Yale Prose, 7:205. I am grateful to David Armitage and Blair Worden for advice on this point. See also my "Juvenal, Charles X Gustavus and Milton's Letter to Richard Jones," *The Seventeenth Century* 9 (1994): 25–34.

devoted to prose as an extended lacuna in his poetic career, we should also see the ten years of government service as constituting a kind of lacuna within his prose career.

This is not in any way to disparage the great achievement of these years, the three Latin *Defences*. Milton was immensely proud of his victory over Salmasius in the first of them and constantly returned to the scene of his triumph ("not without cause, but without end," as Seneca once remarked of the same tendency in Cicero), while Andrew Marvell judged his performance in the second as rising "to the Height of the Roman Eloquence."[49] Rather it is to draw attention to their particular combination of the epideictic and the forensic.[50] Indeed, their generic duality should be insisted upon if only to correct the recent claim that the *Defensio* and the *Defensio Secunda* are "really judicial" while the *Pro Se Defensio* is simply to be classified as epideictic.[51] Certainly, the forensic character of the first two is not in doubt: their titles alone suggest as much. But whereas Cicero's judicial pleas were entered on behalf of an individual client (*Pro Milone*, *Pro Rabirio*, *Pro Sestio*, etc), Milton defends a collective client, the people of England (*Pro Populo Anglicano*), replying first to the charges made by Salmasius in *Defensio Regia* (1649) and then to Pierre Du Moulin's *Regii Sanguinis Clamor ad Coelum adversus Parricidas Anglicanos* (1652) — a work Milton mistakenly attributed to Alexander More. It can hardly be denied, however, that *laudatio* and *vituperatio* are integral features of these works. In the *Defensio*, for example, quite apart from subjecting Salmasius to comprehensive and unremitting denigration, Milton repeatedly denounces the Presbyterians for their hypocrisy while singling out the army and its supporters for praise.[52] Epideictic exercises of this kind feature more prominently still in *Defensio Secunda*. Milton seizes every opportunity, however slight, to expose More's sexual misdemeanours to censure. Equally, invective gives way to panegyric at regular intervals. Thus Queen Christina of Sweden and John Bradshaw receive lengthy trib-

---

[49] Quoted in Cicero, *On Duties*, xi; Marvell to Milton, 2 June 1654, Yale Prose, 4:860.

[50] An earlier example of this combination is Milton's *Colasterion* (March 1645).

[51] Proposed by Philip B. Rollinson, entry s.v. "Rhetoric" in *A Milton Encyclopedia*, gen. ed. W. B. Hunter, 9 vols. (Lewisburg: Bucknell Univ. Press, 1978-83), 7:124.

[52] See Milton, *Political Writings*, xx-xxi; D. Parkin Speer, "Milton's *Defensio Prima*: Ethos and Vituperation in a Polemical Engagement," *Quarterly Journal of Speech* 56 (1970): 277-83.

utes, with the longest and most elaborate reserved for Cromwell himself (though it also advises and cautions him, thus repeating the epideictic-deliberative formula of the sonnet) (4:604–6, 637–39, 666–80).

By way of underlining this, all we need do is note Milton's constant use throughout these works of a particularly sophisticated form of vituperation (sophisticated in Neo-Latin circles at least): name-calling. In *Defensio Secunda*, for example, More's Latinized surname permits an elaborate series of puns on *morus* (foolish and mulberry tree in Latin), *moros* and *sukomoros* (foolish and fig-mulberry in Greek), all of which Milton scurrilously brings to bear on More's notorious liaisons in a Geneva garden (4:566). Milton's penchant for this kind of word play, alleged to be of an astonishing "variety and dullness" and to stem from the "absurd suggestion that a person's name has any relation to his character," has been deemed "indefensible."[53] But even here Milton was following Ciceronian precedent.[54] In the *Verrines*, Cicero unfurls a sequence of puns on *verrere* (to sweep) and *verres* (boar-pig), culminating in the famous *ambiguitas*, "ius verrinum," meaning both "the administration of Verres" and "pork gravy."[55] It is true that Cicero passed them off as jokes which had done the rounds, but he used them nevertheless. And they surfaced again whenever classical writers discussed the role of *urbanitas* in oratory; although they had reservations, Cicero's prestige was such that they could not entirely disown the practice.[56]

It is especially misleading, however, to classify *Pro Se Defensio* as purely epideictic. Milton's reply to More's *Fides Publica* (1654) and *Supplementum* (1655) is in fact the most determinedly forensic work that he ever composed. This is clear from the moment that Milton lays a formal charge against More, taken from Justinian's *Institutes*, and framed so that he can be convicted as an accessory to the publication of the *Clamor* even if — as Milton now admits — he was not its author (4:713). Nor is it surprising to find Milton turning once more to the *Verrines*. There was one obvious parallel which he duly notes; that, like Verres, More fled from Geneva

---

[53] See Yale Prose, 4:114, 545, 565n.
[54] See chap. 24, "On Notation" in Milton's *Art of Logic*, Yale Prose, 8:294–5.
[55] Cicero, *Verrines*, 1:350 (2.2.21.52); 2:401 (2.4.43.95); 1:253 (2.1.46.121).
[56] See Tacitus, *Dialogus sub oratoribus*, 23; Quintilian, *Institutio*, 2:467–69 (6.3.55).

before his prosecution was complete.⁵⁷ But Milton also faced some of the same difficulties that Cicero did in presenting his case. Just as Cicero found it hard to trace the proceeds of extortion to Verres personally, so Milton labored to implicate More personally in the publication of the *Clamor*. And, again like Verres, More had produced a stream of inartifical evidence — letters, testimonials, and certificates — which had to be discounted or discredited. Indeed, with More seeking to bolster his reputation in this way, and Milton to dismantle it, forensic argument is by the end submerged in *laus* and *vituperatio*.

Despite the vigor and inventiveness with which More is prosecuted, recent commentators have agreed in finding Milton "considerably less certain" about the value of what he was doing in *Pro Se Defensio*. They suggest he was burdened by what was "no longer a heroic task" and even that he felt the need to "defend himself from himself."⁵⁸ These strains are most evident in the peroration, where Milton expressly confronts the problems of epideictic oratory:

> We who as youths [*adolescentes*] under so many masters are accustomed to sweat in the shade [*exudare in umbra*] at eloquence, deciding that its demonstrative force lies in vituperation no less than in praise, do bravely dismember, at the desk to be sure, the names of ancient tyrants. If chance allows, we kill Mezentius over again in rank [*putidis*] antitheta, or, in the sad bellowing of enthymemes more carefully devised than his own bull, we burn alive Phalaris of Agrigentum. In the college precincts [*xysto*] or school of rhetoric [*palaestra*], of course; for in the state we commonly adore, or rather worship such men, and call them most mighty, most powerful, most august. And yet it would be proper either not to have spent one's first youth shadily secluded [*umbratiles*] in games, or, when it is needful to our country, when the commonwealth re-

---

⁵⁷ See Yale Prose, 4:756, 766, 813. The Yale editor, Kester Svendsen, overlooks the second of these allusions. In fact, Milton's Latin, "Lucium Crassum poenituisse olim ferunt, quod Caium Carbonem unquam in judicium vocavisset" (*The Works of John Milton*, gen. ed. F. Patterson, 18 vols. [New York: Columbia Univ. Press, 1931–38], 9:162), is taken directly from Cicero, *Verrines*, 2:2–4 (2.3.1.3).

⁵⁸ David Loewenstein, *Milton and the Drama of History: Historical Vision, Iconoclasm and the Literary Imagination* (Cambridge: Cambridge Univ. Press, 1990), 171n; Nicholas von Maltzahn, *Milton's "History of Britain": Republican Historiography in the English Revolution* (Oxford: Clarendon Press, 1991), 67.

quires it, casting practice-swords [*rudibus*] aside, now to venture into the sun, and dust, and field of battle [*in solem ac pulverem atque aciem audere*], now to exert real brawn, brandish real arms, seek a real enemy. With many a weapon, we pursue in one direction the Sophists and Suffeni, in another the Pharisees and Simons, the Hymenaeuses and Alexanders, for these, indeed, are ancients; the same appearing today and brought to life in the church, we praise with eulogies bestowed upon them, we honour with professorships, and stipends, and chairs, incomparable men that they are, most learned and most saintly.[59]

Much of this has a familiar ring, most notably the apparent echo of Milton's refusal in *Areopagitica* to "praise a fugitive and cloister'd virtue" which "slinks out of the race, where that immortall garland is to be run for, not without dust and heat" (2:515). And the vignette of students paradoxically sweating in the shade seems to recall the "preposterous exaction" derided in *Of Education*. Milton even essays a pastiche of grisly schoolboy humour, the game evidently being to match tyrants with rhetorical *figurae*. Thus Mezentius, whose favored method of execution was to bind the victim to a decaying corpse in what Virgil called a "ghastly embrace," is himself despatched with an antitheton (or "opposition of terms disagreeing" as John Hoskins defined the figure).[60] Similarly, Phalaris, who roasted his victims in a hollow brazen bull, meets his fate enclosed in an enthymeme (a syllogism with a suppressed premise).

But to dwell on the familiarity of these materials is to miss the point that, for Milton, still to be saying the same kind of things is a sign that matters have not improved since 1644, and may even have got worse. In particular, he suggests, the mechanism of praise and blame has gone badly awry. It is easy to denounce ancient wrongdoers, but their modern counterparts in church and state, far from being censured and struck down, are honored and applauded, as shown by the titles and professorships awarded to More (intriguingly, Milton provides no examples of the phenomenon drawn from political life). More's European progress from appointment to appointment, as traced by Milton, becomes an object lesson in the decline

---

[59] The translation is adapted from that given in Yale Prose, 4:795; the Latin is taken from Milton, *Works*, 9:222–24.

[60] See Virgil, *Aeneid*, 8:485–89; for Hoskins' definition, see L. A. Sonnino, *A Handbook to Sixteenth-Century Rhetoric* (London: Routledge, 1968), 61.

of epideictic as an instrument of public morality. Even after proceedings began against him at Geneva in 1648, More had the effrontery to solicit testimonials from the authorities; anxious to avoid scandal, they colluded in a whitewash to the extent of placing the charges against him on file and supplying references which he could take to his new post at Middelburg. More's conduct both there and in Amsterdam, where he moved next, scandalized his employers; but despite this, and despite public exposure in *Defensio Secunda*, he set about gathering testimonials from all quarters for his reply to Milton before moving on, yet again, to Charenton.[61] What compounded the offence was that these attestations issued from protestant and republican sources, including the venerable theologian John Diodati and the city-state of Geneva.

Of course, Milton plays up these difficulties so as to throw into relief his own singularity in overcoming them. In keeping with this, he freely admits that his own "youth [*adolescens*]" was spent entirely in "literary leisure [*otio literarum*]." But none of this has prevented him from discharging "an office neither displeasing to God, unsalutary to the church, nor unuseful to the state."[62] However, these protestations do not succeed in dispelling an underlying note of disenchantment which stems in part from the nature of the sources upon which Milton draws for the peroration. Thus the vignette of students triumphing rhetorically over tyrants is in direct imitation of a scene depicted by Juvenal in his seventh satire ("De Sterilitate Studiorum").[63] The metaphor of shade and light was a classical commonplace, often employed by Roman writers when contrasting a life in the shade (*umbra* had the same connotations as "ivory towers" for us) and a life lived in the full glare (*lux forensis*) of public life, frequently combining this with a contrast between the mock battles and weapons used when training under cover and actual combat in the open air.[64] But Milton, as his Latin vocabulary shows, specifically had in mind Cicero's use of these metaphors when discussing oratory itself. In *De oratore*, for example, Cicero insists that it is necessary for oratory to

---

[61] For these details see Svendsen's introduction, Yale Prose, 4:687–93 and further references given there.

[62] Yale Prose, 4:796; Milton, *Works*, 9:226.

[63] See Juvenal, *Satires*, 7:150–54. For Milton's use of Juvenal's epigram, *crambe repetita* ("réchauffé cabbage"), see *Works*, 7:224 and 9:166.

[64] For these metaphors, see J. P. V. D. Balsdon, *Life and Leisure in Ancient Rome* (London: Bodley, 1969), 136–37, 383n.

be conducted out of this sheltered [*umbratili*] training-ground at home, right into action, into the dust [*in pulverem*] and uproar, into the camp and the fighting-line of public debate [*in aciem forensem*]; she must face putting everything to the proof and test the strength of her talent, and her secluded preparation must be brought forth into the daylight of reality.[65]

In *Orator*, after praising the achievements of Isocrates, Cicero proceeds nevertheless to dismiss epideictic as "more fit for the parade than for the battle; set apart for the gymnasium and the palaestra, it is spurned and rejected in the forum." Such games must be left behind when we "enter into the keenest of the fray [*in aciem*]."[66] And in *Brutus* — the work clearly uppermost in Milton's mind at this point — Cicero similarly dismisses the work of Demetrius of Phaleron:

his training was less for the field than for the parade-ground [*palaestra*]. He entertained rather than stirred his countrymen; for he came forth into the heat and dust [*in solem et pulverem*] of action, not from the soldier's tent, but from the shady retreat [*umbraculis*] of the great philosopher Theophrastus.[67]

What the Ciceronian subtext of the peroration in fact bespeaks is a turning away from epideictic oratory.

By August 1655, Milton had clearly reached the limits of what he could do in singing the praises of the Protectorate. Although he continued with his offical duties, what happened next, as is agreed on all sides, was a retreat from *negotium* into *otium* as he took up a number of cherished literary projects including *The History of Britain* and *Paradise Lost*. As for public affairs, Milton maintained a stony four-year silence (comparable in many ways to his earlier refusal to comment on the course of events between 1645 and 1649) until his astonishing dismissal of the Protectorate in 1659. But while it is true that Milton only resumed a deliberative stance in 1659, this may be to overlook the mordant irony embodied in the two works which he did publish in 1658 — his edition of *The Cabinet-Council*, which he took (mistakenly) to be the work of Sir Walter Ralegh,

---

[65] Cicero, *De oratore*, 1:108–9 (1.34.157).

[66] Cicero, *Orator*, 336–38 (13.42).

[67] Cicero, *Brutus*, trans. G. Hendrickson, Loeb Classical Library (London: Heinemann, 1952), 42–43 (9.37–38).

and a further edition of his own *Pro Populo Anglicano Defensio*. The first was an example of the advice book, a genre which epitomized the Renaissance statecraft which Milton otherwise loathed but which also (so we must assume) served to reflect the current decline in political morality, while the second was the most prestigious vindication of the Commonwealth regime which Cromwell had overthrown.[68] Taken together, they offered a poignant reminder of what the English republic had once been and a caustic comment on what it had since become.

---

[68] For a fuller account of these publications, see my "Milton and the Protectorate in 1658," in Armitage et al., *Milton and Republicanism*, 181–205.

DAVID LOEWENSTEIN

The Powers of the Beast: Gerrard Winstanley and Visionary Prose of the English Revolution

IN ONE OF HIS RICHLY FIGURATIVE AND DRAMATIC PROSE WORKS, the apocalyptic *Fire in the Bush* (March 1650), the Digger writer Gerrard Winstanley uses a terrifying image of evil based upon the great red Dragon of Revelation 12 to represent ecclesiastical power: the most dreadful form of kingly power, "clergy power," he writes, "makes a man a sinner for a word, and so he sweeps the Stars of Heaven downe with his tayle, he darkens Heaven and Earth, and defiles body and mind."[1] Winstanley's striking image conveys the frightening character of the professional clergy in his age: throughout the figurative prose of his visionary tracts he depicts that ecclesiastical institution as a monstrous Antichristian power. Winstanley's passage suggests, moreover, that language and interpretation themselves could be exploited by institutional powers as dark instruments of tyranny and bondage which restrain "the liberty of the inward man" (469) — and that they continued to be employed oppressively even after the English Revolution of 1648–49. This oppressive use of language was itself a manifestation of the great apocalyptic conflicts of his unsettled age between the powers of darkness and light, flesh and spirit, bondage and righteousness, property and community, and selfishness and Reason

---

[1] *The Works of Gerrard Winstanley*, ed. George H. Sabine (Ithaca: Cornell Univ. Press, 1941), 469. Quotations from Winstanley's works, except for his early works of 1648 not printed by Sabine, are taken from this edition, hereafter cited as *Works*, and page references are cited parenthetically in my text.

(Winstanley's name for God or the Spirit). Indeed, as Winstanley explained in one of his early tracts, he chose to call the "King of righteousnesse" by the name of Reason precisely because he himself had "been held under darknesse by that word [God]" (105).

One of the most gifted radical religious writers of seventeenth-century England, Winstanley produced all his remarkable visionary works between 1648 and 1652, a time of great political and religious upheaval, as well as social conflict. His more than twenty pamphlets, letters, and broadsides appeared during the period of the dramatic republican revolution which overthrew the monarchy and the House of Lords and established the Commonwealth under what turned out to be the largely unrevolutionary regime of the Rump Parliament.[2] In effect, Winstanley believed that even after the second civil war, Pride's Purge of Parliament, and the execution of Charles I, "kingly power," as he called it, continued to exist in many different Antichristian shapes and forms in the newly erected Commonwealth: state rulers, the clergy, the army, lawyers, and landlords were all contributing to an elaborate and ensnaring system of coercive institutional power which oppresses the poor of the earth and keeps England itself in bondage and under the curse. The great danger in his unsettled age, Winstanley perceived, was that one form of tyranny would replace another, though it might assume new and ensnaring shapes; this condition would merely perpetuate the class conflict that had troubled England under the legacy of Norman power reinforced by the reign of Charles I.[3] In *Fire in the Bush*, Winstanley observed that "as yet the power and dominion of the Prince of darknesse rules every where" and "the Dragon is not yet cast out" (472, 477); and in his final pamphlet, *The Law of Freedom in a Platform* (1652), he told Cromwell (to whom that work is

---

[2] Believing that it had not lived up to its revolutionary origins, Winstanley told Parliament in 1650 that "truly there is abundance of Rust about your Actings" (354). Studies of the Rump and its shortcomings as a revolutionary regime include David Underdown, *Pride's Purge: Politics in the Puritan Revolution* (Oxford: Clarendon Press, 1971), chap. 9; Blair Worden, *The Rump Parliament* (Cambridge: Cambridge Univ. Press, 1974); and Austin Woolrych, *Commonwealth to Protectorate* (Oxford: Clarendon Press, 1982).

[3] That fear of renewed tyranny and bondage in the Republic was powerfully expressed by other radical writers as well, especially the embittered Levellers: see e.g., John Lilburne, *Englands New Chains Discovered* (London, 1649) and *The Second Part of Englands New Chaines Discovered* (London, 1649). On class conflict in Winstanley's age, see Brian Manning, *The English People and the English Revolution, 1640–1649* (London: Heinemann, 1976).

dedicated) that "Kingly Power remains in power still in the hands of those who have no more right to the Earth then our selves" (507). Indeed, the bulk of Winstanley's tracts provide an acute analysis of the complex network of power and oppression which he believed continued to operate in subtle forms under the new Republic. His prose works offer a particularly compelling instance of the way a major writer of the period — the one who most movingly articulated the perspective of poor Englishmen — attempted to interpret, shape, and criticize the unsettling processes of revolution which disrupted the Stuart monarchy and the Church of England, while stimulating radical sectarianism, social protest, and millenarian expectations.

Winstanley's politics, heretical religious ideas, and radical theory of economics — his perception that political, spiritual, and individual freedom begin with economic freedom and common ownership of the land (making the earth "a common treasury to all") — have received valuable attention from historians of the English Revolution, including D. W. Petegorsky, George Sabine, Christopher Hill, G. E. Aylmer, Perez Zagorin, Olivier Lutaud, among others. These scholars have studied the works of Winstanley, as well as the Digger experiment in communism of 1649-50 which he led, in relation to the radical sociopolitical and religious milieu and thought of mid-seventeenth-century England.[4] What is too often missing

---

[4] See, for example, D. W. Petegorsky, *Left-Wing Democracy in the English Civil War* (1940); Perez Zagorin, *A History of Political Thought in the English Revolution* (London: Routledge and Kegan Paul, 1954), chap. 4; Christopher Hill, *The World Turned Upside Down: Radical Ideas During the English Revolution* (Harmondsworth: Penguin, 1975), chap. 7; Hill, "The Religion of Gerrard Winstanley," *Past and Present Supplement*, no. 5 (1978); Hill, "Winstanley and freedom," in *Freedom and the English Revolution: Essays in History and Literature*, ed. R. C. Richardson and G. M. Ridden (Manchester: Manchester Univ. Press, 1986), 151–68; George Juretic, "Digger no Millenarian: The Revolutionizing of Gerrard Winstanley," *Journal of the History of Ideas* 36 (1975): 263–80; C. H. George, "Gerrard Winstanley: A Critical Retrospect," in *The Dissenting Tradition*, ed. C. Robert Cole and Michael E. Moody (Athens, OH: Ohio Univ. Press, 1975), 191–225; Olivier Lutaud, *Winstanley: Socialisme et Christianisme sous Cromwell* (Paris: Marcel Didier, 1976); Lotte Mulligan, John K. Graham, and Judith Richards, "Winstanley: A Case for the Man as He Said He Was," *Journal of Ecclesiastical History* 28 (1977): 57–75; J. C. Davis, *Utopia and the Ideal Society: A Study of English Utopian Writing, 1516–1700* (Cambridge: Cambridge Univ. Press, 1981), chap. 7; G. E. Aylmer, "The Religion of Gerrard Winstanley," in *Radical Religion in the English Revolution*, ed. J. F. McGregor and Barry Reay (Oxford: Clarendon Press, 1984); F. D. Dow, *Radicalism in the English Revolution, 1640–1660* (Oxford: Basil Blackwell, 1985), 74–80. I have not noted important differences of opinion among these scholars; but as will become clearer in this essay, I agree with those (e.g., Aylmer and Hill) who stress interconnections between Winstanley's

from such historical studies, however, is a fuller examination of the mythopoeic, aesthetic, and verbal dimensions and texture of Winstanley's writings — not as features to be considered in isolation from his sociopolitical and religious world, but rather as features which intersect with Winstanley's distinct revolutionary vision and scrutiny of Antichristian power in its multiple shapes. Winstanley acutely perceives that the politics of class oppression and exploitation, as well as religious orthodoxy, are interconnected with issues of language and artfulness; this dimension of Winstanley's writing especially deserves more critical attention from commentators.[5] As we shall see, Winstanley, like his contemporary Milton, was in his own way sensitive to the implications of verbal and artful equivocation in an age of revolution and its ambiguous aftermath — even on the part of political and ecclesiastical authorities which had opposed kingly power during the revolutionary decade of the 1640s.

At the same time Winstanley himself is often intensely poetic in his political and religious writings, recreating biblical myths and images as a means of representing the great spiritual and political conflicts of his unsettled age: his fantastic recreation of Daniel's apocalyptic vision of the four great beasts in *Fire in the Bush* will serve as a key example later in this discussion. But Winstanley, who does not read scriptural texts and history literally, also gives fresh allegorical interpretations to other potent myths such as Cain versus Abel, Jacob versus Esau, Michael versus the Dragon, and the myth of Eden itself. As he observes in *Fire in the Bush*, "whether there was any such outward things or no, it matters not much, if thou seest all within" (462): and so the radical visionary writer, deriving his authority from the Spirit within, is free to reinterpret scriptural texts and myths. These he invests with urgent religious and political significance, as

---

radical theology and politics. On these interconnections, see also Andrew Bradstock, "Sowing in Hope: the Relevance of Theology to Gerrard Winstanley's Political Programme," *The Seventeenth Century* 6, no. 2 (1991): 189–204.

[5] For examples of helpful studies which have begun to explore literary or rhetorical dimensions of Winstanley's pamphlets, see Thomas N. Corns, *Uncloistered Virtue: English Political Literature, 1640–1660* (Oxford: Clarendon Press, 1992), 146–74; and T. Wilson Hayes, *Winstanley the Digger: A Literary Analysis of Radical Ideas in the English Revolution* (Cambridge, Mass.: Harvard Univ. Press, 1979), a study which examines the typological method of biblical analysis in Winstanley's writings, as well as his alchemical metaphors. See also Nigel Smith, *Literature and Revolution in England, 1640–1660* (New Haven: Yale Univ. Press, 1994), 172–76, and, for Winstanley's idiosyncratic use of the Bible, John R. Knott, *The Sword of the Spirit: Puritan Responses to the Bible* (Chicago: Univ. of Chicago Press, 1980), chap. 4.

he interrogates the multiple and interconnected forms of Norman power in his revolutionary age, and as he represents his millennial expectations for a fundamental transformation of the existing social order. He envisions a new age of universal salvation for all to be established by the spreading of the power of righteousness as Christ begins to rise up in his sons and daughters, the saints and True Levellers, and as Abel triumphs over Cain, Jacob over Esau, and Michael over the Dragon. Like many other radical Puritan writers of his age, Winstanley draws heavily upon the books of Daniel and Revelation in order to engage in millennial speculation.[6] But in his unorthodox prose, we shall see, he gives apocalyptic and millenarian discourse his own original inflection and highly distinctive mythopoeic expression.

From his earliest tracts, Winstanley depicted himself as an inwardly inspired prophetic writer, "drawn forth by the Spirit to write" (101; cf. 194, 199) his visionary works, a claim that would become especially characteristic of prophetic Quaker writers in the 1650s who found themselves guided by the Spirit within and who therefore rejected all outward religious forms. "Written in the Light of inward experience," he announces on the title page of *Several Pieces Gathered into One Volume* (1649), and following "the Spirits inward workings,"[7] Winstanley declares freely the Law of Righteousness within, as well as his communist message: his visionary texts and radical prophecies are, as he puts it in *The New Law of Righteousnes*, "the Declarations of the Lord through his servant" (204), not texts or visions generated second-hand from books or study or any form of human learning.[8] And so from the beginning of *Fire in the Bush*, Winstanley distances his visionary writing, and its internal inspiration and power,

---

[6] For a concentrated study of the politics of apocalypticism and millenarianism in Winstanley's period, see John P. Laydon, "The Kingdom of Christ and the Powers of the Earth: The Political Uses of Apocalyptic and Millenarian Ideas in England, 1648–1653" (Ph.D. diss., Cambridge Univ., 1977). See also Bernard Capp, "The Political Dimension of Apocalyptic Thought," in *The Apocalypse in English Renaissance Thought and Literature*, ed. C. A. Patrides and Joseph Wittreich (Ithaca: Cornell Univ. Press, 1984), 109–18.

[7] *Several Pieces Gathered into one Volume* (London, 1649), title page and sig. A3v. This is the second edition of five of Winstanley's works, a collection printed for the radical publisher Giles Calvert; the unique copy, from which I quote here, appears in the Manchester Central Library.

[8] Beginning with his early works Winstanley is critical of "whosoever preaches from his book, and not from the anointing" (*The Mysterie of God, Concerning the whole Creation, Mankinde* [London, 1648], 37); he himself claims to "have writ nothing but what was given me of my Father" (sig. A2v). Cf. his address "To the Reader" in *Several Pieces*.

from all human and ecclesiastical authorities, as well as all customary and established forms of divine worship: "This following declaration of the word of Life was a free gift to me from the Father himselfe; And I received it not from men" (445). The inwardly inspired Winstanley writes as one of God's messengers through whom the Spirit itself speaks.

A highly talented allegorical writer, Winstanley takes biblical myths and apocalyptic language and creatively transforms them to express a distinctive socio-economic vision of the Fall, social change, and power in mid-seventeenth-century England. His mythmaking expresses with urgency his criticisms of the Revolution and its shortcomings during the years of the republican regime which, though claiming to represent the power of the people, in fact did little to alleviate "the crie of the poore" (472).[9] While stressing the apocalyptic and sociopolitical dimensions of Winstanley's revolutionary vision, as well as the vivid and potent language expressing it, this essay highlights the ways aesthetic and sociopolitical issues intersect in his radical religious writing, especially *Fire in the Bush*. Arguably the most visionary and mythopoeic of his Digger writings, that work illustrates strikingly how linguistic, mythic, religious, and sociopolitical concerns converge in Winstanley's unorthodox prophetic discourse.

* * *

Among the most dramatic of his metaphorically rich works, *Fire in the Bush* is an apocalyptic tract addressed to the churches "IN THE PRESBYTERIAN, INDEPENDENT, OR ANY OTHER FORME OF PROFESSION" (445) — by which Winstanley means the university-trained, professional clergy of his age. His tract was published in March 1650, more than a year after his conversion to communism, that crucial event in his career which occurred between December 1648 and January 1649 at the climactic moment of the English Revolution itself.[10] In this visionary text, where Winstanley's theology and social radicalism are fused, he assumes a fiercely prophetic stance, often admonishing earthly and institutional powers: his impulse to write was a "gift . . . from the Father himselfe . . .

---

[9] On this failure in the Commonwealth, see Woolrych, *Commonwealth to Protectorate*, 7; Underdown, *Pride's Purge*, 284.

[10] On the tract's composition and date, see Keith Thomas, "The Date of Gerrard Winstanley's *Fire in the Bush*," *Past and Present* 42 (1969): 160–62. Winstanley published only seven of the thirteen chapters he intended to write for this apocalyptic text: see *Works*, 449.

the voyce was in my very heart and mouth, ready to come forth; goe send it to the Churches" (445). In his mythopoeic work, moreover, Winstanley recreates biblical images and language — from Genesis and especially from Daniel and Revelation — as a means of giving dramatic immediacy and apocalyptic urgency to his writing and to his attacks on orthodox political and ecclesiastical institutions and established beliefs; and to express his intense vision of the heated and ongoing battle between spirit and flesh, the Lamb and the Dragon raging within the self and "within the garden mankinde" (460). Winstanley makes highly original and idiosyncratic use of scriptural myths and language, along with their figurative qualities, to represent his socio-economic vision of the Fall or the curse (as he often calls it), the clashing of spiritual forces, and the multiple shapes of Antichristian power still operating in his age. Biblical myths and eschatological metaphors take on fresh potency as they assume urgent contemporary sociopolitical implications, suggesting the interdependence of the political and theological dimensions of his visionary writing.[11]

Thus the Fall itself in Winstanley's vision, which eschews the Calvinist Puritan doctrine of original sin emphasized by the orthodox clergy, is not a distant event to be blamed on Adam who died six thousand years ago. Rather, it is a historical process unfolding within us all, just as the Serpent itself lies within. Moreover, it is directly linked to the human creation of private property, which results in the pursuit of outward objects and in enclosures (i.e., the "dividing of the Earth into parcells" and hedging the weak out of the earth [490]), as well as the artful craft of buying and selling, and which then leads to discontent, divisions, and wars — a kind of vicious, competitive Hobbesian state of nature characterized by a restless desire of power after power. And so driven out of the Garden by the Serpent "blinde Imagination," this self-alienated mankind "is like the Beasts of the field, who live upon objects without them," while being filled "with feares, doubts, troubles, evill surmisings and grudges" (452). Similarly, the great apocalyptic battle between the powers of Michael and the Dragon will take place not at some distant point in the future, but indeed is taking place at this very moment in history — within the souls and hearts of each individual, as well as within the culture at large:[12]

---

[11] Since Winstanley wrote and published *Fire in the Bush* nearly a year after he began the Digger experiment (in April 1649), it is hard to agree with Juretic's thesis that "once he began his Digging cooperative Winstanley's ideas became rapidly secularized" (Juretic, "The Revolutionizing of Gerrard Winstanley," 269). For connections between theological and political modes of thought in Winstanley, cf. Corns, *Uncloistered Virtue*, 170, 172.

[12] The internal character of that apocalyptic battle is likewise highlighted in the

"These two powers are *Michaell* and the Dragon, and this battaile is fought in Heaven, (that is, in mankinde, in the garden of *Eden*) where God principally resolves to set up his throne of righteous government.... And this battaile in our age of the world, growes hotter and sharper then formerly" (457).

In the prose of *Fire in the Bush*, furthermore, that sense of the alienated, restless self, fallen from a state of innocence and tormented within, is heightened through Winstanley's striking use of a dramatic voice at a number of points: thus, for example, mankind, looking inwardly, wonders to himself, "oh what have I done, how am I falne? all outward content in objects flies away, and I am left naked, and want Light, life, and rest within" (459). Reconfiguring the myth of the Fall in terms of the invention of private property and the politics of capitalism (here conceived as buying and selling the land, that common treasury for both rich and poor), Winstanley's allegorical and dramatic prose gives the conflict between spiritual forces urgent contemporary socio-economic significance:

> For now saith the Buyer, this parcell of Land is mine. I have paid the fruit of my labours for it, to be properly my owne. But the younger brother comes in, and saith, the land is our portion by creation as well as yours, and we give no consent to be shut out; therefore what authority had you to buy, or the other to sell; by thus doing you cheat us, and cast us out of the Earth; And from hence now divisions and wars begins to arise betweene the brothers.

Winstanley's use of dramatic voices here sharpens the sense of the immediacy of the spiritual conflict, as he radically reinterprets the mythic struggle between the warring brothers Cain and Abel, the son of bondage and the son of freedom, in terms of "the cheating Art of buying and selling" (490) which continues to his very day: such an ominous crafty art, we shall see, Winstanley perceived as a manifestation of Antichristian power operating in his age of social crisis and class oppression.[13]

Winstanley's apocalyptic mythmaking, however, can best be illustrated by looking at one of the most forceful of his vivid symbolic passages of

---

subtitle of Winstanley's tract: *The spirit burning, not consuming, but purging mankinde. Or, The great battell of God Almighty, between Michaell the seed of life, and the great red dragon, the curse fought within the spirit of man* (*Works*, 72).

[13] For Winstanley's other uses of a dramatic voice, see *Fire in the Bush*, 460–61, 488, 489.

writing in *Fire in the Bush* — or anywhere in Winstanley's prose works, for that matter. This long visionary section provides a striking example of the way Winstanley combines political representation and creative myth-making with an almost Blakean imagination: he recalls and expands the Book of Daniel's apocalyptic vision of the four great beasts or worldly kingdoms rising out of the chaos of the great sea (see Dan. 7:2-12), a favorite passage in Winstanley's age for millenarian interpretation.[14] In order to convey the potency and texture of Winstanley's visionary writing, it is worth examining crucial details of that allegorical prophecy — and the distinctive sociopolitical interpretation Winstanley gives it — at some length:

> These foure powers are the foure Beasts, which *Daniel* saw rise up out of the Sea.... And this Sea is the bulke and body of man-kinde, which is that Sea, and waters, upon which the Spirit of God is said sometimes to move; for out of Mankinde arises all that darknesse and Tyranny that oppresses it selfe; And though these Beasts appear divers, one from another, yet they are all one in their power; for Imaginary-selfe ruling in mans heart, is the Father that created and bred them all.

Although each beast is different from the others, as the Book of Daniel indicates, Winstanley stresses that they are really "all one in their power," and he proceeds to give the symbolic creatures contemporary significance that expresses his urgent sociopolitical concerns and prophetic vision of the rule of the Serpent in its fourfold external power. In Winstanley's mythic version all the fantastic beasts are indeed human creations rising "up out of the deceived heart of mankinde" (464): kingly power, the institutional church, the law, and private property are thus visible manifestations of the Dragon or dark power within humankind. External tyranny, according to Winstanley, whatever shapes it assumes or power it manifests, always derives from an internal origin. The first beast, like a lion with eagle wings (representing Babylon in the Bible), is symbolic of the con-

---

[14] See e.g., the Fifth Monarchy prophetess Mary Cary's political interpretation of this visionary scriptural text in her millenarian work *The Little Horns Doom & Downfall* (London, 1651), 2–8. For Cary the vision becomes a means of interpreting the late King Charles's power in relation to the Roman Beast to which England was subjected; Winstanley's visionary rendering has a much greater socio-economic dimension. See also the near-Digger text, *More Light Shining in Buckinghamshire* (1649), which is reproduced in *Works*, 635–36.

quering "Kingly Power": dividing the creation with the sword, it gives "the Earth to some, denying the Earth to others"; and his eagle wings are symbolic of the swiftness with which this power conquers and divides what it takes (465). The second beast, appearing like a bear and commanded to devour flesh in Daniel's vision, represents the power of the predatory and "selfish Lawes, which is full of covetousnesse" (465), as it devours the fearful and helpless poor: the three ribs in this beast's mouth represent in Winstanley's allegorical vision a series of hellish torments including the power of prisons, the power of whipping and banishment, and the power of hanging and burning.[15]

Indeed, Winstanley's terrifying allegory of power becomes increasingly elaborate — symbolic of a great cosmic drama and the "fruitfull generation" (468) and branching forth of the interconnected powers of Antichrist — as he continues to expand upon Daniel's vision (while also recalling the worldly and tyrannical beast rising from the sea in Rev. 13): thus the third beast rising up resembles "a Leopard, spotty" (that it is "spotty" is symbolic of its impurity),[16] and this becomes in Winstanley's vision the "thieving Art of buying and selling the Earth with her fruits one to another," while its four wings represent "Policy, Hypocrisie, Self-Love, and hardnesse of Heart; for this Beast is a true self-Lover, to get the Earth to himselfe, to lock it up in Chests and barnes, though others starve for want." Furthermore, its four heads — all supporting the beast's tyranny and enslaving others to it — become in Winstanley's interpretation "the power of the sword," "the power of the Law," "the power of the covetous Imaginary Clergie," and the power of "a blinde deceived Heart, over-awed with feare of men" (465-66). In effect, Winstanley is engaging in his own highly original mythmaking as he takes and radically revises a prophetic scriptural text to represent his perception of the acute social crisis, economic oppression, and class conflict dividing his age.

But the grimmest beast of all is the fourth — "the Imaginary Clergy-Power . . . more terrible and dreadful then the rest" (466) — since he, "the Father" of them all, has begotten the other three devouring beasts out of himself: "the other Beasts," Winstanley observes, "are this Beasts sons, he bred them" and they have "their strength and succour from him" (467,

---

[15] On "Prisons, Whips, and Gallows" as "the torments of this Hell" under kingly power, see Winstanley's *Watch-Word to the City of London* in *Works*, 324.

[16] Cf. the Ranter writer Abiezer Coppe's reference to the "unspotted beauty and majesty" of "even base things" in the title page to *A Second Fiery Flying Roule* (London, 1649).

468).[17] In a sense he resembles the Satan of Book 2 of *Paradise Lost* who has begotten out of himself his own monstrous and allegorical progeny who are self-generating: "he knows / His end with mine involv'd" (2.806-7) observes Sin of her son, the grim devouring Death. The "little horne" arising out of the ten horns of Winstanley's dreadful clergy beast — and which, in Daniel, wages war against the saints and persecutes them (Dan. 7:21-22, 25) — becomes "Ecclesiasticall power" (469) in Winstanley's historical myth, the dominion and rule of church establishment supported by the might of kingly power. This, then, is Winstanley's potent way of expressing the interconnections which exist in his age between political and institutional ecclesiastical powers. The learned clerical beast is more menacing too, as we shall see in a moment, because he cunningly employs the tyrannizing power of language itself. All these Antichristian beasts, "with all their heads and hornes," reign in power "while propriety" — or the cursed institution of private ownership in Winstanley's distinctive vision — "rules as King" (466); and all "oppresse, burden, and destroy universall Love ... who is the Sonne of righteousnesse" (467). Thus Winstanley's eschatological representation of the various powers of the world, as he creatively revises scriptural prophecy and myths and gives them a fresh potency, assumes a distinct and individualistic sociohistorical interpretation. It expresses with great poetic vividness Winstanley's response to the existing social and religious order and economic and legal system which continues, in the period of the newly erected English Commonwealth, to oppress the poor of the earth and control their common lands[18] — not only by means of physical force, but also by means of ambiguous verbal and artful practices. As Winstanley perceived, Antichristian "Tyrannie" could indeed be "a subtile, proud and envious Beast" (*The New Law of Righteousnes*, 198) which operates in multiple forms and ways.

Like Milton in his antiprelatical and antimonarchical tracts, Winstanley in his visionary discourse is passionately concerned with exposing the

---

[17] Cf. Winstanley's early apocalyptic tract *The Breaking of the Day of God* (London, 1648), 106, where his allegorical imagination begins to work in a similar fashion and is no less intensely anti-ecclesiastical: the Dragon and the Leopard, he writes, "committed fornication together; then they begat this Beast (or Ecclesiasticall power) to kill and suppress, not men and women simply, but the manifest appearance of God in them."

[18] For responses by radical writers to the social, ecclesiastical, economic, and legal order which contributed to class conflict and the oppression of the poor in this age, see Manning, *The English People and the English Revolution*, esp. chap. 9.

multiple shapes and images of "Clergy power" and "Kingly power," along with the other two Antichristian powers he saw operating and proliferating in his age: "All these Beasts," as he calls them in *Fire in the Bush*, may "differ in shape, and yet they agree all in one oppressing power, supporting one another; one cannot live without another.... These foure beasts are all very fruitfull; for from them, as from foure Fountaines, or Monarchs, springs up divers heads and hornes; that is, severall spreadings forth, of selfish tyrannicall Power, whereby the Creation is opprest and burdened" (466). Using dramatic language, the Independent divine John Owen commented to the House of Commons in April 1649 about the manifestations and web of Antichristian power: "The opening, unravelling, and revealing the Antichristian interest, interwoven, and coupled together in civill and spirituall things, into a State opposite to the kingdom of the Lord Jesus, is the great discovery of these dayes."[19] Engaged himself in unravelling the complex network of Antichristian powers in the new Commonwealth, Winstanley would add that the "Antichristian interest" is no less interwoven in "economic things" or "propriety." Indeed, Winstanley finds that these interconnected forms of worldly power, oppression, and institutional authority regularly manifest themselves not only through the power of the sword but through craft, cunning, artfulness, and subtle uses of language: "these [Beasts] rise up by craft," he observes, "supported by the kingly power" (467). Even "buying and selling" the earth, that cause of inequality, is an "Imaginary" and "crafty Art" (464, 531, 532), as he calls it in his tracts, "the neat art of thieving and suppressing fellow-creatures" (188) and cheating the poor commoners of England out of their rightful land. This is the subtle art and power of Cain and Esau operating in his age. As Winstanley puts it in his final tract, *The Law of Freedom*, such subtle forms of *"the Power and Government of the Beast"* manifest "the cunning Machavilian spirit" which fills "the heart of Mankind with enmity and ignorance, pride and vain-glory"; and that "subtle spirit of darkness" is promoted in the present economic system by the agents of kingly and clergy power (531-32).

Moreover, like Milton, the Digger writer acutely perceived in his own way that tyranny was an equivocal art that especially exploits verbal ambiguity: this Milton had learned in the 1640s from intensely scrutinizing the paltering language and behavior of a prevaricating Presbyterian clergy — not to mention the verbal equivocation of the king himself.[20] Indeed,

---

[19] John Owen, *The Shaking and Translating of Heaven and Earth* (London, 1649), 35.
[20] For a discussion of Milton's responses to the equivocal behavior of clergy and

Winstanley perceives that the institutional power of the Beast becomes treacherous not only when it is maintained by the power of the sword, but particularly when it operates at a subtle verbal level — in the cunning and dark uses of "speaking words" (475). Addressing his "brethren" of the churches at the opening of *Fire in the Bush*, Winstanley notes how their "verball profession" reveals them serving "the government of darknesse" (445, 447) and in his pamphlet he ominously characterizes the clerical beast — the learned ministry — as "a King, understanding dark sayings, and he shall by craft deceive many" (467). Winstanley's visionary writing offers an acute analysis of "that spirit which in words [the Churches] *seeme* to professe" (445; emphasis added) as they practice their "teaching Art" (467–68).

Winstanley thus begins this prophetic tract by attacking the "verball profession" of the preaching clergy and (what he calls elsewhere) their "close dissimulation" (171): "for you acknowledge Christ in words, and the Dragon in your actions" (448) — actions like imposing tithes on the poor of the earth, which Winstanley and other religious radicals regarded as "the greatest sin of oppression" (238) and Norman power, and behind which might be detected the Antichristian power of the Beast itself.[21] The learned clergy not only put on "a shew of holiness, or spiritual doctrine" (523) and "pretend to be saviours of the people" (472), suggesting the theatricalism of Antichristian powers in Winstanley's age. Their crafty covetousness is also manifested by their linguistic practices. The preaching clergy use subtle, "deceitfull words" (469) and "insinuating" (387) language as an instrument of power to awe and ensnare the poor and common people, and "to bewitch [them] to conforme" (470), as Winstanley puts it in *Fire in the Bush*. Thus, as he observes throughout his pamphlets, they use a "multitude of words" (219, 291, 365, 563) to confound and delude the simple or common people, making them more dependent upon clerical authority and interpretation. Winstanley is profoundly suspicious of the artifice of "verbal worship" practiced by a pharisaical professional ministry — "blinde guides," "painted sepulchers," and "enemies to the Gospel" and the inner workings of the Holy Spirit

---

kingly powers, see my essay "'An Ambiguous Monster': Representing Rebellion in Milton's Polemics and *Paradise Lost*," *Huntington Library Quarterly* 55 (1992): 295–315.

[21] On the Dragon's power behind tithes, see George Fox, *The Law of God, the Rule for Law-Makers* (London, 1658), 8. On the radical Puritan grounds for objecting to them because they maintained the Antichristian church, see Woolrych, *Commonwealth to Protectorate*, 236.

itself (*The New Law of Righteousnes*, 185, 214). Like the antinomian William Dell, Winstanley perceives that Antichrist "builds up *his Church* by the *Word* without the *Spirit*."[22]

Moreover, Winstanley is acutely sensitive to the way scriptural interpretation or hermeneutics practiced by the professional preachers too has become a treacherous and ensnaring instrument of power and subjection in his age — a subtle means of reinforcing the orthodoxies of the clerical elite, as well as economic exploitation.[23] It is thus an art of what he calls "black interpretation" which draws "a veyle over the truth" of the Scriptures. "The Scriptures of the Bible," he observes in *Fire in the Bush*,

> were written by the experimentall hand of Shepherds, Husbandmen, Fishermen, and such inferiour men of the world; And the Universitie learned ones have got these mens writings; and flourishes their plaine language over with their darke interpretation, and glosses, as if it were too hard for ordinary men now to understand them; and thereby they deceive the simple, and makes a prey of the poore, and cosens them of the Earth, and of the tenth of their labors.[24] (474–75)

Indeed, as Winstanley had put it in his early tract, *Truth Lifting up its Head above Scandals* (1649), the ministers of the gospel are nothing less than cunning artificers "new moulding those Scriptures into their own language" (103–4); they practice "their own inventions" thereby turning the Scriptures "into a lie" (140). Especially vulnerable to such verbal and interpretative arts practiced by such artificers are the plain hearted and common people who have "no guile" and subtlety or "know'st not the wiles of the tempter": such plain heartedness without envy or guile, while associated with "the innocencie of mankinde," can easily be fashioned and molded. As Winstanley's metaphorical prose in *Fire in the Bush* suggests, it is "a state like wax, flexible and easie to take any impression" and "prepared for any stamp" (479–81). Even the love of the "simple hearted" Peter was "changeable" and thus too susceptible to such tempta-

---

[22] William Dell, *The Tryal of Spirits* (London, 1653), 21.

[23] On Winstanley's view of the oppressive theological system of the church, see also Bradstock, "Sowing in Hope," 196–98; Bradstock, however, does not consider Winstanley's perception of the verbal and artful practices employed by the clergy.

[24] Cf. *The Law of Freedom*: "likewise hath the Scriptures of *Moses*, the Prophets, Christ, and his Apostles, been darkened and confounded by suffering Ministers to put their Inferences and Interpretations upon them" (555).

tion: "for when the tryall came," Winstanley reminds his readers, "*Peter* denyed Christ" (480).

Winstanley, then, considers the institutional clergy of his age as no less ambiguous and shifty in their political and religious allegiances than Milton does in *The Tenure of Kings and Magistrates* (1649), where he characterizes the equivocal Presbyterian divines as *Macbeth*-like fiends juggling and paltering with the world by having first borne arms against King Charles and then, later in the 1640s, having altogether switched their position by trying to reinstate him.[25] In Winstanley's words, these equivocal ministers "will serve on any side" and "any Government": "They will serve the Papists, they will serve the Protestants, they will serve the King, they will serve the States" (*A New-Yeers Gift*, 358). Furthermore, like Milton who draws upon the myth of Circe in *Eikonoklastes* (1649) to depict the bewitching effects of Stuart representation and power (there he describes the people as easily "stupifi'd and bewitch'd"), Winstanley perceives that both clergy and kingly powers in the Commonwealth have a seductive and bewitching effect on the common people; and in his works he links these sinister forms of bewitching power with the Beast "in all her shapes and disguises."[26] Kingly power, as well as other guileful forms of Antichristian power, he writes in *Fire in the Bush*, "depend upon the Clergy, to bewitch the people to conforme" (470), for the "Kingly Clergy," as he later notes in *The Law of Freedom*, most effectively preserve their authority and power "among a charmed, befooled and besotted people" (544). Since the "Image of the Beast" reigns within, as well as without, Winstanley envisions that a great "overturning" and social revolution in his age full of institutional craft and "bewitching knavery" (485, 472, 470) must involve not the restless seeking of an external kingdom but the regaining of a new "Kingdome within" (445, 458, 494) the self that will abide — a "new law of righteousnesse" set up within "every man and woman" (206), as he had announced in his first communist tract. "This Seed or Christ then is to be seen within, to save you from the curse within, to free you from bondage within," he writes at the end of *Fire in the Bush*; and so "therefore your publick Ministers bewitches you," he warns his godly readers, "by telling you of a Saviour at

---

[25] See *Complete Prose Works of John Milton*, gen. ed. Don M. Wolfe, 8 vols. (New Haven: Yale Univ. Press, 1953–82), 3:191.

[26] I cite, respectively, from Milton, *Complete Prose Works*, 3:347, and from Winstanley's *Breaking of the Day of God*, 57.

a distance" (496). Such a bewitching clergy power manifests the sorcery and subtlety of the power of Antichrist itself.[27]

In Winstanley's prophetic discourse, then, the Kingdom of Darkness, with its sorcery, oppression, and multiple Norman powers, is reinforced by the deadening and ensnaring uses of language, artfulness, and the fleshly imagination: when we live in a "dark time" associated with the Dragon or Beast, he writes in *A New-Yeers Gift*, we lie "under Types, Shadows, Ceremonies, Forms, Customes ... and heaps of waste words, under which the Spirit of Truth [lies] buried" (377). In *The New Law of Righteousnes* Winstanley had accused the public divines of using "fine language" yet "words without life" (242), in contrast to the living law of righteousness within the hearts of those whom they despise.[28] Words, Winstanley passionately believed, must be lived through action. One response to these and other manifestations of internal and external bondage was popular and symbolic political action, that "pure righteous action" (445) of digging and cultivating the common and waste lands on St. George's Hill, Surrey, since, as he famously stated it in one tract, "action is the life of all, and if thou dost not act, thou dost nothing"; Winstanley was indeed acutely aware that "there are but few that act for freedome" in his age of social and political crisis (*A Watch-Word to the City of London and the Armie* [1649], 315, 317). Another response, however, was his own fiery prophetic writing with its creative purging power, itself an expression of "the burning flame" and "the fire of pure Light" (471, alluding to Dan. 7:11) and the power of the Spirit itself: as he wrote in the subtitle to *Fire in the Bush*, "The Spirit [is] burning, not consuming, but purging Mankinde" (451).

Thus moved in his prose "by Vision, Voyce, and Revelation" (257), Winstanley could respond to the subtle manifestations of worldly powers not only by the provocative and symbolic communal action of digging, but also through his sharp but saving prophetic writing,[29] which at moments

---

[27] For a similar condemnation, see the anonymous near-Digger pamphlet *Light Shining in Buckinghamshire* (1648): "Thy Priests have guld, bewitched, cheated, and betrayed [England] into these tyrants hands with their sorceries onely for their own filthy lucre and bellies sake" (*Works*, 619).

[28] See also Winstanley's remarks about "men that are ful of wast words ... for they have had neither voice, vision, nor revelation to warrant their words" (208); and his observation that "by this multitude of waste discourse, people are blinded" (242-43).

[29] At the end of *The New Law of Righteousnes*, Winstanley observes that his "words may seem sharp to some," yet he writes them "out of love to all [men]" (244), a passage that can be compared to Milton's justification of "things that are sharply spoken, or vehemently written" in *The Reason of Church-Government* (*Complete Prose Works*, 1:803-4).

is no less iconoclastic and burning than the apocalyptic prose of some of his radical religious contemporaries. Writing in an age when the great apocalyptic battle between Michael and the Dragon seems more fierce than ever, he appropriates the forceful, unsettling prophetic language of Haggai 2:6–7, applying it to the contemporary historical moment:[30] the "Imaginary Kingly power" "must be shaken to pieces," the Digger prophet proclaims in *Fire in the Bush*; Christ, who "is coming now once more" to destroy the power of the four great beasts, to deliver the Creation from the curse, and to set all men free, will "shake terribly the Nations, not *England* only, but all Nations ... and of his Kingdome there shall be no end" (463, 445, 464). As Winstanley had put it as early as *Truth Lifting up Its Head*, using militant language, Jesus Christ is a spiritual force able to tread all enemies "powerfully under foot": he is a "travelling army of mighty strength" (132). Though Winstanley himself may fight with "the sword of Love" (471), the iconoclastic and embattled revolutionary writer, whose spiritual "Armour," he tells us in *Fire in the Bush*, "is tryed," would become a mighty leveller too and use his inspired apocalyptic prose to "batter to pieces all the old Lawes" (446, 331), since their Antichristian representatives have made England into "a blinded and a snared generation" (591), as he later put it in *The Law of Freedom*. Like other visionary prose writers in the early years of the Republic — the Ranter Abiezer Coppe in *A Fiery Flying Roll* (1649), inspired by the prophetic authority of Ezekiel, or the millenarian George Foster in *The Sounding of the Last Trumpet* (1650) — Winstanley depicts God and the radical religious writer himself as mighty levellers of economic and social hierarchies in an unsettled time when the lower orders continued to be acutely oppressed and their plight ignored. Echoing the unsettling prophetic language of Ezekiel 21:27 in *Fire in the Bush*, Winstanley warns the great "oppressing powers of the world" that their "overturning, overturning, overturning, is come on to you" (472). So, too, Foster wrote in 1650 that the work of a mighty God and the visionary writer "is now to breake in peeces all things, and to make all things become new: which change is to restore the whole creation from bondage and slaverie"; and Coppe, responding acutely to the oppression of the poor in his extravagant apocalyptic prose, envisioned the Lord and himself as great levellers of "the Great Ones" of the earth — both are "now RISEN to shake terribly the Earth," for "The

---

[30] As Winstanley had already done as early as *The Breaking of the Day of God*, 115.

Eternall God, the mighty Leveller is comming, yea come, even at the door."[31]

In the impassioned prose of *Fire in the Bush*, moreover, the prophetic Digger writer, moved by the Spirit, assumes the visionary warning voice of St. John of Patmos (see Revelation 8:13, 12:12), as he directs his admonitions to those great powers of the earth that have opposed the coming of the kingdom of Christ, as well as a new age of equality, communism, freedom, and spiritual inwardness: "Therefore woe, woe, woe, to the Inhabitants of the Earth; when Christ rises in power, and begins to come in glory with his Saints" (470–71); "then woe, woe, woe, to the imaginary power, that rules the world, he shall be shaken with terror, and fall, and burst asunder" (463). And so while Christ himself is "the greatest, first, and truest Leveller" "tearing to pieces all rule, power and Authority," and one who will "levell mountaines and valleys" (386, 455, 448), Winstanley's own revolutionary prose, with its striking uses of prophetic language and original recreations of scriptural myths, becomes an urgent means of envisioning the coming millennium, a great reformation of the kingdom within, and the Land of Righteousness here on earth.

* * *

Winstanley's visionary writings, and *Fire in the Bush* in particular, I have tried to show, offer a compelling illustration of the way political, religious, aesthetic, and linguistic concerns intersect in the revolutionary discourse of seventeenth-century England. His unorthodox and poetic prose, his mythmaking, his allegorical imagination, his sensitivity (not unlike Milton's) to the powers, dangers, and subtle manipulations of language, scriptural interpretation, and artfulness: all these features suggest a writer whose prophetic and political discourse, as well as his religious radicalism, cannot be divorced from the textual and literary domain. One

---

[31] George Foster, *The Sounding of the Last Trumpet, Or, Severall Visions, declaring the Universall overturning and rooting up of all Earthly Powers in ENGLAND* (London, 1650), 15. Foster's work was published in April 1650, soon after the appearance of *Fire in the Bush*. See Coppe, *A Fiery Flying Roll* (London, 1649), for the Lord as "that mighty Leveller" (2–3, 6), though Coppe also distinguishes himself from the Diggers since he does not engage in "digging-levelling" (2). See also the Digger poet Robert Coster's *A Mite Cast into the Common Treasury* in *Works*, 659. For other examples from this period of God depicted as the great leveller, see Christopher Hill, *The English Bible and the Seventeenth-Century Revolution* (Harmondsworth: Penguin, 1993), 120–21.

of the reasons the Diggers matter, Ronald Hutton has recently stressed, is "because of their contribution to the history of ideas,"[32] a remark certainly confirmed by Winstanley's revolutionary views of an egalitarian economic and social order. But his visionary writing, I have suggested, cannot simply be confined to the history of ideas, however striking Winstanley's ultra-radical ideas may be: his prose matters because its contribution is also literary and aesthetic — Winstanley's rich mythopoeic writing having been stimulated by his responses to his immediate sociopolitical contexts of the 1648-49 Revolution and its ambiguous aftermath during the Republic. His visionary tracts are in their own way imaginative works both interacting with and interrogating political ideology and religious orthodoxies in an age of revolution, as well as the world of state power and social injustice, including their sinister verbal and artful manifestations. Like the anonymous author of *Tyranipocrit, Discovered* (1649), Winstanley understood acutely that tyranny in his age had by no means disappeared with the Revolution and the new Republic, but could be established "in other formes and fashions" which deceive men: thus as that author, who attacked the white devil of hypocrisy, observed, "wee have no need of tyranny in a new fashion, but of a changing of manners and customs, which are evill and prejudiciall to the common-wealth."[33] Like Milton, Winstanley perceived in his own terms that the Satanic power of "Hypocrisie turns himself into divers shapes; yea, sometimes into an Angel of light" (174) who in Milton's words, practices "falsehood under saintly show" (*Paradise Lost* 4.122).[34] This was an age, after all, when kingly power — "the great Antichrist, and Mystery of Iniquity" (530) as Winstanley represented it in his visionary tracts — had been cast out in one tyrannizing form during the Revolution of 1648-49 only to reappear in other subtle "shapes and disguises" in the new Commonwealth.

The visionary and mythopoeic writings of Winstanley, then, should be of particular interest at this moment in critical history when sociohistori-

---

[32] *The British Republic, 1649-1660* (London: Macmillan, 1990), 32. Cf. Zagorin's emphasis on Winstanley as "one of the pre-eminent political thinkers of his time" (*A History of Political Thought in the English Revolution*, 56).

[33] *Tyranipocrit, Discovered with his wiles* (Rotterdam, 1649), 35, 36. Yet even this anonymous author, though similar to Winstanley in his perceptions of hypocrisy and tyranny, did not argue for common ownership: see Aylmer, "The Religion of Winstanley," 115.

[34] Cf. *Fire in the Bush* where "Hypocrisie ... invent[s] much shew of holinesse to compasse his selfish ends" (446).

cal work in Renaissance studies has been prompting scholars to reexamine the complex interactions between the aesthetic and the political, the linguistic and the social. Yet the newer historical criticism has tended to focus its energies (even while bringing in marginal texts) on the court-centered culture of early modern England. The heterodox religious and political writings of a figure like Gerrard Winstanley pose a challenge to literary historians of this period (as well as to historians themselves): the challenge to examine the interaction of aesthetic, social, and religious concerns in less traditional kinds of literary discourses produced during this unsettled age of civil war and revolution. Unorthodox writers in this age of English prose, as Winstanley's visionary works amply illustrate, registered acutely the anxieties generated by a period of uncertain political upheaval and transformation, as they engaged in searching and creative explorations of its cultural and historical implications.

GRAHAM PARRY

In the Land of Moles and Pismires: Thomas Browne's Antiquarian Writings

ALTHOUGH THOMAS BROWNE WAS ALMOST an honorary citizen of the ancient world as a result of his extreme familiarity with every aspect of the history, literature, and learning of Greece and Rome, he did not turn his attention to the specific study of antiquities — the physical remains of the past — until the decade of the 1650s. This was a time when royalist gentlemen up and down the country were taking a new interest in the visible traces of the remote past, perhaps as a way of diverting their minds away from present discontents, perhaps too as a consequence of their exclusion from public life during the Commonwealth years. Certainly this was a decade rich in antiquarian publication. The field was dominated by William Dugdale, who established his preeminence with a succession of authoritative volumes. He brought to completion the researches of Roger Dodsworth, the Yorkshire antiquary, who had been gathering the records of the monastic movement in the middle ages and who was the prime mover of the *Monasticon Anglicanum*, the first volume of which came out under the names of Dodsworth and Dugdale in 1655. Dugdale's masterpiece was *The Antiquities of Warwickshire* of 1656, the most thorough, informative, and well-illustrated of all the county histories of the seventeenth century, a work that has remained the paragon of its genre. This was the volume of which the young Oxford scholar Anthony Wood wrote: "my pen cannot enough describe how [my] tender affections and insatiable desire of knowledge were ravish'd and melted down by reading of that book."[1] Such words indicate something of the eagerness with which

---

[1] *The Life and Times of Anthony Wood*, ed. Andrew Clark (Oxford 1891), 1:209.

studies of antiquities were received by well-educated readers at this time. Dugdale next brought out *The History of St. Paul's* in 1658, another large folio, and one that has left all later ecclesiologists in his debt, for it contains a comprehensive account of the contents and appearance of old St. Paul's Cathedral before it was destroyed by fire in 1666. The many etchings of its tombs and architecture by Wenceslaus Hollar, commissioned by Dugdale, form an invaluable record of the medieval cathedral.

Dugdale's concern with church antiquities was matched in some measure by Thomas Fuller, who published his enormous *Church History of Britain* in 1655. This work dwelt extensively on the early period of Christianity in Britain, before moving slowly through the centuries in a leisurely anecdotal narrative of church affairs until the Reformation; the spirited account of the Church of England in Tudor and Stuart times comes to an abrupt halt with the execution of Charles I and the effective demise of the church. A more solemn exercise in antiquarianism was being carried out in the 1650s by "that Goliath of learning," as Wood called him, James Ussher the archbishop of Armagh, whose lifelong preoccupation with the time-scale of ancient civilizations was being delivered to the world in a succession of chronologies that were published in 1650, 1654 and 1658. These works offered a fully synchronized dating of events in Hebrew, Greek, and Roman history, and connected these events with those in other prominent civilizations of antiquity. Ussher's reputation was extremely high during the 1650s: his books were much remarked, and they opened broad vistas from the present back to the remotest past, even to the beginning of the world.

There had been a lively interest in Roman antiquities in Britain ever since Camden first published his *Britannia* in 1586, and successive editions of that work in the seventeenth century had intensified that interest. The fact that Britain had been part of the Roman empire for four hundred years, and that Roman remains were always turning up in English fields, meant that English gentlemen, educated in the classical tradition, commonly had a curiosity about the Roman inheritance of the nation. Roman antiquities were given renewed prominence in the 1650s by the posthumous publication of Inigo Jones's *Stone-Heng Restored* in 1655 which speculated that the enigmatic structure was a Roman temple, and contained much miscellaneous information about the Roman occupation of Britain. The topography of Roman Britain was intensively explicated by William Burton, an Oxford classicist and Kentish schoolmaster, who published his popular *Commentary on Antoninus his Itinerary* in 1658, a book which attempted to identify the location of Roman towns and camps, the names of which were preserved in a series of military routes dating from the third century known as the Antonine Itinerary.

It was against this background of intensive research and publication that Thomas Browne brought out his own contribution to antiquarian studies, *Hydriotaphia: Urn-Burial*, in 1658, inspired by the recent discovery of some sepulchral urns in a field in Norfolk. The success of this work encouraged him to extend his interest thereafter to barrows and earthworks, and later still to church antiquities. His new reputation as an antiquary brought him into rewarding correspondence with Dugdale, John Evelyn, and John Aubrey, thus linking him to the main lines of contemporary thinking about the remote past.

Urn-Burial is a unique production: part excavation report, part meditation on the mystery of time and the vanity of human wishes. Contemplating these clay vessels and their ashy contents, Browne articulated emotions ignored by most antiquaries, acknowledging in these scanty remains the forlorn hope of men to preserve themselves from oblivion. He spoke of the vast futility of human ambition in the face of time, and recounted the extraordinary designs of men to ensure their posthumous passage through age after age. The accidents of fortune that have frustrated so many splendid schemes to perpetuate bodies, names, and memories add an exquisitely poignant savor to Browne's reflections:

> who can but pity the founder of the Pyramids? Herostratus lives that burnt the Temple of Diana, he is almost lost that built it; Time hath spared the epitaph of Adrian's horse, confounded that of himself. In vain we compute our felicities by the advantage of our good names, since bad have equal durations, and Thersites is like to live as long as Agamemnon.[2]

This is the archaeology of sighs and tears, as Browne recognized when he described the urns as "sad and sepulchral Pitchers, which have no joyful voices; silently expressing old mortality, the ruines of forgotten times."[3]

Browne initially assumed that his Norfolk urns were Roman, though the illustration he provides (with a suitable melancholy quotation from Propertius) makes clear to modern eyes that they are Saxon. He is on the wrong track from the start because of his false assumption that the urns are Roman, but to be fair to him, it must be said that there was no sense at all

---

[2] *Hydriotaphia: Urn-Burial*, chap. 5, in *The Works of the learned Sir Thomas Browne* (London, 1686). ("Hydriotaphia" literally means burial in an urn.) The chapters of *Urn-Burial* are very brief, and succeeding quotations can be readily identified without notes.

[3] *Urn-Burial*: The Epistle Dedicatory.

of the artefacts of the pagan Saxons in his time, or indeed until the end of the eighteenth century. As Browne himself remarked in his prefatory epistle, "The supinity of elder dayes hath left so much in silence, or time hath so martyred the Records, that the most industrious heads do finde no easie worke to erect a new *Britannia*."

The discovery of urns was a commonplace event; many antiquarian books noted similar finds on ancient sites: Camden, Stow, Weever, Dugdale all remark on them briefly, and they are always assumed to be Roman, in part because the word "urn" itself derived from the Latin "urna," and also because cremation was known to be a Roman practice.[4] It is important to Browne that the urns should be Roman, for that puts him in touch with the high civilization of antiquity, and allows him to invoke the illustrious classical names that give such splendor to his discourse. These dull earthen pots command a profound respect because of their Roman origin; indeed, the incinerated fragments they contain offer physical contact with the Romans of the ancient empire, and "remembring the early civility they brought upon these countreys, and forgetting long passed mischiefs, we mercifully preserve their bones, and pisse not upon their ashes."[5]

A review of the burial customs of the Romans arises naturally from contemplation of the urns, and from this rich subject Browne proceeds to the funerary practices of other nations of the ancient world. Greeks, Egyptians, Hebrews, Persians, Babylonians — all had their peculiar forms of burial, and distinctive beliefs concerning the fate of the soul. From all nations he gathers examples of extravagant or flamboyant disposal of the noble dead: in gold or silver urns, in enclosures of glass, beneath pyramids,

---

[4] Browne remarked in another context, and at a later time, on the inexhaustible supply of urns, and on their probable date:

> Now though Urnes have often been discovered in former Ages, many think it strange there should be many still found, yet assuredly there may be great numbers still concealed. For though we should not reckon upon any who were thus buried before the time of the Romans ... nor should account this practice of burning among the Britains higher than Vespasian, when it is aid by Tacitus, that they conformed unto the Manners and Customs of the Romans, and so both Nations might have one way of Burial. [The terminus would be the formal establishment of Christianity in the fourth century.] The Account of the buried persons would amount to about Four Millions, and consequently so great a Number of Urnes dispersed through the Land, as may still satisfy the curiosity of succeeding Times, and arise to all Ages.

From "Concerning some Urnes found in Brampton-Field, 1667," in *The Works of Sir Thomas Browne*, ed. Charles Sayle, 3 vols. (Edinburgh 1927), 3:434.

[5] *Urn-Burial*: The Epistle Dedicatory.

obelisks, tumuli; raised high on pillars or towers, or laid in the beds of rivers; burnt with perfumed woods, or buried amid precious stones. "The Scythians ... made their grave in the air; and the Ichthyophagi or fish-eating nations about Egypt, affected the sea for their grave."

After the macabre cortège of burial customs that opens *Urn-Burial*, Browne devotes his second chapter to the discovery, contents, and condition of the objects that provoked his discourse. Clearly an ancient cemetery had been accidentally located:

> In a Field of old Walsingham, not many monethes past, were digged up between fourty and fifty Urnes, deposited in a dry and sandy soile, not a yard deep, nor farre from one another: Not all strictly of one figure, but most answering these described: Some containing two pounds of bones, distinguishable in skulls, ribs, jawes, thigh-bones and teeth, with fresh impressions of their combustion. Besides the extraneous substances like peeces of small brasse instruments, brazen nippers, and in one some kind of Opale.

The opal was found in the urn that had been given to Thomas Browne by the landowner, and this jewel amid the ashes was the spark that set his imagination on fire, and caused him to see the beauty of buried things. It also suggests to him that the ashes might be those of a woman, and the opal a part of her decoration. He tries by minute and accurate description to assign a rough date to the finds, and to relate them to the Romanized culture of East Anglia in the second and third centuries. His assumption is fortified by the presence of a Roman station five miles away from the cemetery, although he notes that the town adjacent to the urn-field has a Saxon name, Burnham. Browne is disappointed that no Roman coins were found with the urns, nor were they "attended with lacrymatories, lamps, bottles of liquor, and other appurtenances of affectionate superstition" that would prove them to be Roman. But so numerous were Roman finds in Norfolk, and the discovery of coins so common, that he feels justified in believing his urns to be a relic of the Roman occupation, which he proves by many details to have been extensive and populous. He believes, reasonably in the circumstances, that they cannot be older than Boadicea's rising in AD 61, nor later than the establishment of Christianity in the early fourth century, which gave "the final extinction to these bone-fires."

Browne's medical skills come into play when he minutely investigates the contents of the urns. From the character of the fragments of bone, he deduces that many of the remains are those of women and children. Burnt pieces of comb, small containers "handsomely overwrought, like the necks or bridges of musicall instruments," "brazen nippers to pull away hair" confirm his belief that these are female remains. The opal, "yet maintaining a blewish colour," leads him into speculations about why precious objects are placed in graves, and in one of those moments of imaginative association that frequently illuminate Browne's discourse with a strange unearthly light, reminds him of the ring of Cynthia's ghost, who returns from her cremation to upbraid her lover Propertius.[6]

As Browne continues to contemplate the unfamiliar objects amid the ashes, the thought occurs to him that the urns might not be Roman after all; there is nothing classical about them, and he suddenly wonders if they might not belong "unto our Brittish, Saxon or Danish Forefathers?" He remembers that Tacitus had written that "the Romans early wrought so much civility upon the British stock, that they brought them to build temples, to wear the Gown, and study the Romane Laws and Language." It may be "no improbable conjecture" "that they conformed also to their Religion, rites and customs in burials." According to Tacitus, the Germans also burnt their dead; the "Saxons, Jutes and Angles" who settled in England were descended from the Germans, and most probably retained their customs. Moreover, the historians Saxo Grammaticus and Olaus Worm have provided evidence of Gothic cremation and urns in Denmark and Sweden. Browne's intuition here is right on target, and his archeological reasoning is meticulous; he is prevented from recognizing the true nature of his find only by the absence of relevant data. Without examples of urns from an indisputable British, Saxon, or Danish source, and without illustrations of comparable material, he is at a loss. The ancient written record is helpful, but provides "no assured conclusion." Browne understands that the answers to his question lie in the character of the objects themselves, and in their location and in the material remains surrounding them in the earth. But the practice of archaeology has not yet been developed, nor indeed does the word seem known to Browne: he has grasped the principle of it, though, and it will not be long before we find him writing to Sir William Dugdale to tell him to dig methodically and record whatever he finds when it comes to deciphering the enigmatic remains of the past.

After this valuable experience of honest doubt, Browne swings back to the Roman hypothesis as the most likely explanation, for he needs some firm basis for his contemplations. He soars off again into ingenious speculations, beginning in facts, ending in fantasy. He taps his smooth black urn, and notes what a "dully sounding" noise it makes, but this sad sound becomes the preface to a panegyric upon "the artifice of clay": "Hereof

---

[6] Propertius, book IV, vii.

the House of Mausolus was built, thus old Jupiter stood in the Capitoll, and the Statua of Hercules made in the reign of Tarquinius Priscus, [that] was extant in Plinies dayes." Then he spirals back down to his urn, to investigate more closely its contents, and to note that it appears to have been stuffed, at the time of burial, with "long roots of Quich, or Dogs-grass wreathed about the bones." How different, he muses, from the "purple peece of silk" which closed "the Homerical Urne of Patrocles." It is this constant shuffling between the rude provincial burial before him and the glories of the great funerals of antiquity that provides the pleasure of *Hydriotaphia*. He sensationalizes the past in every way, making it live again in imagination, and he brings it before the reader with a rousing immediacy. For example, as he observes that there are no vials of tears, "vessels of oyles and aromaticall liquors" included in his urn, even though these in Roman times were often placed in "noble ossuaries," he simultaneously speculates about the taste of such draughts, which "far exceed the Palats of Antiquity. Liquors not to be computed by years of annual magistrates, but by great conjunctions and the fatal periods of kingdoms."

In small specific ways Browne conveys, amid the frequent excursions of his learned fancy, a detailed and dependable account of the objects that have been recovered. When he subjects some of the unidentifiable fragments in his urn to physical tests, what to first sight appeared to be pieces of wood, added to the cremated ashes, being dropped in water and exposed to flame prove to be bone or ivory. "Our little Iron pins which fastened the Ivory works, held well together and lost not their magneticall quality." Other metal pieces that had remained unrusted were bronze, and began to develop verdigris after exposure to the air.

Having exhausted his urn's capacity for factual information, Browne is free to marvel at the metaphysics of death: the immortality of the soul and the hope of resurrection fill the fourth chapter of his discourse. His review of ancient beliefs and the way these beliefs were emblematized in the ceremonies of the grave is unforgettable. If ever there were a "Thesaurus Sepulchralis" it is here, in *Urn-Burial*, where every conceivable funeral curiosity is engagingly displayed, and many that are inconceivable too. We are told why "the souls of Penelope's Paramours conducted by Mercury chirped like bats, and those that followed Hercules made a noise like a flock of birds." The question is put "Why the Funerall Suppers [of the Greeks] consisted of Egges, Beans, Smallage and Lettuce, since the dead are made to eat Asphodels about the Elizian meadows?" We are reliably informed that a woman is "unctuously constituted for the better pyrall combustion than a man" and regaled with the "irregularities" and "wild enormities" of antique funerals: of emperors half-burnt in the arena, of

Mausolus's ashes swallowed in wine by his widow in a draught of "passionate prodigality," of kings' bones burnt for lime. This is the romance of antiquarianism, the pleasure of rare knowledge exquisitely displayed.

The fifth and final chapter of *Urn-Burial* must be the most sublime and richly orchestrated passage of English ever composed. Sustained with astonishing virtuosity through paragraph after paragraph, it combines the mood of a requiem with the language of epic to evoke a vision of mankind everlastingly at war with time to preserve his identity beyond the grave. It is a meditation that begins in earth, with the Norfolk urns that "in a yard under ground, and thin walls of clay" have "quietly rested under the drums and tramplings of three conquests," and it ends in heaven, where the soul experiences "the Gustation of God, and ingression into the divine shadow." Browne soars far beyond the matters of antiquarianism, and the last chapter of *Urn-Burial* belongs more to religion and philosophy than to the study of the past.

The language and the imaginative flight of ideas of *Urn-Burial* are unique and unmatched, but in its subject matter it has antecedents and models. In particular there was a work of continental scholarship that had a special relevance to Browne's purpose. On two occasions he refers to the recent discovery of the tomb of the fifth-century Frankish king Childeric near Tournai in the Low Countries in 1653. This was a notable occasion in archaeological history, for the grave was carefully excavated and the findings published at Antwerp in 1655 under the splendid title *Anastasis Childerici I, Francorum Regis, sive Thesaurus Sepulchralis* (The Resurrection of Childeric). The author was Jean-Jacques Chiflet, who was physician to the archduke Leopold, Regent of the Austrian Netherlands, and the work was effectively the first methodical excavation report to be printed. Browne possessed this book, as is evident from his marginalia, and Stuart Piggott has suggested that he might have known Chiflet through their common association with the Leiden medical school.[7] At any rate, Browne seems to have been much influenced by this work, which detailed the royal treasures found with the body, and illustrated many of them accurately. Chiflet also attempted to reconstruct the funeral practices of the pagan Franks, and to recreate in small measure the cultural ethos of the Merovingian world over which Childeric had reigned. Although Browne had a humble subject with his ignoble urns, he also had before him this model of an archaeological report that went far beyond the

---

[7] See Stuart Piggott, "Sir Thomas Browne and Antiquity," *Oxford Journal of Archaeology* (1988): 257–69, especially 267.

immediate description of a grave, and he may well have set himself to show that an unremarkable find can give rise to reflections as sublime as any inspired by a royal tomb.

While Chiflet's book may have contributed to Browne's idea of a funerary treatise, other works seem to have shed their influence on *Urn-Burial* as well. John Selden's *De Diis Syriis* (1619), that remarkable disquisition on the gods of Syria and their rites, stood as an example of how a learned curiosity could suffuse a profoundly obscure topic with intellectual delight. More relevantly, the "Discourse of Funeral Monuments" that prefaces John Weever's *Ancient Funerall Monuments* of 1631 parades a similar train of memorable and ingenious deaths, burials, and funeral customs before the reader. The solemn and elevated style of Weever's work also anticipates Browne's magniloquent prose. *Urn-Burial* has much in common too with *De Funeribus Romanorum* (1625) of Johannes Kirchmann, the German scholar from Lübeck, whose compilation was the most thorough account in existence of Roman funeral rites.[8]

To return to "the Land of Moles and Pismires", where antiquaries dwell: with the publication of *Urn-Burial*, Browne acquired an immediate reputation as an opinionist on the remains of the ancient world. Dugdale, as we have seen, applied to him for information and ideas about fenland antiquities when he was writing his *History of Imbanking and Draining*, and it would appear that Browne's tract, "Of Artificial Hills, Mounts or Burrows" was a response to a query from Dugdale about the origins of these mounds he so often met with.[9] Browne's reply is not very satisfactory. They might be Roman, Saxon, or Danish, and are either landmarks or boundary marks, or tombs of great men or fallen soldiers. His evidence is entirely from written sources: Virgil provides details to prove that the Romans raised funerary mounds, Wormius attests to the same custom among the ancient Danes. For the Saxons, however, Browne can only cite Leland's opinion but with no solid detail. Although he advises his correspondent to look for objects in or near the mounds, the same difficulty handicaps him here as in *Urn-Burial*: Browne does not know what Saxon or Danish artefacts look like. He never entertains the thought that some mounds may be pre-Roman, and he has no concept that the ancient Brit-

---

[8] Extracts from all these authors are found in Browne's commonplace books. See Jeremiah Finch, *Sir Thomas Browne* (New York: Collier, 1961), 144 and 236 n. 3.

[9] Dugdale's letter to Browne dated 17 November 1658 refers to this tract on tumuli. See *The Letters of Sir Thomas Browne*, ed. G Keynes, (London: Faber, 1946), 337–39.

ish made anything at all. Browne does stress the value of excavation, however, as the best means of advancing knowledge about field-works.

The correspondence with Dugdale allowed Browne to express his opinion about the fen country of East Anglia in antiquity, based on long familiarity with the region. He is persuaded that originally the fenland was forested, as the remains of large trees in the marshes prove; he imagines the first inhabitants clearing the forests by burning, a practice that is still carried on by the natives of America and Ireland, he notes. Between them, Browne and Dugdale discuss the probable geography of land and sea in Eastern England in remote times, and the causes of change. No cataclysms are required to alter the landscape, but Browne speculates that the climate might change, and he posits the theory of a "great winter," taken from Aristotle, that might have transformed the whole character of the land. He uses the presence of the skeletons of fish as proof that the sea once covered the inland areas; he is, however, puzzled by giant bones that seem like bones of elephants that are continually found in the fenland drainages. They cannot all be the remains of the elephants that Claudius brought over, and there is no record of "succeeding emperors" introducing large numbers of the beasts. He has to admit that "many things prove obscure in subterraneous discoverie."[10] At least he does not ascribe all phenomena of fish bones, shells, and other incongruous remains to the Universal Deluge, but seeks for explanation in geological and climatic change.

In considering the Roman occupation of the fenlands, Browne is able to prove that they must have engaged in very extensive drainage schemes for the improvement of the region, and suggests that these schemes must have involved the forced labor of the British population on a large scale. He imagines a major programme of public works in progress, and the building of causeways across the reclaimed land. His detailed knowledge of the drainage projects undertaken by Claudius, Trajan, and Hadrian in Italy enables him to imagine the nature of the works in Britain. He is knowledgeable too about the construction of Roman roads, and although no "noble consularie wayes" were built in East Anglia, he can identify the surviving roads and admire their composition and durability: "raysed with small stones and gravell, of ample height and latitude, probably occasioning the first name of high wayes, now common unto all roades." He assumes that these Roman highways remained well enough preserved to be used in Saxon times by the Mercians "when they so often invaded and

---

[10] Browne to Dugdale, October 1660, in Keynes, *Letters*, 353–56.

spoiled the East-Angles."[11] These letters to Dugdale are full of suggestive comments that show what a valuable collaborator Browne could be, for all his ideas are brought out by enquiry. He had a most lively sense of Roman Britain; his interest in the British inhabitants is, however, minimal, and he cannot believe that they even possessed the arts of agriculture at the time of the Roman conquest, but were wholly devoted to war.[12]

A fruitful correspondence also developed with John Evelyn, beginning at the time of the publication of *Urn-Burial*, devoted principally to what Evelyn would have called "hortulan antiquities," that is to say ancient gardens and horticulture. Evelyn was clearly drawn to Browne's discourse on *The Garden of Cyrus* that was printed together with *Urn-Burial*. Again, Browne's broad knowledge of Roman life and customs is shown to advantage as he is able to describe so many of the refinements of garden art among the ancient societies. He wrote too for Evelyn a learned tract on customs involving the wearing of garlands among the ancients, with an account of the symbolic flowers used on such occasions, information that Evelyn requested for inclusion in his great study (never yet published in full) of the garden in all its aspects, "Elysium Britannicum."

One final antiquarian exercise of Browne's deserves mention: his account of the tombs and monuments in Norwich Cathedral, which was published posthumously in 1712 under the title "Repertorium." Although the title-page gives 1680 as the date when the work was compiled, it is clear from a letter to John Aubrey that Browne began collecting material for his survey in 1660, when he made the acquaintance of a 91-year-old "understanding-singing man" who was himself a living memorial of ecclesiastical history.[13] Browne had already been taking an interest in church antiquities in 1658, when he was volunteering information about Norwich foundations for the *Monasticon*.[14] "Repertorium" (an index or a catalogue) is in the tradition of Weever's *Ancient Funerall Monuments*, and is in fact a more detailed traversing of the same ground that Weever had covered for that book, for Norwich was one of the dioceses he combed. Browne was motivated to make his record after learning that over a hundred brass inscriptions had been stripped away during the Civil Wars, with the result that many monuments were in danger of sinking into the anonymity he had so eloquently lamented in *Urn-Burial*. His

---

[11] Browne to Dugdale, 11 December 1658, in ibid., 344.
[12] Ibid., 344.
[13] Browne to Aubrey, 24 August 1672, in ibid., 395.
[14] Browne to Dugdale, 16 December 1658, in ibid., 339.

catalogue is a piece of local piety, noting the graves of bishops, clerics, and Norfolk worthies, and giving a brief history of their achievements and lineage. He records coats of arms wherever they occur, but he cannot quote many inscriptions, for most have gone. Weever's collection already proves invaluable, for so much of what he recorded in the later 1620s had been destroyed by 1660. Like so many of his contempories, Browne had no interest in architectural or monumental detail, being concerned only with families, names, and deeds. "Repertorium" is a utilitarian compilation, devoid of the stylistic splendor one might expect of a survey of monuments by Browne. It is enlivened, however, by recollections of the Cathedral before the Civil Wars when all was brightly maintained, including a valuable description of the Combination Sermon formerly "preached in the Summer Time at the Cross in the Green-Yard" to crowded audiences as in an outdoor theatre, with the gentry in galleries and "the rest either stood, or sat in the Green, upon long forms provided for them, paying a Penny or Halfpenny apiece, as they did at S. Paul's Cross in London."[15] He remembers too the iconoclasm of the war times, when the richly-embroidered copes belonging to the cathedral were carried to the market place, along with pieces of the cathedral organ, and all were cast into a fire "with shouting and rejoicing." He recalls climbing to the very top of the steeple when scaffolding was put up at the Restoration, and how strange the country looked from on high. He adds a regretful remark that, according to his estimation, only four monarchs have ever visited Norwich since the Conquest, and on this rather forlorn, provincial note, he ends.

Browne's involvement with local historical studies continued as an undercurrent to the end of his life. His prodigious learning made him an involuntary antiquarian, in fact, for he knew so much about the ancient world from his reading that he was qualified to offer an opinion on virtually any subject relating to antiquity. He developed a genuine if minor interest in field archaeology, and in *Urn-Burial* he raised an insignificant incident into an encounter with the past that reverberated through the intellectual community of the nation. This publication gave Browne a perhaps exaggerated reputation for antiquarian expertise, but it certainly commanded the respect of Dugdale, which was no small achievement, and it elevated his pursuits above those of the many educated country gentlemen in the last third of the seventeenth century for whom antiquarian interests held a firm but minor place.

---

[15] "Repertorium," in Thomas Browne, *Posthumous Works* (London, 1712); in Sayle, *Works*, 3:422.

THOMAS N. CORNS

Bunyan's *Grace Abounding* and the Dynamics of Restoration Nonconformity[1]

CHRISTOPHER HILL'S INFLUENTIAL AND OFTEN ARTICULATED belief that the Restoration of spring 1660 brought to a close the great period of English radicalism received two parallel challenges in the mid-1980s, from R. L. Greaves, who carefully documented the plots and the uprising of the radical underground in the years immediately following 1660, and from N. H. Keeble, whose account of the literary culture of Restoration nonconformity sympathetically explores the stratagems for ideological survival inscribed in the texts of dissenters in that broad spectrum from Richard Baxter to Milton and to Bunyan. Indeed, Hill himself has significantly reappraised his position, and his history of Bunyan and his church — its range is larger than a biography — shares much common ground with Greaves and with Keeble.[2]

The struggle continued. As Keeble concludes, "The literary culture of nonconformity was not moribund but vital."[3] That vitality, however,

---

[1] A version of this essay was presented to the 1993 conference of the Rocky Mountain Medieval and Renaissance Association, Flagstaff, Arizona. I should like to acknowledge the generosity of the British Academy and the University of Wales, Bangor, in awarding grants which subvented my attendance.

[2] Richard L. Greaves, *Deliver Us from Evil: The Radical Underground in Britain, 1660–1663* (Oxford: Oxford Univ. Press, 1986); N. H. Keeble, *The Literary Culture of Nonconformity in Later Seventeenth-Century England* (Leicester: Leicester Univ. Press, 1987); Christopher Hill, *A Turbulent, Seditious, and Factious People: John Bunyan and his Church* (Oxford: Oxford Univ. Press, 1988).

[3] Keeble, 283.

manifested itself in one of the most characteristic and unmistakeable of life-signs: Restoration nonconformity was mobile, it was dynamic. My purpose is to explore that aspect of one of the most powerful and fascinating manifestations of that culture, John Bunyan's spiritual autobiography, *Grace Abounding to the Chief of Sinners*.

But *Grace Abounding* is not one text but three, in that in Bunyan's life time it appeared in at least three principal editions (two other editions did not survive; the sixth adds only a little to the fifth): the first edition of 1666; the third, which carries no date but which its editor, Roger Sharrock, ascribes to the period 1672–1674; and the fifth of 1680. Curiously for a work which has the formal characteristics of autobiography, later editions do not add material later than the time frame of the first edition; there is no account of the later life of the writer. Rather, additional material — very little is deleted in the subsequent revisions — adds details and incidents and anecdotes and explanations within the time frame established. It is a narrative of the first thirty-three years of so of his life, first issued when he was thirty-eight; reissued at the age of forty-four to forty-six; reissued at the age of fifty-two; and finally reissued in the year of his death. The tale gets refined and supplemented, but what happened to the author thereafter is not addressed.

In part that may seem utterly unremarkable; it is an account of spiritual regeneration, and while Bunyan's agonizing version of the Calvinist doctrine of salvation admitted of all sort of uncertainties in the process, the book ends with a strong sense of the eventual justification of the sinner, a stage from which a fall into reprobation could probably not be conceived. But the revisions also produce three texts for significantly different times within the history of nonconformity. The refrain recurs within the text: "at that time," referring to discrete points in the time line from 1628 to 1661 or thereabouts. But the three versions of the text, the third and fifth editions significantly nudged by supplementation, address "that time" at which they were published; and those times need a careful regard to make sense of the document, which begins, I shall argue, as a profound but politically naive testament, but which evolves into a polemic for the revived ambitions of nonconformity in the 1670s.

To define the character of the mid-1660s and of the 1670s I would like, in prefatory fashion, to glance at two other prose works by former republican activists, not soldier-preachers like Bunyan, but an academic, Thomas Sprat, and a civil servant, John Milton. Each is a work of politically adroit reconciliation with the restored Stuart ascendancy.

Sprat's *History of the Royal Society*, published in 1667, is a brazen rewriting of the history of the English academic establishment in the period of the Cromwellian ascendancy. Sprat, who had been an elegiast of Cromwell and panegyrist of his son, enjoyed the patronage of those who had gained from purging of the universities which followed the parliamentarian victory, and his career at Oxford owed much to John Wilkins, Cromwell's brother-in-law and successively master of Wadham and Trinity College, Cambridge. It was among that group of talented Cromwellian placemen, including Seth Ward and William Petty, that the Royal Society had its origins. For the most part, they had scampered aboard the reflagged ship of state in 1660 — Sprat, for example, with alacrity became a priest in holy order (and, after several preferments, the bishop of Rochester). When he rewrote the early history of the Royal Society, however, he presents the experience of the 1650s not as a happy and prosperous one for those in their coterie; rather, their early scientific work was undertaken to take their minds off their country's and their king's suffering:

> It was *Nature* alone, which could pleasantly entertain them, in that estate. The contemplation of that, draws our minds off from past, or present misfortunes, and makes them conquerors over things, in the greatest publick unhappiness.[4]

"Present misfortunes," indeed; Sprat and his associates were toasting themselves before the fire of the Master's lodgings in no small part because of those misfortunes, which had seen the university purged and had opened up the glittering prizes to the able and the ambitious.

Sprat's rewriting of history is unsurprising; many clear-eyed and energetic young men were making the same transition, Pepys, for example, or Wren. It was one route to take in the 1660s, a route eschewed by Milton or by Bunyan. Yet in 1673, two years after Milton had indulged the bloody fantasy of *Samson Agonistes* and the alternative vision of *Paradise Regained* whose transcendent hero rises above all worldly rewards and revenges, he published his own conciliatory initiative in (forgive the paradox) his fiercely anti-Catholic tolerationist tract, *Of True Religion, Haeresy, Schism, and Toleration*. In *Paradise Lost* Milton had represented himself as a solitary hero reenacting past solitary heroism in an *imitatio Christi* that must

---

[4] Thomas Sprat, *The History of the Royal Society*, ed. Jackson I. Cope and Harold Whitmore Jones (1959; Washington: Washington Univ. Press and Routledge, 1966), 56.

remain the role of the godly in an ungodly world.⁵ In *Of True Religion* he offers himself as spokesperson for all Protestant opinion, Baptists and Socinians, Lutherans, Calvinists and Arminians, all united in their commitment to certain central truths and in their animosity to Catholicism; such divisions, in a true church like the Church of England, "needs not tend to the breaking of Communion"; and he writes in glowing terms of the Thirty-Nine Articles and of the Authorized Version.⁶

Milton's seeming apostasy, his readiness to make common cause with all English Protestants and to find the finer features of the established Anglican church, is surprising in ways in which Sprat's is not, in that he has no material ambitions that are served by it. The answers rest in the changing nature of nonconformist experience in the Restoration years. Throughout the 1660s, though Charles exercised occasional whimsicalities about the more exotic creeds and though he began quite tolerantly in his dealings with the more conservative Presbyterian nonconformists, the general attitude of government towards dissent was hostile and sometimes ferocious, and each insurrection, irrespective of how limited its scale or particular its origins, was associated with waves of white terror, of arrests, of expropriations, of executions.⁷ But in the early 1670s the possibilities for advancing towards an endurable toleration changed radically. In 1669 Charles had called for a new vigor in prosecuting conventicles.⁸ In its winter session of 1670/71, the Cavalier Parliament still persisted in its hard line.⁹ But in the spring of 1672, two days before declaring war on the United Provinces, prompted against his own instincts by "his whole ring of trusted advisers," Charles issued his "spectacular royal pronouncement," the Declaration of Indulgence, at a stroke suspending all penal laws against Protestant dissenters and Catholics, allowing the former to meet for worship if they obtained licenses from Charles and the latter to hear mass in private.¹⁰

Suddenly, the case was altered, as much for Bunyan as for Milton. In place of the ideology of the godly remnant, of the martyred saints bearing

---

⁵ See, for example, *Paradise Lost*, 7.24–28, 12.473–85.

⁶ John Milton, *Complete Prose Works*, ed. Don M. Wolfe et al. (New Haven: Yale Univ. Press, 1953–82), 8:422–23, 419–20, 428–29. See Hill, 147.

⁷ Greaves, passim; Ronald Hutton, *Charles II, King of England, Scotland, and Ireland* (1989; Oxford: Oxford Univ. Press, 1991), especially chaps. 7 and 10.

⁸ Hutton, 267.

⁹ Ibid., 275.

¹⁰ Ibid., 284–85.

witness to the true faith, came an opportunity to establish a *modus vivendi* with the government that would permit, in the case of Milton (these are the issues he foregrounds in his pamphlet) the renewal of speculative and controversial theology, in the case of Bunyan the practical work of the Baptist ministry to which he was committed. Milton's maneuver, however, was to make common cause with those politically acceptable Protestants that regarded the toleration of Catholicism as an impossible price; his pamphlet, while making space for Protestant dissent, remains profoundly and explicitly antipathetic to the Stuart court (hence, *inter alia*, his otherwise rather gratuitous attack on "Pride, Luxury, Drunkenness, Whoredom, Cursing, Swearing, bold and open Atheism every where abounding,"[11] a transparent allusion to the court scandals that had reached spectacular proportions and prominence in 1671).[12]

Milton was an old man near to death, and he spoke for no one but himself; Bunyan's response shows a greater sensitivity to his corporate obligations to his religious community, and while the Declaration was rescinded in February 1673 it demonstrated that a nonconformist strategy which opened dialogue with the establishment was once more worth considering.[13]

The fifth edition of *Grace Abounding* was published in 1680 in even giddier times. Most significantly, the popish plot of 1678 had once more offered possibilities for redefining the political nation in ways which could readmit even dissenting Protestants (in the face of a supposed French-inspired conspiracy for a Catholic uprising). The end of the Cavalier Parliament and its replacement by a succession of Exclusion Parliaments marked a shift away from the implacable hostility of Restoration royalists to parliaments which were inherently hostile to the popery detected within the court and sympathetic to the plights of beleaguered fellow Protestants of dissenting persuasion. The Exclusion Crisis was at its critical phase at the time Bunyan's book was reissued. Though the outcome, following Charles's assumption of personal rule after March 1681, proved

---

[11] Milton, 8:438.

[12] Hutton, 278.

[13] On probable organizational responses to the opportunities of the early 1670s, see Hill, 123. On his church's decision to seek licensing under the provision of the Proclamation, see Hill, 145, and R. L. Greaves, "The spirit and the Sword: Bunyan and the Stuart State," in Robert G. Collmer, ed., *Bunyan in Our Time* (Kent, Ohio: Kent State Univ. Press, 1989), 147-48. They bought a barn as a permanent meeting-place, and prepared a considerable list of preachers.

in the short term catastrophic for the dissenters' cause, in 1680 Bunyan's church may well have anticipated that they would return to and enjoy the freedoms they had not known since the 1650s. This dangerous and unstable context relates profoundly to the three principal versions of the text.

The first edition seeks no dialogue with the Restored order. Indeed, the abiding power the text retains for a twentieth-century readership lies in its very introversion, its grim interiorization of experience. The best modern reading, by John Stachniewski, brilliantly displaces earlier attempts to regard it simply as a devotional manual, a straightforwardly paradigmatic working out of a Calvinist scheme of salvation.[14] Stachniewski demonstrates how a dread of reprobation haunts the writer: "His assurance of salvation at one moment can be displaced instantaneously by despair at both early and later stages of the narrative."[15]

Deliverance comes to Bunyan with a parodox of which he is unaware: in prison, in contemplation of the sufferings of his family, in anticipation of his own execution, making "a scrabling shift to clamber up the Ladder," "on the Ladder, with the Rope about my neck," poised, like the republican martyrs of 1661, to make one last testament of faith. Even there, right to the imaginative evocation of the last moments of his life, he is pursued by fears of reprobation — Stachniewski's phrase "the persecutory imagination" so well suits the phenomenon — till, contemplating a "leap off the Ladder even blindfold into Eternitie, sink or swim, come heaven, come hell; Lord Jesus, if thou wilt catch me, do; if not, I will venture for thy Name," a new assurance comes. And it comes in the disembodied voice of the spirit: "I was no sooner fixed upon this resolution, but that word dropped upon me, *Doth Job serve God for nought?* ... Now was my heart full of comfort."[16]

The sensibility so dramatically and vividly produced in this passage is incapable of relating polemically to external reality. If comfort comes from contemplation of one's brutal and spectacular death, throttled on a primitive gallows in some provincial marketplace, practical issues of toleration and amelioration are excluded. Bunyan, casually and incidentally, discloses his distance from the Restoration establishment. The climactic passage is premised on an assumption of legal malpractice; in fact, though he be-

---

[14] John Stachniewski, *The Persecutory Imagination: English Puritanism and the Literature of Religious Despair* (Oxford: Clarendon Press, 1991), chap. 3.

[15] Ibid., 136.

[16] John Bunyan, *Grace Abounding to the Chief of Sinners*, ed. Roger Sharrock (Oxford: Clarendon Press, 1962), 100–101.

lieved himself to be in danger of execution, that was the misperception of "a young Prisoner, and not acquainted with the Laws."[17] No doubt his prosecutors did little to explain his rights. The incidents he selects for description from earlier in his life show an utter disregard for the ideological value they carry. Indeed, his unpuritanical youth is the subject of remorse and horror. *The Book of Sports*, reissued as a Laudian initiative in 1633, encouraged the practice of village games on the sabbath; young Bunyan rather enjoyed them, though practice of them generally differentiated Puritans from Laudians within the church and a strict sabbatarianism was enforced in the 1640s. Bunyan's first sense of his own impending reprobation comes when playing "Cat": "leaving my Cat upon the ground, I looked up to Heaven, and was as if I had ... seen the Lord Jesus looking down upon me."[18]

At that time "a voice did suddenly dart from Heaven into my Soul"; critical moments in the psychomachia are often shaped by just such divine sayings. The text of 1666 posits a close and intimate relationship with the spirit working within Bunyan; indeed, these voices, these inner promptings, have a potent interiority and a privilege that ties Bunyan's theology very closely to that of the most radical sectaries. Though Bunyan's illumination characteristically comes through a biblical phrase, it has all the formal characteristics of inner prompting that first Ranters and then Quakers privileged in their own theological discourse. Rarely is Bunyan pondering the Bible; rather it comes to him in fragments of epiphanic directness. Interestingly, the pivotal episode, discussed above, seems confirmed, not by a quotation, but by a vaguer allusion better tailored to the occasion. It is appropriate to recall Bunyan's phrase, "Doth Job serve God for nought?" Both the Geneva and the Authorized translations have, "Doth Job fear God for nought?" (Job 1:9). "Fear" is too much a presence in *Grace Abounding* and would scarcely differentiate this phase of Bunyan's experience from all the other phases. Bunyan has feared God, has feared the devil, has feared for his family, and has quaked for his soul. Indeed, the shift really marks a progression from fear to assurance. The word dropped on him suitably amended.

"The Bible was precious to me in those days," Bunyan added in 1672.[19] Evidently; many of the additions to the third edition serve to

---

[17] Ibid., 100.
[18] Ibid., 10.
[19] Ibid., 17.

exteriorize Bunyan's perception of holy writ and to make the use of biblical texts seem less like Quaker waiting on the holy spirit. Certainly there are references to text and verse attached to some of the echoes and quotations of the first edition. But Bunyan adds a lot more in the third edition. And he sometimes adds material that is gravid with proof texts and allusion (for example, in par. 286). He more frequently speaks of himself studying the Bible, rather than having the word drop on him: "After this, I found by reading the word, that ..." (par. 71); "I would turn to this Scripture, or that for relief" (par. 145). The exteriorization of the biblical experience takes the form of Bible study; significantly, the master to whom he turns (and who thus underwrites an implicit claim that Bunyan belongs within the broad Protestant tradition) is Martin Luther, whose commentary on Galatians is foregrounded as a cardinal source of comfort: "I found my conclusion in his experience, so largely and profoundly handled, as if his Book had been written out of my heart" (par. 129). Much as Milton had done in the citations appended as a coda to *Tetrachordon* and as he had done in publishing his translation of Martin Bucer,[20] Bunyan demonstrates that his radical heterodoxy can be embedded within a broader tradition which embraced Anglicanism.

"I do prefer this book of Mr. *Luther* upon the *Galathians*, (excepting the Holy Bible) before all the books that ever I have seen, as most fit for a wounded Conscience" (par. 130); here we find him binding himself simultaneously to the Protestant tradition and the Bible. At a stroke, Bunyan distances himself from that radical practice of privileging the spirit within above the text, thus asserting his own remoteness from Ranterism and Quakerism.

That concern with Ranterism surprises, since the heyday of Ranter activity (or at least the heyday for attributing heterodox activity and publication to Ranterism) was 1649-1652. Ranterism had been the media phenomenon of the period of the Rump when it served most usefully as a route by which the Independent congregationalists in power could show their erstwhile Presbyterian allies that they, too, could keep the wilder sects in order.[21] Suddenly, twenty years on, Bunyan introduces a series of

---

[20] Thomas N. Corns, *Uncloistered Virtue: English Political Literature 1640-1660* (Oxford: Clarendon Press, 1992), 51-55 and chap. 3 passim, for an account of Milton's oblique asseveration of his Protestant respectability.

[21] The nature and extent of Ranter activity has been the subject of some fierce controversy since the publication of J. C. Davis's *Fear, Myth and History: The Ranters and*

comments and anecdotes, which demonstrate that, though very briefly he had been drawn to Ranterism and their privileging of the spirit over the word, he came quickly to deprecate them (and their heirs, the Quakers). The anecdotes show that they recognized he was remote from them: "These would . . . condemn me as legal and dark," that is, he held himself still to be governed by the moral precepts of the Law rather than liberated by the spirit within (par. 45; see also par. 161). It is, of course, polemically smart thus to separate Bunyan and his Baptists from wilder groups like Ranters and Quakers. The former had been severely treated in the early 1650s; the latter were singled out for singularly rough treatment in the 1660s. We are seeing another quest for respectability, analogous with Milton's discussed above; analogous, too, with Gerrard Winstanley's attack on the Ranters in his *Vindication of those, whose endeavours is only to make the Earth a common treasury, called Diggers or, Some Reasons given by them against the immoderate use of creatures, or the excessive community of women, called Ranting; or rather Renting* (1650).[22]

Additions also nudge the theology of *Grace Abounding* away from celebration of the spirit within and towards a greater Christocentricity (see, for example, par. 131, 138, 162, 169-71, 174); nor is this the interiorized risen Christ of Ranterism (or of Gerrard Winstanley), but rather an exteriorized, intercessive, and atoning Christ: "my Soul had yet the blessed priviledge to flie to Jesus Christ for Mercy" (par. 174).

Ranters had been associated with extravagant behavior which, whatever its symbolic value, placed them outside the customary codes of respectable conduct. Abiezer Coppe, in the most sensational Ranter pamphlet, had represented himself as

> charging so many Coaches, so many hundreds of men and women of the greater rank, in the open streets, with my hand stretched out, my hat cock't up, staring on them as if I would look thorough them, gnashing with my teeth at some of them.[23]

Of course a different age, and that an age of faith, may well have entertained radically different notions of what constituted anti-social behavior,

---

the Historians (Cambridge: Cambridge Univ. Press, 1986); for an account of the debate and my own view, see *Uncloistered Virtue*, 174-81.

[22] *The Works of Gerrard Winstanley*, ed. George H. Sabine (Ithaca: Cornell Univ. Press, 1941), 397-403.

[23] Abizier Coppe, *A Second Fiery Flying Roule*, in Nigel Smith, ed., *A Collection of Ranter Writings from the 17th Century* (London: Junction, 1983), 105.

and Bunyan retains and even adds to his repertoire of anecdotes about his personal sense of persecution, strengthening the narrative vividness of hearing voices calling to him (par. 93-94). But usually additions serve to gloss extraordinary psychological manifestations, to explain sudden mood swings and the intrusion of obsessional ideas (as in par. 105, which is a sort of commentary on the obsessional mental process he has just described, or the additions to par. 252, that give an account of how the obsessions disabled him from his quotidian responsibilities).

The revisions also acknowledge a public function for the text in that he introduces a certain amount of moralizing material, pointing lessons from his own experience and from his observations which carry an ethical imperative for his readers, as in his comments on the worldy appetitiveness of "old people hunting after the things of this life" and on the believers' inabilities to endure bereavement with Christian optimism and fortitude (par. 85).

Additions to the fifth edition are relative slender; the major transformation of the text has occured with edition three. However, they continue the trends we have discerned. There is a new doctrinal emphasis in his attack on Quakerism, which very significantly focusses on their subordination of holy writ and on their imputed Christological deviation from Protestant orthodoxy:

> 124. The errors that this people then maintained were: 1. That the holy Scriptures were not the Word of God. 2. That every man in the world had the spirit of Christ, grace, faith, &c. 3. That Christ Jesus, as crucified, and dying 1600 years ago, did not satisfy divine justice for the sins of the people. 4. That Christ's flesh and blood was within the saints. 5. That the bodies of the good and bad that are buried in the churchyard shall not arise again. 6. That the resurrection is past with good men already. 7. That that man Jesus, that was crucified between two thieves on Mount Calvary, in the land of Canaan, by Jerusalem, was not ascended up above the starry heavens. 8. That he should not, even the same Jesus that dies by the hands of the Jews, come again at the last day, and as man judge all nations, &c.
>
> 125. Many more vile and abominable things were in those days formented by them, by which I was driven to a more narrow search of the Scriptures, and was, through their light and testimony, not only enlightened, but greatly confirmed and comforted in the truth. (par. 124-25)

Note that this reworking of the account of his experiences in the 1650s aims to distance Baptist dissent from the Quaker movement, which had been the special target for Restoration repression.

The Christocentricity of that doctrinal analysis is the theme of several additions to edition five (for example, in par. 174, 175, 183, 184, 188, and 223). He adds, too, a brief aside on the Calvinist dogma of Election, endorsement of which places him within the Protestant tradition from which the Quakers are excluded:

> Now I saw, that as God had his hand in all providences and dispensations that overtook his Elect, so he had his hand in all the temptations that they had to sin against him, not to animate them unto wickedness, but to chuse their temptations and troubles for them; and also to leave them, for a time, to such sins only as might not destroy, but humble them. (par. 157)

This invokes a rather old-fashioned, pre-Arminian religious sensibility that sharply differentiates Bunyan and his group from any hint of newfangledness.

The concern with supplementing his narrative of psychological experience continues, with the mature Bunyan remarking on and explaining the responses of his younger self, making his powerful subjectivity comprehensible in everyday terms: "I remember ... that I thought I could have spoken of his Love, and his mercy to me, even to the very Crows that sat upon the plow'd lands before me" (par. 92; see also par. 149). The largest single addition, however, is his defense of his own reputation for sexual continence (par. 306–17). He indignantly protests that no one can say "there is any woman in Heaven, or Earth, or Hell, that can say I have at any time, in any place, by day or night, so much as attempted to be naught with them"; "I know not whether there be such a thing as a woman breathing under the Copes of the whole Heaven but by their apparel, their Children, or by common Fame, except my Wife" (par. 313, 314). It has long been recognized that Bunyan introduces these passages to meet a particular charge laid against him, namely that he had been complicit with one Agnes Beaumont, his alleged lover, in the murder of her father.[24] But in the context of the larger strategy, we find Bunyan in

---

[24] Bunyan, *Grace Abounding*, 155–56, 176–80.

1680s having to beat off the old Ranter smear, extended to other sectaries, that community of women characterized their life style.

The final edition to be published in Bunyan's life time was the sixth of 1688. To this he makes very few alterations and additions. But by 1680 his own political expectations may have been sufficiently transformed and his theology rendered more ecumenical, less savagely introverted, for them to have been adequately represented by a text of 1666, however worked over. That decade really belongs to *The Holy War* (1682) and the second part of *The Pilgrim's Progress* (1684/85). Whatever the problems posed to dissent in the revived persecutions of the 1680s, it became once more a dynamic, forward-looking theology, concerned with spiritual and ultimately political revolution, and less obsessed with revisions of the history of the 1650s.

BIBLIOGRAPHY OF WORKS CITED

Primary Sources

Acontius, J. *De Methodo*. Basel, 1558.
Anon. *Light Shining in Buckinghamshire*. London, 1648.
Anon. *Tyranipocrit, Discoverd with his Wiles*. Rotterdam, 1649.
Arderne, James. *Directions concerning . . . Sermons*. Edited by John Mackay. Oxford: Blackwell, London, 1952.
Aristotle. *The "Art" of Rhetoric*. Translated by J. H. Freese. Loeb Classical Library. London: Heinemann, 1959.
———. *Poetics*. Edited and translated by James Hutton. Ithaca: Cornell Univ. Press, 1982.
Ashley, Robert. *Of the Interchangeable Course, or Variety of Things in the Whole World*. London, 1594.
Aubrey, John. *Brief Lives*. Edited by Oliver Lawson Dick. Harmondsworth: Penguin Classics, 1987.
Bacon, Francis. *Apophthegmes New and Old – Collected by the right honourable, Francis Lo[rd] Verulam Viscount. St Albans*. London, 1625.
———. *Sylva Sylvarum or a Naturall Historie in Ten Centuries*. London, 1627.
———. *The Works*. Edited by J. A. Spedding, R. L. Ellis, and D. D. Heath. London, 1857–1874.
———. *The Advancement of Learning*. Edited by G. W. Kitchin. London: J. M. Dent, 1973.
———. *"The Great Instauration" and "New Atlantis"*. Edited by J. Weinberger. Arlington Heights, Ill.: Harlan Davidson, 1980.
———. *Essays*. Edited by Michael J. Hawkins. 1915; repr. London: Everyman, 1994.
Bancroft, Richard. *Daungerous positions and Proceedings published and practised within theis Iland of Brytaine, under pretence of Reformation, and for the presbiterial Discipline*. Edited by R. G. Usher. The Camden Society. London, 1905.
Barnes, Joshua. *Gerania: A New Discovery of a Little Sort of People Anciently Discoursed of, Called Pygmies*. London, 1692.
Baxter, Richard. *A Christian Directory*. London, 1673.
Bolton, Edmund. *The Elements of Armories*. London, 1610.
Bracton. *De legibus et consuetudinibus Angliae*. Edited by G. F. Thompson.

Translated by S. E. Thorne. 4 vols. Cambridge, Mass.: Belknap Press of Harvard Univ., 1968-77.

Browne, Sir Thomas. *The Works of the learned Sir Thomas Browne.* London, 1686.

———. *The Works.* Edited by Charles Sayle, 3 vols. Edinburgh, 1927.

———. *The Letters of Sir Thomas Browne.* Edited by G. Keynes. London: Faber, 1946.

Buck, Sir George. *The History of King Richard III (1619).* Edited by Arthur N. Kincaid. Gloucester: A. Sutton, 1979.

Burton, Robert. *The Anatomy of Melancholy.* London, 1907.

———. *The Anatomy of Melancholy.* Edited by Thomas C. Faulkner, Nicholas K. Kiessling, and Rhonda L. Blair. Oxford: Clarendon Press, 1989.

Cartari, Vincenzo. *Le Imagini de i Dei de gli Antichi.* Venice, 1571.

Cary, Mary. *The Little Horns Doom & Downfall.* London, 1651.

Castiglione, Baldessare. *The Book of the Courtier.* Translated by Thomas Hoby. Edited by Walter Raleigh. London, 1900.

Cicero. *Brutus.* Translated by G. Hendrickson. Loeb Classical Library. London: Heinemann, 1952.

———. *The Verrine Orations [In C. Verrem].* Translated by L. Greenwood. 2 vols. London: Heinemann, 1959.

———. *De oratore.* Translated by E. W. Sutton and H. Rackham. Loeb Classical Library. 2 vols. London: Heinemann, 1959-60.

———. *De inventione.* Translated by H. M. Hubbell. Loeb Classical Library. London: Heinemann, 1960.

———. *De partitione oratoria.* Translated by H. Rackham. Loeb Classical Library. London: Heinemann, 1960.

———. *Orator.* Translated by H. M. Hubbell. Loeb Classical Library. London: Heinemann, 1962.

———. *Ad C. Herennium de ratione dicendi [Rhetorica ad Herennium].* Translated by H. Caplan. Loeb Classical Library. London: Heinemann, 1964.

———. *De officiis.* Edited by W. Miller. Loeb Classical Library. London: Heinemann, 1975.

———. *On Duties.* Edited by M. T. Griffin and M. Atkins. Cambridge Texts in the History of Political Thought. Cambridge: Cambridge Univ. Press, 1991.

Clapham, Henoch. *Aelohim-triune.* London, 1601.

Coppe, Abiezer. *A Second Fiery Flying Roule.* In *A Collection of Ranter Writings from the Seventeenth Century,* edited by Nigel Smith. London: Junction Books, 1983.

Cornwallis, Sir William. *The Encomium of Richard III.* Edited by A. N. Kincaid. London: Turner and Develux, 1977.

Cowley, Abraham. *Works.* 7th ed. London, 1681.
Craik, Sir Henry, ed. *English Prose: Selections.* 5 vols. London, 1894.
Crooke, Helkiah. *Microcosmographia.* London, 1615.
Daniell, David, ed. *Tyndale's Old Testament.* New Haven: Yale Univ. Press, 1992.
Davies, John, of Hereford. *Mirium in Modum.* London, 1602.
——. *Microcosmos.* London, 1603.
——. *Summa totalis.* London, 1607.
Dee, John. *Monas Hieroglyphica Ioannis Dee, Londinensis, ad maximilianum, Dei Gratia Romanorum Bohemiae et Hungariae regem sapientissimum.* Antwerp, 1564.
——. *Propaedeumata aphoristica.* London, 1558, repr. 1568. Repr. and translated by W. Shumaker and J. L. Heilbron, *John Dee on Astronomy, Propaedeumata aphoristica (1558 and 1568), Latin and English.* Berkeley: Univ. of California Press, 1978.
Dell, G. *The Tryal of Spirits.* London, 1653.
Donaldson, Ian. ed. *Ben Jonson.* Oxford: Oxford Univ. Press, 1985.
Dorsch, T. S., ed. *Classical Literary Criticism.* Harmondsworth: Penguin Books, 1965.
Erasmus, Desiderius. *The "Adages" of Erasmus.* Edited by Margaret Mann Phillips. Cambridge: Cambridge Univ. Press, 1964.
——. *Erasmus on his Times: A Shortened Version of the Adages.* Translated by Margaret Mann Phillips. Cambridge: Cambridge Univ. Press, 1967.
Estienne, Henri. *The Act of Making Devises.* Translated by Thomas Blount. London, 1646.
Fabyan, Robert. Vol. 2 of *The Chronicle.* London, 1559.
Foigny, Gabriel de. *A New Discovery of Terra Incognita Australis, or the Southern World. By James Sadeur, a Frenchman.* London, 1693.
Foster, George. *The Sounding of the Last Trumpet, Or, Severall Vision, declaring the Universall overturning and rooting up of all Earthly Powers in ENGLAND.* London, 1650.
Fox, George. *The Law of God, the Rule for Law-Makers.* London, 1658.
Foxe, John. *The Acts and Monuments.* Edited by Stephen Reed Cattley. Revised by Josiah Pratt. 4th ed. 7 vols. London, 1877.
Fraunce, Abraham. *Insignium, Armorum, Emblematum . . .* London, 1588.
Giovio, Paolo. *The Worthy Tract of Paulus Giovius.* Translated by Samuel Daniel. London, 1585.
Godwin, Francis. *The Man in the Moone.* London, 1638.
Goodwin, Thomas. *The Vanity of Thoughts Discovered with their Danger and Cure.* London, 1646.
Gosson, Stephen. *The Schoole of Abuse.* London, 1598. In *English Literary*

Criticism: The Renaissance. Edited by O. B. Hardison. New York: Appleton-Century-Crofts, 1963.
Greville, Sir Fulke. *Life of Sir Philip Sidney*. Edited by Nowell Smith. Oxford, 1907.
Hall, Edward. *Hall's Chronicle*. Edited by H. Ellis. London, 1809.
Hall, John. *The Advancement of Learning*. 1649. Edited by A. K. Croston. Liverpool: Liverpool Univ. Press, 1953.
Hartlib, Samuel. *A Description of the Famous Island of Macaria*. London, 1641.
Hill, Nicholas. *Philosophia Epicurea, Democritiana, Theophrastica proposita simpliciter, non edocta, per Nicolaum Hill Anglum, Londinensum*. Paris, 1601.
Hilliard, Nicholas. *The Arte of Limning*. Edited by Arthur Kinney and Linda Bradley Salomon. Foreword by Sir John Pope-Hennessy. Boston: Northeastern Univ. Press, 1983.
Hobbes, Thomas. *Leviathan*. 1651. Edited by Richard Tuck. Cambridge: Cambridge Univ. Press, 1991.
Hooker, Richard. *Of the Laws of Ecclesiastical Polity*. The Folger Library Edition of the Works of Richard Hooker, gen. ed. W. Speed Hill. 5 vols. Cambridge, Mass.: The Belknap Press of Harvard Univ. Press, 1977–91. Volume 1 (1977), Preface and Books I to IV, edited by Georges Edelen; volume 2 (1977), Book V, edited by W. Speed Hill; volume 3 (1981), Books VI, VII, VIII, edited by P. G. Stanwood; volume 4 (1982), "Attack and Response," edited by John E. Booty; volume 5 (1990), "Tractates and Sermons," texts edited by Laetitia Yeandle and commentary by Egil Grislis; volume 6 (Binghamton, N.Y.: Medieval & Renaissance Texts & Studies, 1993), introductions and commentary for all of the *Ecclesiastical Polity* (Preface, William P. Haugaard; Book I, Lee M. Gibbs; Books II to IV, William P. Haugaard; Book V, John E. Booty; Book VI, Lee M. Gibbs; Books VII and VIII, and Hooker's notes and fragments, Arthur S. McGrade); volume 7, bibliography and indexes, edited by W. Speed Hill, forthcoming.
———. *Works*. Edited by John Keble (1836), 7th ed., rev. R. W. Church and F. Paget. 3 vols. Oxford: Clarendon Press, 1888.
———. *Of the Laws of Ecclesiastical Polity*. An abridged edition. Edited by A. S. McGrade and Brian Vickers. London: Sidgwick & Jackson, 1975.
———. *Of the Laws of Ecclesiastical Polity, Preface, Books I and VIII*. Edited by A. S. McGrade. Cambridge Texts in the History of Political Thought. Cambridge: Cambridge Univ. Press, 1989.
Hyperius, Andreas. *The Practise of Preaching*. Translated by John Ludham. London, 1577.

Early Translation. Edited by H. Ellis. Camden Society Publications, vol. 29. London, 1847.

Walton, Izaak. *The Life of Mr. Richard Hooker*. In *Lives*, edited by George Saintsbury. The World's Classics. London: Oxford Univ. Press, 1927, repr. 1956.

Warton, Thomas. *Poems upon Several Occasions, English, Italian, and Latin, with Translations, by John Milton*. London, 1785.

Wilkins, John. *Ecclesiastes*. London, 1646.

Winstanley, Gerrard. *The Breaking of the Day of God*. London, 1648.

———. *The Mysterie of God, Concerning the whole Creation, Mankinde*. London, 1648.

———. *Several Pieces Gathered into one Volume*. London, 1649.

———. *The Works*. Edited by George H. Sabine. Ithaca: Cornell Univ. Press, 1941.

Wood, Anthony à. *Athenæ Oxoniensis*. London, 1721.

Wotton, Henry. *The Elements of Architecture*. London, 1629. In *Reliquiae Wottonianæ*. London, 1651.

Wroth, Lady Mary. *The Poems*. Edited by Josephine A. Roberts. Baton Rouge: Louisiana State Univ. Press, 1983.

Secondary Sources

Adolph, Robert. *The Rise of Modern Prose Style*. Cambridge, Mass.: Harvard Univ. Press, 1968.

Adelman, Janet. In *Suffocating Mothers: Fantasies of Maternal Origin in Shakespeare's Plays, "Hamlet" to "The Tempest."* New York: Routledge, 1992.

Albanese, Denise. "The *New Atlantis* and the Uses of Utopia." *ELH* 57 (1990): 503–28.

Allen, M. J. B. et al., eds. *Sir Philip Sidney's Achievements*. New York: AMS Press, 1990.

Althusser, Louis. *Lenin and Philosophy and Other Essays*. Translated by Ben Brewster. London: New Left Books, 1971.

Ames, Russell A. *Citizen Thomas More and his Utopia*. Princeton: Princeton Univ. Press, 1949.

Amussen, Susan Dwyer. *An Ordered Society: Gender and Class in Early Modern England*. Oxford: Basil Blackwell, 1988.

Anderson, Benedict. *Imagined Communities: Reflections on the Origins and Spread of Nationalism*. London: Verso, 1983.

Anglo, Sydney. *Spectacle, Pageantry and Early Tudor Policy.* Oxford: Clarendon Press, 1969.

Armitage, David, Armand Himy, and Quentin Skinner, eds. *Milton and Republicanism.* Cambridge: Cambridge Univ. Press, 1995.

Armstrong, Nancy, and Leonard Tennenhouse, eds. *The Violence of Representation.* New York: Routledge, 1989.

Axton, Marie. *The Queen's Two Bodies.* London: Royal Historical Society, 1977.

Aylmer. G. E. "The Religion of Gerrard Winstanley." In *Radical Religion in the English Revolution.* Edited by J. F. McGregor and Barry Reay. Oxford: Clarendon Press, 1984.

Babb, Lawrence. *The Elizabethan Malady: A Study of Melancholia in English Literature from 1580–1642.* East Lansing: Michigan State College, 1951.

Baker-Smith, Dominic. "'Inglorious Glory': 1513 and the Humanist Attack on Chivalry." In *Chivalry in the Renaissance,* edited by Sydney Anglo, 129–44. Woodbridge, Suffolk: Boydell and Brewer, 1990.

Balsdon, J. P. V. D. *Life and Leisure in Ancient Rome.* London: Bodley Head, 1969.

Barish, Jonas A. *Ben Jonson and the Language of Prose Comedy.* Cambridge, Mass.: Harvard Univ. Press, 1960.

Barker, Francis. *The Tremulous Private Body: Essays on Subjection.* London: Methuen, 1984.

Barthes, Roland. *Image–Music–Text.* Edited by Stephen Heath. London: Fontana/Collins, 1977.

———. "La Rochefoucauld: 'Reflections on Sentences and Maxims.'" In *New Critical Essays.* Translated by Richard Howard. New York: Farrar, Strauss & Giroux, 1980; repr. Berkeley: Univ. of California Press, 1990.

Baumann, Uwe. "Thomas More and the Classical Tyrant." *Moreana* 86 (1985): 108–27.

Beacock, Andria. "Notes on Melancholia/Schizophrenia as a Social Disease: Robert Burton, R. D. Laing and *Hamlet.*" *Massachussetts Studies in English* 6 (1979): 1–14.

Bellamy, J. G. *The Law of Treason in England in the Later Middle Ages.* Cambridge: Cambridge Univ. Press, 1970.

———. *The Tudor Law of Treason: An Introduction.* London: Routledge and Kegan Paul, 1979.

Benjamin, Walter. *Illustrations.* Edited by Hannah Arendt. Translated by Harry Zohn. London: Fontana/Collins, 1973.

Bennett, H. S. *English Books and Readers.* Cambridge: Cambridge Univ. Press, 1977.

Princeton: Princeton Univ. Press, 1980.
———. *Biographia Literaria.* Vol. 7 of *The Collected Works of Samuel Taylor Coleridge.* Edited by James Edgell and W. Jackson Bate. London: Routledge and Kegan Paul and Princeton: Princeton Univ. Press, 1983.
———. *Lectures 1808-1819: On Literature.* Vol. 5 of *The Collected Works of Samuel Taylor Coleridge.* Edited by R. A. Foakes. London: Routledge and Kegan Paul and Princeton: Princeton Univ. Press, 1987.
Collinson, Patrick. *The Elizabethan Puritan Movement.* Oxford: Clarendon Press, 1967.
———. *The Religion of Protestants.* Oxford: Clarendon Press, 1982.
Conn, Joey. *Robert Burton and the Anatomy of Melancholy: An Annotated Bibliography of Primary and Secondary Sources.* New York: Greenwood Press, 1988.
Cooper, Helen. *Pastoral: Medieval into Renaissance.* Ipswich: D. S. Brewer/Rowman and Littlefield, 1977.
Corns, Thomas N. *Uncloistered Virtue: English Political Literature 1640-1660.* Oxford: Clarendon Press, 1992.
Croll, Morris W. *Style, Rhetoric and Rhythm.* Edited by J. Max Patrick and Robert O. Evans. Princeton: Princeton Univ. Press, 1966.
Cromartie, A. D. T. "The Printing of Parliamentary Speeches, November 1642-July 1643." *Historical Journal* 33 (1990): 23-44.
The Crowland Chronicle Continuations: 1459-1586. Edited by Nicholas Pronay and John Cox. London: Richard III and Yorkist History Trust, 1986.
Crowley, J. Donald, ed. *Hawthorne: The Critical Heritage.* London: Routledge and Kegan Paul, 1970.
Crowley, Tony. *Proper English? Readings in Language, History, and Cultural Identity.* London: Routldge, 1991.
Curtius, E. R. *European Literature and the Latin Middle Ages.* Translated by W. R. Trask. London: Routledge, 1953.
Darby, Harold S. *Hugh Latimer.* London: Epworth Press, 1954.
Davis, J. C. *Utopia and the Ideal Society: A Study of English Utopian Writing 1516-1700.* Cambridge: Cambridge Univ. Press, 1981.
———. *Fear, Myth and History: The Ranters and the Historians.* Cambridge: Cambridge Univ. Press, 1986.
De Quincey, Thomas. *The Collected Writings of Thomas De Quincey.* Edited by David Masson. 14 vols. Edinburgh, 1889-90.
Dear, Peter, ed. *The Literary Structure of Scientific Arguments.* Philadelphia: Univ. of Pennsylvania Press, 1991.
Derrida, Jacques. *Of Grammatology.* Translated by Gayatri Chakravorty Spivak. Baltimore: Johns Hopkins Univ. Press, 1976.
Dorey, T. A., ed. *Cicero.* London: Routledge, 1964.

Dorsten, Jan van, et al. *Sir Philip Sidney: 1586 and the Creation of a Legend.* Leiden: E. J. Brill, 1986.

Dow, F. D. *Radicalism in the English Revolution, 1640–1660.* Oxford: Basil Blackwell, 1985.

Dowling, P. M. "*Areopagitica* and *Areopagiticus:* the Significance of the Isocratic Precedent." *Milton Studies* 21 (1985): 46–69.

Dubrow, Heather. "The Term Early Modern." *PMLA* 109 (1994): 1025–26.

Dunbabin, J. "Government." In *The Cambridge History of Medieval Political Thought c. 350–c. 1450,* edited by J. H. Burns, 477–519. Cambridge: Cambridge Univ. Press, 1988.

Duncan-Jones, Katherine. "Philip Sidney's Toys." *Proceedings of the British Academy* 46 (1986): 161–78. Repr. in *Sir Philip Sidney: An Anthology of Modern Criticism.* Oxford: Clarendon Press, 1987.

Dzelzainis, M. "Milton, *Macbeth,* and Buchanan." *The Seventeenth Century* 4 (1989): 55–66.

———. "Juvenal, Charles X Gustavus and Milton's Letter to Richard Jones." *The Seventeenth Century* 9 (1994): 25–34.

———. "Milton and the Protectorate in 1658." In *Milton and Republicanism,* edited by David Armitage, Armand Himy, and Quentin Skinner. Cambridge: Cambridge Univ. Press, 1995.

Eccleshall, Robert. "Richard Hooker and the Peculiarities of the English: The Reception of the *Ecclesiastical Polity* in the Seventeenth and Eighteenth Centuries." *History of Political Thought* 2 (1981): 63–117.

———. *Order and Reason in Politics: Theories of Absolute and Limited Monarchy in Early Modern England.* Oxford: Oxford Univ. Press for the Univ. of Hull, 1978.

Edelen, Georges. "Hooker's Style." In *Studies in Richard Hooker: Essays Preliminary to an Edition of His Works,* edited by W. Speed Hill. Cleveland: Press of Case Western Reserve Univ., 1972.

Eisenstein, Elizabeth. *The Printing Press as an Agent of Change.* 2 vols. Cambridge: Cambridge Univ. Press, 1979.

Elam, Keir. *The Semiotics of Theatre and Drama.* London: Methuen, 1980.

Elliott, Robert C. "The Shape of Utopia." *ELH* 30 (1963): 317–34.

Ettin, Andrew V. *Literature and the Pastoral.* New Haven: Yale Univ. Press, 1984.

Fallon, R. T. *Captain or Colonel: The Soldier in Milton's Life and Art.* Columbia: Univ. of Missouri Press, 1984.

Fattori, M., ed. *Francis Bacon, Terminologia e Fortuna nel XVII Secole.* Rome: Ateneo, 1984.

Farmer, Norman K., Jr. *Poets and the Visual Arts in Renaissance England.* Austin: Univ. of Texas Press, 1984.

Faulkner, Robert K. *Richard Hooker and the Politics of a Christian England*. Berkeley: Univ. of California Press, 1981.

Finch, Jeremiah. *Sir Thomas Browne*. New York: Collier, 1961.

Finney, Claude L. *The Evolution of Keats's Poetry*. New York: Russell and Russell, 1963.

Firth, C. H., ed. *The Clarke Papers*. London: The Royal Historical Society, 1992.

Fisch, Harold. "The Puritans and the Reform of Prose Style." *Journal of English Literary History* 19 (1952): 229-47.

Fish, Stanley E., ed. *Seventeenth Century Prose: Modern Essays in Criticism*. New York: Oxford Univ. Press, 1971.

———. *Self-Consuming Artifacts: The Experience of Seventeenth Century Literature*. Berkeley: Univ. of California Press, 1972.

Fowler, Alastair. *Kinds of Literature*. Cambridge: Cambridge Univ. Press, 1982.

Fox, Alistair. "Archetype and Antitype: *The History of King Richard III, The Four Last Things*." Chap. 3 of *Thomas More: History and Providence*. New Haven: Basil Blackwell, 1982.

———. "Thomas More and Tudor Historiography: *The History of King Richard III*." Chap. 7 of *Politics and Literature in the Reigns of Henry VII and VIII*. Oxford: Basil Blackwell, 1989.

Fox, Ruth A. *The Tangled Chain: The Structure of Disorder in the Anatomy of Melancholy*. Berkeley: Univ. of California Press, 1976.

Fox Keller, Evelyne. *Reflections on Science and Gender*. New Haven: Yale Univ. Press, 1984.

Freeman, Rosemary. *English Emblem Books*. London: Chatto & Windus, 1948.

Gairdner, James, ed. *Memorials of Henry VII*. Rolls Series, vol. 10. London, 1858.

Garber, Marjorie. "Descanting on Deformity: Richard III and the Shape of History." In *The Historical Renaissance: New Essays on Tudor and Stuart Literature and Culture*, edited by Heather Dubrow and Richard Strier, 79-103. Chicago: Univ. of Chicago Press, 1988.

Gardiner, S. R. *History of the Commonwealth and the Protectorate*. 4 vols. London, 1903.

George, C. H. "Gerrard Winstanley: A Critical Retrospect." In *The Dissenting Tradition*, edited by C. Robert Cole and Michael E. Moody. Athens, Ohio: Ohio Univ. Press, 1975.

Gilbert, Neil W. *Renaissance Concepts of Method*. New York: Columbia Univ. Press, 1960.

Gilman, Ernest. *The Curious Perspective: Literary and Pictorial Wit in the Seventeenth Century*. New Haven: Yale Univ. Press, 1978.

Gilman, W. E. *Milton's Rhetoric: Studies in his Defense of Liberty*. Columbia: Univ. of Missouri Press, 1939.

Goldberg, Jonathan. *James I and the Politics of Literature*. Baltimore: Johns Hopkins Univ. Press, 1983.

Grant, Patrick. *Literature and the Discovery of Method in the Renaissance*. London: Macmillan, 1985.

Greaves, Richard L. *Deliver Us from Evil: The Radical Underground in Britain, 1660-1663*. Oxford: Oxford Univ. Press, 1986.

———. "The Spirit and the Sword: Bunyan and the Stuart State." In *Bunyan in Our Time*, edited by Robert G. Collmer. Kent, Ohio: Kent State Univ. Press, 1989.

Greenblatt, Stephen. *Renaissance Self-Fashioning: From More to Shakespeare*. Chicago: Univ. of Chicago Press, 1980.

———. *Shakespearean Negotiations: The Circulation of Social Energy in Renaissance England*. Oxford: Clarendon Press, 1988.

Griffin, M. T. *Seneca: A Philosopher in Politics*. Oxford: Clarendon Press, 1976.

Griffiths, R. A. and R. S. Thomas. *The Making of the Tudor Dynasty*. Gloucester, Alan Sutton, 1985.

Guillén, C. "Notes towards the Study of the Renaissance Letter." In *Renaissance Genres: Essays on Theory, History, and Interpretation*. Edited by Barbara Keifer Lewalski. Harvard English Studies, 14. Cambridge, Mass.: Harvard Univ. Press, 1986.

Hackett, Helen. "'Yet Tell Me Some Such Fiction': Lady Mary Wroth's *Urania* and the 'Femininity' of Romance." In *Women, Texts and Histories*, edited by Clare Brant and Diane Purkiss. London: Routledge, 1992.

Hagstrum, Jean. *The Sister Arts: The Tradition of Literary Pictorialism and English Poetry from Dryden to Gray*. Chicago: Univ. of Chicago Press, 1958.

Halpern, Richard. *The Politics of Primitive Accumulation: English Renaissance Culture and the Genealogy of Capital*. Ithaca: Cornell Univ. Press, 1991.

Hammond, Gerald. *The Making of the English Bible*. Manchester: Carcanet Press, 1982.

Hammond, P. W. and Anne F. Sutton. *Richard III: The Road to Bosworth Field*. London: Constable, 1985.

———. *The Battles of Barnet and Tewkesbury*. Gloucester: Sutton, 1990.

Hampton, Timothy. *Writing from History: The Rhetoric of Exemplarity in Renaissance Literature*. Ithaca: Cornell Univ. Press, 1990.

Hanff, Helene. *Q's Legacy*. London: Futura, 1986.

———. *84 Charing Cross Road*. London: Warner Books, 1971; repr. 1992.

Hanham, Alison. *Richard III and his Early Historians 1483-1535*. Oxford: Clarendon Press, 1985.

Hannay, Margaret P. *Philip's Phoenix: Mary Sidney, Countess of Pembroke.* New York: Oxford Univ. Press, 1990.
Harding, Sandra. *The Science Question in Feminism.* Ithaca: Cornell Univ. Press, 1986.
Hardison, O. B. *The Enduring Monument: A Study of the Idea of Praise in Renaissance Literary Theory and Practice.* Chapel Hill: Univ. of North Carolina Press, 1962.
Hassel, R. Chris, Jr. "Perceptions of Providence in *Richard III.*" Chap. 5 of *Songs of Death: Performance, Interpretation, and the Text of* Richard III. Lincoln: Univ. of Nebraska Press, 1987.
Hatto, A. T. "*Venus and Adonis* – and the Boar." *Modern Language Review* 41 (1946): 353-61.
Hay, Denys. *Annalists and Historians: Western Historiography from the Eighth to the Eighteenth Centuries.* London: Methuen, 1977.
Hayes, T. Wilson. *Winstanley the Digger: A Literary Analysis of Radical Ideas in the English Revolution.* Cambridge, Mass.: Harvard Univ. Press, 1979.
Hazlitt, William. *Lectures on the Dramatic Literature of the Age of Elizabeth.* Vol. 6 of *The Complete Works of William Hazlitt.* Edited by P. P. Howe. London and Toronto, 1930-34.
Heinemann, Margot. *Puritanism and Theatre: Thomas Middleton and Opposition Drama Under the Stuarts.* Cambridge: Cambridge Univ. Press, 1980.
Helgerson, Richard. *Forms of Nationhood: The Elizabethan Writing of England.* Chicago: Univ. of Chicago Press, 1992.
Henderson, J. R. "Erasmus on the Art of Letter-Writing." In *Renaissance Eloquence: Studies in the Theory and Practice of Renaissance Eloquence,* edited by J. J. Murphy. Berkeley: Univ. of California Press, 1981.
Hertz, Neil. "Medusa's Head: Male Hysteria under Political Pressure." Chap. 9 (with responses by Catherine Gallagher and Joel Fineman) of *The End of the Line: Essays on Psychoanalysis and the Sublime.* New York: Columbia Univ. Press, 1985.
Hill, Christopher. *The World Turned Upside Down: Radical Ideas During the English Revolution.* Harmondsworth: Penguin, 1975.
———. *Milton and the English Revolution.* London: Faber, 1977.
———. "The Religion of Gerrard Winstanley." *Past and Present Supplement* no. 5 (1978).
———. *The Collected Essays.* Brighton: Harvester, 1985.
———. "Winstanley and Freedom." In *Freedom and the English Revolution: Essays in History and Literature,* edited by R. C. Richardson and G. M. Ridden. Manchester: Manchester Univ. Press, 1986.
———. *A Turbulent, Seditious, and Factious People: John Bunyan and his Church.* Oxford: Oxford Univ. Press, 1988.

———. *The English Bible and the Seventeenth-Century Revolution*. Harmondsworth: Penguin, 1993.
Hill, W. Speed. *Hooker: A Descriptive Bibliography of the Early Editions 1593–1724*. Cleveland: Press of Case Western Reserve Univ., 1970.
——— ed. *Studies in Richard Hooker: Essays Preliminary to an Edition of His Works*. Cleveland: Press of Case Western Reserve Univ., 1972.
———. "Editing Richard Hooker: A Retrospective." *Sewanee Theological Review* 36 (1993): 187–99.
Hodgdon, Barbara. "The Coming On of Time: *Richard III*." Chap. 4 of *The End Crowns All: Closure and Contradiction in Shakespeare's History*. Princeton: Princeton Univ. Press, 1991.
Holinshed, Raphael. Vol. 3 of *Chronicles of England, Scotland, and Ireland*. (Repr. of 2d ed. of 1587). Edited by H. Ellis. 6 vols. London, 1807–8.
Höltgen, Karl J. "Robert Burton's *Anatomy of Melancholy*: Struktur und Gattungsproblematik im Licht der ramistischen Logick." *Anglia* 94 (1976): 388–403.
Hornsby, Samuel. "A Note on the Punctuation in the Authorized Version of the English Bible." *English Studies* 54 (1973): 566–68.
Huet, Marie-Hélène. *Monstrous Imagination*. Cambridge, Mass.: Harvard Univ. Press, 1993.
Hunter, W. B., general ed. *A Milton Encyclopedia*. 9 vols. Lewisburg: Bucknell Univ. Press, 1978–83.
Hutton, Ronald. *The British Republic, 1649–1660*. London: Macmillan, 1990.
———. *Charles II, King of England, Scotland, and Ireland*. Oxford: Oxford Univ. Press, 1991.
Imbrie, A. E. "Defining Nonfiction Genres." In *Renaissance Genres: Essays on Theory, History and Interpretation*, edited by B. K. Lewalski. Harvard English Studies, 14. Cambridge, Mass.: Harvard Univ. Press, 1986.
Jackson, H. J. "Johnson and Burton: *The Anatomy of Melancholy* and *The Dictionary of the English Language*." *English Studies in Canada* 5 (1979): 36–48.
Jardine, Lisa, and Anthony Grafton. "Studied for Action: How Gabriel Harvey read his Livy." *Past and Present* 129 (1991): 30–78.
Jebb, R. C. *The Attic Orators from Antiphon to Isaeus*. 2 vols. London, 1893.
Jed, Stephanie. "The Scene of Tyranny: Violence and the Humanistic Tradition." In *The Violence of Representation*, edited by Nancy Armstrong and Leonard Tennenhouse, 29–44. New York: Routledge, 1977.
Jeffrey, Francis. *Jeffrey's Criticism: A Selection*. Edited by Peter F. Morgan. Edinburgh: Scottish Academic Press, 1983.
Johnson, F. R. *Astronomical Thought in Renaissance England*. Baltimore: Johns Hopkins Press, 1937.

Johnson, Samuel. *Poetry and Prose*. Edited by Mona Wilson. London: Rupert Hart-Davis, 1979.
Jones, R. F. et al. *The Seventeenth Century: Studies in the History of English Thought and Literature from Bacon to Pope*. Stanford: Stanford Univ. Press, 1951.
———. *The Triumph of the English Language*. London: Oxford Univ. Press, 1953.
Jones, W. Garmon. "Welsh Nationalism and Henry Tudor." In *Transactions of the Honorable Society of Cymmrodorion, Session 1917-18* (1919): 1-59.
Joseph, B. L. *Elizabethan Acting*. Oxford: Oxford Univ. Press, 1951.
Jung, C. G. *The Collected Works*. Edited by Herbert Read et al. London: Routledge and Kegan Paul, 1953.
Juretic, George. "Digger no Millenarian: The Revolutionizing of Gerrard Winstanley." *Journal of the History of Ideas* 36 (1975): 263-80.
Kantorowicz, Ernst H. *The King's Two Bodies*. Princeton: Princeton Univ. Press, 1957.
Keeble, N. H. *Richard Baxter: Puritan Man of Letters*. Oxford: Clarendon Press, 1982.
———. *The Literary Culture of Nonconformity in Later Seventeenth-Century England*. Leicester: Leicester Univ. Press, 1987.
Kelley, D. R. "The Theory of History." In *The Cambridge History of Renaissance Philosophy*, edited by Charles B. Schmitt et al., 746-61. Cambridge: Cambridge Univ. Press, 1988.
Kelly, Henry A. *Divine Providence in the England of Shakespeare's Histories*. Cambridge, Mass.: Harvard Univ. Press, 1970.
Kelly, Robert L. "Hugh Latimer as Piers Plowman." *Studies in English Literature* 17 (Winter 1977): 13-26.
Kemp, Anthony. *The Estrangement of the Past: A Study in the Origins of the Modern Historical Consciousness*. New York: Oxford Univ. Press, 1991.
Kennedy, G. *The Art of Rhetoric in the Roman World, 300 B.C.-A.D. 300*. Princeton: Princeton Univ. Press, 1972.
Kenyon, T. A. "The Problem of Freedom and Moral Behaviour in Thomas More's *Utopia*." *Journal of the History of Philosophy* 21 (1983): 349-73.
Keynes, Geoffrey. *The Life of William Harvey*. Oxford: Clarendon Press, 1978.
Kiessling, Nicholas K. *The Library of Robert Burton*. Publications of the Oxford Bibliographical Society n.s. 22. Oxford: Oxford Bibliographical Society, 1988.
King, Bruce. *Seventeenth-Century English Literature*. London: Macmillan, 1982.
King, James Roy. *Studies in Six Seventeenth Century Writers*. Athens, Ohio: Ohio Univ. Press, 1966.

King, John. *English Reformation Literature: The Tudor Origins of the Protestant Tradition*. Princeton: Princeton Univ. Press, 1982.

Kinney, Arthur. *Humanist Poetics: Thought, Rhetoric, and Fiction in Sixteenth-Century England*. Amherst: Univ. of Massachusetts Press, 1986.

Kinney, Daniel. "King's Tragicomedies: Generic Misrule in More's *History of Richard III*." *Moreana* 86 (1985): 128-50.

Kirby, W. J. Torrance. *Richard Hooker's Doctrine of the Royal Supremacy*. Leiden: E. J. Brill, 1990.

Knights, L. C. *Drama and Society in the Age of Johnson*. London, 1937; repr. New York: W. W. Norton, 1968.

Knott, John R. *The Sword of the Spirit: Puritan Responses to the Bible*. Chicago: Univ. of Chicago Press, 1980.

———. *Discourses of Martyrdom in English Literature, 1563-1694*. Cambridge: Cambridge Univ. Press, 1993.

Korkowski, Bud. "Genre and Satiric Strategy in Burton's *Anatomy of Melancholy*." *Genre* 7 (1975): 74-85.

Krapp, G. P. *The Rise of English Literary Prose*. New York, 1915.

Krontiris, Tina. "Breaking the Barriers of Genre and Gender: Margaret Tyler's Translation of The Mirrour of Knighthood." *English Literary Renaissance* 18 (1988): 19-39.

Kugel, James L. *The Idea of Biblical Poetry: Parallelism and its History*. New Haven: Yale Univ. Press, 1981.

Lamb, Charles. *The Letters of Charles Lamb*. Edited by E. V. Lucas. London, 1935.

Lamb, Mary Ellen. *Gender and Authorship in the Sidney Circle*. Madison: Univ. of Wisconsin Press, 1990.

Larkey, S. V. *The Vesalian Compendium of Geminus, and Nicholas Udall's Translation, Their Relation to Vesalius, Caius, Vicary and De Mondevillle*. London: Bibliographical Society, 1933.

Lawn, Brian. *The Rise and Decline of the Scholastic 'Quaestio Disputata': with Special Emphasis on its Use in the Teaching of Medicine and Science*. Leiden: E. J. Brill, 1993.

Laydon, John P. "The Kingdom of Christ and the Powers of the Earth: The Political Uses of Apocalyptic and Millenarian Ideas in England, 1648-1653." Ph.D. diss., Cambridge University, 1977.

Levao, Ronald. *Renaissance Minds and their Fictions: Cusanus, Sidney, Shakespeare*. Berkeley: Univ. of California Press, 1985.

Levine, Joseph M. *Humanism and History: Origins of Modern English Historiography*. Ithaca: Cornell Univ. Press, 1987.

Lewis, C. S. *English Literature in the Sixteenth Century Excluding Drama*. Oxford: Clarendon Press, 1954.

Lindberg, D. C. and R. S. Westman, eds. *Reappraisals of the Scientific Revolution.* Cambridge: Cambridge Univ. Press, 1990.

Lindenbaum, Peter. *Changing Landscapes: Anti-Pastoral Sentiment in the English Renaissance.* Athens: Univ. of Georgia Press, 1986.

Loewenstein, David. *Milton and the Drama of History: Historical Vision, Iconoclasm and the Literary Imagination.* Cambridge: Cambridge Univ. Press, 1990.

———. " 'An Ambiguous Monster': Representing Rebellion in Milton's Polemics and *Paradise Lost.*" *Huntington Library Quarterly* 55 (1992): 295-315.

Logan, George M. *The Meaning of More's Utopia.* Princeton: Princeton Univ. Press, 1983.

Lyons, John D. *Exemplum: The Rhetoric of Example in Early Modern France and Italy.* Princeton: Princeton Univ. Press, 1989.

MacCabe, Colin, ed. *The Talking Cure: Essays in Psychoanalysis and Language.* Basingstoke: Macmillan, 1981.

McCanles, Michael. *The Text of Sidney's Arcadian World.* Durham, N.C.: Duke Univ. Press, 1989.

McClure, N. E., ed. *Letters of John Chamberlain.* Philadelphia: American Philosophical Society, 1939.

McCoy, Richard C. *Sir Philip Sidney: Rebellion in Arcadia.* Brighton: Harvester, 1979.

McCutcheon, Elizabeth. "Denying the Contrary: More's Use of Litotes in the *Utopia.*" In *Essential Articles for the Study of Thomas More,* edited by R. S. Sylvester and G. P. Marc'hadour. Hamden, Conn.: Archon Books, 1977.

McGrade, A. S. "The Coherence of Hooker's *Polity:* The Books on Power." *Journal of the History of Ideas* 24 (1963); 163-82.

McKeon, Michael. *The Origins of the English Novel 1600-1740.* Baltimore: Johns Hopkins Univ. Press, 1987.

Manning, Brian. *The English People and the English Revolution, 1640-1649.* London: Heinemann, 1976.

Marcus, Leah S. "Renaissance/Early Modern Studies." In *Redrawing the Boundaries: The Transformation of English and American Literary Studies,* edited by Stephen Greenblatt and Giles Gunn, 41-63. New York: The Modern Language Association of America, 1992.

———. *Puzzling Shakespeare: Local Reading and its Discontents.* Berkeley: Univ. of California Press, 1988.

Marin, Louis. *Utopiques, Jeux d'espaces.* Paris: Minuit, 1973.

Martin, Christopher. "Misdoubting His Estate: Dynastic Anxiety in Sidney's *Arcadia.*" *English Literary Renaissance* 18 (1988): 369-88.

Meli, F. *Spinoza e due antecedenti italiani dello spinozismo.* Florence, 1934.

Merchant, Carolyn. *The Death of Nature: Women, Ecology and the Scientific Revolution.* San Francisco: Harper and Row, 1983.

Milder, Wolfgang, and Alan Dundas, eds. *The Wisdom of Many: Essays on the Proverb.* New York: Garland, 1981.

Miller, L. "Italian Imprimaturs in Milton's *Areopagitica.*" *Papers of the Bibliographical Society of America* 65 (1971): 345-55.

Miller, Naomi. "'Not much to be marked': Narrative of the Woman's Part in Lady Mary Wroth's *Urania.*" *Studies in English Literature* 29 (1989): 120-37.

Miller, Naomi J., and Gary Waller, eds. *Reading Mary Wroth: Representing Alternatives in Early Modern England.* Knoxville: Univ. of Tennessee Press, 1992.

Miola, Robert S. "Senecan Tyranny: *Richard III, Macbeth.*" Chap. 3 of *Shakespeare and Classical Tragedy: The Influence of Seneca.* New York: Clarendon Press, 1992.

Mitchell, T. N. *Cicero: The Ascending Years.* New Haven: Yale Univ. Press, 1979.

Mitchell, W. Fraser. *English Pulpit Oratory from Andrewes to Tillotson.* London, 1932.

Mitchell, W. J. T. *Iconology: Image, Text, Ideology.* Chicago: Univ. of Chicago Press, 1986.

Montagu, Basil. *Selections from the Works of Taylor, Hooker, Hall and Lord Bacon.* London, 1805.

Montrose, Louis Adrian. "'Shaping Fantasies': Figurations of Gender and Power in Elizabethan Culture." *Representations* 1 (1983): 61-94.

Mueller, Janel M. *The Native Tongue and the Word: Developments in English Prose Style, 1380-1580.* Chicago: Univ. of Chicago Press, 1984.

Mueller, William R. "Robert Burton's 'Satyricall Preface.'" *Modern Language Quarterly* 15 (1954): 28-35.

Mulligan, Lotte, John K. Graham, and Judith Richards. "Winstanley: A Case for the Man as He Said He Was." *Journal of Ecclesiastical History* 28 (1977): 57-75.

Myers, A. R., ed. *English Historical Documents 1327-1485.* London: Eyre and Spottiswoode, 1969.

Neely, Carol Thomas. "Constructing the Subject: Feminist Practice and the New Renaissance Discourses." *English Literary Renaissance* 18 (1988): 5-18.

Nijenhuis, Willem. *Adrianus Saravia (c. 1532-1613).* Leiden: E. J. Brill, 1980.

Nochimson, Richard L. "Burton's *Anatomy:* The Author's Purposes and the Reader's Response." *Forum for Modern Language Studies* 13 (1977): 256-84.

Norbrook, David. *Poetry and Politics in the English Renaissance.* London: Routledge, 1984.
Notestein, Wallace. *The House of Commons 1604-10.* New Haven: Yale Univ. Press, 1971.
Novarr, David. *The Making of Walton's Lives.* Ithaca: Cornell Univ. Press, 1958. Part 3: 197-298.
O'Connor, John J. *Amadis de Gaule and its Influence on Elizabethan Literature.* New Brunswick, N.J.: Rutgers Univ. Press, 1970.
——. "James Hay and the Countess of Montgomery's *Urania.*" *Notes and Queries* 200 (1955): 150-52.
O'Malley, Charles D. *Jacopo Aconcio.* Translated by Delio Cantimori. Rome: Edizioni de Storia e Letteratura, 1955.
Ong, Walter, *Ramus, Method, and the Decay of Dialogue.* 1958; repr. Cambridge, Mass.: Harvard Univ. Press, 1983.
Orgel, Stephen. "Making Greatness Familiar." *Genre* 15 (1982): 41-48.
Owst, G. R. *Literature and Pulpit in Medieval England.* 2d. ed. Oxford: Blackwell, 1961.
Parker, Patricia. *Inescapable Romance: The Poetics of a Mode.* Princeton: Princeton Univ. Press, 1979.
——. *Literary Fat Ladies: Rhetoric, Gender, Property.* London: Methuen, 1987.
Parker, Patricia and Geoffrey Hartman, eds. *Shakespeare and the Question of Theory.* New York: Methuen, 1985.
Parker, W. R. *Milton: A Biography.* 2 vols. Oxford: Clarendon Press, 1968.
Parkin Speer, D. "Milton's *Defensio Prima*: Ethos and Vituperation in a Polemical Engagement." *Quarterly Journal of Speech* 56 (1970); 277-83.
Parry, Graham. *The Golden Age Restor'd: The Culture of the Stuart Court 1603-1640.* Manchester: Manchester Univ. Press, 1981.
Paster, Gail Kern. *The Body Embarrassed: Drama and the Disciplines of Shame in Early Modern England.* Ithaca: Cornell Univ. Press, 1993.
Patterson, Annabel. *Censorship and Interpretation: The Conditions of Writing and Reading in Early Modern England.* Madison: Univ. of Wisconsin Press, 1984.
Peck, Linda Levy. *Court Patronage and Corruption in Early Stuart England.* Boston: Unwin Hyman, 1990.
Perez-Ramos, Antonio. *Francis Bacon's Idea of Science and the Maker's Knowledge Tradition.* Oxford: Clarendon Press, 1988.
Petegorsky, D. W. *Left Wing Democracy in the English Civil War.* London, 1940.
Planché, J. R. *The Pursuivant of Arms.* London, 1873.
Piggott, Stuart. "Sir Thomas Browne and Antiquity." *Oxford Journal of Archaeology* 7 (1988): 257-69.

Pollard, A. F. *Henry VIII*, 2d. ed., introduced by A. G. Dickens. New York: Harper & Row, 1966.
Pollard, A. J. *Richard III and the Princes in the Tower*. Stroud: Alan Sutton, 1991.
Pooley, Roger. *English Prose of the Seventeenth Century, 1590-1700*. New York: Longman, 1992.
———. "Language and Loyalty: plain style at the Restoration." *Literature and History* 6 (1980): 2-18.
———. "Prospects for Research in Seventeenth Century Prose." *Prose Studies* 10 (1987): 9-17.
Porter, Roy. *A Social History of Madness*. London: Weidenfeld and Nicholson, 1987.
Potter, Jeremy. *Good King Richard? An Account of Richard III and his Reputation 1483-1983*. London: Constable, 1983.
Praz, Mario. *Studies in Seventeenth Century Imagery*. 2d ed. Rome: Ediz. di Storia e Letteratura, 1964.
Quilligan, Maureen. "Lady Mary Wroth: Female Authority and the Family Romance." In *Unfolded Tales: Essays on Renaissance Romance*, edited by George Logan and Gordon Teskey. Ithaca: Cornell Univ. Press, 1989.
Rackin, Phyllis. *Stages of History. Shakespeare's English Chronicles*. Ithaca: Cornell Univ. Press, 1990.
Randolph, M. C. "The Medical Concept in English Renaissance Satiric Theory: Its Possible Relations and Implications." *Studies in Philology* 38 (1941): 125-57.
Reedy, Gerard. *Robert South (1634-1716)*. Cambridge: Cambridge Univ. Press, 1992.
Renaker, David. "Robert Burton and Ramist Method." *Renaissance Quarterly* 24 (1971): 210-20.
Rhodes, Neil. *Elizabethan Grotesque*. London: Routledge and Kegan Paul, 1980.
———. *The Power of Eloquence and English Renaissance Literature*. Hemel Hempstead: Harvester Wheatsheaf and New York: St. Martin's Press, 1992.
Rivers, Isabel. *Reason, Grace and Sentiment: the language of religion and ethics in England, 1660-1780*. Cambridge: Cambridge Univ. Press, 1991.
Roberts, Josephine A. "An Unpublished Literary Quarrel Concerning the Suppression of Mary Wroth's *Urania*." *Notes and Queries* 222 (1977): 532-35.
———. "Radigund Revisited: Perspectives on Women Rulers in Lady Mary Wroth's *Urania*." In *The Renaissance Englishwoman in Print*, edited by Anne M. Haselkorn and Betty S. Travitsky. Amherst: Univ. of Massachusetts Press, 1990.

———. "Labyrinths of Desire: Lady Mary Wroth's Reconstruction of Romance." *Women's Studies* 19 (1991): 183-92.
Robinson, Forrest G. *The Shape of Things Known: Sidney's Defence in its Philosophical Tradition.* Cambridge, Mass.: Harvard Univ. Press, 1972.
Ross, Charles. *Edward IV.* London: Eyre Methuen, 1974.
———. *Richard III.* Berkeley: Univ. of California Press, 1981.
Rossi, Paolo. *Giacomo Aconcio.* Milan: Storia Universale della Filosofia, 1952.
Rotuli Parliamentorum. Edited by J. Strachey et al. 6 vols. London, 1704-35.
Rudnytsky, Peter. "More's *History of King Richard III* as an Uncanny Text." In *Contending Kingdoms; Historical, Psychological, and Feminist Approaches to the Literature of Sixteenth-Century England and France,* edited by Marie-Rose Logan and Peter Rudnytsky, 149-72. Detroit: Wayne State Univ. Press, 1991.
Rymer, Thomas. *Foedera, Conventiones et Litterae,* 20 vols. London, 1704-1705.
Saintsbury, George. *A History of English Prose Rhythm.* London, 1912.
Salzman, Paul. *English Prose Fiction 1558-1700: A Critical History.* Oxford: Clarendon Press, 1985.
———. "Contemporary References in Mary Wroth's *Urania.*" *Review of English Studies* 29 (1978): 178-81.
Samuel, Irene. "Milton on the Province of Rhetoric." *Milton Studies* 10 (1977): 177-93.
Sawday, Jonathan. *The Body Emblazoned: Dissection and the Human Body in Renaissance Culture.* London: Routledge, 1995.
———. "The Fate of Marsyas: Dissecting the Renaissance Body." In *Renaissance Bodies: The Human Figure in English Culture, c. 1540-1660,* edited by Lucy Gent and Nigel Llewellyn. London: Reaktion Books, 1990.
Saxl, Fritz. "Veritas Temporis Filia." In *Philosophy and History,* edited by R. Klibansky and H. J. Paton, 2d ed., 197-222. New York: Harper and Row, 1963.
Schmidt-Biggeman, Wolfgang. *Topica Universalis, eine Modellgeschichte humanistischer und barocker Wissenschaft.* Hamburg: Felix Meiner Verlag, 1983.
Sharpe, Kevin, ed. *Faction and Parliament: Essays on Early Stuart History.* Oxford: Clarendon Press, 1978.
———. *Criticism and Compliment: The Politics of Literature in the England of Charles I.* Cambridge: Cambridge Univ. Press, 1987.
———. "Faction at the Early Stuart Court." *History Today* 33 (1983): 39-46.
Shaw, W. A. *A History of the English Church during the Civil Wars and under the Commonwealth 1640-1660.* 2 vols. London, 1900.

Shuger, Debora Kuller. *Habits of Thought in the English Renaissance*. Berkeley: Univ. of California Press, 1990.
Sinfield, Alan. "Power and Ideology: An Outline Theory and Sidney's *Arcadia*." *ELH* 52 (1985): 259–77.
Sinson, Janice C. *John Keats and The Anatomy of Melancholy*. London: Keats–Shelley Memorial Association, 1971.
Sisson, C. J. *The Judicious Marriage of Mr. Hooker and the Birth of The Laws of Ecclesiastical Polity*. Cambridge: Cambridge Univ. Press, 1940.
Skerpan, Elizabeth. *The Rhetoric of Politics in the English Revolution 1642–1660*. Columbia: Univ. of Missouri Press, 1992.
Skinner, Q. R. D. *The Foundations of Modern Political Thought*. 2 vols. Cambridge: Cambridge Univ. Press, 1978.
———. "'Scientia civilis' in Classical Rhetoric and in the early Hobbes." In *Political Discourse in Early Modern Britain*, edited by Nicholas Phillipson and Quentin Skinner, 67–93. Cambridge: Cambridge Univ. Press, 1993.
Skretkowicz, Victor. "Symbolic Architecture in Sidney's *New Arcadia*." *Review of English Studies* n.s. 33 (1982): 177–79.
Smith, Logan Pearsall, ed. *Donne's Sermons: Selected Passages with an Essay*. Oxford, 1919.
Smith, Nigel. *Literature and Revolution in England, 1640–1660*. New Haven: Yale Univ. Press, 1994.
Smith, R. E. *Cicero the Statesman*. Cambridge: Cambridge Univ. Press, 1966.
Sommervill, J. P. "Richard Hooker, Hadrian Saravia, and the Advent of the Divine Right of Kings." *History of Political Thought* 4 (1983): 229–45.
Sonnino, L. A. *A Handbook to Sixteenth-Century Rhetoric*. London: Routledge, 1968.
Stachniewski, John. *The Persecutory Imagination: English Puritanism and the Literature of Religious Despair*. Oxford: Clarendon Press, 1991.
Starobinski, Jean. "La Melancholie de L'Anatomiste." *Tel Quel* 10 (1962): 21–29.
Steinberg, Leo. *The Sexuality of Christ in Renaissance Art and Modern Oblivion*. New York: Pantheon Books, 1983.
Stephens, James. *Francis Bacon and the Style of Science*. Chicago: Univ. of Chicago Press, 1975.
Strong, Roy. *Henry, Prince of Wales and England's Lost Renaissance*. London: Thames and Hudson, 1986.
Sulfridge, Cynthia W. "Intimate Narratives: Narrator-Reader Relationships in Three Renaissance Precursors of *Tristram Shandy*." Ph.D. diss., Johns Hopkins University, 1978.
Sutton, Anne F. and P. W. Hammond, eds. *The Coronation of Richard III: The Extant Documents*. New York: St. Martin's Press, 1984.

Swift, Caroline Ruth. "Female Identity in Lady Mary Wroth's Romance *Urania*." *English Literary Renaissance* 14 (1984): 328-46.

Tennenhouse, Leonard. "Violence done to Women on the Renaissance Stage." In *The Violence of Representation*, edited by Nancy Armstrong and Leonard Tennenhouse, 77-97. London: Routledge, 1977.

Thomas, A. H. and I. D. Thornley, eds. *The Great Chronicle of London*. London, 1938.

Thomas, I. "Mediaeval Aftermath: Oxford Logic and Logicians of the Seventeenth Century." In *Oxford Studies Presented to Daniel Callus*. Oxford: Clarendon Press for the Oxford Historical Society, 1964.

Thomas, Keith. "The Date of Gerrard Winstanley's *Fire in the Bush*." *Past and Present* 42 (1969): 160-62.

Thoreau, Henry David. *"Walden" and "Civil Disobedience."* Introduced by Michael Meyer. Harmondsworth: Penguin Books, 1983.

Tillman, James S. "The Satirist Satirized: Burton's Democritus Jr." *Studies in the Literary Imagination* 10 (1977): 256-84.

Trevor-Roper, H. "The Great Tew Circle." Chap. 4 of *Catholics, Anglicans and Puritans*. London: Secker and Warburg, 1987.

Trimpi, Wesley. "The Meaning of Horace's *Ut Pictura Poesis*." *Journal of the Warburg and Courtauld Institutes* 36 (1973): 1-34.

Tuck, Richard. *Philosophy and Government 1572-1651*. Ideas in Context. Cambridge: Cambridge Univ. Press, 1993.

Tudor-Craig, Pamela. *Richard III: National Portrait Gallery 27 June-7 October 1973*. London: National Portrait Gallery, 1973.

Underdown, David. *Pride's Purge: Politics in the Puritan Revolution*. Oxford: Clarendon Press, 1971.

Vernant, Jean-Pierre. "A 'Beautiful Death' and the Disfigured Corpse in Homeric Epic." Chap. 2 of *Mortals and Immortals: Collected Essays*. Edited by F. Zeitlin. Princeton: Princeton Univ. Press, 1991.

Vickers, Brian. *Francis Bacon and Renaissance Prose*. Cambridge: Cambridge Univ. Press, 1968.

———. "Epideictic and Epic in the Renaissance." *New Literary History* 14 (1982): 500-13.

———. *In Defence of Rhetoric*. Oxford: Clarendon Press, 1988.

Vickers, Brian and N. S. Struever. *Rhetoric and the Pursuit of Truth: Language Changes in the Seventeenth and Eighteenth Centuries*. Los Angeles: William Andrews Clark Library, 1985.

Vickers, Nancy. "Diana Described: Scattered Woman and Scattered Rhyme." *Critical Inquiry* 8 (1981): 265-79.

von Maltzahn, Nicholas. *Milton's "History of Britain": Republican Historiography in the English Revolution*. Oxford: Clarendon Press, 1991.

Wagner, Anthony R. *Heralds and Heraldry in the Middle Ages*, 2d ed. Oxford: Oxford Univ. Press, 1956.
Waller, Gary. "The Countess of Pembroke and Gendered Reading." In *The Renaissance Englishwoman in Print*, edited by Anne M. Haselkorn and Betty S. Travitsky. Amherst: Univ. of Massachusetts Press, 1990.
———. "Mother/Son, Father/Daugbter, Brother/Sister, Cousins: the Sidney Family Romance." *Modern Philology* 88 (1991): 401–14.
———. "The Sidney Family Romance: Mary Wroth and Gender Construction in Early Modern England." In *Reading Mary Wroth: Representing Alternatives in Early Modern England*, edited by Naomi J. Miller and Gary Waller. Knoxville: Univ. of Tennessee Press, 1992.
———. *The Sidney Family Romance: Mary Wroth, William Herbert and the Early Modern Construction of Gender*. Detroit: Wayne State Univ. Press, 1993.
Watson, Robert N. "Kinship and Kingship: Ambition in Shakespeare's Major Histories." Chap. 1 of *Shakespeare and the Hazards of Ambition*. Cambridge, Mass.: Harvard Univ. Press, 1984.
White, Helen C. *Social Criticism in Popular Religious Literature of the Sixteenth Century*. New York: Macmillan, 1944.
Williams, Ethel Carleton. *Anne of Denmark*. London: Longman, 1970.
Williamson, George. *The Senecan Amble: A Study in Prose Form from Bacon to Collier*. Chicago: Univ. of Chicago Press, 1951.
Willmott, Robert Aris. *Conversations at Cambridge*. London, 1836.
———. *Precious Stones: Aids to Reflection from Prose Writers of the Sixteenth, Seventeenth and Eighteenth Centuries*. London, 1850.
Winterbottom, M. "Quintilian and Rhetoric." In *Empire and Aftermath: Silver Latin 2*, edited by T. A. Dorey, 79–97. London: Routledge, 1975.
Wittreich, J. A. "Milton's *Areopagitica*: Its Isocratic and Ironic Contexts." *Milton Studies* 4 (1972): 101–15.
Wolfley, Lawrence C. "Sidney's visual-didactic poetic: some complexities and limitations." *Journal of Medieval and Renaissance Studies* 6 (1976): 217–41.
Wood, Charles T. *Joan of Arc and Richard III: Sex, Saints and Government in the Middle Ages*. New York: Oxford Univ. Press, 1988.
Wooden, Warren W. *John Foxe*. Boston: Twayne, 1983.
Woolrych, Austin. "Milton and Cromwell: 'A Short but Scandalous Night of Interruption?'" In *Achievements of the Left Hand: Essays on the Prose of John Milton*, edited by M. Lieb and J. T. Shawcross. Amherst: Univ. of Massachusetts Press, 1974.
———. *Commonwealth to Protectorate*. Oxford: Clarendon Press, 1982.
———. "Cromwell as Soldier." In *Oliver Cromwell and the English Revolution*, edited by J. Morrill. London: Longman, 1990.

Worden, Blair. *The Rump Parliament.* Cambridge: Cambridge Univ. Press, 1974.

———. "Toleration and the Cromwellian Protectorate." In *Persecution and Toleration.* Studies in Church History 21, edited by W. J. Sheils. Oxford, 1984.

Wright, N. "Milton's Use of Latin Formularies." *Studies in Philology* 40 (1943): 390–98.

Zagorin, Perez. *A History of Political Thought in the English Revolution.* London: Routledge and Kegan Paul, 1954.

———. *Milton: Aristocrat & Rebel: the Poet and his Politics.* Rochester, N.Y.: D. S. Brewer, 1992.

INDEX

Acontius (Giacomo Aconzio) 161–62
Admonitionists 76–77, 82
Adolph, Robert 9
Amadis de Gaule 122–23
Anne of Denmark 114–15
Aristotle 180–81, 205–6
Aubrey, John 134n.
Augustine, St. 51
Aurelianus, Coelius 154

Bacon, Sir Francis 2–3, 5–6, 7, 8–9, 16–17, 84, 127–28, 139–46, 147–72, 173–74, 193
Barclay, John 116
Barish, Jonas 9
Barthes, Roland 152n., 179
Barrow, Isaac 3
Baxter, Richard 73
Benjamin, Walter 181
Bolton, Edmund 96
Browne, Sir Thomas 2, 5–7, 12, 84, 87, 247–58
Buck, Sir George 37n., 50n., 55
Buckingham, George Villiers, Duke of 112–13, 124
Bunyan, John 13–14, 73, 259–70
Burton, Robert 2, 5, 11, 14, 21, 126, 173–202
Burton, William 248–49
Bush, Douglas 173–74

Calvin, Jean 155–56
Camden, William 248
Cartari, Vincenzo 94
Cary, Mary 235n.
Cave, Terence 184

Celsus, Aurelius Cornelius 155, 160
Chamberlain, John 111
Charles I, King 214–15, 228
Charles II, King 262
Chiflet, Jean-Jacques 254–55
Cicero and Ciceronianism 8, 16, 147–52, 160, 203–26
Clarendon, Edward Hyde, Earl of 12, 75–76
Coleridge, Samuel Taylor 1–5
Coppe, Abiezer 236n., 243, 267
Cornwallis, Sir William 37n.
Cosin, John 89
Coverdale, Miles 66
Cowley, Abraham 202
Craik, Sir Henry 7
Cranmer, Thomas 4, 58
Croll, Morris W. 8–10, 15
Cromwell, Oliver 218–19, 221, 228
Crooke, Helkiah 197–98

Dee, John 157–60, 170n.
Defoe, Daniel 73
Dell, William 240
Denny, Edward 110–12, 119, 121, 124
De Quincey, Thomas 3
Derrida, Jacques 191n.
Descartes, René 186
Dodsworth, Roger 247
Donne, John 7–8, 12, 16
Dugdale, Sir William 247–50, 255–58
Du Moulin, Pierre 220

Edward IV, King 56

Index 299

Elizabeth I, Queen 17–18
Erasmus 27, 29, 41n., 42–43n., 50, 80–81n., 192, 208
Estienne, Henri 102, 104–5
Euripides 211
Evelyn, John 257

Fabyan, Robert 44–45
Fish, Stanley 9–11, 174, 177, 190n.
Foigny, Gabriel de 127
Foster, George 243–44
Foxe, John 57–58, 64, 69n.
Fuller, Thomas 248

Galen 199
Garber, Marjorie 36–37n., 53n.
Gauden, John 78
Goodwin, Thomas 185–86
Gosson, Stephen 101
Greville, Fulke 113, 116

Hall, Edward 44–46
Hall, John 198–99
Halpern, Richard 128–30
Hanff, Helene 7–8
Hardyng, John 36
Harriot, Thomas 170n.
Harvey, William 196, 198n.
Hawthorne, Nathaniel 6
Hazlitt, William 2–3
Henry VII, King 46–47, 50
Henry, Prince 115
Herbert, George 88–89
Herbert, William 114–15, 118
Hill, Christopher 259
Hill, Nicholas 159–60
Hilliard, Nicholas 95–96
Hippocrates 154–55, 157, 195–96
Hobbes, Thomas 173, 186–87, 191, 195
Holinshed, Raphael 44–46
Hollar, Wenceslaus 248
Hooker, Richard 3, 12–13, 16, 75–90
Hyperius, Andreas 68

Isocrates 26, 205, 211, 225

James I, King (of England) 79, 112–16
Jeffrey, Francis 3
Johnson, Samuel 5, 188–93
Jones, Inigo 248
Jones, R. F. 9, 150
Jonson, Ben 4, 116, 175–76, 180, 182, 186–88, 190–91, 194–95
Joyce, James 179, 181
Juvenal 224

Keats, John 2, 201
Keeble, N. H. 259
Kirchmann, Johannes 255

Lamb, Charles 2, 4
Latimer, Hugh 4, 12, 15–16, 57–74
Laurentius (André Du Laurens) 197
Leavis, F. R. 7
Leonardo da Vinci 197
Le Roy, Louis 163–64
Lewis, C. S. 73, 79
Lipsius, Justus 9
Lloyd, Humfrey 156n.
Locke, John 175, 187–88, 191–92, 202
Lucian 54, 191
Luther, Martin 266

Machiavelli, Niccolò 41n.
Marin, Louis 135
Marvell, Andrew 220
Marx, Karl 42n.
Melanchthon, Philip 155
Melville, Herman 5–6
Milton, John 13, 16, 41–42, 84, 185n., 203–26, 230, 237–38, 241, 242n., 245, 261–63, 266
Montagu, Basil 4
Montaigne, Michel de 9
More, Alexander 220–24
More, Sir Thomas 12–13, 17, 19, 23, 35–36, 84, 125–46

Morton, Cardinal John 51n.
Muret, Marc-Antoine 9

Nashe, Thomas 21
Nedham, Marchamont 218

Ong, Walter 161n., 199
Owen, John 217–218, 238

Paracelsus 96
Pembroke, Mary Sidney, Countess of 11
Perkins, William 68
Piers Plowman 63–64
Piscator, Johann 155–56, 160
Plato 126, 205
Plutarch 192
Politian 95
Pooley, Roger 11
Propertius 252
Puttenham, George 93n., 94, 100

Quiller-Couch, Sir Arthur 7–8, 18
Quintilian 192, 205–6, 214

Rainsborough, Thomas 63
Ralegh, Sir Walter 167–70, 225
Ramus, Peter 162–63, 199n.
Ranter writing 24, 33–34, 236n., 243, 266–67, 270
Rawley, Walter 167–70
Reuchlin, Johann 19–20
Richard III, King 35–56
Royal Society 149n., 175, 201–2, 261
Rufinianus, Julius 154

Salmasius 220
Salmon, Joseph 33–34
Selden, John 255
Seneca 8–9, 148
Shakespeare, William 10, 24, 39n., 45n., 50, 51, 53, 125
Shore, 'Jane' 52, 54
Sidney, Sir Philip 4, 13, 14–15, 91–108, 109–10, 113–16, 122–23, 207

Skelton, John 64
Smith, Logan Pearsall 7–8
South, Robert 73
Spenser, Edmund 4
Sprat, Thomas 12, 16, 261–62
Stachniewski, John 264–65
Sterne, Laurence 188
Stubbes, Philip 112

Tacitus 8, 49n., 252
Taylor, Jeremy 1–4, 6, 16
Tesauro, Emmanuele 94
Tey, Josephine 40
Thoreau, Henry David 6
Tillotson, John 73
Trevor-Roper, Hugh 204
Tyler, Margaret 123
Tyndale, William 12, 15, 19–34, 58

Udall, Nicholas 24
Ussher, Archbishop James 248

Vane, Sir Henry 218–19
Vergil, Polydore 45–46
Vesalius, Andreas 196–200, 202
Vickers, Brian 9, 149–50

Wakefield, Robert 20–26, 34
Walton, Isaak 78–79
Warton, Thomas 185
Webster, Noah 5–6
Weever, John 255, 257–58
Whythorne, Thomas 33
Williamson, George 9
Willmott, Robert Aris 4
Wilson, Thomas 71
Winstanley, Gerrard 13, 15–16, 73, 227–46, 267
Wood, Anthony à 178, 183, 189, 247–48
Wotton, Sir Henry 99–100
Wroth, Lady Mary 17–18, 109–24

Young, Robert 181

NOTES ON CONTRIBUTORS

NEIL RHODES is Reader in English Renaissance Literature at the University of St Andrews. He is the author of *The Power of Eloquence and English Renaissance Literature* (1992), editor of the Penguin *John Donne: Selected Prose* (1987) and a contributor to the Oxford Collected Works of Thomas Middleton. He is also the author of *Elizabethan Grotesque* (1980) and has collaborated with Yoshiko Uèno on a Japanese language version of the same book (1989).

GERALD HAMMOND is John Edward Taylor Professor of English at the University of Manchester. He is the author of *The Reader and Shakespeare's Young Man Sonnets* (1974), *The Making of the English Bible* (1984), *Fleeting Thing: English Poets and Poems 1616–1660* (1990), and *Horseracing: A Book of Words* (1992), as well as editions of Skelton, Ralegh, and Richard Lovelace and a number of articles on Renaissance poetry and prose.

DANIEL KINNEY teaches English and Comparative Literature at the University of Virginia. He has written numerous studies of Medieval and Renaissance genres and modes of reception and is a prize-winning translator and editor; currently he is also the general editor of the Delaware edition of Abraham Cowley's *Complete Works*.

N. H. KEEBLE is Professor of English at the University of Stirling. His publications include editions of texts by Richard Baxter, John Bunyan and Lucy Hutchinson; an anthology illustrating *The Cultural Identity of Seventeenth-century Women* (1994); studies of *Richard Baxter* (1982) and of *The Literary Culture of Nonconformity* (1987); and (with Geoffrey F. Nuttall) a two-volume *Calendar* of Baxter's correspondence (1991). He is currently working on a study of the 1660s.

P. G. STANWOOD is Senior Professor of English and former director of graduate studies at the University of British Columbia. He has edited texts by John Cosin, John Donne, Jeremy Taylor, and William Law, and is the editor of *Of the Laws of Ecclesiastical Polity* (Books VI, VII and VIII) in the Folger Library Edition of the Works of Richard Hooker and also of *Poetry and Politics: New Essays on Milton and His World* (1995). *The Sempiternal Season: Studies in Seventeenth-Century Devotional Writing* (1993) is a collection of his own essays.

CLAIRE PRESTON is Fellow in English at Sidney Sussex College, Cambridge, and Newton Trust Lecturer in the Faculty of English, Cambridge University. She has written about Shakespeare, Jonson, Sidney, Thomas Browne, and Edith Wharton.

PAUL SALZMAN is Senior Lecturer in the School of English, La Trobe University, Melbourne. He is the author of *English Prose Fiction 1558-1700* and has edited two collections of early prose fiction for Oxford World's Classics, as well as a selection of Aphra Behn's fiction and poetry. He is currently completing a book about the writing of 1621.

SUSAN BRUCE is Lecturer in English at the University of Keele. She has published articles on various aspects of early modern English Literature, and is currently at work on a book on the early modern utopian imagination.

STEPHEN CLUCAS is Lecturer in Renaissance Studies at Birkbeck College, University of London. His present work is largely in the sphere of interdisciplinary and cultural history. He has published articles on Samuel Hartlib, Giordano Bruno, John Dee and Thomas Harriot, and is currently working on an intellectual biography of Henry Percy, 9th Earl of Northumberland (1564-1632).

JONATHAN SAWDAY is Senior Lecturer in English at the University of Southampton. He is the author of *The Body Emblazoned: Dissection and the Human Body in Renaissance Culture* (1995), and co-editor (with Thomas Healy) of *Literature and the English Civil War* (1990).

MARTIN DZELZAINIS is Lecturer in English at Royal Holloway, University of London. He has edited Milton's *Political Writings* for Cambridge Texts in the History of Political Thought (1991) and is the author of several articles on Milton, Clarendon and Hobbes. He is currently working on a study of the ideological origins of the English Revolution.

Contributors

DAVID LOEWENSTEIN is Professor of English at the University of Wisconsin-Madison. He is the author of *Milton and the Drama of History: Historical Vision, Iconoclasm, and the Literary Imagination* (1990) and of *Milton: "Paradise Lost"* (1993). He has also co-edited *Politics, Poetics and Hermeneutics in Milton's Prose* (1990) and *The Emergence of Quaker Writing: Dissenting Literature in Seventeenth-Century England* (1995). With Ann Hughes and Thomas N. Corns, he is editing the works of Gerrard Winstanley for Clarendon Press.

GRAHAM PARRY teaches at the University of York. He is the author of several books on the cultural and intellectual life of the seventeenth century, including *The Golden Age Restor'd* (1981) and *The Trophies of Time: English Antiquaries of the Seventeenth Century* (1996).

THOMAS N. CORNS is Professor of English at the University of Wales, Bangor. He is author of *Uncloistered Virtue: English Political Literature, 1640–1660* (1992) and *Regaining "Paradise Lost"* (1994), and editor of *The Cambridge Companion to English Poetry, Donne to Marvell* (1993). With Ann Hughes and David Loewenstein, he is editing the works of Gerrard Winstanley for Clarendon Press.

WITHDRAWN from the Alma College Library